The Good Society

A BOOK OF READINGS

The Good Society

A BOOK OF READINGS

edited with an introduction by
ANTHONY ARBLASTER
and STEVEN LUKES

METHUEN & CO LTD
11 NEW FETTER LANE · LONDON · EC4

First published 1971 by Methuen & Co Ltd
11 New Fetter Lane, London EC4
© 1971 by A. Arblaster and S. Lukes
Printed in Great Britain by
Butler and Tanner Ltd
Frome and London

SBN (hardbound) 416 08350 1
SBN (paperback) 416 08430 3

CONTENTS

v

ACKNOWLEDGEMENTS

The editors and publishers wish to thank the following for permission to reproduce extracts from the works listed below:

Allen & Unwin, Ltd for Fyodor Dostoevsky, 'The Journal of an Author', *The Dream of a Queer Fellow and the Pushkin Speech*, trans. S. Koteliansky and J. Middleton Murry (1960), and Bertrand Russell, *Roads to Freedom: Socialism, Anarchism and Syndicalism* (1918) and J. Lively (ed. and trans.), 'Étude sur la Souveraineté' (1884), *The Works of Joseph de Maistre* (1965); Edward Arnold, Ltd for E. M. Forster, 'The Challenge of Our Time', *Two Cheers for Democracy* (1951); G. Bell & Sons, Ltd for R. H. Tawney, *The Acquisitive Society* (1948); Blackwell & Mott, Ltd for David McLellan (ed. and trans.), 'Notes on James Mill', *Karl Marx: Early Texts* (1971), F. M. H. Markham (ed. and trans.), 'Henri, Comte de Saint-Simon: "On Social Organization"', *Saint-Simon: Selected Writings* (1952), and H. S. Reiss (ed. and trans.), 'Novalis: "Die Christenheit Oder Europa"', *The Political Thought of the German Romantics* (1955); Cambridge University Press for M. Oakeshott (ed.), 'Benito Mussolini: "La Dottrina de Fascismo"', *The Social and Political Doctrines of Contemporary Europe* (1940); Jonathan Cape, Ltd for C. Lévi-Strauss, *The Scope of Anthropology*, trans. S. D. and R. A. Paul (1967) and C. A. R. Crosland, *The Future of Socialism* (1964); Clarendon Press, Oxford, for T. M. Knox (ed. and trans.), 'The German Constitution', *Hegel's Political Writings* (1964); Mrs Margaret Cole for G. D. H. Cole, *Guild Socialism Re-Stated* (Leonard Parsons, 1920); William Collins, Sons & Co., Ltd for Boris Pasternak, *Dr Zhivago*, trans. Max Hayward and Manya Harari (1958); Communist Party of Great Britain and Penguin Books, Ltd for N. Bukharin and E. Preobrazhensky, *The ABC of Communism*, trans. E. and C. Paul (1922) (Penguin edition,

1969); Constable & Co., Ltd for Robert Michels, *Political Parties* (1915), trans. E. and C. Paul (1959); J. M. Dent & Sons, Ltd for Robert Owen, *A New View of Society and Other Writings*, introduction by G. D. H. Cole, Everyman's Library Edition (1963) and Jean-Jacques Rousseau, *The Social Contract and Discourses*, trans. with introduction by G. D. H. Cole, Everyman's Library Edition (1958); André Deutsch Ltd for G. and D. Cohn-Bendit, *Obsolete Communism: The Left-Wing Alternative* (1968); Encyclopaedia Britannica International, Ltd for Peter A. Kropotkin, 'Anarchism', *Encyclopaedia Britannica*, Vol. I, 14th edition (1926); Faber & Faber, Ltd for J. P. Mayer, 'Max Weber on Bureaucratization in 1909', from Appendix I, *Max Weber and German Politics* (1944) and T. S. Eliot, *The Idea of a Christian Society* (© 1939 by T. S. Eliot, renewed 1967 by Esme Valerie Eliot); Faber & Faber, Ltd and Random House, Inc. for W. H. Auden, 'Reading', *The Dyer's Hand and Other Essays* (1962), and 'Vespers', *Collected Shorter Poems, 1927–1957* (1955); The Free Press (New York) for David Riesman, *Individualism Reconsidered* (1954),and K. H. Wolff (trans.), *The Sociology of Georg Simmel* (1950); The Freedom Press for Pierre-Joseph Proudhon, *General Idea of the Revolution in the Nineteenth Century* (1951), trans. J. B. Robinson (1923); Victor Gollancz, Ltd and Random House, Inc. for Paul Goodman, *Growing Up Absurd* (1961); William Heinemann, Ltd for Fyodor Dostoevsky, *The Brothers Karamazov*, trans. Constance Garnett (1960); Independent Labour Party for Eduard Bernstein, *Evolutionary Socialism: A Criticism and Affirmation*, trans. E. C. Harvey (1909); the Institute of Phenomenological Studies for D. Cooper (ed.), 'Liberation from the Affluent Society', *Herbert Marcuse: The Dialectics of Liberation* (1968); the Estate of the late Mrs Frieda Lawrence and Laurence Pollinger, Ltd for E. D. McDonald (ed.), 'Democracy', Part 1, *Phoenix: The Posthumous Papers of D. H. Lawrence* (© 1964 by the Estate of Frieda Lawrence Ravagli); Lawrence & Wishart, Ltd for V. I. Lenin, 'State and Revolution', *Selected Works* (1969); Little, Brown & Co. for Walter Lippmann, *The Good Society* (1937); The London School of Economics and Political Science for Sidney and Beatrice Webb, *A Constitution for the Socialist Commonwealth of Great Britain* (1920); McGraw-Hill Book Company for Gaetano Mosca, 'Elementi di Scienza Politica', trans. as Chapters 12–17 of *The Ruling Class*, ed. A. Livingstone (1939); Macmillan & Co., Ltd for A. A. Berle, *The Twentieth-Century Capitalist Revolution* (1955) and J. M. Keynes, *A General Theory of Employment, Interest and Money* (1960); Methuen & Co., Ltd for M. Oakeshott, 'On Being Conservative', *Rationalism in Politics* (1962); Oxford University

Press for William Blake, 'An Ancient Proverb', *William Blake: Complete Writings* (1966) and Ernest Renan, 'What is a Nation?', trans. A. Zimmern in *Modern Political Doctrines* (1939); The Pareto Fund (New York) for A. Livingstone (ed.), *Vilfredo Pareto: The Mind and Society* (1935); Penguin Books, Ltd for Thomas Paine, *Rights of Man* (Pelican, 1969), and Leo Tolstoy, *Anna Karenin*, trans. Rosemary Edmunds (1954); Sir Karl Popper, Routledge & Kegan Paul, Ltd and Basic Books, Inc. for Sir Karl Popper, 'Utopia and Violence', *Conjectures and Refutations* (1969); Routledge & Kegan Paul, Ltd for J. C. F. von Schiller, *On the Aesthetic Education of Man* (1954), Karl Mannheim, *Man and Society in an age of Reconstruction* (1940) and Friedrich von Hayek, 'Individualism: True and False', *Individualism and Economic Order* (1949); Routledge & Kegan Paul, Ltd and The Free Press for Émile Durkheim, *Professional Ethics and Civic Morals*, trans, C. Brookfield (1957); Routledge & Kegan Paul, Ltd and Stanford University Press by the Board of Trustees of the Leland Stanford Junior University for Ralf Dahrendorf, *Class and Conflict in an Industrial Society* (1959); Sigmund Freud Copyrights, Ltd, The Institute of Psycho-Analysis and The Hogarth Press, Ltd for Sigmund Freud, 'Civilization and Its Discontents', *The Standard Edition of the Complete Psychological Works of Sigmund Freud*, ed. and trans. James Strachey (1961); Sonia Brownell and Secker & Warburg, Ltd for George Orwell, *Homage to Catalonia* (1938) (© 1952 by Sonia Brownell Orwell); The Viking Press, Inc. for Lionel Trilling (ed.), *The Portable Matthew Arnold* (1949); C. A. Watts & Co., Ltd for T. Bottomore (ed.), *Karl Marx: Early Writings* (1963); Weidenfeld & Nicolson, Ltd for Jean Antoine Nicolas Caritat, Marquis de Condorcet, *Sketch for the Progress of the Human Mind*, trans. J. Barraclough (1955); M. B. Yeats for William Butler Yeats, 'At Galway Races' (© 1940 by Bertha Georgie Yeats), and 'Coole Park and Ballylee' (© 1961 by Bertha Georgie Yeats), from *The Collected Poems of William Butler Yeats* (1963).

Every effort has been made to trace copyright holders, but in several cases they could not be found. The editors and publishers wish to apologize for consequent omissions.

INTRODUCTION

We hope that this book will prove to be subversive in at least two ways. First, we have deliberately ignored the conventional academic demarcation lines which separate political and social theory from any wider, less systematic or more polemical discussion of social and political issues, in literature or in manifestos. We hope that our anthology contains enough evidence to demonstrate that poets, novelists and essayists, as well as politicians and revolutionaries, make their own uniquely valuable contributions to the discussion of the issues which specialists in political and social theory are sometimes apt to regard as their private preserve.

Second, we hope to bring out the crucial importance, in such a discussion, of values and ideals – especially where claims are made to 'realism', 'neutrality' and 'objectivity'. Social and political ideals do not merely constitute one subject among others for social and political theorizing – the subject-matter of so-called 'normative theory'. They are a central, integral and indispensable part of all such theorizing, not least when it claims to be free of them. We hope that our selection will give some idea of the range of the ideals that have been historically influential during the last two centuries. Different thinkers have found their ideal societies in the past, the future and the present, while others believe their ideals to be virtually unrealizable, and yet others denounce the very pursuit of ideals (which, as we will try to show, does not mean that they have none themselves). We also hope to show the range of reasons and justifications that different thinkers have advanced in support of their ideals, ranging from the most general and *a priori* appeals to the nature of the universe and of man to claims based on the empirical data of sociology, anthropology and psychology. It is, we believe, a major task of social and political theory to inquire into how different social and political ideals might rationally be justified, whether some are more justifiable than others, and why. An indispensable first step in such an inquiry is a consideration of the best arguments for the widest possible range of such ideals – to be found, we claim, in the pages of thinkers such as those we have selected.

This introduction aims to do three things: first, to suggest that all the positions represented in this book have an evaluative basis, from the most 'realistic' to the most 'utopian', and indeed that this very distinction is tendentious and misleading; second, to give some idea of the range of value positions represented, and of the justifications advanced in their support; and third, to trace some of the basic continuities, and some of the significant changes, suggested by our selection from the social and political thought of the period since the French and Industrial Revolutions.

I

It might have been expected that an anthology entitled *The Good Society* would be a collection only of radical and utopian writings. But that very expectation is a product of the view that, on the one hand, there are those who are 'realistic', with a concrete sense of the actual, concerned, in varying degrees, with reforming it in the light of the possible – and, on the other hand, the myth-makers and ideologists, utopians dedicated to the construction and imposition of abstract models, or blueprints, of 'the good society'.

Edmund Burke was among the first to launch an attack on ideological and utopian politics as such, on all attempts, starting from universal first principles, to draw up blueprints of what an ideal society would be like and make them into realities. Such attempts were at odds with 'reason, and order, and peace, and virtue, and fruitful penitence' and led to 'madness, discord, vice, confusion, and unavailing sorrow'.[1] Many since have followed his example, particularly in the period since the Russian Revolution. Such contemporary writers as Walter Lippmann, Friedrich Hayek, Sir Karl Popper and Seymour Martin Lipset – all of whom are represented here – attack, from their various positions, the idea of utopia as an illusion which is at best misleading and most often cruel and dangerous in its consequences. At times, this attack is linked, explicitly or implicitly, with an even wider assault on the role of general principles in politics, the

[1] Except where indicated, all the quotations in this Introduction are from the selections in this volume.

invocation and application of which are described and condemned by Michael Oakeshott as 'rationalism in politics'.

The opposition between 'realism' and 'utopianism' is characteristically used by those who see themselves as adhering to the former – indeed, a 'utopia' can be defined as any ideal regarded by a 'realist' as impractical or unrealizable. Though expressed in many different ways, and with varying degrees of explicitness, this distinction is operative in the thought of many of the writers we have selected – though what counts as 'realistic' clearly differs from thinker to thinker. At one extreme, there is de Maistre, for whom 'royalty is *the natural government*', and who sees government as 'a true religion', with 'its dogmas, its mysteries, its priests', condemning reason when applied to politics as corrosive and dangerous – 'the mortal enemy of any association whatever': De Maistre sees his doctrine as proved by 'well-attested facts'. On the other hand, de Tocqueville seeks to disabuse 'those who have constructed for themselves an ideal democracy, a glittering dream, which they believe can be easily realized . . .'. A well-known case is that of the political sociologist Robert Michels, discoverer of the 'iron law of oligarchy', who made an assault on what he saw as democratic illusions. For Michels:

> A realistic view of the mental condition of the masses shows beyond question that even if we admit the possibility of moral improvement in mankind, the human materials with whose use politicians and philosophers cannot dispense in their plans of social reconstruction are not of a character to justify excessive optimism. Within the limits of time for which human provision is possible, optimism will remain the exclusive privilege of utopian thinkers.

It does not, however, need a lifetime of study to see that the objections of the 'anti-utopians' are very seldom of a purely logical or empirical character. Those accused of utopianism are not most frequently criticized simply for being inconsistent or self-contradictory (though see the last passage from Bentham, on direct democracy). Nor is the critique confined to the charge that they advocate the impossible, although this has certainly been a common allegation. The most common and the most passionately advanced charge against them has been that what they recommend as an ideal condition of human society, and the means required for achieving it, are undesirable, because destructive of those moral values and institutions which the anti-utopians wish to sustain or preserve.

Utopia for the latter is not a bright vision, but a horrific nightmare, or at best a delusion which it is better not to attempt to realize, not merely because the attempt is sure to fail, but also because of the appalling moral and social costs which such efforts have and always will incur. Thus Lippmann writes, using the phrase that we have taken for our title:

> The Good Society has no architectural design. There are no blueprints. There is no mold in which human life is to be shaped. . . .
>
> The supreme architect, who begins as a visionary, becomes a fanatic, and ends as a despot. For no one can be the supreme architect of society without employing a supreme despot to execute the design.

Popper argues similarly that 'the Utopian method, which chooses an ideal state of society as the aim which all our political actions should serve, is likely to produce violence' and that 'the Utopian engineers who design and execute the Utopian blueprint' must 'become omniscient as well as omnipotent. They become gods.' And Oakeshott attacks those who seek 'to turn a private dream into a public and compulsory manner of living'.

Implicit in the arguments of Burke against the French Revolution and its English supporters, explicit in the words of Lippmann and in the passage from Pasternak's *Doctor Zhivago* which we have included, is the belief that life, the whole of human life, is too large a thing to come within the scope of the conscious and deliberate restructuring of society. 'Reshaping life!', Pasternak's hero scornfully exclaims:

> People who can say that have never understood a thing about life – they have never felt its breath, its heart – however much they have seen or done. They look on it as a lump of raw material which needs to be processed by them, to be ennobled by their touch. But life is never a material, a substance to be moulded. If you want to know, life is the principle of self-renewal, it is constantly renewing and remaking and changing and transfiguring itself, it is infinitely beyond your or my theories about it.

The sphere of politics, in other words, is, or ought to be, limited, and therefore, as Oakeshott argues in the passage we have taken from his essay 'On Being Conservative', the proper role of government is also limited. A good society, for thinkers of this kind, will be one which accepts these general principles as guidelines for its political life, and others which underlie them. Here, as always, in criticizing what are held to be utopian plans and projects, a different view as to what general principles should determine the life and structure of society is implied, and this is bound to be so, since criticisms of utopianism are essentially moral and evaluative, implying not an unattainable moral neutrality, but simply a different moral standpoint or vision.

This can be illustrated by reference to a particular social principle which figures very largely in a great many of the passages in this book – the principle of social equality (though the same point could be made with respect to liberty, or democracy or justice). For writers as various as Rousseau, Babeuf, Shelley, Bakunin, Matthew Arnold, William Morris, Lenin and George Orwell, social and economic equality broadly conceived is an essential part of a good society, of which their conceptions are in many other respects very different from each other. It is, however, a commonplace that equality, like utopia itself, is said to be an unattainable goal. But when we turn to those writers in this collection who do not share a thoroughgoing commitment to equality, we find that they characteristically dispute not simply its feasibility but, more fundamentally, its desirability.

In the passages from Burke, Coleridge and Carlyle, and in one of the two poems by Yeats, 'Coole Park and Ballylee, 1931', it is a frankly and traditionally hierarchical society that is held up for our admiration. Edmund Burke defends the derivation of political and social power from birth and property:

> Some decent, regulated pre-eminence, some preference (not exclusive appropriation) given to birth, is neither unnatural, nor unjust, nor impolitic.

Coleridge, in a less traditional way, develops his notion of a 'clerisy', a 'national church' of the enlightened, whose object is 'civilization with freedom'—'to secure and improve that civilization, without which the nation could be neither permanent nor progressive'. Carlyle proclaims the need for 'Aristocracy and Priesthood, a Governing Class and a Teaching Class', while Yeats extols the cultural continuity of an aristocracy.

From a quite different position, Saint-Simon and Comte also argue for a hierarchical society, though here the social structure is intended to be functionally organized and meritocratic: as Comte says, science provides a new basis for the 'idea of social subordination'. There are comparable visions of a well-organized, technocratic structure to be found in the Webbs and Karl Mannheim. Even Fourier, usually described as a utopian socialist, argues that the principle governing the new, scientifically based system of organizing industry and agriculture, the discovery of which he so proudly proclaims, is 'incompatible with equality', since it requires contrasts, competition and 'very active rivalries'.

Liberal thinkers and even moderate socialists, taking up positions between, let us say, Burke on the one hand and Condorcet on the other, couple their advocacy of piecemeal reforms with a general defence of some sorts of inequality. Hayek, Keynes and C. A. R. Crosland exemplify this kind of approach. For Hayek 'true individualism is not equalitarian in the modern sense of the word': though

> profoundly opposed to all prescriptive privilege, to all protection, by law or force, of any rights not based on rules equally applicable to all persons, it also denies government the right to limit what the able or fortunate may achieve. It is equally opposed to any rigid limitation of the position individuals may achieve, whether this power is used to perpetuate inequality or to create equality.

Keynes, writing in the mid-thirties, declared his belief

> that there is social and psychological justification for significant inequalities of incomes and wealth, but not for such large disparities as exist today. There are valuable human activities which require the motive of money-making and the environment of private wealth-ownership for their full fruition.

And C. A. R. Crosland is, or was in the mid-fifties, 'sure that a definite limit exists to the degree of equality which is desirable', since the relentless pursuit of equality would lead only to 'some drab extreme'.

It would be seriously misleading to suggest that any of these writers are no more than 'realistic' or 'objective' critics of the 'impossible' goal of complete social and economic equality. On the contrary, all of them, for different reasons, and to different degrees, see some forms of inequality as permanently desirable. Hence some kind of inequality, and in some cases a hierarchy of power, or status, or wealth or birth, form elements in their conceptions of a good society. They are not to be distinguished from those thinkers commonly regarded as utopians by their having *no* general principles or *no* general idea of what society should be like—although it is often implied that just such a distinction can be drawn.

Traditionalist conservatives, organizing technocrats, dogmatic and pragmatic liberals and piecemeal social reformers—although they attack socialists, anarchists and other radicals for attempting to produce blueprints of the desired future society (which very few of the latter do in any detailed way) – are only able to do so by reference to rival conceptions of the good society. The anti-utopians are apt to claim, nevertheless, that their approach to politics is radically different from that of those they see as utopians. The latter are said to be dogmatic, doctrinaire and inflexible, while they are naturally flexible and realistic, accepting Kant's dictum that 'out of the crooked timber of humanity no straight thing was ever made'.

On the evidence presented in this book, and widely available elsewhere, there seems no reason to accept this trite contrast. It is not self-evident that Burke is less dogmatic in his commitment to tradition, or Oakeshott to his belief in limited government, or Hayek to 'true' individualism, or Lipset and Riesman in their commitment to the fundamental excellence of American democracy than is Condorcet in his commitment to the possibility of unlimited human perfection, or Lenin in his commitment to communism, or Proudhon and Kropotkin in their devotion to the anarchist ideal. Some may disagree. If our extracts do not convince them, we hope they will look further, for it is a central aim of this book to lead people on (or back) to the texts from which we have extracted these passages.

A further claim often made by those who draw a distinction between realists and utopians is that the zeal of the latter for the hypothetical future happiness of mankind leads them to sacrifice the real happiness which is available to those living in the present. This charge is made by one of the speakers in our passage from Alexander Herzen and it has been echoed in this century by Popper, among many others. An adequate discussion of this claim would require a full study, not only of so-called 'utopian' ideas, but also of their influence upon political action as compared with that of more material factors, including pressing political necessities. That we cannot attempt, but would offer only one general observation. It cannot necessarily be assumed that the sacrifice of present benefit will *not* yield a greater benefit to future generations. Nor can it be assumed that a refusal to make sacrifices in the present will not have bad or cruel consequences for a generation yet unborn. Inaction has its consequences as well as action, and they are not necessarily happier ones.

Another contrast between the 'utopians' and their critics made, for example, by Lippmann and Hayek is that the former are committed to the overall planning and regimentation of society, and this is held to be either impossible on account of the sheer complexity of social phenomena (which the utopians characteristically choose to simplify), or undesirable, as reducing the freedom of individuals and groups to pursue their own purposes and lead their own lives. Once more, we do not have the space for a full discussion of this issue, but will again confine ourselves to a single observation. It is very striking how many of those described as utopian, whether they are labelled communist, socialist or anarchist, or whether they altogether elude tidy classification, agree in looking forward to a future in which government and every kind of constraining authority will be reduced to a minimum.

This, it is clear from our extracts, is one point at which communism, socialism and anarchism converge. Marx, Lenin and Mao, and Robert Owen, William Morris and G. D. H. Cole share with avowed anarchists, like Godwin, Proudhon, Bakunin, Kropotkin, and others such as Tolstoy, Oscar Wilde, Russell and Paul Goodman, the vision of a society in which the voluntary principle is dominant, in which there is the greatest possible equality, not only of wealth and status, but also of power, in which there are the fewest possible externally imposed rules and laws, and the least need for an authority to enforce them.

The picture of communism and socialism as committed to the continuous and unlimited increase of the power of the state over society arises from a study of history, rather than a close study of ideas. For it is striking how many socialist thinkers, both Marxist and non-Marxist, have in their writings looked forward with confidence and hope to the eventual withering away of the state; as Lenin puts it, 'So long as the state exists there is no freedom. When there is freedom, there will be no state.' It is, of course, fair to point out that there are some famous socialist writers for whom this vision apparently has no appeal, or else no relevance. But it is equally fair to point out that these are not those socialists to whom the utopian label is most habitually attached. Eduard Bernstein and the Webbs are normally regarded as stalwarts of the more 'realistic' traditions of social democracy. Yet it is in the extracts from these writers that we find the heaviest emphasis being placed on the centralizing, planning and organizational elements in socialism, while Crosland, representing contemporary social democracy, would, we suspect, simply not think it worthwhile to peer so far into a wholly hypothetical and most unlikely future as to anticipate the disappearance of the state.

One essential difference between all these self-styled realists and those they see as utopian comes down to a *moral* difference in their attitudes to the present and to the future. The so-called utopians do not in general accept the view of Lippmann, Hayek, Oakeshott and, for that matter, John Stuart Mill, that the major need *in the present* is that the role of government and the state should be as limited as they would like it to be in the future. As Michels somewhat over-emphatically puts it, they tend to combine 'pessimism regarding the present, with rosy optimism and immeasurable confidence regarding the future'. The difference is fundamentally an evaluative one, a difference of moral vision. The anti-utopians look with relative satisfaction, or at least with resignation, upon what Oakeshott calls 'the current condition of human circumstances': either it does not require radical improvement or else it would be interfering folly to attempt it. Men are what they are and can never be expected to be radically different. Social life has its own laws and its own momentum, compared to which human attempts to prescribe and bring into existence a new pattern of society are irredeemably clumsy, usually destroying more of value than they can ever hope to create. This view is especially clear among liberal writers. Constant, Humboldt, Mill, Herbert Spencer, T. H. Green and Mosca, and, in our own time, E. M. Forster, Keynes, Berle, Riesman and Dahrendorf do not all take an equally strong stand against every extension of governmental power and activity: they have differing principles setting different limits to the activities of the liberal state. Nevertheless, like the Arcadian in Auden's anti-utopian poem, they look with instinctive suspicion upon such extensions and activities because of the great value they attach to the liberty, self-development, privacy and autonomy of the individual. Society and authority must allow scope for the individual to exercise initiative and choice – what else can give meaning to his life?

For the most part, those accused of utopianism see the present condition of human circumstances very differently. The immediate choice, as they see it, is not between the extension of state power and the preservation or extension of individual liberty and choice, but whether or not to leave power in the hands of groups of men based upon private concentrations of wealth and upon social class. Their eyes are fixed upon the grim facts of social and economic inequality and oppression, which, they argue, make nonsense of any claim that all individuals are equally free or enjoy equal opportunities for the exercise of initiative and choice. They share a faith in the future – though they differ very widely indeed about how to bring it nearer. At one extreme are Bakunin, protesting 'against everything which resembles, either closely or distantly, communism or State socialism' and Kropotkin envisaging that 'the voluntary associations which already now begin to cover all the fields of human activity would take a still greater extension so as to substitute themselves for the State in all its functions'. At the other are Marx and Engels, seeking to bring about the 'Communist revolution . . . the most radical rupture with traditional property relations' and Lenin, so bitterly criticized by Rosa Luxemburg for seeking to bring about socialism by 'Decree, dictatorial force . . . , draconian penalties, rule by terror . . .'. But, unlike the anti-utopians and the liberals, all these writers agree that, until equality is established, arguments that focus on limiting the role of present governments are simply disguised pleas to allow the continuance of inequality and oppression.

We have been arguing that the distinction between realism and utopianism is itself a misleading and value-loaded, indeed polemical distinction, serving to conceal the value premises from which it is made. In fact, its use is not confined to the conservative, or liberal, or moderate socialist 'realists'. It is typically used by Marxists – and was, in particular, used by Marx and Engels with reference to such writers as Owen, Fourier and Saint-Simon, who offer, as they say in *The Communist Manifesto*, 'phantastic pictures of future society, painted at a time when the proletariat is still in a very undeveloped state'. Thus we have selected a passage from Engels's *Socialism: Utopian and Scientific*, and Rosa Luxemburg, in the passage we include, contrasts 'scientific socialism' with 'the utopian varieties'. Yet Owen criticizes those who 'have been governed . . . by mere illusions of the imagination, in direct opposition to existing facts'. And anarchists, too, see themselves as realists; even Kropotkin claims that the anarchist ideal is 'not a utopia, constructed on the *a priori* method, after a few desiderata have been taken as postulates. It is derived . . . from *an analysis of tendencies* that are at work already . . .'. One man's realism is another man's utopia. Indeed history may show the utopian to have been a realist. As Oscar Wilde writes:

> A map of the world that does not include Utopia is not worth even glancing at, for it leaves out the one country at which Humanity is always landing. And when Humanity lands there, it looks out, and, seeing a better country, sets sail. Progress is the realization of Utopias.

The distinction is a misleading one, because the boundaries between what is 'realistic' and what is 'unrealistic', setting what are seen as the limits of possibility in achieving social change, are themselves in large part value-determined – and, indeed, they vary, not only in different times and places, but from thinker to thinker. This is true even where claims are made, as by Freud, to have identified some 'indestructible feature of human nature' which allegedly sets such limits. The distinction is further misleading, as we have tried to suggest, because it is generally taken to imply that those thinkers called utopian have a monopoly of dogmatism, or show, as a body, a greater indifference to human happiness or a greater addiction to centralized planning and the principle of authority than their critics.

The positions of both sides, then, have an evaluative basis. This is not to say that all positions are equally valid or equally invalid – that choosing between them is entirely subjective, a mere matter of taste. We have tried to gather together passages which marshal some of the best available attempts to defend a very wide range of evaluative positions. It is up to the reader to assess these various attempts for their plausibility. But the various positions are all to be seen as equally evaluative. Ironically, even conservative thinkers like Burke and Oakeshott, who insist most strongly on the impossibility of devising universal recipes for good government or a good society, who emphasize, in Burke's words, that the 'circumstances are what render every civil and political scheme beneficial or noxious to mankind', cannot avoid enunciating what are essentially general principles to which any good society should conform; indeed, their entire social and political theories rest on such principles. Even more ironically, the same can be said of those deeply sceptical thinkers like Freud and Pareto who seek to show that the social ideals of others are simply illusory rationalizations of their interests and desires. The passages we have chosen from their writings should suffice to show that they too make crucial and ineradicable evaluative assumptions.

II

We began by saying that we hope to indicate both the range of social and political ideals and the range of justifications offered in their support.

There are a few thinkers who find their ideal society located wholly in the past. Among our most distinctive examples are the early German Romantic, Novalis, looking back to the 'fine magnificent times when Europe was a Christian country'; Thomas Carlyle, romanticizing the 'rugged stalwart ages: full of earnestness, of a rude God's truth'; and Joseph de Maistre, recalling the 'ages of belief' and drawing theocratic lessons from history. These thinkers derive reactionary conclusions from their idealized pictures of medieval Europe, but many others, including some socialists, find, in their conceptions of the Middle Ages, support for a variety of different proposals. Thus Comte sees his 'speculative class' as the modern functional equivalent of the medieval Church, while both Durkheim and Cole seek to recreate the guilds in a new form; and a medieval nostalgia is of central importance to the thought of Morris and John Ruskin (from whom, unfortunately, we were unable to find a suitable passage). But medieval Europe is not the only historical source of inspiration. There is the case of Dostoevsky, seeking salvation in Russia's organic native traditions, and there is Schiller, who hopes that the future will see a recovery of the unalienated, harmonious existence once achieved in the civilization of classical Greece. (There are, incidentally, some very remarkable echoes of Schiller in Marx, both of them seeing man as fragmented within the division of labour, but potentially able to develop 'the harmony of his being'.) And, though he says that '[o]ne does not go backwards', Mussolini's fascism, as our passages from him show, clearly does so.

Those who look forward to the future realization of imagined possibilities range from the most moderate reformists to the most extreme radicals, and from those, like Adam Smith and the majority of liberals, who believe that society, if left unhindered, tends to evolve naturally towards its ideal condition, to those, like Fourier and most of the socialists, who believe that such a condition can only be the end result of conscious and planned intervention in history. Again, there are those who contemplate an ideal society without conflict – like Rousseau, who hopes that men will come to 'cherish one another mutually as brothers [and] to will nothing contrary to the will of society', or Robert Owen, who desires that there should 'not be any counteraction of wishes and desires among men'. There are others, like Mill, who welcome dissent and debate and certain kinds of conflict and competition, or, like Mao, believe that 'society at all times develops through continual contradictions'. There are those with an unbounded optimism in the power of reason, from Paine, Godwin and Shelley to Russell, and there is D. H. Lawrence, seeking to liberate men from ideals – 'superimposed from above, from the mind' – into 'free spontaneity'. There are those who stress aesthetic ideals of creativity and self-development from Schiller and Marx to Marcuse, and, in a different way, Oscar Wilde and W. H. Auden; and there are those like Comte who believe that 'the aesthetic point of view' is 'concerned only with the faculties of expression, which must ever hold a secondary place', and those, including Rousseau, Durkheim and Tawney, who take a severe and high-minded view of morality. There are utilitarians, from Bentham and Owen to the Webbs; and others from Rousseau and Kant onwards (the extracts from whom suggest something of what the second owed to the first) who appeal to other moral principles not reducible to utilitarianism. There are those who set an absolute value on equality, like Babeuf; or on liberty (though variously conceived) like Constant, Humboldt, Hegel, Mill and Green; or on participatory democracy, like Rosa Luxemburg and G. D. H. Cole; or on community, like Renan; or, like Bakunin, on justice.

If those who take an optimistic view of future possibilities are often criticized as utopian, there are other writers (often those who make this criticism) who are in their way a great deal more audacious than most so-called utopians dare to be. For they have discovered their good society, not in a romanticized past nor an unrealized future, but here and now, in the present. For a number of contemporary writers its precise location is (or was) the United States of America. For Berle, Riesman and Lipset, contemporary America *is* the good society. 'What is there in Pericles' famous praise of Athens that does not apply to us, in some or even in extended measure?' asks Riesman rhetorically, while Lipset declares that democracy, as practised in the United States, 'is the good society itself in operation'. Contemporary socialists are often criticized for proclaiming the realization of a socialist utopia in Russia, or China, or Cuba, yet here are texts which in their complacency and selective perception surely equal the most rose-tinted pictures which have come from the Left. It is doubtful whether any serious American or Western writer could now find it possible to write in the vein of our extracts from Berle, Riesman, Lipset and Dahrendorf.

Finally, there are those thinkers who doubt that unduly optimistic ideals can be realized, or else denounce the attempt to do so. They either seek to make the best of what they see as inevitable trends, like de Tocqueville, Gaetano Mosca, Georg Simmel, Max Weber and Michels, or they adapt their ideals to accommodate what they see as the 'realities'. As we have already seen, such 'realism' is no less evaluative than all the other views we have considered.

Attempts to support all these views with reasons are too various to be reviewed here, but it may be helpful to hint at their range. At one extreme there are highly general appeals to cosmic principles, as when Burke writes of 'the great primeval contract of eternal society, linking the lower with the higher natures, connecting the visible and invisible world' and when Fourier refers to the 'harmonies of the universe', or when Comte and Spencer refer to general principles at work in nature. Then there are widely divergent, and not always explicit, assumptions about human nature – about the general principles governing human behaviour and specifying the possibilities of human satisfaction. And, at the other extreme, there are appeals to empirical evidence to substantiate such possibilities, as when Marx finds a relative freedom from alienation among French socialist workers and in a French workman returning from San Francisco (see the remarkable footnote from the first of the passages from *Capital*), or when Lévi-Strauss refers to the 'particular wisdom' of so-called 'primitive societies' or T. S. Eliot speaks of 'the operation of a social–religious–artistic complex' among these societies 'which we should emulate upon a higher plane'. Again, the evidence may be imaginatively re-created in the form of fiction, as in Tolstoy's portrayal of communal labour. Such empirical evidence, both historical and contemporary, is of the greatest relevance to the justification and assessment of social and political ideals, bearing on their relation to actual historical tendencies, on the feasibility of their realization, and on its potential benefits and costs. Appealing to such evidence is one way of extending the boundaries of 'realism'.

III

We have arranged the passages in chronological order based upon dates of birth of the writers, rather than freezing them into over-simple categories. It is nevertheless possible to pick out certain recurring themes and attitudes. It is possible to notice both the continuity and the change within particular traditions of social and political thinking.

The period covered by this anthology is that which is both inaugurated and dominated by two great revolutions – the Industrial Revolution which began in Britain, and the French Revolution. The processes set in motion by that double revolution – the processes of industrialization and urbanization, the formation of new social classes, new political movements, aspirations and ideologies – are, in one way or another, the natural and inevitable preoccupation of virtually all the writers in our collection. Their reactions, interpretations and prescriptions are immensely varied, but some shared elements can be discovered.

Some of the first writers in this anthology greet the new age with hope and confidence. They are ready to celebrate it, in Bentham's words, as 'a busy age; in which knowledge is rapidly advancing towards perfection' and 'every thing teems with discovery and improvement'. Adam Smith shares this mood. This confidence in industrialization is shared by later writers of a rather different type, like Robert Owen and Fourier, Saint-Simon and Comte, and, to some extent, Marx. But with them it is a faith of a more qualified kind. They do not suppose that industrialization will *automatically* bring benefits to every section of the community, as did Adam Smith. But they do accept that its beneficial potential is enormous, and that what is essentially required is a rational form of organization to ensure that this potential is realized.

This strain of confidence in industrialization is incorporated into socialist thought, in which this beneficial potential is stressed, as is the tension between it and a system of organizing production – capitalism – which systematically obstructs that potentiality. Industrialization also creates a new class, the urban proletariat, whose resistance to their own exploitation and oppression is to provide the key to the liberation of mankind as a whole – a thesis stated or assumed in all the Marxist writers we have included.

But confidence was not perhaps the commonest reaction to industrialization. Many at least of our chosen writers, including some socialists, were less convinced of the future benefits of industrialization than they were impressed, and oppressed, by the social problems it had already created, to say nothing of the immediate horrors of the new industrial cities and towns. They were concerned with the lack of any kind of real community in the new urban conglomerations, with the absence of a stable and interlocking social structure, with the atomization of society (for which the theory of society descending from Adam Smith through Bentham and Mill to Spencer provided an analytical parallel) into a collection of isolated, and so, in some theories, reduced and alienated individuals. Concerns of this kind are reflected in the passages from Schiller, Coleridge, Fourier, Carlyle, Comte, and, of course, Marx and Engels. Where these writers differ is in the great range of remedies, or panaceas, they offer for this social malaise. Concern with this condition, and the offering of remedies for it, is one of the recurring themes of this book. One response to it was to devise ways of introducing organization and above all morality into economic life – a response common to Durkheim, Tawney and G. D. H. Cole. Another distinctive response is Eliot's sketch of what he thought a Christian society would be like, conscious as he was that 'the organization of society on the principle of private profit, as well as public destruction, is leading both to the deformation of humanity by unregulated industrialism, and to the exhaustion of natural resources. . . .'

Eliot's vision, as he was well aware, had much in common with the hier-archical structure Coleridge had outlined in *On the Constitution of Church and State*. Another, very different, writer who is concerned with the creation, or re-creation, of community is Paul Goodman, and he too looks back to Coleridge, and to the passage we have printed here. Another response is in Yeats's short poem, 'At Galway Races'. D. H. Lawrence's desire for an authentic democracy can be seen in the same context. Perhaps even the national unity preached by fascism can be partially understood as a response to atomization. There is certainly support for this suggestion in the passage from Mussolini we have included.

One characteristic form of this brooding concern with the reduction and alienation of the individual man is the preoccupation with the nature of work. How is work to be made meaningful? Or is that impossible, and should attention be concentrated instead on what the later Marx calls 'the realm of freedom' outside work? These questions are discussed by writers as various as Fourier, Marx, Tolstoy, William Morris, Oscar Wilde, Georg Simmel, Russell, Tawney, Riesman, Goodman and Che Guevara. The intensity and the continuity of the discussion alone are enough to indicate that this is one of the central problems of industrial societies.

We have already suggested something that should be made explicit: that for a series of thinkers, who have many differences among them-selves, what industrial society requires above all is rational organization. Attitudes towards this requirement vary. Some, like Weber and to some extent Simmel, tend to regard it gloomily as a disagreeable but unavoid-able necessity, whose evils we must take every care to guard against. Others, from Saint-Simon and Comte to Mannheim and the Webbs, wel-come the advent of a planned society in place of the chaos of illogicalities and injustices which preceded it.

But against those who see in planning the right rational response to an industrial civilization, there are those who interpret planning as yet another manifestation of all that is most sinister and inhuman in such a civilization – its powerful tendencies to the regimentation, control, organ-ization and manipulation of individual human beings. The more planning, the less spontaneity. The more organization, the less scope there is for individual initiative and self-expression. Some oppose planning and organization with the slogan *laissez-faire*, like Herbert Spencer and Hayek, and to some extent Mill and Keynes. (Other liberals, like Forster, warn against their moral dangers while acknowledging their economic necessity.) The opposition of the anarchists is less ambiguous, because it is egalitarian as *laissez-faire* was not, and more thorough-going.

Anarchism has often been analysed, and dismissed, as a primitive reaction against industrialism as such. In terms of the history of anarchist movements, this has some truth; in terms of ideas, it has a great deal less, and the continuing appeal of anarchism derives in part from the fact that its challenge to the rational, organizing character of advanced industrial society has its roots in ordinary experience. Many people have a sense of crushed spontaneity, or self-expression repressed. The anarchists would agree with Freud that present society is founded upon repression. They would not accept his view that every society must be.

The other revolution, in France, provoked a similar variety of response. Burke and de Maistre were among the first to perceive its appalling implications for traditional principles, and denounced it accordingly. They were followed by many others who, if they did not denounce the event, deplored the pernicious principles which it had spread all through Europe and far beyond. Interestingly, in one of his early writings which we reproduce here, Hegel advanced a nuanced critique of the Jacobin tendencies of the Revolution from an essentially liberal perspective, criticizing the quality of life 'engendered in a modern state where everything is regulated from the top downwards, where nothing with any general implications is left to the management and execution of interested parties of the people'. Others, such as Paine, Condorcet, Godwin, William Blake (though not in the four lines quoted here), Gracchus Babeuf, Saint-Simon and Wordsworth greeted the Revolution with enthusiasm – though in the case of Wordsworth this was (as the first of our selections from him shows) short-lived. They heard in the Revolution the death-knell of the ecclesiastical and secular tyrannies which had oppressed men for so long. They were confident that liberty, equality and popular sovereignty would spread from France, and America, outward to every corner of the earth. The eighteenth-century dream of the Heavenly City, of 'the absolute perfection of the human race', now seemed capable of realization. The dark ages of ignorance and superstition were now to be superseded by the age of reason.

A second generation of radicals kept the faith alive. It included Shelley, whose thinking owed so much to that of his father-in-law, Godwin, and William Hazlitt, who continued to uphold the essential democratic principle of government by the people. But the radicalism of Paine and

Hazlitt does not survive as an independent tradition of thought: it is absorbed into the more economically and socially conscious thinking of the socialists and anarchists. Yet these too continue to look back to the Revolution. Thus Bakunin seeks to 'proclaim anew that great principle of the French Revolution: that every man should have the material and moral means of developing all his humanity', and even Bernstein sees (revisionist) socialism as carrying further the Revolution's work.

Meanwhile, another important tradition had emerged – a liberal tradition which, initially at least, is distinct from Burkean conservatism as well as from political and social radicalism. It is clearly adumbrated in Kant, and among its first representatives are Wilhelm von Humboldt and Benjamin Constant; later in the nineteenth century there follow de Tocqueville and Mill, Herzen and Matthew Arnold. For all of these writers, individual liberty is the greatest of social values, and most of them agree in seeing it as threatened by another principle to which liberalism is at least in theory committed: democracy. Arnold agrees explicitly with de Tocqueville that democracy has got to be accepted, because, in the modern world, it is an irresistible force. But they look on it with suspicion. We are already a long way from Hazlitt's *vox populi vox Dei*. For these liberals, popular sovereignty constitutes possibly an even greater threat to the freedom, and therefore to the individuality, of the individual than the older forms of tyranny. This attitude to democracy becomes part of the permanent furniture of modern liberalism, and it is one of the factors which link modern liberalism with modern conservatism. There are others. As we have already noted, liberals like Popper join conservatives like Lippmann in attacking utopianism, while a contemporary advocate of *laissez-faire* like Hayek is naturally regarded as a conservative, even though he echoes a 'progressive' nineteenth-century liberal like Mill. On the other hand, Green's liberalism, as our extract from him shows, stressing 'the liberation of the powers of all men equally for contributions to a common good', and limitations on freedom of contract, points in the direction of socialism. Finally, E. M. Forster represents a continuing and permanently valuable strand in the whole history of liberalism (a strand reaching right back to Constant), with his firm emphasis on 'the importance of personal relationships and the private life' and on '*laisser-faire* . . . in the world of the spirit'.

Traditions of thought change, although some change less than others. Many writers in the Marxist socialist tradition follow fairly closely the lines of thought set out by its founders, though the reader may find it interesting to trace the divergences evident even in these passages. Compare, for example, Marx's fundamental and continuing commitment to a 'real community' in which 'individuals obtain their freedom in and through their association' and everyone has 'the means of cultivating his gifts in all directions', with Engels's Saint-Simonian stress upon the need to eliminate anarchy and waste and to replace 'the government of persons' by 'the administration of things', by 'systematic, definite organization' – a theme echoed and developed by Bukharin and Preobrazhensky. It is interesting to see what Lenin, in one of his most 'utopian' passages, derives from the very passages from Marx and Engels that we have included (the implications of which Stalin was later to explain away). Then there is Rosa Luxemburg's fundamentalist critique of what she saw as the inexorable consequences of Lenin's practice, declaring, in words reminiscent of anarchism, that 'socialism by its very nature cannot be decreed' and proclaiming the need to involve the 'whole mass of the people' in public life. Another critic of bureaucratic tendencies is Mao Tse-Tung, seeking to combine in an original synthesis the ideals of Marxism-Leninism with traditional ideals of social harmony 'long cherished by the Chinese people'. And in the passages of most recent origin, those by Marcuse, Guevara and the brothers Cohn-Bendit, there is a renewed stress on the anti-authoritarian character of socialism, which witnesses to the continuing liveliness and relevance of anarchist as well as more orthodoxly socialist ideas.

Some Marxists still, like Engels and Lenin, denounce 'anarchism', and, for that matter, 'utopianism' as well. But the anarchists and utopians can fairly respond to this by asking why it is that the states which are supposedly founded upon Marxist-Leninist principles are still so flagrantly non-socialist and non-libertarian in so many respects, and why they do not seem to be perceptibly advancing towards the class-less, state-less society envisaged by all the great socialist theorists. The relation between end and means, between the goal and the path towards it, is now seen to be far closer and more complex than has sometimes been supposed. As Marcuse writes:

these aesthetic needs and goals must from the beginning be present in the reconstruction of society, and not only at the end or in the far future. Otherwise the needs and satisfactions which reproduce a repressive society would be carried over into the new society. Repressive men would carry over their repression into the new society.

Active discussion about social and political ideals, so far from being obsolete, as was suggested by many Western writers a decade ago, has taken on a new lease of life. People are once more seriously arguing about the principles on which a good society ought to be founded. In so doing they are, as our book shows, contributing to a long-standing and continuous debate in which thinkers and writers of many persuasions have taken part. We hope that this book will cast a little light upon current discussions by illustrating, in however compressed a fashion, the contributions such thinkers and writers have made to it and the historical context in which it takes place.

Our selection of authors is, obviously, determined by our own judgements of historical and intellectual significance and contemporary relevance, and it makes no pretence of any illusory 'comprehensiveness'. As for our selection of passages, we have tried hard to satisfy a number of criteria. Sadly, in applying these criteria, we found that a number of thinkers whom we would have wished to include, proved recalcitrant, among them Ruskin, Nietzsche, Sorel and Trotsky.

We have tried to select passages which show a thinker's evaluative standpoint – which go some way toward answering the question, 'What does he stand for?' and toward revealing his reasons for taking the stand that he does. Since we believe that values and ideals form a crucial and integral part of social and political theorizing, it can be especially illuminating to seek out those passages which bring out the principles governing the social order each thinker sees as desirable – providing, so to speak, a kind of privileged access to his thought. Such passages may reveal a thinker's most basic assumptions, making sense of much else that he says.

Beyond this basic criterion of selection, we have tried to find passages that are particularly representative of a thinker's tone of voice and of the ideas which are distinctively his. Sometimes, as with Hegel, Spencer and Russell, this involves taking an early text, on the assumption that it presents ideas that remain central and integral to his thinking, whatever other important changes that thinking may undergo. In other cases, as with Bentham, Saint-Simon, Mill and Marx, we have selected writings dating from different stages in a writer's development. Whenever we were faced with a choice between well-known passages, on the one hand, and less familiar or less accessible passages, on the other, we have chosen the latter.

Finally, we have tried to find passages which relate to each other, both in terms of subject-matter and of allusions to one another's ideas. We have already said enough to show the considerable continuity of themes, differently treated. But there are also a great number of cross-references – both explicit and implicit – in the passages we have included. Thus (to mention only some of those that are explicit), Babeuf quotes Condorcet; Godwin refers to Rousseau; Hegel refers to 'would-be philosophers and teachers of the rights of man'; Mill refers to Bentham and Humboldt; Herzen to Rousseau; Engels to the anarchists; Arnold to de Tocqueville; Bernstein to Rousseau, Babeuf and the anarchists; Freud to communists and socialists; Durkheim to the classical economists, the utilitarians and the Kantians; Simmel and Michels to Proudhon; Lenin to Marx, Engels and the anarchists; Rosa Luxemburg to Lenin; Russell to Kropotkin and Guild Socialism; Forster to Mussolini; Mussolini to Adam Smith, Bentham, de Maistre, Saint-Simon, Owen, Fourier, Humboldt, Marx and Renan; Eliot to D. H. Lawrence; Pasternak to Tolstoyism; Marcuse to Marx; Hayek to Burke, Saint-Simon and de Tocqueville; Lévi-Strauss to Saint-Simon; Riesman to Adam Smith and Dostoevsky; Paul Goodman to Coleridge; and Crosland to William Morris and the Webbs.

In fact, the book as a whole can be read, to some extent, as a reconstructed debate within and between several different traditions of social and political thought. In this way, we hope that it may give some idea of their historical significance and their contemporary relevance.

Many friends and colleagues have joined in the pleasure of compiling this book, making suggestions of thinkers and passages, not all of which we have acted upon. We wish especially to thank David Lloyd-Jones for his help in checking the (difficult) translation from Fourier, and David McLellan for his felicitous translation of the passage from Marx's notebook on James Mill. We also owe debts of gratitude to Chris Allen, John Birtwhistle, John Corina, Aidan Foster-Carter, Jonathan Glover, Barbara Goodwin, Jasper Griffin, Christopher Hitchens, Jack Lively, Jackie Lukes, Ira Magaziner, Derek Parfit, Carole Pateman, John Torrance and David Wiltshire.

We have removed footnotes from the selected passages where they are merely references or contribute nothing to the author's argument. Where already available translations are used, we have tried to find the best and clearest; but the passages from Babeuf, Constant, Fourier, de Tocqueville and Bakunin, and the first two passages from Saint-Simon have been specially translated for this volume by Steven Lukes.

PART I

Jean-Jacques Rousseau
(1712–1778)

THE HEALTH-GIVING
AIR OF LIBERTY

If I had had to make choice of the place of my birth, I should have preferred a society which had an extent proportionate to the limits of the
human faculties; that is, to the possibility of being well governed: in which
every person being equal to his occupation, no one should be obliged to
commit to others the functions with which he was entrusted: a State, in
which all the individuals being well known to one another, neither the
secret machinations of vice, nor the modesty of virtue should be able to
escape the notice and judgement of the public; and in which the pleasant
custom of seeing and knowing one another should make the love of
country rather a love of the citizens than of its soil.

I should have wished to be born in a country in which the interest of the
Sovereign and that of the people must be single and identical; to the end
that all the movements of the machine might tend always to the general
happiness. And as this could not be the case, unless the Sovereign and the
people were one and the same person, it follows that I should have wished
to be born under a democratic government, wisely tempered.

I should have wished to live and die free; that is, so far subject to the
laws that neither I, nor anybody else, should be able to cast off their
honourable yoke: the easy and salutary yoke which the haughtiest necks
bear with the greater docility, as they are made to bear no other.

I should have wished then that no one within the State should be able
to say he was above the law; and that no one without should be able to
dictate so that the State should be obliged to recognize his authority. For,
be the constitution of a government what it may, if there be within its
jurisdiction a single man who is not subject to the law, all the rest are
necessarily at his discretion. And if there be a national ruler within, and
a foreign ruler without, however they may divide their authority, it is

impossible that both should be duly obeyed, or that the State should be well governed.

I should not have chosen to live in a republic of recent institution, however excellent its laws; for fear the government, being perhaps otherwise framed than the circumstances of the moment might require, might disagree with the new citizens, or they with it, and the State run the risk of overthrow and destruction almost as soon as it came into being. For it is with liberty as it is with those solid and succulent foods, or with those generous wines which are well adapted to nourish and fortify robust constitutions that are used to them, but ruin and intoxicate weak and delicate constitutions to which they are not suited. Peoples once accustomed to masters are not in a condition to do without them. If they attempt to shake off the yoke they still more estrange themselves from freedom, as, by mistaking for it an unbridled licence to which it is diametrically opposed, they nearly always manage, by their revolutions, to hand themselves over to seducers, who only make their chains heavier than before. The Roman people itself, a model for all free peoples, was wholly incapable of governing itself when it escaped from the oppression of the Tarquins. Debased by slavery, and the ignominious tasks which had been imposed upon it, it was at first no better than a stupid mob, which it was necessary to control and govern with the greatest wisdom; in order that, being accustomed by degrees to breathe the health-giving air of liberty, minds which had been enervated or rather brutalized under tyranny, might gradually acquire that severity of morals and spirit of fortitude which made it at length the people of all most worthy of respect. I should, then, have sought out for my country some peaceful and happy Republic of an antiquity that lost itself, as it were, in the night of time: which had experienced only such shocks as served to manifest and strengthen the courage and patriotism of its subjects; and whose citizens, long accustomed to a wise independence, were not only free, but worthy to be so.

Dedication to the 'Discourse on the Origin and Foundation of Inequality' (1755), in J.-J. Rousseau, *The Social Contract, and Discourses*, trans. with introd. by G. D. H. Cole, Everyman ed. (London, Dent, 1913), 1958 ed., pp. 144–6.

. . . . .

Let our country then show itself the common mother of her citizens; let the advantages they enjoy in their country endear it to them; let the government leave them enough share in the public administration to make them feel that they are at home; and let the laws be in their eyes only the guarantees of the common liberty. These rights, great as they are, belong to all men: but without seeming to attack them directly, the ill-will of rulers may in fact easily reduce their effect to nothing. The law, which they thus abuse, serves the powerful at once as a weapon of offence, and as a shield against the weak; and the pretext of the public good is always the most dangerous scourge of the people. What is most necessary, and perhaps most difficult, in government, is rigid integrity in doing strict justice to all, and above all in protecting the poor against the tyranny of the rich. The greatest evil has already come about, when there are poor men to be defended, and rich men to be restrained. It is on the middle classes alone that the whole force of the law is exerted; and they are equally powerless against the treasures of the rich and the penury of the poor. The first mocks them, the second escapes them. The one breaks the meshes, the other passes through them.

It is therefore one of the most important functions of government to prevent extreme inequality of fortunes; not by taking away wealth from its possessors, but by depriving all men of means to accumulate it; not by building hospitals for the poor, but by securing the citizens from becoming poor. The unequal distribution of inhabitants over the territory, when men are crowded together in one place, while other places are depopulated; the encouragement of the arts that minister to luxury and of purely industrial arts at the expense of useful and laborious crafts; the sacrifice of agriculture to commerce; the necessitation of the tax-farmer by the maladministration of the funds of the State; and in short, venality pushed to such an extreme that even public esteem is reckoned at a cash value, and virtue rated at a market price: these are the most obvious causes of opulence and of poverty, of public interest, of mutual hatred among citizens, of indifference to the common cause, of the corruption of the people and of the weakening of all the springs of government. Such are the evils, which are with difficulty cured when they make themselves felt, but which a wise administration ought to prevent, if it is to maintain, along with good morals, respect for the laws, patriotism and the influence of the general will.

But all these precautions will be inadequate, unless rulers go still more to the root of the matter. I conclude this part of public economy where I ought to have begun it. There can be no patriotism without liberty, no liberty without virtue, no virtue without citizens; create citizens, and you have everything you need; without them, you will have nothing but debased slaves, from the rulers of the State downwards. To form citizens is not the work of a day; and in order to have men it is necessary to educate them when they are children. It will be said, perhaps, that whoever has men to govern, ought not to seek, beyond their nature, a perfection of which they are incapable; that he ought not to desire to destroy their passions; and that the execution of such an attempt is no more desirable than it is possible. I will agree, further, that a man without passions would certainly be a bad citizen; but it must be agreed also that, if men are not taught not to love some things, it is impossible to teach them to love one object more than another – to prefer that which is truly beautiful to that which is deformed. If, for example, they were early accustomed to regard their individuality only in its relation to the body of the State, and to be aware, so to speak, of their own existence merely as a part of that of the State, they might at length come to identify themselves in some degree with this greater whole, to feel themselves members of their country and to love it with that exquisite feeling which no isolated person has save for himself; to lift up their spirits perpetually to this great object, and thus to transform into a sublime virtue that dangerous disposition which gives rise to all our vices. Not only does philosophy demonstrate the possibility of giving feeling these new directions; history furnishes us with a thousand striking examples. If they are so rare among us moderns, it is because nobody troubles himself whether citizens exist or not, and still less does anybody think of attending to the matter soon enough to make them. It is too late to change our natural inclinations, when they have taken their course, and egoism is confirmed by habit: and it is too late to lead us out of ourselves when once the human ego, concentrated in our hearts, has acquired that contemptible activity which absorbs all virtue and constitutes the life and being of little minds. How can patriotism germinate in the midst of so many other passions which smother it? And what can remain, for fellow-citizens, of a heart already divided between avarice, a mistress, and vanity?

From the first moment of life, men ought to begin learning to deserve to live; and, as at the instant of birth we partake of the rights of citizenship, that instant ought to be the beginning of the exercise of our duty. If there are laws for the age of maturity, there ought to be laws for infancy, teaching obedience to others: and as the reason of each man is not left to be the sole arbiter of his duties, government ought the less indiscriminately to abandon to the intelligence and prejudices of fathers the education of their children, as that education is of still greater importance to the State than to the fathers: for, according to the course of nature, the death of the father often deprives him of the final fruits of education; but his country sooner or later perceives its effects. Families dissolve, but the State remains.

Should the public authority, by taking the place of the father, and charging itself with that important function, acquire his rights by discharging his duties, he would have the less cause to complain, as he would only be changing his title, and would have in common, under the name of *citizen*, the same authority over his children, as he was exercising separately under the name of *father*, and would not be less obeyed when speaking in the name of the law, than when he spoke in that of nature. Public education, therefore, under regulations prescribed by the government, and under magistrates established by the Sovereign, is one of the fundamental rules of popular or legitimate government. If children are brought up in common in the bosom of equality; if they are imbued with the laws of the State and the precepts of the general will; if they are taught to respect these above all things; if they are surrounded by examples and objects which constantly remind them of the tender mother who nourishes them, of the love she bears them, of the inestimable benefits they receive from her and of the return they owe her, we cannot doubt they will learn to cherish one another mutually as brothers, to will nothing contrary to the will of society, to substitute the actions of men and citizens for the futile and vain babbling of sophists, and to become in time defenders and fathers of the country of which they will have been so long the children.

I shall say nothing of the Magistrates destined to preside over such an education, which is certainly the most important business of the State. It is easy to see that if such marks of public confidence were conferred on slight grounds, if this sublime function were not, for those who have worthily discharged all other offices, the reward of labour, the pleasant and honourable repose of old age and the crown of all honours, the whole enterprise would be useless and the education void of success. For wherever the lesson is not supported by authority, and the precept by example, all instruction is fruitless; and virtue itself loses its credit in the mouth of one who does not practise it. But let illustrious warriors, bent under the weight of their laurels, preach courage: let upright Magistrates, grown white in the purple and on the bench teach justice. Such teachers as these would thus get themselves virtuous successors, and transmit from age to age, to generations to come, the experience and talents of rulers, the courage and virtue of citizens, and common emulation in all to live and die for their country.

I know of but three peoples which once practised public education, the Cretans, the Lacedemonians and the ancient Persians: among all these it was attended with the greatest success, and indeed it did wonders among the two last. Since the world has been divided into nations too great to admit of being well governed, this method has been no longer practicable, and the reader will readily perceive other reasons why such a thing has never been attempted by any modern people. It is very remarkable that the Romans were able to dispense with it; but Rome was for five hundred years one continued miracle which the world cannot hope to see again. The virtue of the Romans, engendered by their horror of tyranny and the crimes of tyrants, and by an innate patriotism, made all their houses so many schools of citizenship; while the unlimited power of fathers over their children made the individual authority so rigid that the father was more feared than the Magistrate, and was in his family tribunal both censor of morals and avenger of the laws.

Thus a careful and well-intentioned government, vigilant incessantly to maintain or restore patriotism and morality among the people, provides beforehand against the evils which sooner or later result from the indifference of the citizens to the fate of the Republic, keeping within narrow bounds that personal interest which so isolates the individual that the State is enfeebled by his power, and has nothing to hope from his goodwill. Wherever men love their country, respect the laws and live simply, little remains to be done in order to make them happy; and in public administration, where chance has less influence than in the lot of individuals, wisdom is so nearly allied to happiness, that the two objects are confounded.

'Discourse on Political Economy' (1755), in ibid., pp. 249–54.

THE SYSTEM OF NATURAL LIBERTY

. . . Every individual who employs his capital in the support of domestic industry, necessarily endeavours so to direct that industry, that its produce may be of the greatest possible value.

The produce of industry is what it adds to the subject or materials upon which it is employed. In proportion as the value of this produce is great or small, so will likewise be the profits of the employer. But it is only for the sake of profit that any man employs a capital in the support of industry; and he will always, therefore, endeavour to employ it in the support of that industry of which the produce is likely to be of the greatest value, or to exchange for the greatest quantity either of money or of other goods.

But the annual revenue of every society is always precisely equal to the exchangeable value of the whole annual produce of its industry, or rather is precisely the same thing with that exchangeable value. As every individual, therefore, endeavours as much as he can both to employ his capital in the support of domestic industry, and so to direct that industry that its produce may be of the greatest value; every individual necessarily labours to render the annual revenue of the society as great as he can. He generally, indeed, neither intends to promote the public interest, nor knows how much he is promoting it. By preferring the support of domestic to that of foreign industry, he intends only his own security; and by directing that industry in such a manner as its produce may be of the greatest value, he intends only his own gain, and he is in this, as in many other cases, led by an invisible hand to promote an end which was no part of his intention. Nor is it always the worse for the society that it was no part of it. By pursuing his own interest he frequently promotes that of the society more effectually than when he really intends to promote it. I have never known much good done by those who affected to trade for the public good. It is an affectation, indeed, not very common among mer-chants, and very few words need be employed in dissuading them from it.

What is the species of domestic industry which his capital can employ, and of which the produce is likely to be of the greatest value, every indi-vidual, it is evident, can, in his local situation, judge much better than any statesman or lawgiver can do for him. The statesman, who should attempt to direct private people in what manner they ought to employ their capitals, would not only load himself with a most unnecessary attention, but assume an authority which could safely be trusted, not only to no single person, but to no council or senate whatever, and which would no-where be so dangerous as in the hands of a man who had folly and pre-sumption enough to fancy himself fit to exercise it.

It is thus that every system which endeavours, either, by extraordinary encouragements, to draw towards a particular species of industry a greater share of the capital of the society than what would naturally go to it; or, by extraordinary restraints, to force from a particular species of industry some share of the capital which would otherwise be employed in it, is in reality subversive of the great purpose which it means to promote. It retards, instead of accelerating, the progress of the society towards real wealth and greatness; and diminishes, instead of increasing, the real value of the annual produce of its land and labour.

All systems either of preference or of restraint, therefore, being thus completely taken away, the obvious and simple system of natural liberty establishes itself of its own accord. Every man, as long as he does not violate the laws of justice, is left perfectly free to pursue his own interest his own way, and to bring both his industry and capital into competition with those of any other man, or order of men. The sovereign is completely discharged from a duty in the attempting to perform which he must always be exposed to innumerable delusions, and for the proper performance of which no human wisdom or knowledge could ever be sufficient; the duty of superintending the industry of private people and of directing it towards the employments most suitable to the interest of the society. According to the system of natural liberty, the sovereign has only three duties to attend to; three duties of great importance, indeed, but plain and intelligible to common understandings: first, the duty of protecting the society from the violence and invasion of other independent societies;

secondly the duty of protecting, as far as possible, every member of the society from the injustice or oppression of every other member of it, or the duty of establishing an exact administration of justice; and, thirdly, the duty of erecting and maintaining certain public works and certain public institutions, which it can never be for the interest of any individual, or small number of individuals, to erect and maintain; because the profit could never repay the expense to any individual or small number of individuals, though it may frequently do much more than repay it to a great society.

An Inquiry into the Nature and Causes of the Wealth of Nations (1776), paperback ed. (London, Methuen, 1961), vol. I, pp. 477–8; vol. II, pp. 208–9.

Immanuel Kant
(1724–1804)

LIBERTY, EQUALITY AND POPULAR SOVEREIGNTY

The LIBERTY of every Member of the State AS A MAN, is the first Principle in the constitution of a rational Commonwealth. I would express this Principle in the following form: 'No one has a right to compel me to be happy in the peculiar way in which he may think of the well-being of other men; but everyone is entitled to seek his own happiness in the way that seems to him best, if it does not infringe the liberty of others in striving after a similar end for themselves when their Liberty is capable of consisting with the Right of Liberty in all others according to possible universal laws.' – A Government founded upon the principle of Benevolence towards the people – after the analogy of a *father* to his children, and therefore called a *paternal Government* – would be one in which the Subjects would be regarded as children or minors unable to distinguish what is beneficial or injurious to them. These subjects would be thus compelled to act in a merely passive way; and they would be trained to expect solely from the Judgement of the Sovereign and just as he might will it, merely out of his goodness, all that *ought* to make them happy. Such a Government would be the greatest conceivable *Despotism*; for it would present a Constitution that would abolish all Liberty in the Subjects and leave them no Rights. It is not a *paternal* Government, but only a *patriotic* Government that is adapted for men who are capable of Rights, and at the same time fitted to give scope to the good-will of the ruler. By 'patriotic' is meant that condition of mind in which everyone in the State – the Head of it not excepted – regards the Commonwealth as the maternal bosom, and the country as the paternal soil out of and on which he himself has sprung into being, and which he also must leave to others as a dear inheritance. Thus, and thus only, can he hold himself entitled to protect the Rights of his fatherland by laws of the common will, but not to subject it

34

to an unconditional purpose of his own at pleasure. – This Right of Liberty thus belongs to him as a man, while he is a Member of the Commonwealth; or, in point of fact, so far as he is a being capable of rights generally.

The EQUALITY of every member of the State AS A SUBJECT, is the second Principle in the Constitution of a rational Commonwealth. The formula of this Principle may be put thus: 'Every Member of the Commonwealth has rights against every other that may be enforced by compulsory Laws, from which only the Sovereign or Supreme Ruler of the State is excepted, because he is regarded not as a mere Member of the Commonwealth, but as its Creator or Maintainer; and he alone has the Right to compel without being himself subject to compulsory Law.' All, however, who live *under* Laws in a State, are its subjects; and, consequently, they are subjected to the compulsory Law, like all other members of the Commonwealth, one only, whether an individual Sovereign or a collective body, constituting the Supreme Head of the State, and as such being accepted as the medium through which alone all rightful coercion or compulsion can be exercised. For, should the Head of the State also be subject to compulsion, there would no longer be a Supreme Head, and the series of members subordinate and superordinate would go on upwards *ad infinitum*. Again, were there in the State two such powers as persons exempt from legal compulsion, neither of them would be subject to compulsory Laws, and as such the one could do no wrong to the other; which is impossible.

Out of this idea of the Equality of men as Subjects in the Commonwealth, there arises the following formula: 'Every Member of the State should have it made possible for him to attain to any position or rank that may belong to any subject, to which his talent, his industry or his fortune may be capable of raising him; and his fellow-subjects are not entitled to stand in the way by any *hereditary* prerogative forming the exclusive privilege of a certain class, in order to keep him and his posterity for ever below them.'

For, all Right just consists in restriction of the Liberty of another to the condition that is consistent with my Liberty according to a universal Law; and Public Right in a Commonwealth is only the product of actual legislation conformable to this principle and conjoined with power, in virtue of which all who belong to a nation as its subjects find themselves in a rightful state – *status juridicus* – constituted and regulated by law. And, as such, this state is in fact a condition of Equality, inasmuch as it is determined by the action and reaction of free-wills limiting one another, according to the universal law of Freedom; and it thus constitutes the Civil State of human Society. Hence the *inborn* Right of all individuals in this sphere (that is considered as being prior to their having actually entered upon juridical action) to bring compulsion to bear upon any others, is entirely *identical and equal throughout*, on the assumption that they are always to remain within the bounds of unanimity and concord in the mutual use of their Liberty. Now birth is not an *act* on the part of him who is born, and consequently it does not entail upon him any inequality in the state of Right, nor any subjection under laws of compulsion other than what is common to him, with all others, as a subject of the one supreme legislative Power; and, therefore, there can be no inborn privilege by way of Right in any member of the Commonwealth as a subject, before another fellow-subject. Nor, consequently, has anyone a right to transmit the privilege or prerogative of the *Rank* which he holds in the Commonwealth to his posterity so that they should be, as it were, qualified by birth for the rank of nobility; nor should they be prevented from attaining to the higher stages in the gradations of social rank, by their own merit. Everything else that partakes of the nature of a thing and does not relate to personality, may be bequeathed; and, since such things may be acquired as property, they may also be alienated or disposed. Hence after a number of generations a considerable inequality in external circumstances may arise among the members of a Commonwealth, producing such relations as those of Master and Servant, Landlord and Tenant, etc. These circumstances and relations, however, ought not to hinder any of the subjects of the State from rising to such positions as their talent, their industry and their fortune may make it possible for them to fill. For otherwise such a one would be qualified to coerce without being liable to be coerced by the counter action of others in return; and he would rise above the stage of being a fellow-subject. Further, no man who lives under the legalized conditions of a Commonwealth, can fall out of this equality otherwise than by his own crime, and never either by compact or through any military occupancy.[1] For he cannot by any legal act, whether of himself or of another, cease to be the owner of himself, or enter into the class of domestic cattle, which are used for all sorts of services at will and are maintained in this condition without their consent as long as there is a will to do it, although under the limitation – which is sometimes sanctioned even by religion, as among the Hindoos – that they are not to be

[1] Occupatio bellica.

mutilated or slain. Under any conditions, he is to be regarded as happy who is conscious that it depends only on himself – that is on his faculty or earnest will – or on circumstances which he cannot impute to any other, and not on the irresistible will of others, that he does not rise to a stage of Equality with others who as his fellow-subjects have no advantage over him as far as Right is concerned.

The SELF-DEPENDENCY of a member of the Commonwealth AS A CITIZEN, or fellow-legislator, is the third principle or condition of Right in the State. In the matter of the legislation itself, all are to be regarded as free and equal *under* the already existing public Laws; but they are not to be all regarded as equal in relation to the right to give or *enact* these laws. Those who are not capable of this right are, notwithstanding, subjected to the observance of the laws as members of the Commonwealth, and thereby they participate in the protection which is in accordance therewith; they are, however, not to be regarded as *Citizens* but as protected fellow-subjects. – All right, in fact, depends on the laws. A public law, however, which determines for all what is to be legally allowed or not allowed in their regard, is the act of a public Will, from which all right proceeds and which therefore itself can do no wrong to anyone. For this, however, there is no other Will competent than that of the *whole* people, as it is only when all determine about all that each one in consequence determines about himself. For it is only to himself that one can do no wrong. But if it be another will that is in question, then the mere will of anyone different from it, could determine nothing for it which might not be wrong; and consequently the law of such a will would require another law to limit its legislation. And thus no particular will can be legislative for a Commonwealth. – Properly speaking, in order to make out this, the ideas of the external Liberty, Equality and *Unity* of the will of all, are to be taken into account; and for the last of these *Self-dependency* is the condition, since the exercising of a vote is required when the former two ideas are taken along with it. The fundamental law thus indicated, which can only arise out of the universal united will of the people, is what is called the '*Original Contract*'.

Now anyone who has the right of voting in this system of Legislation, is a *Citizen* as distinguished from a Burgess; he is a *citoyen* as distinguished from a *bourgeois*. The quality requisite for this status, in addition to the natural one of not being a child or a woman, – is solely this, that the individual is his *own master* by right (*sui juris*); and, consequently, that he has some property that supports him, – under which may be reckoned any art or handicraft, or any fine art or science. Otherwise put, the condition in those cases in which the citizen must acquire from others in order to live, is that he only acquires it by alienation of what is his own, and not by a consent given to others to make use of his powers; and consequently that he *serves* no one but the Commonwealth, in the proper sense of the term. In this relation those who are skilled in the arts, and large or small proprietors, are all equal to one another; as in fact each one is entitled only to one vote.

Furthermore, *all* who have this right of voting must agree in order to realize the Laws of public justice, for otherwise there would arise a conflict of right between those who were not in agreement with it, and the others who were; and this would give rise to the need of a higher principle of right that the conflict might be decided. A universal agreement cannot be expected from a whole people; and consequently it is only a plurality of voices, and not even of those who immediately vote in a large nation, but only of their delegates as representative of the people that can alone be foreseen as practically attainable. And hence, even the principle of making the majority of votes suffice as representing the general consent, will have to be taken as by compact; and it must thus be regarded as the ultimate basis of the establishment of any Civil Constitution.

'The Principles of Political Right' (1793), in *Kant's Principles of Politics*, ed. and trans. W. Hastie (Edinburgh, T. & T. Clark, 1891), pp. 36–8, 39–44, 45–6.

Edmund Burke
(1729–1797)

LIBERTY, PROPERTY AND CONTINUITY

I flatter myself that I love a manly, moral, regulated liberty as well as any gentleman of that society, be he who he will; and perhaps I have given as good proofs of my attachment to that cause, in the whole course of my public conduct. I think I envy liberty as little as they do, to any other nation. But I cannot stand forward, and give praise or blame to anything which relates to human actions, and human concerns, on a simple view of the object, as it stands stripped of every relation, in all the nakedness and solitude of metaphysical abstraction. Circumstances (which with some gentlemen pass for nothing) give in reality to every political principle its distinguishing colour and discriminating effect. The circumstances are what render every civil and political scheme beneficial or noxious to mankind. Abstractedly speaking, government, as well as liberty, is good; yet could I, in common sense, ten years ago, have felicitated France on her enjoyment of a government (for she then had a government) without inquiry what the nature of that government was, or how it was administered? Can I now congratulate the same nation upon its freedom? Is it because liberty in the abstract may be classed amongst the blessings of mankind, that I am seriously to felicitate a madman, who has escaped from the protecting restraint and wholesome darkness of his cell, on his restoration to the enjoyment of light and liberty? Am I to congratulate a highwayman and murderer, who has broke prison, upon the recovery of his natural rights? This would be to act over again the scene of the criminals condemned to the galleys, and their heroic deliverer, the metaphysic knight of the sorrowful countenance.

When I see the spirit of liberty in action, I see a strong principle at work; and this, for a while, is all I can possibly know of it. The wild *gas*, the fixed air, is plainly broke loose: but we ought to suspend our judgement until the first effervescence is a little subsided, till the liquor is cleared, and until we see something deeper than the agitation of a troubled and frothy surface. I must be tolerably sure, before I venture publicly to congratulate men upon a blessing, that they have really received one. Flattery corrupts both the receiver and the giver; and adulation is not of more service to the people than to kings. I should therefore suspend my congratulations on the new liberty of France, until I was informed how it had been combined with government; with public force; with the discipline and obedience of armies; with the collection of an effective and well-distributed revenue; with morality and religion; with the solidity of property; with peace and order; with civil and social manners. All these (in their way) are good things too; and, without them, liberty is not a benefit whilst it lasts, and is not likely to continue long. The effect of liberty to individuals is, that they may do what they please: we ought to see what it will please them to do, before we risk congratulations, which may be soon turned into complaints. Prudence would dictate this in the case of separate, insulated, private men; but liberty, when men act in bodies, is *power*. Considerate people, before they declare themselves, will observe the use which is made of *power*; and particularly of so trying a thing as *new* power in *new* persons, of whose principles, tempers and dispositions they have little or no experience, and in situations, where those who appear the most stirring in the scene may possibly not be the real movers.

You will observe, that from Magna Charta to the Declaration of Rights, it has been the uniform policy of our constitution to claim and assert our liberties, as an *entailed inheritance* derived to us from our forefathers, and to be transmitted to our posterity; as an estate specially belonging to the people of this kingdom, without any reference whatever to any other more general or prior right. By this means our constitution preserves a unity in so great a diversity of its parts. We have an inheritable crown; an inheritable peerage; and a House of Commons and a people inheriting privileges, franchises and liberties, from a long line of ancestors.

This policy appears to me to be the result of profound reflection; or rather the happy effect of following nature, which is wisdom without reflection, and above it. A spirit of innovation is generally the result of a selfish temper and confined views. People will not look forward to posterity, who never look backward to their ancestors. Besides, the people of England well know, that the idea of inheritance furnishes a sure principle of conservation and a sure principle of transmission; without at all excluding a principle of improvement. It leaves acquisition free; but it secures what it acquires. Whatever advantages are obtained by a state proceeding on these maxims, are locked fast as in a sort of family settlement; grasped as in a kind of mortmain for ever. By a constitutional policy, working after the pattern of nature, we receive, we hold, we transmit our government and our privileges, in the same manner in which we enjoy and transmit our property and our lives. The institutions of policy, the goods of fortune, the gifts of providence, are handed down to us, and from us, in the same course and order. Our political system is placed in a just correspondence and symmetry with the order of the world, and with the mode of existence decreed to a permanent body composed of transitory parts; wherein, by the disposition of a stupendous wisdom, moulding together the great mysterious incorporation of the human race, the whole, at one time, is never old, or middle-aged, or young, but, in a condition of unchangeable constancy moves on through the varied tenor of perpetual decay, fall, renovation and progression. Thus, by preserving the method of nature in the conduct of the state, in what we improve, we are never wholly new; in what we retain, we are never wholly obsolete. By adhering in this manner and on those principles to our forefathers, we are guided not by the superstition of antiquarians, but by the spirit of philosophic analogy. In this choice of inheritance we have given to our frame of polity the image of a relation in blood; binding up the constitution of our country with our dearest domestic ties; adopting our fundamental laws into the bosom of our family affections; keeping inseparable, and cherishing with the warmth of all their combined and mutually reflected charities, our state, our hearths, our sepulchres and our altars.

Through the same plan of a conformity to nature in our artificial institutions, and by calling in the aid of her unerring and powerful instincts to fortify the fallible and feeble contrivances of our reason, we have derived several other, and those no small benefits, from considering our liberties in the light of an inheritance. Always acting as if in the presence of canonized forefathers, the spirit of freedom, leading in itself to misrule and excess, is tempered with an awful gravity. This idea of a liberal descent inspires us with a sense of habitual native dignity, which prevents that upstart insolence almost inevitably adhering to and disgracing those who are the first acquirers of any distinction. By this means our liberty becomes a noble freedom. It carries an imposing and majestic aspect. It has a pedigree and illustrating ancestors. It has its bearings, and its ensigns armorial. It has its gallery of portraits; its monumental inscriptions; its records, evidences and titles. We procure reverence to our civil institutions on the principle upon which nature teaches us to revere individual men; on account of their age, and on account of those from whom they are descended. All your sophisters cannot produce anything better adapted to preserve a rational and manly freedom than the course that we have pursued, who have chosen our nature rather than our speculations, our breasts rather than our inventions, for the great conservatories and magazines of our rights and privileges.

Believe me, Sir, those who attempt to level, never equalize. In all societies, consisting of various descriptions of citizens, some description must be uppermost. The levellers therefore only change and pervert the natural order of things; they load the edifice of society, by setting up in the air what the solidity of the structure requires to be on the ground. The associations of tailors and carpenters, of which the republic (of Paris, for instance) is composed, cannot be equal to the situation, into which, by the worst of usurpations, an usurpation on the prerogatives of nature, you attempt to force them.

The Chancellor of France at the opening of the States, said, in a tone of oratorical flourish, that all occupations were honourable. If he meant only, that no honest employment was disgraceful, he would not have gone beyond the truth. But in asserting that anything is honourable, we imply some distinction in its favour. The occupation of a hairdresser, or of a working tallow-chandler, cannot be a matter of honour to any person – to say nothing of a number of other more servile employments. Such descriptions of men ought not to suffer oppression from the state; but the state suffers oppression, if such as they, either individually or collectively, are permitted to rule. In this you think you are combating prejudice, but you are at war with nature.[1]

---

[1] *Ecclesiasticus*, chap. xxxviii. verses 24, 25. 'The wisdom of a learned man cometh by opportunity of leisure: and he that hath little business shall become wise.' – 'How can he get wisdom that holdeth the plough, and that glorieth in the goad; that driveth oxen; and is occupied in their labours; and whose talk is of bullocks?'

Ver. 27. 'So every carpenter and work-master that laboureth night and day,' etc.

Ver. 33. They shall not be sought for in public counsel, nor sit high in the congregation: they shall not sit on the judge's seat, nor understand the sentence of judgement; they cannot declare justice and judgement, and they shall not be found where parables are spoken.'

Ver. 34. 'But they will maintain the state of the world.'

I do not determine whether this book be canonical, as the Gallican church (till

I do not, my dear Sir, conceive you to be of that sophistical, captious spirit, or of that uncandid dullness, as to require, for every general observation or sentiment, an explicit detail of the correctives and exceptions, which reason will presume to be included in all the general propositions which come from reasonable men. You do not imagine, that I wish to confine power, authority, and distinction to blood, and names, and titles. No, Sir. There is no qualification for government but virtue and wisdom, actual or presumptive. Wherever they are actually found, they have, in whatever state, condition, profession or trade, the passport of Heaven to human place and honour. Woe to the country which would madly and impiously reject the service of the talents and virtues, civil, military or religious, that are given to grace and to serve it; and would condemn to obscurity everything formed to diffuse lustre and glory around a state! Woe to that country too, that, passing into the opposite extreme, considers a low education, a mean contracted view of things, a sordid, mercenary occupation, as a preferable title to command! Everything ought to be open; but not indifferently to every man. No rotation; no appointment by lot; no mode of election operating in the spirit of sortition, or rotation, can be generally good in a government conversant in extensive objects. Because they have no tendency, direct or indirect, to select the man with a view to the duty, or to accommodate the one to the other. I do not hesitate to say, that the road to eminence and power from obscure condition, ought not to be made too easy, nor a thing too much of course. If rare merit be the rarest of all rare things, it ought to pass through some sort of probation. The temple of honour ought to be seated on an eminence. If it be opened through virtue, let it be remembered too, that virtue is never tried but by some difficulty and some struggle.

Nothing is a due and adequate representation of a state, that does not represent its ability, as well as its property. But as ability is a vigorous and active principle, and as property is sluggish, inert and timid, it never can be safe from the invasions of ability, unless it be, out of all proportion, predominant in the representation. It must be represented too in great masses of accumulation, or it is not rightly protected. The characteristic essence of property, formed out of the combined principle of its acquisition and conservation, is to be *unequal*. The great masses therefore which excite envy, and tempt rapacity, must be put out of the possibility of

---

lately) has considered it, or apocryphal, as here it is taken. I am sure it contains a great deal of sense and truth.

danger. Then they form a natural rampart about the lesser properties in all their gradations. The same quantity of property, which is by the natural course of things divided among many, has not the same operation. Its defensive power is weakened as it is diffused. In this diffusion each man's portion is less than what, in the eagerness of his desires, he may flatter himself to obtain by dissipating the accumulations of others. The plunder of the few would indeed give but a share inconceivably small in the distribution to the many. But the many are not capable of making this calculation; and those who lead them to rapine never intend this distribution.

The power of perpetrating our property in our families is one of the most valuable and interesting circumstances belonging to it, and that which tends the most to the perpetuation of society itself. It makes our weakness subservient to our virtue; it grafts benevolence even upon avarice. The possessors of family wealth, and of the distinction which attends hereditary possession (as most concerned in it), are the natural securities for this transmission. With us the House of Peers is formed upon this principle. It is wholly composed of hereditary property and hereditary distinction; and made therefore the third of the legislature; and, in the last event, the sole judge of all property in all its subdivisions. The House of Commons too, though not necessarily, yet in fact, is always so composed, in the far greater part. Let those large proprietors be what they will, and they have their chance of being amongst the best, they are, at the very worst, the ballast in the vessel of the commonwealth. For though hereditary wealth, and the rank which goes with it, are too much idolized by creeping sycophants, and the blind, abject admirers of power, they are too rashly slighted in shallow speculations of the petulant, assuming, shortsighted coxcombs of philosophy. Some decent, regulated pre-eminence, some preference (not exclusive appropriation) given to birth, is neither unnatural, nor unjust, nor impolitic.

To avoid therefore the evils of inconstancy and versatility, ten thousand times worse than those of obstinacy and the blindest prejudice, we have consecrated the state, that no man should approach to look into its defects or corruptions but with due caution; that he should never dream of beginning its reformation by its subversion; that he should approach to the faults of the state as to the wounds of a father, with pious awe and trembling solicitude. By this wise prejudice we are taught to look with horror on those children of their country, who are prompt rashly to hack that aged parent in pieces, and put him into the kettle of magicians, in hopes that by their poisonous weeds, and wild incantations, they may regenerate the paternal constitution, and renovate their father's life.

Society is indeed a contract. Subordinate contracts for objects of mere occasional interest may be dissolved at pleasure – but the state ought not to be considered as nothing better than a partnership agreement in a trade of pepper and coffee, calico or tobacco, or some other such low concern, to be taken up for a little temporary interest, and to be dissolved by the fancy of the parties. It is to be looked on with other reverence; because it is not a partnership in things subservient only to the gross animal existence of a temporary and perishable nature. It is a partnership in all science; a partnership in all art; a partnership in every virtue, and in all perfection. As the ends of such a partnership cannot be obtained in many generations, it becomes a partnership not only between those who are living, but between those who are living, those who are dead and those who are to be born. Each contract of each particular state is but a clause in the great primeval contract of eternal society, linking the lower with the higher natures, connecting the visible and invisible world, according to a fixed compact sanctioned by the inviolable oath which holds all physical and all moral natures, each in their appointed place. This law is not subject to the will of those, who by an obligation above them, and infinitely superior, are bound to submit their will to that law. The municipal corporations of that universal kingdom are not morally at liberty at their pleasure, and on their speculations of a contingent improvement, wholly to separate and tear asunder the bands of their subordinate community, and to dissolve it into an unsocial, uncivil, unconnected chaos of elementary principles. It is the first and supreme necessity only, a necessity that is not chosen, but chooses, a necessity paramount to deliberation, that admits no discussion, and demands no evidence, which alone can justify a resort to anarchy. This necessity is no exception to the rule; because this necessity itself is a part too of that moral and physical disposition of things, to which man must be obedient by consent or force: but if that which is only submission to necessity should be made the object of choice, the law is broken, nature is disobeyed, and the rebellious are outlawed, cast forth and exiled, from this world of reason, and order, and peace, and virtue, and fruitful penitence, into the antagonist world of madness, discord, vice, confusion and unavailing sorrow.

Reflections on the Revolution in France (1790), Everyman ed. (London, Dent, 1910), pp. 6–7, 31–3, 46–9, 93–4.

Thomas Paine
(1737–1809)

MUTUAL DEPENDENCE AND
RECIPROCAL INTEREST

Great part of that order which reigns among mankind is not the effect of government. It has its origin in the principles of society and the natural constitution of man. It existed prior to government, and would exist if the formality of government was abolished. The mutual dependence and reciprocal interest which man has upon man, and all the parts of a civilized community upon each other, create that great chain of connection which holds it together. The landholder, the farmer, the manufacturer, the merchant, the tradesman and every occupation, prospers by the aid which each receives from the other, and from the whole. Common interest regulates their concerns, and forms their law; and the laws which common usage ordains, have a greater influence than the laws of government. In fine, society performs for itself almost everything which is ascribed to government.

To understand the nature and quantity of government proper for man, it is necessary to attend to his character. As Nature created him for social life, she fitted him for the station she intended. In all cases she made his natural wants greater than his individual powers. No one man is capable, without the aid of society, of supplying his own wants; and those wants, acting upon every individual, impel the whole of them into society, as naturally as gravitation acts to a centre.

But she has gone further. She has not only forced man into society, by a diversity of wants, which the reciprocal aid of each other can supply, but she has implanted in him a system of social affections, which, though not necessary to his existence, are essential to his happiness. There is no period in life when this love for society ceases to act. It begins and ends with our being.

If we examine, with attention, into the composition and constitution of man, the diversity of his wants, and the diversity of talents in different men for reciprocally accommodating the wants of each other, his propensity to society and consequently to preserve the advantages resulting from it, we shall easily discover that a great part of what is called government is mere imposition.

Government is no farther necessary than to supply the few cases to which society and civilization are not conveniently competent; and instances are not wanting to show, that everything which government can usefully add thereto, has been performed by the common consent of society, without government.

For upwards of two years from the commencement of the American war, and to a longer period in several of the American States, there were no established forms of government. The old governments had been abolished, and the country was too much occupied in defence, to employ its attention in establishing new governments; yet during this interval, order and harmony were preserved as inviolate as in any country in Europe. There is a natural aptness in man, and more so in society, because it embraces a greater variety of abilities and resource, to accommodate itself to whatever situation it is in. The instant formal government is abolished, society begins to act. A general association takes place, and common interest produces common security.

So far is it from being true, as has been pretended, that the abolition of any formal government is the dissolution of society, that it acts by a contrary impulse, and brings the latter the closer together. All that part of its organization which it had committed to its government, devolves again upon itself, and acts through its medium. When men, as well from natural instinct, as from reciprocal benefits, have habituated themselves to social and civilized life, there is always enough of its principles in practice to carry them through any changes they may find necessary or convenient to make in their government. In short, man is so naturally a creature of society, that it is almost impossible to put him out of it.

Formal government makes but a small part of civilized life; and when even the best that human wisdom can devise is established, it is a thing more in name and idea, than in fact. It is to the great and fundamental principles of society and civilization – to the common usage universally consented to, and mutually and reciprocally maintained – to the unceasing circulation of interest, which, passing through its million channels, invigorates the whole mass of civilized man – it is to these things, infinitely more than to anything which even the best instituted government can perform, that the safety and prosperity of the individual and of the whole depends.

The more perfect civilization is, the less occasion has it for government, because the more does it regulate its own affairs, and govern itself; but so contrary is the practice of old governments to the reason of the case, that the expenses of them increase in the proportion they ought to diminish. It is but few general laws that civilized life requires, and those of such common usefulness, that whether they are enforced by the forms of government or not, the effect will be nearly the same. If we consider what the principles are that first condense men into society, and what the motives that regulate their mutual intercourse afterwards, we shall find, by the time we arrive at what is called government, that nearly the whole of the business is performed by the natural operation of the parts upon each other.

Man, with respect to all those matters, is more a creature of consistency than he is aware, or than governments would wish him to believe. All the great laws of society are laws of nature. Those of trade and commerce, whether with respect to the intercourse of individuals, or of nations, are laws of mutual and reciprocal interest. They are followed and obeyed, because it is the interest of the parties so to do, and not on account of any formal laws their governments may impose or interpose.

Rights of Man (1791), Pelican ed. (London, Penguin, 1969), pp. 185–7.

Jean Antoine Nicolas Caritat, Marquis de Condorcet (1743–1794)

THE ABSOLUTE PERFECTION OF THE HUMAN RACE

Our hopes for the future condition of the human race can be subsumed under three important heads: the abolition of inequality between nations, the progress of equality within each nation and the true perfection of mankind. Will all nations one day attain that state of civilization which the most enlightened, the freest and the least burdened by prejudices, such as the French and the Anglo-Americans, have attained already? Will the vast gulf that separates these peoples from the slavery of nations under the rule of monarchs, from the barbarism of African tribes, from the ignorance of savages, little by little disappear?

Is there on the face of the earth a nation whose inhabitants have been debarred by nature herself from the enjoyment of freedom and the exercise of reason?

Are those differences which have hitherto been seen in every civilized country in respect of the enlightenment, the resources and the wealth enjoyed by the different classes into which it is divided, is that inequality between men which was aggravated or perhaps produced by the earliest progress of society, are these part of civilization itself, or are they due to the present imperfections of the social art? Will they necessarily decrease and ultimately make way for a real equality, the final end of the social art, in which even the effects of the natural differences between men will be mitigated and the only kind of inequality to persist will be that which is in the interests of all and which favours the progress of civilization, of education and of industry, without entailing either poverty, humiliation or dependence? In other words, will men approach a condition in which everyone will have the knowledge necessary to conduct himself in the ordinary affairs of life, according to the light of his own reason, to preserve his mind free from prejudice, to understand his rights and to exercise them in accordance with his conscience and his creed; in which everyone will become able, through the development of his faculties, to find the means of providing for his needs; and in which at last misery and folly will be the exception, and no longer the habitual lot of a section of society?

Is the human race to better itself, either by discoveries in the sciences and the arts, and so in the means to individual welfare and general prosperity; or by progress in the principles of conduct or practical morality; or by a true perfection of the intellectual moral or physical faculties of man, an improvement which may result from a perfection either of the instruments used to heighten the intensity of these faculties and to direct their use or of the natural constitution of man?

In answering these three questions we shall find in the experience of the past, in the observation of the progress that the sciences and civilization have already made, in the analysis of the progress of the human mind and of the development of its faculties, the strongest reasons for believing that nature has set no limit to the realization of our hopes.

The time will therefore come when the sun will shine only on free men who know no other master but their reason; when tyrants and slaves, priests and their stupid or hypocritical instruments will exist only in works of history and on the stage; and when we shall think of them only to pity their victims and their dupes; to maintain ourselves in a state of vigilance by thinking on their excesses; and to learn how to recognize and so to destroy, by force of reason, the first seeds of tyranny and superstition, should they ever dare to reappear amongst us.

In looking at the history of societies we shall have had occasion to observe that there is often a great difference between the rights that the law allows its citizens and the rights that they actually enjoy, and, again, between the equality established by political codes and that which in fact exists amongst individuals: and we shall have noticed that these differences were one of the principal causes of the destruction of freedom in the Ancient republics, of the storms that troubled them and of the weakness that delivered them over to foreign tyrants.

These differences have three main causes: inequality in wealth; inequality in status between the man whose means of subsistence are hereditary and the man whose means are dependent on the length of his life, or, rather, on that part of his life in which he is capable of work; and, finally, inequality in education.

. . . . . .

From such time onwards the inhabitants of a single country will no longer be distinguished by their use of a crude or refined language; they will be able to govern themselves according to their own knowledge; they will no longer be limited to a mechanical knowledge of the procedures of the arts or of professional routine; they will no longer depend for every trivial piece of business, every insignificant matter of instruction on clever men who rule over them in virtue of their necessary superiority; and so they will attain a real equality, since differences in enlightenment or talent can no longer raise a barrier between men who understand each other's feelings, ideas and language, some of whom may wish to be taught by others but, to do so, will have no need to be controlled by them, or who may wish to confide the care of government to the ablest of their number but will not be compelled to yield them absolute power in a spirit of blind confidence.

This kind of supervision has advantages even for those who do not exercise it, since it is employed for them and not against them. Natural differences of ability between men whose understanding has not been cultivated give rise, even to savage tribes, to charlatans and dupes, to clever men and men readily deceived. These same differences are truly universal, but now they are differences only between men of learning and upright men who know the value of learning without being dazzled by it; or between talent or genius and the common sense which can appreciate and benefit from them; so that even if these natural differences were greater, and more extensive than they are, they would be only the more influential in improving the relations between men and promoting what is advantageous for their independence and happiness.

These various causes of equality do not act in isolation; they unite, combine and support each other and so their cumulative effects are stronger, surer and more constant. With greater equality of education there will be greater equality in industry and so in wealth; equality in wealth necessarily leads to equality in education: and equality between the nations and equality within a single nation are mutually dependent.

So we might say that a well-directed system of education rectifies natural inequality in ability instead of strengthening it, just as good laws remedy natural inequality in the means of subsistence, and just as in societies where laws have brought about this same equality, liberty, though subject to a regular constitution, will be more widespread, more complete than in the total independence of savage life. Then the social art will have fulfilled its aim, and of assuring and extending to all men enjoyment of the common rights to which they are called by nature.

The real advantages that should result from this progress, of which we can entertain a hope that is almost a certainty, can have no other term than that of the absolute perfection of the human race; since, as the various kinds of equality come to work in its favour by producing ampler sources of supply, more extensive education, more complete liberty, so equality will be more real and will embrace everything which is really of importance for the happiness of human beings.

Sketch for the Progress of the Human Mind (1795), trans. June Barraclough (London, Weidenfeld & Nicolson, 1955), pp. 173–5, 179, 183–4.

HAPPINESS AND REPRESENTATIVE DEMOCRACY

The age we live in is a busy age; in which knowledge is rapidly advancing towards perfection. In the natural world, in particular, every thing teems with discovery and with improvement. The most distant and recondite regions of the earth traversed and explored – the all-vivifying and subtle element of the air so recently analysed and made known to us – are striking evidences, were all others wanting, of this pleasing truth.

Correspondent to *discovery* and *improvement* in the natural world, is *reformation* in the moral; if that which seems a common notion be, indeed, a true one, that in the moral world there no longer remains any matter for *discovery*. Perhaps, however, this may not be the case: perhaps among such observations as would be best calculated to serve as grounds for reformation, are some which, being observations of matters of fact hitherto either incompletely noticed, or not at all would, when produced, appear capable of bearing the name of discoveries: with so little method and precision have the consequences of this fundamental axiom, *it is the greatest happiness of the greatest number that is the measure of right and wrong*, been as yet developed.

Be this as it may, if there be room for making, and if there be use in publishing, *discoveries* in the *natural* world, surely there is not much less room for making, nor much less use in proposing, *reformation* in the *moral*. If it be a matter of importance and of use to us to be made acquainted with *distant* countries, surely it is not a matter of much less importance, nor of much less use to us, to be made better and better acquainted with the chief means of living happily *in our own*. If it be of importance and of use to us to know the principles of the element we breathe, surely it is not of much less importance nor of much less use to comprehend the principles, and endeavour at the improvement of those *laws*, by which alone we breathe it in security.

That arrangement of the materials of any science may, I take it, be termed a *natural* one, which takes such properties to characterize them by, as men in general are, by the common constitution of man's *nature*, disposed to attend to: such, in other words, as *naturally*, that is readily, engage and firmly fix the attention of any one to whom they are pointed out. The materials, or elements here in question, are such actions as are the objects of what we call Laws or Institutions.

Now then, with respect to actions in general, there is no property in them that is calculated so readily to engage, and so firmly to fix the attention of an observer, as the *tendency* that may have *to*, or *divergency* (if one may so say) *from*, that which may be styled the common *end* of all of them. The end I mean is *Happiness*: and this *tendency* in any act is what we style its *utility*: as this *divergency* is that to which we give the name of *mischievousness*. With respect then to such actions in particular as are among the objects of the Law, to point out to a man the *utility* of them or the mischievousness, is the only way to make him see *clearly* that property of them which every man is in search of; the only way, in short, to give him *satisfaction*.

From *utility* then we may denominate a *principle*, that may serve to preside over and govern, as it were, such arrangement as shall be made of the several institutions or combinations of institutions that compose the matter of this science: and it is this principle, that by putting its stamp upon the several names given to those combinations, can alone render *satisfactory* and *clear* any arrangement that can be made of them.

Governed in this manner by a principle that is recognized by all men, the same arrangement that would serve for the jurisprudence of any one country, would serve with little variation for that of any other.

'A Fragment on Government' (1776), Preface, in *A Fragment on Government and An Introduction to the Principles of Morals and Legislation*, ed. with an introd. by W. Harrison (Oxford, Blackwell, 1948), pp. 3, 24–5.

What, then, is the best *form* of government? This question may itself be clothed in an indefinite number of forms. What is the most eligible?

what is the most desirable? what is the most expedient? what is the most right and proper? and so on. In whatsoever form clothed, it is resolvable into these two: What is the end to which it is your will to see the arrangements employed in the delineation of it directed? What are the several arrangements by which, in the character of *means*, it is your opinion that that same end, in so far as attainable, is most likely to be attained?

To write an answer to this question – to write on the subject which it holds up to view – is virtually, is in effect, from beginning to end, to write an answer to one or other, or both of these questions.

To the first, my answer is – the greatest happiness of all the several members of the community in question, taken together, is the end to which it is my desire to see all the arrangements employed in the delineation of it directed. *That* being taken for the end, to which it is right and proper that all legislative arrangements be directed, my opinion is, that so far as they go, the proposed arrangements which here follow would be in a higher degree conducive to it than any other could be, that could be proposed in a work which was not particularly adapted to the situation of any one country, to the exclusion of all others.

Should it be asked, *What* is the community which, by the description of the community in question, you have in view? my answer is – any community, which is as much as to say every community whatsoever.

CIVIL OR DISTRIBUTIVE LAW
General Object

Of law in general, and of this branch in particular, the principal object is to give security to rights; viz. to such as it finds in existence, and such others, as under and in virtue of such arrangements as it finds in existence, are, from time to time, successively brought into existence; to wit, either by such events as take place without the operation of human will, such as deaths and other casualties, and the produce of the elements of the three kingdoms of nature – the mineral, the vegetable and the animal; and such as are brought into existence by the operation of the human will, such as voluntary contracts, and ordinances of the administrative branch of government.

In comparison with the security thus afforded for rights in general, such benefits as belong to this or that one of the three remaining heads, under one or other of which, all the as-yet-unmentioned benefits, which it is in the nature of government to confirm or secure, may be classed, are but of secondary importance; to wit, subsistence, meaning incidental arrangements for securing national subsistence against incidental causes of failure; abundance, meaning continual increase to that which is a common matter of subsistence and abundance; and equality, meaning the giving to the several masses of the matter of wealth in the possession of different individuals, such approach and perpetual tendency to absolute equality, as shall not be inconsistent with the security which ought to be afforded to the rights relative to property, and the rights relative to condition in life.

Security, subsistence, abundance and equality – by these then will be presented to view the several subordinate or particular ends, most immediately in contact with, and branching out from, the only legitimate and universal end of government.

In every government, which has for its object and effect the pursuit of the happiness of the governors at the expense and by the correspondent sacrifice of the happiness of the governed, oppression at large will be the habitual and unintermitted practice of the government in all its ranks.

The only species of government which has or can have for its object and effect the greatest happiness of the greatest number, is, as has been seen, a democracy: and the only species of democracy which can have place in a community numerous enough to defend itself against aggression at the hands of external adversaries, is a representative democracy.

A democracy, then, has for its characteristic object and effect, the securing its members against oppression and depredation at the hands of those functionaries which it employs for its defence, against oppression and depredation at the hands of foreign adversaries and against such internal adversaries as are not functionaries.

Every other species of government has necessarily, for its characteristic and primary object and effect, the keeping of the people or non-functionaries in a perfectly defenceless state, against the functionaries their rulers; who being, in respect of their power and the use they are disposed and enabled to make of it, the natural adversaries of the people, have for their object the giving facility, certainty, unbounded extent and impunity, to the depredation and oppression exercised on the governed by the governors.

The arrangements which afford a promise of operating as securities to the fabric of government, against corruption, and corruptive influence – against that dry rot, to which all government stands exposed, by the nature of the materials of which it must everywhere be composed, may, it is believed, be comprehended all of them, under one or other of the heads following, viz.:

1. Minimizing the quantity of power in the hands of the functionaries.
2. Minimizing the quantity of the matter of wealth at the disposal of functionaries.
3. Minimizing the quantity of the matter of wealth, employed as pay of functionaries.
4. Applying legal counterforces to the power of functionaries.
5. Applying moral counterforces to the power of functionaries.
6. Exclusion of factitious honour, or say factitious dignity.
7. Exclusion of all other factitious instruments of delusive influence.

As in the case of every other act, so in the case of every act of government: add the power to the will, the act takes place: take away either, the act does not take place.

The problem is – throughout the whole field of legislation, how to prevent the sinister sacrifice: leaving at the same time unimpaired, both the will and the power to perform whatsoever acts may be in the highest degree conducive to the only right and proper end of government.

The powers, by the exercise of which government is carried on, cannot be exercised by all in the same manner at the same time. Any such proposition as this, that the best government is that in which the powers of government are all of them exercised by all the members of the community at the same time, would be a self-contradictory proposition: by it would be asserted the existence of a government, and at the same time, in the same community, the non-existence of any government.

The exercise of the powers of government consists in the giving of directions or commands, positive and prohibitive; and incidentally in securing compliance through the application of rewards and punishments.

In and by every such exercise is implied a separation of the whole members of the community into two classes, namely the governors and the governed – the rulers and those over whom rule is exercised.

But though consistently with the continued existence of government, it is impossible that the separation should, as to the two classes themselves, be otherwise than perpetual; not so is the existence of the same individual in both these classes, so it be at different points of time. Of each class, the whole population might migrate into the other: those who are governors at one moment may be all of them governed, and not governors, during the second moment; while those who are governed during the first moment may be governors during the second moment.

In comparison with the governed, the governors must, in every community, be a small number; for those by whom the operations of government are carried on, cannot during that time be carrying on operations of any other sort. The greatest portion of the labouring time of the greatest number must at all times be employed in the securing of the means of subsistence to the whole.

By whom, then, and how, shall this distinction be made? By what cause or causes shall it be determined who, at each moment, shall be the governor, and who the governed?

The greatest happiness principle requires that, be the governors who they may – be the powers of government exercised by them what they may – it is of the will of the governed, that during each moment their existence in that situation should be the result: that it is to say, that after having been placed, they should at certain intervals of no great length, be displaceable by the governed.

The governed cannot all of them be exercising the immediate powers of government, but at stated times they may all of them exercise the function of declaring who the individuals shall be by whom those same immediate powers shall be exercised.

'The Constitutional Code' (1818–1830), as reproduced in *The Works of Jeremy Bentham*, ed. J. Bowring (Edinburgh, William Tait, 1843), vol. IX, pp. 7, 11, 47, 49, 95.

Joseph de Maistre
(1753–1821)

MEN ARE BORN FOR
MONARCHY

Human reason left to its own resources is completely incapable *not only of creating but also of conserving any religious or political association*, because it can only give rise to disputes and because, to conduct himself well, man needs beliefs, not problems. His cradle should be surrounded by dogmas; and, when his reason awakes, all his opinions should be given, at least all those relating to his conduct. Nothing is more vital to him than *prejudices*. Let us not take this word in bad part. It does not necessarily signify false ideas, but only, in the strict sense of the word, any opinions adopted without examination. Now, these kinds of opinion are essential to man; they are the real basis of his happiness and the palladium of empires. Without them, there can be neither religion, morality, nor government. There should be a state religion just as there is a state political system; or rather, religion and political dogmas, mingled and merged together, should together form a *general* or *national mind* sufficiently strong to repress the aberrations of the individual reason which is, of its nature, the mortal enemy of any association whatever because it gives birth only to divergent opinions.

All known nations have been happy and powerful to the degree that they have faithfully obeyed this national mind, which is nothing other than the destruction of individual dogmas and the absolute and general rule of national dogmas, that is to say, useful prejudices. Once let everyone rely on his individual reason in religion, and you will see immediately the rise of anarchy of belief or the annihilation of religious sovereignty. Likewise, if each man makes himself the judge of the principles of government you will see immediately the rise of civil anarchy or the annihilation of political sovereignty. Government is a true religion; it has its dogmas, its mysteries, its priests; to submit it to individual discussion is to destroy it; it has life only through the national mind, that is to say, political faith, which is a *creed*. Man's primary need is that his nascent reason should be curbed under a double yoke; it should be frustrated, and it should lose itself in the national mind, so that it changes its individual existence for another communal existence, just as a river which flows into the ocean still exists in the mass of water, but without name and distinct reality.

What is patriotism? It is this national mind of which I am speaking; it is individual *abnegation*. Faith and patriotism are the two great thaumaturges of the world. Both are divine. All their actions are miracles. Do not talk to them of scrutiny, choice, discussion, for they will say that you blaspheme. They know only two words, *submission* and *belief*; with these two levers, they raise the world. Their very errors are sublime. These two infants of Heaven prove their origin to all by creating and conserving; and if they unite, join their forces and together take possession of a nation, they exalt it, make it divine and increase its power a hundredfold. . . .

But can you, insignificant man, light this sacred fire that inflames nations? Can you give a common soul to several million men? Unite them under your laws? Range them closely around a common centre? Shape the mind of men yet unborn? Make future generations obey you and create those age-old customs, those conserving *prejudices*, which are the father of the laws and stronger than them? What nonsense! . . .

There is no doubt that, in a certain sense, reason is good for nothing. We have the scientific knowledge necessary for the maintenance of society; we have made conquests in mathematics and what is called natural science; but, once we leave the circle of our needs, our knowledge becomes either useless or doubtful. The human mind, ever restless, proliferates constantly succeeding theories. They are born, flourish, wither and fall like leaves from the trees; the only difference is that their year is longer.

And in the whole of the moral and political world, what do we know, and what are we able to do? We *know* the morality handed down to us by our fathers, as a collection of dogmas or useful prejudices adopted by the national mind. But on this point we owe nothing to any man's individual reason. On the contrary, every time this reason has interfered, it has perverted morality.

In politics, we *know* that it is necessary to respect those powers established we know not how or by whom. When time leads to abuses capable of altering the root principle of a government, we *know* that it is necessary to remove these abuses, but without touching the principle itself, an act of delicate surgery; and we *are able* to carry through these salutary reforms until the time when the principle of life is totally vitiated and the death of the body politic is inevitable. . . .

Wherever the individual reason dominates, there can be nothing great, for everything great rests on a belief, and the clash of individual opinions left to themselves produces only scepticism which is destructive of every-thing. General and individual morality, religion, laws, revered customs, useful prejudices, nothing is left standing, everything falls before it; it is the universal dissolvent.

Let us return again to basic ideas. Any *institution* is only a political edifice. In the physical and the moral order, the laws are the same; you cannot build a great edifice on narrow foundations or a durable one on a moving or transient base. Likewise, in the political order, to build high and to build for centuries, it is necessary to rely on an opinion or a belief broad and deep: for if the opinion does not hold the majority of minds and is not deeply rooted, it will provide only a narrow and transient base.

Now, if you seek the great and solid bases of all possible institutions of the first and second order, you will always find religion and patriotism.

And if you reflect still further, you will find that these two things are identical, for there is no true patriotism without religion. You will see it shine out only in the ages of belief, and it always fades and dies with it. Once man divorces himself from the divinity, he corrupts himself and everything he touches. His actions are misguided and end only in destruction. As this powerful binding force weakens in the state, so all the conserving virtues weaken in proportion. Men's characters become degraded, and even good actions are paltry. A murderous selfishness relentlessly presses on public spirit and makes it fall back before it, like those enormous glaciers of the high Alps that can be seen advancing slowly but frighteningly on the area of living things and crushing the useful vegetation in their path.

But once the idea of the divinity is the source of human action, this action is fruitful, creative and invincible. An unknown force makes itself felt on all sides, and animates, warms, vivifies all things. However much human ignorance and corruption have soiled this great idea with errors and crimes, it no less preserves its incredible influence. . . .

It can be said in general that all men are born for monarchy. This form of government is the most ancient and the most universal. . . . Monarchical government is so natural that, without realizing it, men identify it with sovereignty. They seem tacitly to agree that, wherever there is no king, there is no real *sovereign*. . . .

This is particularly striking in everything that has been said on both sides of the question that formed the subject of the first book of this work. The adversaries of divine origin always hold a grudge against *kings* and talk only of *kings*. They do not want to accept that the authority of kings comes from God: but it is not a question of *royalty* in particular but of *sovereignty* in general. Yes, all sovereignty derives from God; whatever form it takes, it is not the work of man. It is one, absolute and inviolable of its nature. Why, then, lay the blame on royalty, as though the inconveniences which are relied on to attack this system are not the same in any form of government? Once again, it is because royalty is *the natural government* and because in common discourse men confuse it with sovereignty by disregarding other governments, just as they neglect the exception when enunciating the general rule. . . .

Man must always be brought back to history, which is the first and indeed the only teacher in politics. Whoever says that man is born for liberty is speaking nonsense. If a being of a superior order undertook the *natural history* of man, surely he would seek his directions in the history of facts. When he knew what man is and has always been, what he does and has always done, he would write; and doubtless he would reject as foolish the notion that man is not what he should be and that his condition is contrary to the laws of creation. The very expression of this proposition is sufficient to refute it.

History is experimental politics; and just as, in the physical sciences, a hundred books of speculative theories disappear before a single experiment, in the same way in political science no theory can be allowed if it is not the more or less probable corollary of well-attested facts. If the question is asked, 'What is the most natural government to man?' history will reply, *It is monarchy*.

This government no doubt has its drawbacks, like every other, but all the declamations that fill the books of the day on these kinds of abuses can only rouse pity for their authors. It is pride and not reason which gives rise to them. Once it is rigorously established that nations are not made for the same government, that each nation has that which is best for it, above all that 'liberty is not open to every nation, and that the more we ponder on this principle laid down by Montesquieu, the more apparent its truth appears', we can no longer understand what the diatribes against the vices of monarchical government are about. If their aim is to make the unfortunate people who are destined to bear the disadvantages feel them more sharply, it is a most barbaric pastime; if their aim is to urge men to revolt against a government made for them, it is a crime beyond description.

But the subjects of monarchies are by no means reduced to taking refuge from despair in philosophic meditations; they have something better to do which is to gain full knowledge of the excellence of their government and to learn not to envy others. . . .

Let us go on to examine the principal characteristics of monarchical government. . . .

Monarchy is a *centralized* aristocracy. At all times and in all places, aristocracy dominates. Whatever form is given to governments, birth and wealth always take the first rank, and nowhere is their rule more harsh than where it is not founded on the law. But in a monarchy the king is the centre of this aristocracy: the latter, here, as elsewhere, still rules, but it rules in the name of the king, or, if you like, the king is guided by the understanding of the aristocracy. . . .

Avoiding all exaggeration, it is certain that the government of a single man is that in which the vices of the sovereign have the least effect upon the governed.

'Study on Sovereignty' (1884), trans. in *The Works of Joseph de Maistre*, ed. J. Lively (London, Allen & Unwin, 1965), pp. 108–11, 113–15.

William Godwin
(1756–1836)

THE EQUALIZATION OF
CONDITIONS

Government then being first supposed necessary for the welfare of mankind, the most important principle that can be imagined relative to its
structure, seems to be this; that, as government is a transaction in the
name and for the benefit of the whole, every member of the community
ought to have some share in the selection of its measures. The arguments
in support of this proposition are various.

First, it has already appeared that there is no satisfactory criterion,
marking out any man, or set of men, to preside over the rest.

Secondly, all men are partakers of the common faculty, reason; and may
be supposed to have some communication with the common instructor,
truth. It would be wrong in an affair of such momentous concern, that
any chance for additional wisdom should be rejected; nor can we tell, in
many cases, till after the experiment, how eminent any individual may be
found, in the business of guiding and deliberating for his fellows.

Thirdly, government is a contrivance instituted for the security of
individuals; and it seems both reasonable, that each man should have a
share in providing for his own security, and probable, that partiality and
cabal will by this means be most effectually excluded.

Lastly, to give each man a voice in the public concerns comes nearest
to that fundamental purpose of which we should never lose sight, the
uncontrolled exercise of private judgement. Each man will thus be
inspired with a consciousness of his own importance, and the slavish
feelings that shrink up the soul in the presence of an imagined superior,
will be unknown.

Admitting then the propriety of each man having a share in directing
the affairs of the whole in the first instance, it seems necessary that he
should concur in electing a house of representatives, if he be the member

of a large state; or, even in a small one, that he should assist in the appointment of officers and administrators; which implies, first, a delegation of authority to these officers, and, secondly, a tacit consent, or rather an admission of the necessity, that the questions to be debated should abide the decision of a majority.

But to this system of delegation the same objections may be urged, that were cited from Rousseau under the head of a social contract. It may be alleged that, 'if it be the business of every man to exercise his own judgement, he can in no instance surrender this function into the hands of another'.

To this objection it may be answered, first, that the parallel is by no means complete, between an individual's exercise of his judgement in a case that is truly his own, and his exercise of his judgement in an article where the province of a government is already admitted. If there be something contrary to the simplest ideas of justice in such a delegation, this is an evil inseparable from political government. The true and only adequate apology of government is necessity; the office of common deliberation is solely, to supply the most eligible means of meeting that necessity.

Secondly, the delegation we are here considering, is not, as the word in its most obvious sense may seem to imply, the act of one man committing to another, a function which, strictly speaking, it became him to exercise for himself. Delegation, in every instance in which it can be reconciled with justice, proposes for its object the general good. The individuals to whom the delegation is made, are either more likely, from talents or leisure, to perform the function in the most eligible manner, or there is at least some public interest requiring that it should be performed by one or a few persons, rather than by every individual for himself. This is the case, whether in that first and simplest of all political delegations, the prerogative of a majority, or in the election of a house of representatives, or in the appointment of public officers. Now all contest, as to the person who shall exercise a certain function and the propriety of resigning it, is frivolous, the moment it is decided how and by whom it can most advantageously be exercised. It is of no consequence that I am the parent of a child, when it has once been ascertained that the child will live with greater benefit under the superintendence of a stranger.

Lastly, it is a mistake to imagine that the propriety of restraining me, when my conduct is injurious, rises out of any delegation of mine. The justice of employing force upon certain emergencies, was at least equally cogent before the existence of society. Force ought never to be resorted to but in cases of absolute necessity; and, when such cases occur, it is the duty of every man to defend himself from violation. There is therefore no delegation necessary on the part of the offender; but the community, in the censure it exercises over him, puts itself in the place of the injured party.

From what is here stated, we may be enabled to form the clearest and most unexceptionable idea of the nature of government. Every man, as was formerly observed, has a sphere of discretion; that sphere is limited by the co-ordinate sphere of his neighbour. The maintenance of this limitation, the office of taking care that no man exceeds his sphere, is the first business of government. Its powers, in this respect, are a combination of the powers of individuals to control the excesses of each other. Hence is derived to the individuals of the community, a second and indirect province, of providing, by themselves or their representatives, that this control is not exercised in a despotical manner, or carried to an undue excess.

It will not be right to pass over a question that will inevitably suggest itself to the mind of the reader. 'If an equalization of conditions be to take place, not by law, regulation or public institution, but only through the private conviction of individuals, in what manner shall it begin?' In answering this question it is not necessary to prove so simple a proposition, as that all republicanism, all reduction of ranks and immunities, strongly tends towards an equalization of conditions. If men go on to improve in discernment, and this they certainly will with peculiar rapidity, when the ill-constructed governments which now retard their progress are removed, the same arguments which showed them the injustice of ranks, will show them the injustice of one man's wanting that which, while it is in the possession of another, conduces in no respect to his well-being.

It is a common error to imagine, 'that this injustice will be felt only by the lower orders who suffer from it'; and from thence to conclude 'that it can only be corrected by violence'. But in answer to this it may, in the first place, be observed that all suffer from it, the rich who engross, as well as the poor who want. Secondly, it has been endeavoured to be shown in the course of the present work, that men are not so entirely governed by self-interest, as has frequently been supposed. It appears, if possible, still more clearly, that the selfish are not governed solely by sensual gratification or the love of gain, but that the desire of eminence and distinction is, in different forms, a universal passion. Thirdly, and principally, the progress of truth is the most powerful of all causes. Nothing can be more improbable than to imagine, that theory, in the best sense of the word, is not essentially connected with practice. That which we can be persuaded clearly and distinctly to approve, will inevitably modify our conduct. When men shall habitually perceive the folly of individual splendour, and when their neighbours are impressed with a similar disdain, it will be impossible they should pursue the means of it with the same avidity as before.

It will not be difficult to trace, in the progress of modern Europe from barbarism to refinement, a tendency towards the equalization of conditions. In feudal times, as now in India and other parts of the world, men were born to a certain station, and it was nearly impossible for a peasant to rise to the rank of a noble. Except the nobles, there were no men that were rich; for commerce, either external or internal, had scarcely an existence. Commerce was one engine for throwing down this seemingly impregnable barrier, and shocking the prejudices of nobles, who were sufficiently willing to believe that their retainers were a different species of beings from themselves. Learning was another, and more powerful engine. In all ages of the church we see men of the basest origin rising to the highest eminence. Commerce proved that others could rise to wealth beside those who were cased in mail; but learning proved that the low-born were capable of surpassing their lords. The progressive effect of these ideas may easily be traced. Long after learning began to unfold its powers, its votaries still submitted to those obsequious manners and servile dedications, which no man reviews at the present day without astonishment. It is but lately that men have known that intellectual excellence can accomplish its purposes without a patron. At present, among the civilized and well informed, a man of slender income, but of great intellectual powers and a firm and virtuous mind, is constantly received with attention and deference; and his purse-proud neighbour who should attempt to treat him superciliously, is sure to encounter a general disapprobation. The inhabitants of distant villages, where long-established prejudices are slowly destroyed, would be astonished to see how comparatively small a share wealth has, in determining the degree of attention with which men are treated in enlightened circles.

These no doubt are but slight indications. It is with morality in this respect as it is with politics. The progress is at first so slow as, for the most part, to elude the observation of mankind; nor can it be adequately perceived but by the contemplation and comparison of events during a considerable portion of time. After a certain interval, the scene is more fully unfolded, and the advances appear more rapid and decisive. While wealth was every thing, it was to be expected that men would acquire it, though at the expense of conscience and integrity. The abstract ideas of justice had not yet been so concentred, as to be able to overpower what dazzles the eye, or promises a momentary gratification. In proportion as the monopolies of rank and corporation are abolished, the value of super-fluities will decline. In proportion as republicanism gains ground, men will be estimated for what they are, and not for their accidental appendages.

Let us reflect on the gradual consequences of this revolution of opinion. Liberality of dealing will be among its earliest results; and, of consequence, accumulation will become less frequent and enormous. Men will not be disposed, as now, to take advantage of each other's distresses. They will not consider how much they can extort, but how much it is reasonable to require. The master-tradesman who employs labourers under him, will be disposed to give a more ample reward to their industry; which he is at present enabled to tax, chiefly by the accidental advantage of possess-ing a capital. Liberality on the part of his employer will complete in the mind of the artisan, what ideas of political justice will probably have begun. He will no longer spend the surplus of his earnings in that dis-sipation, which is one of the principal of those causes that at present subject him to the arbitrary pleasure of a superior. He will escape from the irresolution of slavery and the fetters of despair, and perceive that independence and ease are scarcely less within his reach than that of any other member of the community. This is an obvious step towards the still further progression, in which the labourer will receive entire whatever the consumer may be required to pay, without having a capitalist, and idle and useless monopolizer, as he will then be found, to fatten upon his spoils.

The same sentiments that lead to liberality of dealing, will also lead to liberality of distribution. The trader, who is unwilling to grow rich by extorting from his customers or his workmen, will also refuse to become rich by the not inferior injustice, of withholding from his indigent neighbour the gratuitous supply of which he stands in need. The habit which was created in the former case of being contented with moderate gains, is closely connected with the habit of being contented with slender accumulation. He that is not anxious to add to his heap, will not be reluctant by a benevolent distribution to prevent its increase. Wealth was at one period almost the single object of pursuit that presented itself to the gross and uncultivated mind. Various objects will hereafter divide men's attention, the love of liberty, the love of equality, the pursuits of art and the desire of knowledge. These objects will not, as now, be confined to a few, but will gradually be laid open to all. The love of liberty obviously leads to a sentiment of union, and a disposition to sympathize in the concerns of others. The general diffusion of truth will be productive of general improvement; and men will daily approximate towards those views according to which every object will be appreciated at its true value. Add to which, that the improvement of which we speak is public, and not individual. The progress is the progress of all. Each man will find his sentiments of justice and rectitude echoed by the sentiments of his neighbours. Apostacy will be made eminently improbable, because the apostate will incur, not only his own censure, but the censure of every beholder.

Enquiry concerning Political Justice and its Influence on Morals and Happiness (1793), 3rd ed., corrected G. G. and J. Robinson (London, 1798), (2 vols.), vol. I, pp. 214–18 and vol. II, pp. 548–53 (Bk. III, Ch. III and Bk. VIII, Ch. X).

William Blake
(1757–1827)

AN ANCIENT PROVERB

An Ancient Proverb

Remove away that black'ning church:
Remove away that marriage hearse:
Remove away that man of blood:
You'll quite remove the ancient curse.

'An Ancient Proverb' (1793), in *Complete Writings* (London, O.U.P., 1966), p. 176.

J. C. F. von Schiller
(1759–1805)

THE AESTHETIC STATE

Whence comes this disadvantageous relation of individuals in spite of all the advantages of the race? Why was the individual Greek qualified to be the representative of his time, and why may the individual modern not dare to be so? Because it was all-uniting Nature that bestowed upon the former, and all-dividing intellect that bestowed upon the latter, their respective forms.

It was culture itself that inflicted this wound upon modern humanity. As soon as enlarged experience and more precise speculation made necessary a sharper division of the sciences on the one hand, and on the other, the more intricate machinery of States made necessary a more rigorous dissociation of ranks and occupations, the essential bond of human nature was torn apart, and a ruinous conflict set its harmonious powers at variance. The intuitive and the speculative understanding took up hostile attitudes upon their respective fields, whose boundaries they now began to guard with jealousy and distrust, and by confining our activity to a single sphere we have handed ourselves over to a master who is not infrequently inclined to end up by suppressing the rest of our capacities. While in one place a luxuriant imagination ravages the hard-earned fruits of the intellect, in another the spirit of abstraction stifles the fire at which the heart might have warmed itself and the fancy been enkindled.

This disorder, which Art and learning began in the inner man, was rendered complete and universal by the new spirit of government. It was not, indeed, to be expected that the simple organization of the first republics would outlive the ingenuousness of their early manners and conditions; but instead of rising to a higher animal life it degenerated to a common and clumsy mechanism. That zoophyte character of the Greek States, where every individual enjoyed an independent life and, when need arose, could become a whole in himself, now gave place to an ingenious piece of machinery, in which out of the botching together of a vast number of lifeless parts a collective mechanical life results. State and Church, law and customs, were now torn asunder; enjoyment was separated from labour, means from ends, effort from reward. Eternally chained to only one single little fragment of the whole, Man himself grew to be only a fragment; with the monotonous noise of the wheel he drives everlastingly in his ears, he never develops the harmony of his being, and instead of imprinting humanity upon his nature he becomes merely the imprint of his occupation, of his science. But even the meagre fragmentary association which still links the individual members to the whole, does not depend on forms which present themselves spontaneously (for how could such an artificial and clandestine piece of mechanism be entrusted to their freedom?), but is assigned to them with scrupulous exactness by a formula in which their free intelligence is restricted. The lifeless letter takes the place of the living understanding, and a practised memory is a surer guide than genius and feeling.

If the community makes function the measure of a man, when it respects in one of its citizens only memory, in another a tabulating intellect, in a third only mechanical skill; if, indifferent to character, it here lays stress upon knowledge alone, and there pardons the profoundest darkness of the intellect so long as it co-exists with a spirit of order and a law-abiding demeanour – if at the same time it requires these special aptitudes to be exercised with an intensity proportionate to the loss of extension which it permits in the individuals concerned – can we then wonder that the remaining aptitudes of the mind become neglected in order to bestow every attention upon the only one which brings in honour and profit? We know indeed that vigorous genius does not make the boundaries of its concern the boundaries of its activity; but mediocre talent consumes the whole meagre sum of its strength in the concern that falls to its lot, and it must be no ordinary head that has something left over for private pursuits without prejudice to its vocation. Moreover, it is seldom a good recommendation with the State when powers exceed commissions, or when the higher spiritual requirements of the man of genius furnish a rival to his office. So jealous is the State for the exclusive possession of its servants, that it will more easily bring itself (and who can blame it?) to share its man with a Cytherean than with a Uranian Venus![1]

And so gradually individual concrete life is extinguished, in order that

[1] As presiding over earthly and spiritual love respectively.

the abstract life of the whole may prolong its sorry existence, and the State remains eternally alien to its citizens because nowhere does feeling discover it. Compelled to disburden itself of the diversity of its citizens by means of classification, and to receive humanity only at second hand, by representation, the governing section finally loses sight of it completely, confounding it with a mere patchwork of the intellect; and the governed cannot help receiving coldly the laws which are addressed so little towards themselves. Finally, weary of maintaining a bond which is so little alleviated for it by the State, positive society disintegrates (as has long since been the fate of the majority of European States) into a moral state of Nature, where open force is only one *more* party, hated and eluded by those who make it necessary, and respected only by those who can dispense with it.

And just as form gradually approaches him from without, in his dwelling, his furniture, his clothing, it begins finally to take possession of Man himself, to transform at first only the outward but ultimately the inward man. The lawless leap of joy becomes a dance, the shapeless gesture a graceful and harmonious miming speech; the confused noises of perception unfold themselves, begin to obey a rhythm and weld themselves into song. While the Trojan host with shrill cries storms like a flight of cranes across the battlefield, the Greek army approaches quietly, with noble tread.[1] There we see only the arrogance of blind strength, here the triumph of form and the simple majesty of law.

A lovelier necessity now links the sexes together, and the sympathy of hearts helps to maintain the bond which was knitted only capriciously and inconstantly by desire. Released from its sullen chains, the quieter eye apprehends form, soul gazes into soul, and out of a selfish exchange of lust there grows a generous interplay of affection. Desire extends and exalts itself into love as mankind arises in its object, and the base advantage over sense is disdained for the sake of a nobler victory over the will. The need to please subjects the man of force to the gentle tribunal of taste; lust can be robbery, but love must be a gift. For this loftier prize he can contend through form alone, not through matter. He must cease to approach feeling as force, and to confront the intellect as a phenomenon; in order to please liberty, he must concede it. And just as Beauty resolves the conflict of natures in its simplest and purest example, in the eternal opposition of the sexes, so does she resolve it – or

[1] *Iliad*, III, 1–9.

at least aims at resolving it – in the intricate totality of society, and reconciles everything gentle and violent in the moral world after the pattern of the free union which she there contrives between masculine strength and feminine gentleness. Weakness now becomes sacred, and unbridled strength disgraceful; the injustice of Nature is rectified by the generosity of the chivalric code. The man whom no force may confound is disarmed by the tender blush of modesty, and tears stifle a revenge which no blood could slake. Even hatred pays heed to the gentle voice of honour, the victor's sword spares the disarmed foe and a hospitable hearth smokes for the fugitive on the dreaded shore where of old only murder awaited him.

In the midst of the awful realm of powers, and of the sacred realm of laws, the aesthetic creative impulse is building unawares a third joyous realm of play and of appearance, in which it releases mankind from all the shackles of circumstance and frees him from everything that may be called constraint, whether physical or moral.

If in the *dynamic* state of rights man encounters man as force and restricts his activity, if in the *ethical* state of duties he opposes him with the majesty of law and fetters his will, in the sphere of cultivated society, in the *aesthetic* state, he need appear to him only as shape, confront him only as an object of free play. *To grant freedom by means of freedom* is the fundamental law of this kingdom.

The dynamic state can only make society possible, by curbing Nature through Nature; the ethical State can only make it (morally) necessary, by subjecting the individual to the general will; the aesthetic State alone can make it actual, since it carries out the will of the whole through the nature of the individual. Though need may drive Man into society, and Reason implant social principles in him, Beauty alone can confer on him a *social character*. Taste alone brings harmony into society, because it establishes harmony in the individual. All other forms of perception divide a man, because they are exclusively based either on the sensuous or on the intellectual part of his being; only the perception of the Beautiful makes something whole of him, because both his natures must accord with it. All other forms of communication divide society, because they relate exclusively either to the private sensibility or to the private skilfulness of its individual members, that is, to what distinguishes between one man and another; only the communication of the Beautiful unites society, because it relates to what is common to them all. We enjoy the pleasures of the senses simply as individuals, and the race which lives within us has no share in them; hence we cannot extend our sensuous pleasures into being universal, because we cannot make our own individuality universal. We enjoy the pleasures of knowledge simply as race, and by carefully removing every trace of individuality from our judgement; hence we cannot make our intellectual pleasures universal, because we cannot exclude the traces of individuality from the judgement of others as we do from our own. It is only the Beautiful that we enjoy at the same time as individual and as race, that is, as *representatives* of the race. Sensuous good can make only *one* happy man, since it is based on appropriation, which always implies exclusion; it can also make this one man only partially happy, because the personality does not share in it. Absolute good can bring happiness only under conditions which are not to be universally assumed; for truth is only the reward of renunciation, and only a pure heart believes in the pure will. Beauty alone makes all the world happy, and every being forgets its limitations as long as it experiences her enchantment.

No pre-eminence, no rival dominion is tolerated as far as taste rules and the realm of the Beautiful extends. This realm stretches upward to the point where Reason governs with unconditional necessity and all matter ceases; it stretches downwards to the point where natural impulse holds sway with blind compulsion and form has not yet begun; indeed, even on these outermost boundaries, where its legislative power has been taken from it, taste still does not allow its executive power to be wrested away. Unsocial desire must renounce its selfishness, and the agreeable, which otherwise allures only the senses, must cast the toils of charm over spirits too. Necessity's stern voice, Duty, must alter its reproachful formula, which resistance alone can justify, and honour willing Nature with a nobler confidence. Taste leads knowledge out of the mysteries of science under the open sky of common sense, and transforms the perquisite of the schools into a common property of the whole of human society. In its territory even the mightiest genius must resign its grandeur and descend familiarly to the comprehension of a child. Strength must let itself be bound by the Graces, and the haughty lion yield to the bridle of a Cupid. In return, taste spreads out its soothing veil over physical need, which in its naked shape affronts the dignity of free spirits, and conceals from us the degrading relationship with matter by a delightful illusion of freedom. Given wings by it, even cringing mercenary art rises from the dust, and at the touch of its wand the chains of thraldom drop away from the lifeless and the living alike. Everything in the aesthetic

State, even the subservient tool, is a free citizen having equal rights with the noblest; and the intellect, which forcibly moulds the passive multitude to its designs, must here ask for its assent. Here, then, in the realm of aesthetic appearance, is fulfilled the ideal of equality which the visionary would fain see realized in actuality also; and, if it is true that fine breeding matures earliest and most completely near the throne, we are bound to recognize here too the bountiful dispensation which seems often to restrict mankind in the actual, only in order to incite him into the ideal world.

But does such a State of Beauty in Appearance really exist, and where is it to be found? As a need, it exists in every finely tuned soul; as an achievement we might perhaps find it, like the pure Church, or the pure Republic, only in a few select circles where it is not the spiritless imitation of foreign manners but people's own lovely nature that governs conduct, where mankind passes through the most complex situations with eager simplicity and tranquil innocence, and has no need either to encroach upon another's freedom in order to assert his own, or to display gracefulness at the cost of dignity.

On the Aesthetic Education of Man (1795), trans. R. Snell (London, Routledge, 1954), paperback ed. (New York, Ungar), pp. 39–42, 136–40.

Gracchus Babeuf
(1760–1797)

THE REPUBLIC OF EQUALS

MANIFESTO OF THE EQUALS

Real equality: the final aim of the social art

Condorcet, *Sketch for a Historical Picture of the Progress of the Human Mind.*

People of France!

For fifteen centuries you have lived in slavery, and in consequence in misery. For six years, you have scarcely been able to breathe in the anticipation of independence, happiness and equality.

Equality! the primary natural desire! the primary need of man and the chief bond of every legitimate association! People of France, you have been no more favoured than the other nations which vegetate on the unhappy earth! Everywhere and always is the poor human species abandoned to more or less crafty forms of cannibalism, and serves as a plaything for every ambition, a prey for every tyranny. Everywhere and always, men are lulled with fine words; nowhere and never do they obtain the reality with the word. Since time immemorial it has been hypocritically repeated to us that men are equal; and from time immemorial the most degrading and the most extensive inequality weighs insolently upon the human race. For as long as there have been civil societies the noblest attribute of man has been acknowledged without question, but not in one single instance has it yet been realized. Equality has been nothing but a beautiful and sterile fiction of the law. Today when it is demanded in a louder voice, we are answered thus: 'Be silent, you wretched people! Real equality is nothing but a chimera; content yourselves with conditional equality: you are all equal before the law. What more do you, rabble, need? What more do we need? Legislators, rulers, rich property-owners, listen in your turn.

We are equal, are we not? That principle remains uncontested, because, without being accused of madness, no one can seriously suggest that night is day.

Very well! We henceforth demand to live and die equal as we were born. We desire real equality or death – that is what we need.

And we will have it, this real equality, whatever the price. Woe to those who stand between us and it! Woe to anyone seeking to resist so firm a desire.

The French Revolution was but the forerunner of another much greater and much more solemn revolution, which will be the last.

The people has routed kings and priests in coalition against it: it will do the same to the new tyrants, the new political hypocrites seated in the places of the old.

What more do we need than equality of rights?

We do not merely need that equality which is inscribed in the Declaration of the Rights of Man and of the Citizen; we desire it in our midst, under the roofs of our houses. We will agree to anything for its sake, we will make a clean sweep of everything just for the satisfaction of enjoying it. Perish, if need be, all the arts, so long as we retain equality.

Legislators and rulers, who have as little wit as you have good faith, rich and ruthless property-owners, in vain do you seek to neutralize our sacred enterprise by saying: 'They are only repeating the demand for that agrarian law demanded many times before now.'

Calumnators, be silent in your turn, and, in the silence of confusion, listen to our demands dictated by nature and based on justice.

The agrarian law or the distribution of the land was the spontaneous desire of certain unprincipled soldiers, of certain mobs impelled by their instinct rather than by reason. We aim at something more sublime and more equitable, namely the common good, or the community of goods! Not just individual property of land: *the land belongs to no one*. We demand, we desire the common enjoyment of the fruits of the land: the fruits are for everyone.

We declare ourselves no longer able to endure that the very great majority of men should toil and sweat at the service and at the good pleasure of a tiny minority.

For long enough, for too long have less than a million individuals disposed of what belongs to more than twenty millions of their fellow-men, their equals.

May it finally come to an end, this great scandal, in which our descendants will refuse to believe! Let the appalling distinctions between rich and poor, great and small, masters and servants, rulers and ruled, finally disappear.

Let there be no other difference between men than that of age and sex. Since all have the same needs and the same faculties, let them henceforth have the same education and the same diet. They are content with the same sun and the same air for all; why should not the same portion and the same quality of nourishment not suffice for each of them?

But already the enemies of the most natural order of things that is conceivable declaim against us: 'Agents of disorder and anarchy', they say to us, 'you only seek massacres and plunder.'

People of France,

We will not waste our time in answering them, but we will say to you: the holy task which we are undertaking has no other aim than to put an end to civil disputes and to public misery.

Never has a grander design been conceived or put into operation. At long intervals, some men of genius, some wise men, have spoken of it in low and trembling voices. None of them has had the courage to speak the whole truth.

The moment for great measures has come. The evil is at its worst; it covers the face of the earth. Chaos, under the name of politics, has reigned for too many centuries. May everything return to order and regain its place. In the name of equality, may the elements of justice and of happiness be organized. The moment has come to found the Republic of Equals, that great refuge open to all men. The days of general restitution have arrived. Wailing families, come and sit at the common table laid by nature for all her children.

People of France,

The purest of all glories has thus been reserved for you! Yes, it is you who will be the first who must offer to the world this moving spectacle.

Old habits, old prejudices, will once more seek to hinder the establishment of the Republic of Equals. The organization of real equality, the sole equality which responds to all needs, without creating victims or exacting sacrifices, will not perhaps please everyone at first. The egoistic and the ambitious will tremble with rage. Those who possess unjustly will cry out at injustice.

Exclusive enjoyments, solitary pleasures, personal comforts will be the source of keen regret to some individuals deadened to the sufferings of others. The lovers of absolute power, the vile tools of arbitrary authority, will find it painful to allow their splendid leaders to be brought down to the level of real equality. Their short-sightedness makes it difficult for them to foresee the coming future of common happiness; but what do a few thousand malcontents matter, in the face of a mass of entirely happy men, astonished to have sought so long a happiness that is within their grasp.

On the morrow of this real revolution, they will say, in amazement: 'How can it be? The common happiness depends on so little! We have only to desire it. Ah! Why did we not desire it sooner? Did we need to be told of it so many times?' Yes, without doubt; if there is a single man on the earth who is more resolute and more powerful than his fellows, his equals, then the equilibrium is destroyed: crime and unhappiness are upon the earth.

People of France,

What is the sign that will henceforth enable you to recognize the excellence of a constitution? . . . Only that which is based entirely on real equality can be fit for you and satisfy all your wants.

The aristocratic charters of 1791 and 1795 fastened your chains instead of breaking them. That of 1793 was, in fact, a great step towards real equality, which had not yet been approached so closely; but it did not yet attain the goal and did not achieve the common happiness, the principle of which it none the less solemnly consecrated.

People of France,

Open your eyes and your hearts to the fullness of happiness. Acknowledge and proclaim with us the Republic of Equals.

'Manifeste des Égaux' (1796), in *Les Précurseurs Français du Socialisme de Condorcet à Proudhon*, ed. Maxime Leroy (Paris, Éditions du Temps Présent, 1948), pp. 63–70. (Translated by Steven Lukes.)

Henri, Comte de Saint-Simon
(1760–1825)

SCIENTISTS, ARTISTS AND INDUSTRIALISTS

... the fundamental basis of the old political system was, on the one hand, a state of ignorance, the result of which was that judgements about the means for securing the well-being of society did not depend on observations, but depended only on mere intuitions.

And, on the other hand, a state of incompetence prevailed in the arts and crafts which (rendering peoples incapable of producing wealth, by working on raw materials) left them no other means of enriching themselves than seizing the raw materials in the possession of other peoples.

As a result of industrial progress, peoples have acquired the means of prospering all at the same time, by enriching themselves through peaceful labours.

On the other hand, positive knowledge has been acquired, phenomena of all kinds have been observed, and philosophy, based upon experience, today contains principles which can guide peoples towards morality and well-being much more certainly than metaphysics can.

Given this state of affairs, there exist the means and thus the necessity of establishing a new political system.

The fundamental bases of a new system are therefore, on the one hand, a state of civilization which provides men with the means of employing their faculties in a way which is useful to others and profitable to themselves.

And, on the other hand, it is based on a state of enlightenment with the consequence that society, aware of the means it must employ to improve its lot, can be guided by principles, and no longer has any need to give arbitrary powers to those whom it entrusts with the task of administering its affairs.

It is not the way powers are divided which constitutes the difference between the systems; it is the difference in the nature and the quantity of powers exercised by the rulers over the ruled.

All forms of government are applicable to all political systems.[1]

So long as the rulers are considered as the most important, the most capable and the most useful men in society; so long as their leaders are given immense salaries in order to increase their status and their power; so long as the nation leaves to them the task of choosing the means they judge most suitable to perfect its morality and secure its tranquillity, as well as its prosperity; so long as they are chosen, on the one hand, from the class of metaphysicians (that is, persons who, still subject to blind belief and with only a superficial knowledge, seek to reason on the basis of general facts) and, on the other hand, from the military class (persons whose most exalted occupation consists in perfecting the means of conflict between men) – for so long the nation will remain entangled in the old system. It will remain subject to that system, whatever form of government it adopts, whether that form be republican, aristocratic, pure monarchy or constitutional monarchy. It will remain subject to the old system whether it finds its military leaders among the descendants of feudal families or among the descendants of serfs, whether its intellectual leaders are taken from among the theologians or from the metaphysicians who have been trained in law schools.

The nation will only find itself set upon the threshold of the new political existence it must embrace, when it has a clear consciousness of the total immorality and total monstrosity of the social regime to which it has remained subject hitherto; when, having opened its eyes to the combined methods of force and cunning which the nobility and the clergy have used so as to exploit it to their advantage, it will decide to dismantle completely that old machine, and replace it by a new one that will be conceived and organized according to principles derived from a healthy morality and true philosophy; when it will recognize that its government will inevitably be arbitrary so long as its leaders are taken from military men and metaphysicians, when it will recognize that its rulers will of necessity be despotic so long as they are regarded by society as the most important persons in the State, those who are most useful to it and who deserve, in consequence, the highest honours; when finally (having

[1] I do not mean by this that the forms of government and the manner of dividing power are matters of indifference. I simply mean that these matters have only a secondary importance.

grasped that its prosperity can only result from the progress of the sciences, the fine arts and the useful arts), it will regard scientists, artists and artisans as the men that are most useful to it, and consequently as those to whom it must accord the highest degree of honour. That will be a happy epoch for the human race, when the functions of the rulers will be reduced to being no more than those of ushers in schools: the ushers are charged with doing no more than maintaining order; it is the teachers who have the task of directing the work of the pupils. It must be the same with the State; scientists, artists and artisans must direct the work of the nation; the rulers must be occupied only with the task of preventing that work from being hindered.

Fifty thousand acres of land (and more if this is judged suitable) will be chosen from among the most picturesque sites, crossed by roads and canals. These areas will be devoted to serving as places of rest for travellers and as pleasurable abodes for the inhabitants of the neighbourhood.

Each of these gardens will contain a museum of natural products, as well as of industrial products, of the surrounding areas. They will also contain dwelling-places for artists who wish to stop there, and there will always be provision for a certain number of musicians whose function will be to inflame the inhabitants of the canton with the passion whose development circumstances will require for the greater good of the nation.

The whole of the soil of France should become a superb English park, embellished with all that the fine arts can add to the beauties of nature. For a long time luxury has been concentrated in the palaces of kings, in the residences of princes, in the mansions and chateaux of a few powerful men. This concentration is very harmful to the general interests of society, because it tends to establish two distinct levels of civilization, two different classes of men, that of persons whose intelligence is developed by the habitual sight of works of fine art, and that of men whose faculties of imagination remain undeveloped, since the physical work that exclusively occupies them in no way stimulates their intelligence.

Present conditions are favourable to making luxury national. Luxury will become useful and moral when the entire nation enjoys it. It is to our century that the honour and advantage have been reserved of putting to immediate use, through political combinations, the progress achieved in the exact sciences and in the fine arts since the brilliant epoch of their regeneration.

'L'Organisateur' (1819–20), in *Œuvres de Saint-Simon et d'Enfantin* (Paris, Dentu, 1865–78), vol. XX, pp. 38–43, 52–3. (Translated by Steven Lukes.)

The mechanism of social organization was inevitably very complicated so long as the majority of individuals remained in a state of ignorance and improvidence which rendered them incapable of administering their own affairs. In this state of incomplete intellectual development they were swayed by brutal passions which urged them to revolt and every kind of anarchy.

In such a situation, which was the necessary prelude to a better social order, it was necessary for the minority to be organized on military lines, to obtain a monopoly of legislation, and so to keep all power to itself, in order to hold the majority in tutelage and subject the nation to strong discipline. Thus the main energies of the community have till now been directed to maintaining itself as a community, and any efforts directed to improving the moral and physical welfare of the nation have necessarily been regarded as secondary.

Today this state of affairs can and should be completely altered. The main effort should be directed to the improvement of our moral and physical welfare; only a small amount of force is now required to maintain public order, since the majority have become used to work (which eliminates disorder) and now consists of men who have recently proved that they are capable of administering property, whether in land or money.

As the minority no longer has need of force to keep the proletarian class in subordination, the course which it should adopt is as follows:

(1) A policy by which the proletariat will have the strongest interest in maintaining public order.

(2) A policy which aims at making the inheritance of landed property as easy as possible.

(3) A policy which aims at giving the highest political importance to the workers.

Such a policy is quite simple and obvious, if one takes the trouble to judge the situation by one's own intelligence, and to shake off the yoke enforced on our minds by the political principles of our ancestors – principles which were sound and useful in their own day, but are no longer applicable to present circumstances. The mass of the population is now composed of men (apart from exceptions which occur more or less equally in every class) who are capable of administering property whether in land or in money, and therefore we can and must work directly for the improvement of the moral and physical welfare of the community.

The most direct method of improving the moral and physical welfare of the majority of the population is to give priority in State expenditure to ensuring work for all fit men, to secure their physical existence; spreading throughout the proletarian class a knowledge of positive science; ensuring for this class forms of recreation and interests which will develop their intelligence.

We must add to this the measures necessary to ensure that the national wealth is administered by men most fitted for it, and most concerned in its administration, that is to say the most important industrialists.

Thus the community, by means of these fundamental arrangements, will be organized in a way which will completely satisfy reasonable men of every class.

There will no longer be a fear of insurrection, and consequently no longer a need to maintain large standing armies to suppress it; no longer a need to spend enormous sums on a police force; no longer a fear of foreign danger, for a body of thirty millions of men who are a contented community would easily repel attack, even if the whole human race combined against them.

We might add that neither princes nor peoples would be so mad as to attack a nation of thirty millions who displayed no aggressive intentions against their neighbours, and were united internally by mutual interests.

Furthermore, there would no longer be a need for a system of police-spying in a community in which the vast majority had an interest in maintaining the established order.

The men who brought about the Revolution, the men who directed it, and the men who, since 1789 and up to the present day, have guided the nation, have committed a great political mistake. They have all sought to improve the governmental machine, whereas they should have subordinated it and put administration in the first place.

They should have begun by asking a question the solution of which is simple and obvious. They should have asked who, in the present state of morals and enlightenment, are the men most fitted to manage the affairs of the nation. They would have been forced to recognize the fact that the scientists, artists and industrialists, and the heads of industrial concerns are the men who possess the most eminent, varied, and most positively useful ability, for the guidance of men's minds at the present time. They would have recognized the fact that the work of the scientists, artists and industrialists is that which, in discovery and application, contributes most to national prosperity.

They would have reached the conclusion that the scientists, artists and leaders of industrial enterprises are the men who should be entrusted with administrative power, that is to say, with the responsibility for managing the national interests; and that the functions of government should be limited to maintaining public order.

'On Social Organization' (1825), trans. in *Saint-Simon, Selected Writings,* ed. F. M. H. Markham (Oxford, Blackwell, 1952), pp. 76–9.

Benjamin Constant de Rebecque
(1767–1830)

LIBERTY AS THE TRIUMPH OF INDIVIDUALITY

For forty years I have stood for the same principle: liberty in all things, in religion, in philosophy, in literature, in industry, in politics. By liberty I understand the triumph of individuality, as much over the authority which aspired to govern by despotism, as over the masses who claim the right to subject the minority to the majority. Despotism has no rights. The majority has the right to compel the minority to respect order: but everything which does not interfere with order, everything which is merely private, such as opinion; everything which, in the expression of opinion, does not harm others, whether by provoking physical violence or by denying a contrary expression; everything which, in the sphere of industry, allows rival industries to operate freely – all this is individual, and cannot legitimately be subjected to the power of society.

I have expressed all my thoughts about all these matters. Perhaps I will equally displease, in matters of religion, both the devout and the unbelievers, or at least those who have embraced unbelief as a dogmatic doctrine. As for the history of our troubles, I will displease both the well-intentioned admirers of Robespierre and Saint-Just, and the enemies of Malesherbes and La Fayette; and, with respect to the empire, both the devoted partisans of Napoleon and his detractors. Perhaps my aversion for the protective rules which have for so long shackled the progress of our literature will earn me the enmity of those who proclaim the necessity of imitation, because for them originality is impossible.

What does it matter? These things have no importance so long as they are merely personal opinions. Someone who merely wishes, in his own particular interest and to attain a personal end, to pass through a crowd, must be able to get round those near him without bumping into them and to edge past them without disturbing them.

But when one has no other end than fully to understand the great crisis which has been in preparation for two centuries and evident for the last forty years, and to support the movement which carries the entire human race towards a better system of ideas and institutions, one can and one must say all that one thinks.

The crisis which is occurring before our eyes, despite the resistance of some, and the declamations of others, and without the knowledge of the masses who are occupied in bringing it about, is not the last crisis that will change the face of the world. After the changes which befall us today, many more will follow in the future. But those destructions, or rather ultimate deliverances, are reserved for another epoch. Let us not anticipate future times: let us get to the bottom of the doctrines which the times have brought into being and which they are strengthening.

In matters of government, the most absolute equality of rights distributed among all the individuals gathered together in the body of the nation must be and soon will be, in all civilized countries, the first condition for the existence of all governments. Their functions will differ, their forms will be combined in such a way as to maintain order; but fixed limits will be set to all power, because power is only the means and because the maintenance and exercise of rights are the end. In consequence there will be possible variations and progressive changes in the functions, the forms, the extent, the competence and the names of power. But beneath these various names and these diverse forms, its basis will necessarily be the equality of rights which we have just indicated; and all those who possess these rights will be entitled to combine in their defence, that is, to participate in some way or other in the making of the laws that will determine the influence of government.

In matters of political economy, there will be, regarding property, respect and protection because property is a legal convention, necessary to the epoch: but the disposition, the division, the sub-division, the circulation and the distribution of property will encounter no restriction and no obstacle because the unlimited freedom to maintain, to alienate, to parcel out, to alter the nature of property is, in our social state, the inherent right, the essential requirement of all those who own property. All types of property will be equally sacred in the eyes of the law: but each will take the position and enjoy the influence assigned to it by the nature of things. Industrial property will be placed, without the law interfering with it, higher than landed property with every day that passes, because, as we have said elsewhere, landed property is the value of the thing;

industrial property the value of the man. Moreover, in relation to industry, there will be freedom, competition and the absence of all interference by authority, whether to save individuals from their own mistakes (they must learn by experience) or else to secure for the public the best objects of consumption (their experience must guide their choices); and every monopoly, every privilege, every corporation protected to the detriment of individual activity and individual enterprise will disappear never to return.

In matters of opinion, beliefs and knowledge, there will be complete neutrality on the part of government, because government, composed of men of the same nature as those it governs, does not have, any more than they do, incontestable opinions, certain beliefs, or infallible knowledge. At the most, they will be granted the power to collect and preserve all the materials of instruction, to establish depositories, open to all, from which everyone may draw at will, in order to make use of them in his own fashion, without any direction being imposed upon him.

Such is, I believe, the social state towards which the human race is beginning to advance. To attain that social state is the necessity, and will in consequence be the destiny, of the epoch. To wish to remain on this side of it would be far from wise: to wish to go beyond it would be premature.

During this time, many things that will become superfluous will still be envisaged as necessary; many that will become necessary will be considered as problematic, paradoxical, perhaps even criminal. Let us not concern ourselves with them; to each age its task.

Preface to 'Mélanges de Littérature et de Politique' (1829), in *Œuvres*, ed. A. Roulin (Paris, Gallimard, 1957), pp. 835–8. (Translated by Steven Lukes.)

Wilhelm von Humboldt
(1767–1835)

LIBERTY, INDIVIDUALITY AND INDEPENDENCE

... some means must be provided to connect the governing and governed classes of the nation together – to secure the former in the possession of the power confided to them, and the latter in the enjoyment of what
freedom remains after this necessary deduction. Different methods have
been adopted in different States for this purpose: in some, it has been
sought to strengthen the physical power of the government (a plan somewhat perilous for freedom); in others, the accomplishment of this end has
been attempted by bringing contending and counterbalancing forces into
opposition; and in others, by diffusing throughout the nation a spirit
favourable to the constitution. The last method we have mentioned,
although often productive of beautiful results (as we notice more especially
in antiquity), has too hurtful a tendency on the individual development of
the citizen, too easily induces one-sidedness in the national character, and
is therefore most foreign to the system we have proposed. According to
this, we should rather look for a constitution which should have the least
possible positive or special influence on the character of the citizens, and
would fill their hearts with nothing but the deepest regard for the rights of
others, combined with the most enthusiastic love for their own liberty. I
shall not here attempt to discover which constitution may be supposed to
resemble this most faithfully. Such an investigation belongs evidently to
a strict theory of politics; and I shall content myself with a few brief
considerations, which may serve to show more clearly the possibility of
such a constitution. The system I have proposed tends to strengthen and
multiply the private interests of the citizen, and it may therefore seem
calculated in that way to weaken the public interest. But it interweaves
the two so closely together, that the latter seems rather to be based on the
former; and especially so appears to the citizen, who wishes to be at once

secure and free. Thus then, with such a system, that love for the constitution might be most surely preserved, which it is so often vainly sought to cultivate in the hearts of the citizens by artificial means. In this case of a State, moreover, in which the sphere of action is so narrow and limited, a less degree of power is necessary, and this requires proportionately less defence. Lastly, it follows of course, that, as power and enjoyment are often to be sacrificed on both sides to secure given results, in order to protect both from a greater loss, the same necessary accommodations are to be supposed in the system we have propounded.

I have now succeeded, then, in answering the question I proposed myself, as far as my present powers would allow, and have traced out the sphere of political activity, and confined it within such limits as seemed to me most conducive and necessary to man's highest interests. In this endeavour I have invariably set out with a view to discover what was *best* in the several cases; although it might not be uninteresting to ascertain what course was most strictly accordant with the principles of *right*. But when a State union has once proposed to itself a certain aim, and has voluntarily prescribed certain limits to its activity, those ends and limits are naturally in accordance with right, so long as they are such that those who defined them were adequate to their important task. Where such an express determination of ends and limits has not been made, the State must naturally endeavour to bring its activity within the sphere which abstract theory prescribes, but must also be guided by the consideration of such obstacles, as, if overlooked, would lead to far more hurtful consequences. The nation can always demand the adoption of such a theory, in so far as these obstacles render it practicable, but no further. I have not hitherto taken these obstacles into consideration, but have contented myself with developing the pure and abstract theory. I have in general aimed at discovering the most favourable position which man can occupy as member of a political community. And it has appeared to me to be that in which the most manifold individuality and the most original independence subsisted, with the most various and intimate union of a number of men – a problem which nothing but the most absolute liberty can ever hope to solve. To point out the possibility of a political organization which should fall as little short of this end as possible, and bring man nearer to such a position, has been my strict design in these pages, and has for some time been the subject of all my thoughts and researches. I shall be satisfied to have shown that this principle should be, at least, the guiding one in all political constitutions, and the system which is based upon it the high ideal of the legislator.

These ideas might have been forcibly illustrated by historical and statistical considerations, if both were directed to this end. On the whole there seems to me to be much need of reform in statistical science. Instead of giving us the mere data of area, population, wealth and industry in a State, from which its real condition can never be fully and accurately determined, it should proceed from a consideration of the real state of the country and its inhabitants, and endeavour to convey the extent and nature of their active, passive and enjoying powers, with such gradual modifications as these receive, either from the force of national union, or from the influence of the political organization. For the State constitution and the national union, however closely they may be interwoven with each other, should not be confounded together. While the State constitution, by the force of law, or custom, or its own preponderating power, imparts a definite relation to the citizens, there is still another which is wholly distinct from this – chosen of their own free-will, infinitely various and in its nature ever-changing. And it is strictly this last – the mutual freedom of activity among all the members of the nation – which secures all those benefits for which men longed when they formed themselves into a society. The State constitution itself is strictly subordinate to this, as to the end for which it was chosen as a necessary means; and, since it is always attended with restrictions in freedom, as a necessary evil.

It has, therefore, been my secondary design in these pages to point out the fatal consequences which flow for human enjoyment, power and character, from confounding the free activity of the nation with that which is enforced upon its members by the political constitution.

The Sphere and Duties of Government (1791, first pub. posthumously), J. Coulthard (London, Trubner, 1854), pp. 187–90.

G. W. F. Hegel
(1770–1831)

THE FREE ACTIVITY OF
THE CITIZENS

Of course on the political theories of our day, partly propounded by would-be philosophers and teachers of the rights of man and partly realized in tremendous political experiments, everything we have excluded from the necessary concept of public authority (except what is most important of all, language, education, manners and religion) is subjected to the immediate activity of the supreme public authority and in such a way that it is settled by that authority itself and driven by it down to the last detail.

It is to be taken for granted that the highest public authority must carry the supreme oversight of these afore-mentioned aspects of the domestic relationships of a people and their organization (which has been settled by chance and ancient arbitrary decisions); equally obvious is it that these aspects may not hinder the chief activity of the state, since on the contrary this activity must secure itself before all else, and to this end it is not to spare the subordinate systems of rights and privileges. Nevertheless, it is one great virtue of the old states in Europe that while the public authority is secure so far as its needs and its progress are concerned, it leaves free scope to the citizens' own activity in details of the administration, judicial and others, partly in the nomination of the necessary officials, partly in the management of current affairs and the administration of law and customary usages.

The size of modern states makes it quite impossible to realize the ideal of giving every free individual a share in debating and deciding political affairs of universal concern. The public authority must be concentrated in one centre for deciding these matters and, as government, for executing these decisions. If this centre is secure on its own account in virtue of the awe of the masses, and is immutably sacrosanct in the person of a monarch appointed in accordance with a natural law and by birth, then a public authority may without fear or jealousy freely hand over to subordinate systems and bodies a great part of the relationships arising in society and their maintenance according to the laws. Each estate, city, town, commune, etc., can itself enjoy freedom to do and to execute what lies within its area.

Just as laws on these matters have gradually proceeded as a hallowed tradition directly from custom itself, so the constitution, the organization of the lower jurisdiction, the rights of the citizens therein – i.e. rights of municipal management, collection of taxes, whether national or those necessary for the municipalities themselves and the legal application of the latter – all these things and those connected with them have been set up by native impulse. They have grown up of themselves, and since ever they saw the light they have maintained themselves similarly.

The organization of the ecclesiastical establishments, which is so far-reaching, has just as little been created by the supreme public authority, and the whole ecclesiastical estate maintains and perpetuates itself more or less internally. The huge sums paid annually in a large state for the poor, and the consequential and wide-ranging arrangements which pervade all parts of a country, are not defrayed by levies which the state would have to adjust, nor is it at the state's command that the whole system is maintained and carried on. The mass of the relevant property and contributions depends on foundations and gifts by individuals, and so does the whole system and its administration and realization, without any dependence on the highest public authority. Most of the internal social arrangements for each special sphere of need have been made by the free action of the citizens, and their continuation and life has been maintained by just this freedom, which has been undisturbed by any jealousy or anxiety on the part of the supreme public authority, except that of course the government sometimes supports them and sometimes checks the over-abundant growth of one provision of this sort which might otherwise suppress other necessary provisions.

However, in recent theories, carried partly into effect, the fundamental presupposition is that a state is a machine with a single spring which imparts movement to all the rest of the infinite wheel-work, and that all institutions implicit in the nature of a society should proceed from the supreme public authority and be regulated, commanded, overseen and conducted by it.

The pedantic craving to determine every detail, the illiberal jealousy of [any arrangement whereby] an estate, a corporation, etc., adjusts and manages its own affairs, this mean carping at any independent action by the citizens which would only have some general bearing and not a bearing on the public authority, is clothed in the garb of rational principles. On these principles not a shilling of the public expenditure on poor relief in a country of twenty or thirty million inhabitants may be incurred unless it has first been not merely allowed but actually ordered, controlled and audited by the supreme government. The appointment of every village schoolmaster, the expenditure of every penny for a pane of glass in a village school or a village hall, the appointment of every toll-clerk or court officer or local justice of the peace, is to be an immediate emanation and effect of the highest authority. In the whole state every mouthful of food is brought from the ground that produces it to the mouth that eats it along a line examined, computed, adjusted, and directed by state, law and government.

This is no place to argue at length that the centre, as the public authority, i.e. the government, must leave to the freedom of the citizens whatever is not necessary for its appointed function of organizing and maintaining authority and thus for its security at home and abroad. Nothing should be so sacrosanct to the government as facilitating and protecting the free activity of the citizens in matters other than this. This is true regardless of utility, because the freedom of the citizens is inherently sacrosanct.

But, as regards utility, if we are to reckon what advantage is produced by the citizens' management of their affairs through special bodies, their courts, their appointments to the offices entailed in these, etc., then the reckoning is threefold. The first calculation concerns something tangible, namely the money which flows on this system into the hands of the supreme public authority; the second concerns intelligence and the excellence with which everything happens in a machine at a uniform pace in accordance with the shrewdest calculation and the wisest ends; but the third concerns the vitality, the contented mind, and free and self-respecting self-awareness which arises when the individual will participates in public affairs so far as their ramifications are matters of indifference to the supreme public authority.

On the first reckoning, the tangible one, the state whose principle is universal mechanism fancies, without hesitation, that it has the advantage over the state which leaves detail in great part to the rights and individual action of its citizens. But it must be noticed in general that the machine state cannot possibly have the advantage unless it imposes heavier taxes on everyone. Since it takes over all branches of government, the administration of justice, etc., it must be burdened at the same time with the expense of all this, and if the whole machine is organized as a universal hierarchy, then this expense must be covered by systematic taxation. On the other hand, (i) if the state hands over to the individual bodies interested the making of arrangements requisite for such purely contingent and individual matters as the administration of justice, educational expenses, contributions in support of the poor, etc., and also for providing the cost of these, then it sees these costs defrayed otherwise than in the form of taxes. The man who requires a judge or an attorney or a teacher, or who cares for the poor of his own volition, pays and pays then only; there is no question of a tax; no one pays for a court, an attorney, a teacher, a priest unless he needs one. (ii) If, for the lower official appointments in the court or the management of municipal or corporation affairs, one of the members of one of these bodies is chosen, then he is paid by the honour which thereby accrues to him, while if he is supposed to be the servant of the state, then he has to demand pay from the state because here this inner honour is lacking. These two points, (i) and (ii), even if, as is not to be expected, more money might have to be contributed by the people under (i), produce the following effects: the first produces the difference that no one pays out money for something he does not need, for something which is not a universal requirement of the state; while the second produces an actual saving for everybody. The net result is that the people feel themselves treated under (i) with reason and by necessity and under (ii) with trust and freedom: (ii) constitutes the prime difference revealed by the second and third modes of reckoning.

A mechanical hierarchy, highly intellectual and devoted to noble ends, evinces no confidence whatever in its citizens and can thus expect nothing from them. It has no assurance in any action not ordered, carried out and arranged by itself; thus it bans free-will gifts and sacrifices; it displays to its subjects its conviction of their lack of intellect, its contempt for their capacity to assess and do what is compatible with their private interests, and its belief in general profligacy. Thus it cannot hope for any vital action, any support from its subjects' self-respect.

There is a difference here so great as to be beyond the grasp of the statesman who allows for nothing which cannot be reckoned in hard cash. It shows itself primarily in the ease and welfare, the honesty and contentment of the inhabitants in one state, as compared with the dullness, the baseness (continually lapsing into shamelessness) and the poverty [of those] in another. Where, in things of the greatest moment, it is only the contingent aspect of the event that lies on the surface, a state of the latter kind determines this contingency and makes it necessary.

It makes an infinite difference whether the public authority is so organized that everything on which it can count is in its own hands while for this very reason it can count on nothing else, or whether apart from what is in its own hands it can count also on the free devotion, the self-respect and the individual effort of the people – on an all-powerful invincible spirit which the hierarchical system has renounced and which has its life only where the supreme public authority leaves as much as possible to the personal charge of the citizens. How dull and spiritless a life is engendered in a modern state where everything is regulated from the top downwards, where nothing with any general implications is left to the management and execution of interested parties of the people – in a state like what the French Republic has made itself – is to be experienced only in the future, if indeed this pitch of pedantry in domination can persist. But what life and what sterility reigns in another equally regulated state, in the Prussian, strikes anyone who sets foot in the first town there or sees its complete lack of scientific or artistic genius, or assesses its strength otherwise than by the ephemeral energy which a single genius has been able to generate in it for a time by pressure.

Thus we do not merely distinguish in a state, on the one hand, the necessary element which must lie in the hands of the public authority and be directly determined by it, and, on the other, the element which is necessary indeed simply for the social unification of a people but which for the public authority is in itself contingent. We also regard that people as fortunate to which the state gives a free hand in subordinate general activities, just as we regard a public authority as infinitely strong if it can be supported by the free and unregimented spirit of its people.

'The German Constitution' (1799–1802, first pub. posthumously), in *Hegel's Political Writings*, trans. T. M. Knox with an Introductory Essay by Z. A. Pelczynski (Oxford, Clarendon Press, 1964), pp. 159–64.

William Wordsworth
(1770–1850)

THE GOVERNMENT OF EQUAL RIGHTS
AND INDIVIDUAL WORTH

O friend! I know not which way I must look
For comfort, being, as I am, opprest,
To think that now our life is only drest
For show; mean handy-work of craftsman, cook,
Or groom! – We must run glittering like a brook
In the open sunshine, or we are unblest:
The wealthiest man among us is the best:
No grandeur now in nature or in book
Delights us. Rapine, avarice, expense,
This is idolatry; and these we adore:
Plain living and high thinking are no more:
The homely beauty of the good old cause
Is gone; our peace, our fearful innocence,
And pure religion breathing household laws.

'Sonnet of Indignation' (written in London: September 1802).

But though untaught by thinking or by books
To reason well of polity or law
And nice distinctions, then on every tongue,
Of natural rights and civil, and to acts
Of Nations, and their passing interests,
(I speak comparing these with other things)
Almost indifferent, even the Historian's Tale

Prizing but little otherwise than I priz'd
Tales of the Poets, as it made my heart
Beat high and fill'd my fancy with fair forms,
Old Heroes and their sufferings and their deeds;
Yet in the regal Sceptre, and the pomp
Of Orders and Degrees, I nothing found
Then, or had ever, even in crudest youth,
That dazzled me; but rather what my soul
Mourn'd for, or loath'd, beholding that the best
Rul'd not, and feeling that they ought to rule.

For, born in a poor District, and which yet
Retaineth more of ancient homeliness,
Manners erect, and frank simplicity,
Than any other nook of English Land,
It was my fortune scarcely to have seen
Through the whole tenor of my School-day time
The face of one, who, whether Boy or Man,
Was vested with attention or respect
Through claims of wealth or blood; nor was it least
Of many debts which afterwards I owed
To Cambridge, and an academic life
That something there was holden up to view
Of a Republic, where all stood thus far
Upon equal ground, that they were brothers all
In honour, as in one community,
Scholars and Gentlemen, where, furthermore,
Distinction lay open to all that came,
And wealth and titles were in less esteem
Than talents and successful industry.
Add unto this, subservience from the first
To God and Nature's single sovereignty,
Familiar presences of awful Power
And fellowship with venerable books
To sanction the proud workings of the soul,
And mountain liberty. It could not be
But that one tutor'd thus, who had been form'd
To thought and moral feeling in the way
This story hath described, should look with awe

Upon the faculties of Man, receive
Gladly the highest promises, and hail
As best the government of equal rights
And individual worth. And hence, O Friend!
If at the first great outbreak I rejoiced
Less than might well befit my youth, the cause
In part lay here, that unto me the events
Seemed nothing out of nature's certain course,
A gift that rather was come late than soon.

               Yet not the less,
Hatred of absolute rule, where will of One
Is law for all, and of that barren pride
In them who, by immunities unjust,
Betwixt the Sovereign and the People stand,
His helper and not theirs, laid stronger hold
Daily upon me, mix'd with pity too
And love; for where hope is there love will be
For the abject multitude. And when we chanc'd
One day to meet a hunger-bitten Girl,
Who crept along, fitting her languid gait
Unto a Heifer's motion, by a cord
Tied to her arm, and picking thus from the lane
Its sustenance, while the girl with her two hands
Was busy knitting, in a heartless mood
Of solitude, and at the sight my Friend
In agitation said, ' 'Tis against *that*
Which we are fighting,' I with him believed
Devoutly that a spirit was abroad
Which could not be withstood, that poverty
At least like this, would in a little time
Be found no more, that we should see the earth
Unthwarted in her wish to recompense
The industrious, and the lowly Child of Toil,
All institutes for ever blotted out
That legalized exclusion, empty pomp
Abolish'd, sensual state and cruel power
Whether by edict of the one or few,
And finally, as sum and crown of all,

Should see the People having a strong hand
In making their own Laws, whence better days
To all mankind.

The Prelude (1805 Version), Book 9, lines 200–53 and 501–32.

Robert Owen
(1771–1858)

THE HAPPINESS SYSTEM

Long before I came to reside among you, it had been my chief study to discover the extent, causes and remedy of the inconveniences and miseries which were perpetually recurring to every class in society.

The history of man informed me that innumerable attempts had been made, through every age, to lessen these evils; and experience convinced me that the present generation, stimulated by an accession of knowledge derived from past times, was eagerly engaged in the same pursuit. My mind at a very early period took a similar direction; and I became ardently desirous of investigating to its source a subject which involved the happiness of every human being.

It soon appeared to me, that the only path to knowledge on this subject had been neglected; that one leading in an opposite direction had alone been followed; that while causes existed to compel mankind to pursue such direction, it was idle to expect any successful result: and experience proves how vain their pursuit has been.

In this inquiry, men have hitherto been directed by their inventive faculties, and have almost entirely disregarded the only guide that can lead to true knowledge on any subject – experience. They have been governed, in the most important concerns of life, by mere illusions of the imagination, in direct opposition to existing facts.

Having satisfied myself beyond doubt with regard to this fundamental error; having traced the ignorance and misery which it has inflicted on man, by a calm and patient investigation of the causes which have continued this evil, without any intermission from one generation to another; and having also maturely reflected on the obstacles to be overcome, before a new direction can be given to the human mind; I was induced to form the resolution of devoting my life to relieve mankind from this mental disease and all its miseries.

It was evident to me that the evil was universal; that, in practice, none was in the right path – no, not one; and that, in order to remedy the evil, a different one must be pursued. That the whole man must be re-formed on fundamental principles the very reverse of those in which he had been trained; in short, that the minds of all men must be born again, and their knowledge and practice commence on a new foundation.

Satisfied of the futility of the existing modes of instruction, and of the errors of the existing modes of government, I was well convinced that none of them could ever effect the ends intended; but that, on the contrary, they were only calculated to defeat all the objects which human instructors and governors had proposed to attain.

I found, on such a patient consideration of the subject as its importance demanded, that to reiterate precept upon precept, however excellent in theory, while no decisive measures were adopted to place mankind under circumstances in which it might be possible to put those precepts in practice, was but a waste of time. I therefore determined to form arrangements preparatory to the introduction of truths, the knowledge of which should dissipate the errors and evils of all the existing political and religious systems.

Be not alarmed at the magnitude of the attempt which this declaration opens to your view. Each change, as it occurs, will establish a substantial and permanent good, unattended by any counteracting evil; nor can the mind of man, formed on the old system, longer interpose obstacles capable of retarding the progress of those truths which I am now about to unfold to you. The futile attempts which ignorance may for a short time oppose to them, will be found to accelerate their introduction. As soon as they shall be comprehended in all their bearings, every one will be compelled to acknowledge them, to see their benefits in practice to himself and to each of his fellow-creatures; for, by this system, none, no not one, will be injured. It is a delightful thought, an animating reflection, a stimulus to the steady prosecution of my purpose, beyond – nay, far beyond – all that riches, and honour, and praise can bestow, to be conscious of the possibility of being instrumental in introducing a practical system into society, the complete establishment of which *shall give happiness to every human being through all succeeding generations*. And such I declare was the sole motive that gave rise to this Institution, and to all my proceedings.

The events which have yet occurred far exceed my most sanguine anticipations, and my future course now appears evident and straightforward. It is no longer necessary that I should silently and alone exert myself for your benefit and the happiness of mankind. The period is arrived when I may call numbers to my aid, and the call will not be in vain. I well knew the danger which would arise from a premature and abrupt attempt to tear off the many-folded bandages of ignorance, which kept society in darkness. I have therefore been many years engaged, in a manner imperceptible to the public, in gently and gradually removing one fold after another of these fatal bands, from the mental eyes of those who have the chief influence in society. The principles on which the practical system I contemplate is to be founded, are now familiar to some of the leading men of all sects and parties in this country, and to many of the governing powers in Europe and America. They have been submitted to the examination of the most celebrated universities in Europe. They have been subjected to the minute scrutiny of the most learned and acute minds formed on the old system, and I am fully satisfied of their inability to disprove them. These principles I will shortly state.

Every society which exists at present, as well as every society which history records, has been formed and governed on a belief in the following notions, assumed as *first principles*:

First, – That it is in the power of every individual to form his own character.

Hence the various systems called by the name of religion, codes of law and punishments. Hence also the angry passions entertained by individuals and nations towards each other.

Second, – That the affections are at the command of the individual.

Hence insincerity and degradation of character. Hence the miseries of domestic life, and more than one-half of all the crimes of mankind.

Third, – That it is necessary that a large portion of mankind should exist in ignorance and poverty, in order to secure to the remaining part such a degree of happiness as they now enjoy.

Hence a system of counteraction in the pursuits of men, a general opposition among individuals to the interests of each other and the necessary effects of such a system – ignorance, poverty and vice.

Facts prove, however –

First, – That character is universally formed *for*, and not *by*, the individual.

Second, – That *any* habits and sentiments may be given to mankind.

Third, – That the affections are *not* under the control of the individual.

Fourth, – That every individual may be trained to produce far more than he can consume, while there is a sufficiency of soil left for him to cultivate.

Fifth, – That nature has provided means by which population may be at all times maintained in the proper state to give the greatest happiness to every individual, without one check of vice or misery.

Sixth, – That any community may be arranged, on a due combination of the foregoing principles, in such a manner, as not only to withdraw vice, poverty and, in a great degree, misery, from the world, but also to place *every* individual under circumstances in which he shall enjoy more permanent happiness than can be given to *any* individual under the principles which have hitherto regulated society.

Seventh, – That all the assumed fundamental principles on which society has hitherto been founded are erroneous, and may be demonstrated to be contrary to fact. And –

Eighth, – That the change which would follow the abandonment of those erroneous maxims which bring misery into the world, and the adoption of principles of truth, unfolding a system which shall remove and for ever exclude that misery, may be effected without the slightest injury to any human being.

Here is the groundwork, – these are the data, on which society shall ere long be re-arranged; and for this simple reason, that it will be rendered evident that it will be for the immediate and future interest of every one to lend his most active assistance gradually to reform society on this basis. I say *gradually*, for in that word the most important considerations are involved. Any sudden and coercive attempt which may be made to remove even misery from men will prove injurious rather than beneficial. Their minds must be gradually prepared by an essential alteration of the circumstances which surround them, for any great and important change and amelioration in their condition. They must be first convinced of their blindness: this cannot be effected, even among the least unreasonable, or those termed the best part of mankind, in their present state, without creating some degree of irritation. This irritation, must then be tranquillized before another step ought to be attempted; and a general conviction must be established of the truth of the principles on which the projected change is to be founded. Their introduction into practice will then become easy – difficulties will vanish as we approach them – and, afterwards, the desire to see the whole system carried immediately into effect will exceed the means of putting it into execution.

The principles on which this practical system is founded are not new;

separately, or partially united, they have been often recommended by the sages of antiquity, and by modern writers. But it is not known to me that they have ever been thus combined. Yet it can be demonstrated that it is only by their being *all brought into practice together* that they are to be rendered beneficial to mankind; and sure I am that this is the earliest period in the history of man when they could be successfully introduced into practice.

I do not intend to hide from you that the change will be great. 'Old things shall pass away, and all shall become new.'

But this change will bear no resemblance to any of the revolutions which have hitherto occurred. These have been alone calculated to generate and call forth all the evil passions of hatred and revenge: but that system which is now contemplated will effectually eradicate every feeling of irritation and ill will which exists among mankind. The whole proceedings of those who govern and instruct the world will be reversed. Instead of spending ages in telling mankind what they ought to think and how they ought to act, the instructors and governors of the world will acquire a knowledge that will enable them, in one generation, to apply the means which shall cheerfully induce each of those whom they control and influence, not only to think, but to act in such a manner as shall be best for himself and best for every human being. And yet this extraordinary result will take place without punishment or apparent force.

Under this system, before commands are issued it shall be known whether they can or cannot be obeyed. Men shall not be called upon to assent to doctrines and to dogmas which do not carry conviction to their minds. They shall not be taught that merit can exist in doing, or that demerit can arise from not doing that over which they have no control. They shall not be told, as at present, that they must love that which, by the constitution of their nature, they are compelled to dislike. They shall not be trained in wild imaginary notions, that inevitably make them despise and hate all mankind out of the little narrow circle in which they exist, and then be told that they must heartily and sincerely love all their fellow-men. No, my friends, that system which shall make its way into the heart of every man, is founded upon principles which have not the slightest resemblance to any of those I have alluded to. On the contrary, it is directly opposed to them; and the effects it will produce in practice will differ as much from the practice which history records, and from that which we see around us, as hypocrisy, hatred, envy, revenge, wars, poverty, injustice, oppression and all their consequent misery, differ from that genuine charity and sincere kindness of which we perpetually hear, but which we have never seen, and which, under the existing systems, we never can see.

That charity and that kindness admit of no exception. They extend to every child of man, however he may have been taught, however he may have been trained. They consider not what country gave him birth, what may be his complexion, what his habits or his sentiments. Genuine charity and true kindness instruct, that whatever these may be, should they prove the very reverse of what we have been taught to think right and best, our conduct towards him, our sentiments with respect to him, should undergo no change; for, when we shall see things as they really are, we shall know that this our fellow-man has undergone the same kind of process and training from infancy which we have experienced; that he has been as effectually taught to deem his sentiments and actions right, as we have been to imagine ours right and his wrong; when perhaps the only difference is, that we were born in one country, and he in another. If this be not true, then indeed are all our prospects hopeless; then fierce contentions, poverty and vice, must continue for ever. Fortunately, however, there is now a superabundance of facts to remove all doubt from every mind; and the principles may now be fully developed, which will easily explain the source of all the opinions which now perplex and divide the world; and their source being discovered, mankind may withdraw all those which are false and injurious, and prevent any evil from arising in consequence of the varieties of sentiments, or rather of feelings, which may afterwards remain.

In short, my friends, the New System is founded on principles which will enable mankind to *prevent*, in the rising generation, almost all, if not all of the evils and miseries which we and our forefathers have experienced. A correct knowledge of human nature will be acquired; ignorance will be removed; the angry passions will be prevented from gaining any strength; charity and kindness will universally prevail; poverty will not be known; the interest of each individual will be in strict unison with the interest of every individual in the world. There will not be any counteraction of wishes and desires among men. Temperance and simplicity of manners will be the characteristics of every part of society. The natural defects of the few will be amply compensated by the increased attention and kindness towards them of the many. None will have cause to complain; for each will possess, without injury to another, all that can tend to his comfort, his well-being and his happiness. – Such will be the certain consequences of the introduction into practice of that system for which I have been silently preparing the way for upwards of five-and-twenty years.

'An Address to the Inhabitants of New Lanark' (1816), in *A New View of Society and Other Writings*, Everyman's Library (London, Dent, 1927, reprinted 1963), pp. 93–5, 109–13.

Samuel Taylor Coleridge
(1772–1834)

MAKING MEN AND CITIZENS

After these introductory preparations, I can have no difficulty in setting forth the right idea of a national Church as in the language of Queen Elizabeth the third great venerable estate of the realm; the first being the estate of the land-owners or possessors of fixed property, consisting of the two classes of the Barons and the Franklins; and the second comprising the merchants, the manufacturers, free artisans and the distributive class. To comprehend, therefore, the true character of this third estate, in which the reserved Nationalty was vested, we must first ascertain the end or national purpose, for which such reservation was made.

Now, as in the first estate the permanency of the nation was provided for; and in the second estate its progressiveness and personal freedom; while in the king the cohesion by interdependence, and the unity of the country, were established; there remains for the third estate only that interest which is the ground, the necessary antecedent condition, of both the former. These depend on a continuing and progressive civilization. But civilization is itself but a mixed good, if not far more a corrupting influence, the hectic of disease, not the bloom of health, and a nation so distinguished more fitly to be called a varnished than a polished people, where this civilization is not grounded in cultivation, in the harmonious development of those qualities and faculties that characterize our humanity. We must be men in order to be citizens.

The Nationalty, therefore, was reserved for the support and maintenance of a permanent class or order with the following duties. A certain smaller number were to remain at the fountain heads of the humanities, in cultivating and enlarging the knowledge already possessed, and in watching over the interests of physical and moral science; being, likewise, the instructors of such as constituted, or were to constitute, the remaining more numerous classes of the order. The members of this latter and far more numerous body were to be distributed throughout the country, so as not to leave even the smallest integral part or division without a resident guide, guardian and instructor; the objects and final intention of the whole order being these – to preserve the stores and to guard the treasures of past civilization, and thus to bind the present with the past; to perfect and add to the same, and thus to connect the present with the future; but especially to diffuse through the whole community and to every native entitled to its laws and rights that quantity and quality of knowledge which was indispensable both for the understanding of those rights, and for the performance of the duties correspondent: finally, to secure for the nation, if not a superiority over the neighbouring states, yet an equality at least, in that character of general civilization, which equally with, or rather more than, fleets, armies and revenue, forms the ground of its defensive and offensive power. The object of the two former estates of the realm, which conjointly form the State, was to reconcile the interests of permanence with that of progression – law with liberty. The object of the national Church, the third remaining estate of the realm, was to secure and improve that civilization, without which the nation could be neither permanent nor progressive.

That, in all ages, individuals who have directed their meditations and their studies to the nobler characters of our nature, to the cultivation of those powers and instincts which constitute the man, at least separate him from the animal, and distinguish the nobler from the animal part of his own being, will be led by the supernatural in themselves to the contemplation of a power which is likewise super-human; that science, and especially moral science, will lead to religion, and remain blended with it – this, I say, will in all ages be the course of things. That in the earlier ages, and in the dawn of civility, there will be a twilight in which science and religion give light, but a light refracted through the dense and the dark, a superstition; – this is what we learn from history, and what philosophy would have taught us to expect. But I affirm that in the spiritual purpose of the word, and as understood in reference to a future state, and to the abiding essential interest of the individual as a person, and not as the citizen, neighbour or subject, religion may be an indispensable ally, but is not the essential constitutive end, of that national institute, which is unfortunately, at least improperly, styled the Church; a name which in its best sense is exclusively appropriate to the Church of Christ. If this latter be *ecclesia*, the communion of such as are called out of the world, that is, in reference to the especial ends and purposes of that communion; this other might more expressively have been entitled *enclesia*, or an order of men chosen in and of the realm, and constituting an estate of that realm. And in fact, such was the original and proper sense of the more appropriately named clergy. It comprehended the learned of all names, and the clerk was the synonym of the man of learning. Nor can any fact more strikingly illustrate the conviction entertained by our ancestors respecting the intimate connection of this clergy with the peace and weal of the nation, than the privilege formerly recognized by our laws, in the well-known phrase, 'benefit of clergy'.

Deeply do I feel, for clearly do I see, the importance of my theme. And had I equal confidence in my ability to awaken the same interest in the minds of others, I should dismiss as affronting to my readers all apprehension of being charged with prolixity, while I am labouring to compress in two or three brief chapters the principal sides and aspects of a subject so large and multilateral as to require a volume for its full exposition; – with what success will be seen in what follows, commencing with the Churchmen, or (a far apter and less objectionable designation) the national Clerisy.

The Clerisy of the nation, or national Church, in its primary acceptation and original intention, comprehended the learned of all denominations, the sages and professors of the law and jurisprudence, of medicine and physiology, of music, of military and civil architecture, of the physical sciences, with the mathematical as the common organ of the preceding; in short, all the so-called liberal arts and sciences, the possession and application of which constitute the civilization of a country, as well as the theological. The last was, indeed, placed at the head of all; and of good right did it claim the precedence. But why? Because under the name of theology or divinity were contained the interpretation of languages, the conservation and tradition of past events, the momentous epochs and revolutions of the race and nation, the continuation of the records, logic, ethics and the determination of ethical science, in application to the rights and duties of men in all their various relations, social and civil; and lastly, the ground-knowledge, the *prima scientia* as it was named – philosophy, or the doctrine and discipline of ideas.[1]

---

[1] That is, of knowledges immediate, yet real, and herein distinguished in kind from logical and mathematical truths, which express not realities, but only the necessary forms of conceiving and perceiving, and are therefore named the formal or abstract sciences. Ideas, on the other hand, or the truths of philosophy, properly so called, correspond to substantial beings, to objects the actual subsistence of which is implied

Theology formed only a part of the objects, the theologians formed only a portion of the clerks or clergy, of the national Church. The theological order had precedency indeed, and deservedly; but not because its members were priests, whose office was to conciliate the invisible powers, and to superintend the interests that survive the grave; nor as being exclusively, or even principally, sacerdotal or templar, which, when it did occur, is to be considered as an accident of the age, a mis-growth of ignorance and oppression, a falsification of the constitutive principle, not a constituent part of the same. No, the theologians took the lead, because the science of theology was the root and the trunk of the knowledges that civilized man, because it gave unity and the circulating sap of life to all other sciences, by virtue of which alone they could be contemplated as forming, collectively, the living tree of knowledge. It had the precedency because, under the name theology, were comprised all the main aids, instruments and materials of national education, the *nisus formativus* of the body politic, the shaping and informing spirit, which, educing or eliciting the latent man in all the natives of the soil, trains them up to be citizens of the country, free subjects of the realm. And lastly, because to divinity belong those fundamental truths, which are the common ground-work of our civil and our religious duties, not less indispensable to a right view of our temporal concerns, than to a rational faith respecting our immortal well-being. Not without celestial observations can even terrestrial charts be accurately constructed. And of especial importance is it to the objects here contemplated, that only by the vital warmth diffused by these truths throughout the many, and by the guiding light from the philosophy, which is the basis of divinity, possessed by the few, can either the community or its rulers fully comprehend, or rightly appreciate, the permanent distinction and the occasional contrast between cultivation and civilization; or be made to understand this most valuable of the lessons taught by history, and exemplified alike in her oldest and her most recent

---

in their idea, though only by the idea revealable. To adopt the language of the great philosophic Apostle, they are *spiritual realities that can only spiritually be discerned,* and the inherent aptitude and moral preconfiguration to which constitutes what we mean by ideas, and by the presence of ideal truth and of ideal power, in the human being. They, in fact, constitute his humanity. For try to conceive a man without the ideas of God, eternity, freedom, will, absolute truth, of the good, the true, the beautiful, the infinite. An animal endowed with a memory of appearances and of facts might remain. But the man will have vanished, and you have instead a creature, *more subtle than any beast of the field,* but likewise *cursed above every beast of the field; upon the belly must it go and dust must it eat all the days of its life.* But I recall myself from a train of thoughts little likely to find favour in this age of sense and selfishness.

records – that a nation can never be a too cultivated, but may easily become an over-civilized, race.

I may be allowed, therefore, to express the final cause of the whole by the office and purpose of the greater part; and this is, to form and train up the people of the country to be obedient, free, useful, organizable subjects, citizens and patriots, living to the benefit of the State, and prepared to die for its defence. The proper object and end of the national Church is civilization with freedom; and the duty of its ministers, could they be contemplated merely and exclusively as officiaries of the national Church, would be fulfilled in the communication of that degree and kind of knowledge to all, the possession of which is necessary for all in order to their civility. By civility I mean all the qualities essential to a citizen, and devoid of which no people or class of the people can be calculated on by the rulers and leaders of the State for the conservation or promotion of its essential interests.

> *On the Constitution of Church and State* (1830) (London, William Pickering, 1839), chs. V and VI, pp. 45–52 and 58.

Charles Fourier
(1772–1837)

THE SYSTEM OF SOCIAL HARMONY

... Our wise men extol to us the virtues of co-operative action, yet what co-operation is there to be seen in these industrial small-holdings, this anti-social cacophony! How is it that they have waited for three thousand years before proposing the principle that it is Association and not fragmented small-holdings that is the destiny of man, and that until the theory of domestic Association is known, man has not yet attained his destiny?

In order to appreciate the correctness of this principle, let us reflect upon the vast amount of knowledge which agriculture demands, and upon the impossibility for the villager to muster on his own one-twentieth of the means that would be at the command of the perfect agronomist. Not only would he need considerable capital: in addition he would need the knowledge distributed among one hundred expert minds and among two hundred consummate practitioners. Moreover, it would be necessary to render immortal the agronomist endowed with these numerous items of knowledge at present scattered among three hundred theoreticians and practitioners. If the landlord in question were to die without leaving behind a successor of equal talent, the arrangements he would have made would immediately be jeopardized, and the canton would rapidly decline.

It is only within the Association that one will be able to combine in perpetuity the talents and the capital whose co-operation I have just imagined; the Association is thus the sole system on which the Creator can have calculated, for, supposing it to have been applied to cantons of about fifteen hundred inhabitants, it will collect together in each canton that vast body of knowledge which will perpetuate itself through corporate transmission. A son certainly inherits no knowledge from his father, but given a canton of fifteen hundred inhabitants, there will be found individuals suitable to inherit the talent of competent members by whom they will have been schooled. These transmissions of talent are an essential feature of the *series of the passions*, a tendency which I will describe below and which governs all the industrial details of the associative state.

The more one discourses upon this hypothesis of Association, the more one is convinced that civilized agriculture, based on domestic small-holdings, is the very opposite of the destiny of man, and that it is necessary to look for the secret of how to associate large masses of men. Small numbers could not rise to the requirements of large-scale economy, nor could they combine the variety of knowledge required for the perfection of each branch of cultivation and administration.

I have given some idea of the thoughtlessness of thirty centuries of learned men who have neglected to research into the associative procedure now finally discovered.

We are going to consider its principal feature, namely *industrial attraction* – a feature by means of which we will overcome all the obstacles that have from the beginning arrested the progress of science.

Hitherto, politics and morality have failed in their aim of making people like work: one sees wage-earners and the whole popular class more and more inclined to idleness; one sees them in towns adding Monday's unemployment to that of Sunday; working without enthusiasm, slowly and with revulsion.

In order to chain them to industrious activity, no other means are known, apart from slavery, than the fear of hunger and of punishments. If, however, such activity is the destiny assigned us by the Creator, then how can one believe that he wishes us to be brought to it by violence, and that he could not have brought into play some more noble principle of operation, some lure capable of transforming labours into pleasures!

God alone is invested with the power of distributing attraction; he only wishes to govern the operation of the universe and its creatures by means of attraction; and in order to tie us to agriculture and manufacturing, he has devised a system of *industrial attraction* which, once organized, will distribute a host of allurements among the functions of cultivation and manufacture. It will attach to them enticements that are more tempting perhaps than those of our present feasts, balls and public displays; which is to say that in the associative state the people will find their work so pleasant and stimulating that they will not agree to abandon it for an offer of feasts, balls and public displays if these are planned for the hours of the industrial sessions.

Associative work, in order to exercise such a strong attraction upon the people, will have to differ in every way from the repulsive forms that render it so odious in present conditions. Associative industry, in order to become attractive, will have to fulfil the following seven conditions:

1. That each worker be associated, and paid by dividend, not wages;
2. That everyone, man, woman and child, be rewarded in proportion to three faculties: *capital, labour* and *talent*;
3. That the industrial sessions be varied about eight times a day, since enthusiasm cannot be sustained for more than one and a half hours or two hours in the exercise of an agricultural or manufacturing function;
4. That these be exercised by teams of friends spontaneously combined, and aroused and stimulated by very active rivalries;
5. That the workshops and plots present to the worker the enticements of elegance and cleanliness;
6. That the division of labour be carried to the ultimate degree, so as to allot to each sex and to each age-group the functions that are appropriate to it;
7. That in this distribution, everyone, man, woman or child, fully enjoys the right to work or the right to engage at any time in whatever branch of work it suits him to choose, so long as he can prove his honesty and skill.

Finally, that the people enjoy in this new social order a guarantee of well-being and of a minimum sufficient for the present and future, and that this guarantee relieves them of all anxiety for themselves and their relatives.

One finds all these features combined in the associative mechanism whose discovery I have published; and as I am going to demonstrate them in great detail during the course of this work, we may begin by discussing the hypothesis of industrial attraction implied by this mechanism.

I have said above that it alone will suffice to remove all the obstacles which have, for three thousand years, paralysed the social spirit. Let us judge it in the light of three problems, from which one may derive conclusions concerning all others.

1. *The elimination of poverty.* Poverty arises largely from idleness; but when people will find industry as inviting as feasts are today, idleness will no longer be able to exist; it will be transformed into an ardour to be industrious, the product of which will amply suffice to eliminate poverty.

2. *The prevention of discords.* These arise for the most part from poverty. Now, if it is proved that the Association and industrial attraction have the

power to increase productivity threefold, they will eliminate the main source of discords, namely poverty.

3. *A guaranteed minimum for the people.* The means to this end is the vast product which the associative regime will furnish. Its characteristic of attracting men towards work will remove the danger that guaranteeing subsistence to the poor would incur in present conditions by providing an incentive to idleness: but there will be no risk in making them an advance of a minimum of 400 francs when they will know that they should create from it at least 600, by devoting themselves to work that has become pleasure and been transformed into a perpetual holiday.

Thus, all good things flow at once from this feature of *industrial attraction* enjoyed by the associative order. This feature depends upon a tendency that is quite unknown amongst us, and which I will describe by the term, *unitary series of the passions* or the *contrasted, competitive, but co-ordinating series.* This operation, from which there flow so many social marvels, could have been discovered at the first stages of civilization, if men had applied themselves to some research into the associative mechanism, the unpardonable neglect of which has delayed its discovery.

The opportunities for advantage of which I have given an idea should be enough to stimulate men's inclinations. The philosophers, in order to excuse their apathy concerning this great problem, object that *this would be too wonderful,* that so much perfection is not made for men – a curious reason for neglecting research! The more dazzling the results, the more should the prospect of them excite men to aim at establishing the system of Association.

It will be said that men's passions are opposed to it, that it is impossible to keep together in a domestic unit three or four families, without knavery, differences of character and domineering pretensions soon leading to discords, above all among the women, who would fall out within a week.

I know this, but we will see in the course of this work that the harmony that is impossible between ten families becomes very practicable among a hundred, distributed according to the system that I have called the *unitary series of the passions,* a system which can only be applied to large numbers and not to ten families.

In this new mechanism, the passions, and inequalities of fortune and character, far from being opposed to the bonds of association, are the means of maintaining them. All contrasts here become useful: thus our prejudices represent to us as an obstacle what is, on the contrary, a means of Association, and for proof it will be seen in this treatise that it would be impossible to associate a hundred families that are equal in fortune and uniform or very similar in character. The operation called the *unitary series of the passions* is incompatible with equality.

Since economy can only arise from large groupings, God must have adapted his associative plan to large numbers. Hence the fact that small Associations of six, eight or ten families are internally irreconcilable, and would be so even if one tried to apply to them the associative procedure (the *series of the passions*) which cannot be adapted to such small groupings.

Outside their development through the unitary series, the passions are nothing but demonic forces, unchained tigers, which led the moralists to believe that our passions were our enemies. On the contrary, it is the mechanism of civilization and barbarism which is the enemy of the passions and of human beings, in so far as it does not submit to the associative bonds desired by God.

Let us here introduce a provisional definition of that tendency which I call the *contrasted, competitive, but co-ordinating series of the passions*. It is the lever which moves the entire system of social harmony: the discovery of this system opened the way to the realization of happiness; its discovery is throughout the universe a condition *sine qua non*. The social world cannot, on any planet, attain unity, nor ascend to a happy destiny before the invention of this mechanism for implementing the series of the passions, research into which is the essential task of genius. The other sciences, even the most accurate, such as mathematics, are nothing but vain knowledge for us, so long as we ignore the science of the associative mechanism, which gives birth to wealth, unity and happiness.

At its first appearance, a discovery appears ridiculous if one compares it with known methods. The first person to announce the invention of gunpowder and its prodigious effects, in mines, artillery, etc., must have met with nothing but incredulity and accusations of seeing visions. Nevertheless, what is more universally recognized today than these amazing effects of gunpowder?

It is, I admit, a pretty improbable scheme I am announcing – to associate three hundred families that are unequal in fortune and to pay each person, man, woman and child, according to the three faculties, *capital*, *labour* and *talent*. More than one reader will think it very amusing to say: 'Let the author try to associate only three families, let him try to reconcile in one and the same abode three families in an associative community, combining their purchases and expenditures, and in a perfect harmony of the passions, of character and of authority; when he has succeeded in reconciling three associated housewives, then we will believe he can unite thirty or three hundred.'

I have already answered this argument which it is useful to reproduce (since on this point repetitions will often prove necessary). I have observed that *since economies can only arise from large groupings, God must have composed an associative theory applicable to large numbers and not to three or four families.*

An objection that is, on the face of it, more reasonable and which it is necessary to refute more than once, is that which refers to social discords. How can one reconcile passions, conflicts of interests, incompatible characters and in short the innumerable differences which engender so many discords?

It will be clear that I propose to make use of a totally unknown lever, whose properties cannot be assessed before I have explained them. The series of contrasted passions draws nothing but sustenance from those differences which disorient civilized politics. It operates like the labourer who from a pile of dirt extracts the seeds of wealth; the rubbish, the mud, the dung and the filthy substances which only serve to soil and infect our houses become for him sources of prosperity. It is the same with the disgusting passions for which politics can find no use. Thanks to the lever which I call the *series of contrasts* we are going to transform into precious materials all these fermenting-agents of social turmoil. The more numerous they are, the more the series will be graduated, contrasted and conducive to co-ordinated dynamism.

One must thus avoid raising objections in advance against a system whose characteristics one does not yet understand. One must, following the precepts of philosophy, believe that nature is not limited to means that are already known, and, following the dictates of reason, that God – whose providence is universal – has not created the passions, the elements of social mechanics, without providing us with some means of employing these materials usefully: a means the discovery of which our false methods have hitherto delayed. Humanity waited 4,000 years before inventing the stirrup and carriage-braces, which any good simple person could discover and which were unknown in Athens and Rome. Should one be surprised that an immense calculation, such as that of the series of the passions, has eluded the contemporary sciences which have not even sought it and have not conceived of its existence?

The more benefits an invention promises, the more demanding must the reader be concerning its proofs. If my theory were not in concordance with the established sciences, everyone would be entitled to suspect me of merely having an urge to systematize, and would be entitled to modify my plan of Association according to his own fantasies. It will only be worthy of confidence in so far as it combines together, and provides, in a single scheme, the framework for, the associative mechanics of the passions and the other known harmonies of the universe.

'Théorie de l'unité universelle' (1822), vol. II, introduction in *Œuvres complètes de Fourier*, 2nd ed. (Paris, Société pour la propagation et pour la réalisation de la théorie de Fourier, 1841), vol. III, pp. 12–19, 29–31. (Translated by Steven Lukes.)

THE DREAM OF CHRISTENDOM

Those were fine, magnificent times when Europe was a Christian country, when one Christendom inhabited this civilized continent and one great common interest linked the most distant provinces of this vast spiritual empire. – Dispensing with great secular possessions, *one* sovereign governed and united the great political forces. – Immediately under him was an enormous guild, open to all, which carried out his commands and eagerly strove to consolidate his beneficent power. Every member of this society was everywhere honoured; and if the common people sought from him comfort or help, protection or advice, gladly and generously tendering to his various needs, by way of recompense, he in his turn gained protection, respect and audience from his superiors. They were the elect, armed with miraculous powers and treated as children of heaven, whose presence and affection dispensed manifold blessings. Their proclamations inspired childlike faith. Mankind could serenely go about its daily business on earth, for these holy men safeguarded the future, forgave every sin and obliterated and transfigured all life's discolourations. They were the experienced pilots on the vast uncharted seas in whose care mankind could disparage all storms and count on safely reaching and landing on the shores of its true home. The wildest and most insatiable desires had to yield to the reverence and obedience commanded by their words. Peace emanated from them. – They preached nothing but love of our holy and beautiful lady of Christendom, who endowed with divine power, was ready to rescue every believer from the most terrible dangers. They told of saintly men, long dead, who had resisted earthly temptations through their attachment and fidelity to the blessed mother and her sweet, celestial child, and who had thus attained divine honour and were now beneficent protectors of their living brethren, willing helpers in need, intercessors for human frailties and the powerful friends of mankind before the throne of heaven. With what serenity did men leave beautiful congregations in churches full of mystery, adorned with stirring pictures, filled with sweet fragance and enriched by sacred exalting music. There the consecrated relics of former godfearing persons were gratefully preserved in precious containers. – And the divine goodness and omnipotence, the beneficent might of these blessed pious beings were revealed in these relics through glorious miracles and signs. In the same way, lovers keep a lock of hair or the letters of their dead sweethearts and sustain their sweet ardour with such objects till death reunites them. Everything that had belonged to these beloved persons was collected with ardent care, and to obtain or even only to touch so consoling a relic was accounted the greatest good fortune. Now and then divine grace seemed to have visited some strange image or tomb in particular, to which men flocked from all parts with beautiful offerings and departed having received heaven's gifts of inner peace and bodily health in return. This mighty peace-loving society assiduously sought to let all men share this beautiful faith, and sent its members into all continents of the world to proclaim everywhere the gospel of life and to make the kingdom of heaven the only kingdom in this world. The wise sovereign of the Church rightly opposed any presumptuous development of human capacities at the expense of religious sense as also any untimely and dangerous discoveries in the sphere of knowledge. Thus he forbade bold thinkers to assert publicly that the earth is merely an insignificant planet, for he knew well that men in losing their respect for their residence and their earthly home would also lose respect for their celestial home and for their race. They would prefer limited knowledge to infinite faith and come to despise all that is great and awe-inspiring, regarding it merely as the dead effect of scientific law. All the wise and respected men of Europe assembled at his court. All treasures flowed thither, destroyed Jerusalem was avenged and Rome itself became Jerusalem, the sacred seat of divine rule on earth. Princes submitted their disputes to the father of Christendom, willingly laid their crowns and their magnificence at his feet, and indeed considered it an augmentation of their glory to spend as members of this high guild the evening of their lives in divine meditation within the solitary walls of monasteries. How beneficent this government was, how appropriate this institution to man's inner nature is shown by the powerful aspirations of all other human forces, the harmonious development of all abilities, the immense height reached by individuals in all spheres of the sciences of life and of the arts, and by the trade in spiritual and physical goods which flourished everywhere in Europe and as far as the most distant Indies.

Such were the main features of this truly Catholic and Christian age. But mankind was not yet mature or educated enough for this splendid kingdom. It was a first love that died under the pressure of commercial life, a love whose memory was ousted by egotistical cares and whose bond was afterwards denounced as a deceit and an illusion and condemned in the light of later experiences; and then destroyed for ever by a large section of Europeans. This great inner schism accompanied as it was by destructive wars was a remarkable sign of what culture can do to spiritual awareness, or at least of the temporary harmfulness of culture at a certain level. That eternal awareness cannot be destroyed, but it can be dimmed, paralysed and displaced by other senses. In an old community spiritual inclinations and pride of race diminish and men grow accustomed to applying all their thoughts and endeavours solely to the means of achieving comfort; their needs and the arts of satisfying them become more complicated; avaricious man needs so much time to acquaint himself with these arts and to acquire skill in their exercise, that no time remains for quiet recollection, for attentive contemplation of the inner world. In cases of conflict present interest seems to mean more to him; so the beautiful flowers of his youth, faith and love, wilt and give way to the cruder fruits of knowledge and possession. In late autumn people look back on spring as on a childish dream and hope naïvely that the filled granaries will last for ever. Some degree of solitude seems necessary for the development of higher insight, and if the world is too much with us we must suffocate many a seed of spiritual growth and drive away the gods who flee the restless tumult of social distractions and the negotiation of petty affairs. Besides, we are dealing with times and periods which surely must be cyclic, an alternation of opposite tendencies? Is it not their very nature to be impermanent, to wax and to wane, and is not also a resurrection, a rejuvenation in new and vital form certainly to be expected of them with complete certainty. Progressive, ever-increasing evolutions on an ever-increasing scale are the stuff of history.

What has not so far reached perfection will do so in a future attempt or in one later still; nothing that history has seized upon is ephemeral; it re-emerges renewed in ever richer forms from countless metamorphoses.

Now we turn to the political spectacle of our time. The ancient and the new worlds are in a state of struggle, the imperfection and terrible phenomena bear witness to the imperfections and destitution of previous institutions.

How would it be if here too, as in the sciences, a closer and more varied connection and contact of the European states were first and foremost the historical aims of war, if Europe were now to be rescued from her previous slumber, if Europe wanted to awaken again, if a state of all the states, a political theory of science were to confront us! Should then the hierarchy, that symmetrical and basic norm of the state, be the principle of the community of states as it is the intellectual view of the body politic? It is impossible for secular forces to find their own equilibrium, a third element which is both secular and supernatural can alone fulfil this task. No peace can be concluded among the disputing powers, for all peace is merely an illusion and an armistice; and from the point of view of the cabinets and of common conviction no union is conceivable. Both elements have great and necessary claims and must put them forward since they are impelled by the spirit of the world and of mankind. Both are ineradicable powers of the human soul; on the one hand, veneration of the ancient world, loyalty to the historical constitution, love of the patriarchal monuments and the ancient and glorious state family, and joy in obedience; on the other hand, the delightful feeling of freedom, the unqualified expectation of vast domains, pleasure in what is new and young, informal contact with all fellow citizens, pride in man's universality, joy in personal rights and in the property of the whole, and strong civic sense. Neither should hope to destroy the other, all conquests mean nothing, for the innermost capital of every kingdom does not lie behind walls of earth and cannot be taken by storm.

Who knows whether there has been enough of war, but it will never cease unless the palm-branch is grasped, which a spiritual power alone can offer. Blood will continue to stream over Europe till the nations become aware of their terrible madness which drives them round in circles, and till, moved and calmed by sacred music, they approach former altars in motley throngs to undertake works of peace and celebrate with hot tears a great banquet of love as a festival of peace on the smoking battlefields. Only religion can reawaken Europe, make the people secure and instal Christendom with a new magnificence in its old office of peacemaker in the world, visible to the whole world.

Do nations possess all the attributes of man except that sacred organ – his heart? Do they not, as men do, become friends at the coffins of their beloved ones and do they not forget all hostility when divine mercy speaks to them when they are united by one misfortune, one lament, one feeling which fills their eyes with tears? Are they not stirred by infinite power of sacrifice and surrender, and do they not long to be friends and allies? Where is now that ancient, blessed belief in the government of God on earth which alone can bring salvation? Where is that divine trust of men in one another, that sweet devotion in the outpourings inspired by God, that all-embracing spirit of Christendom?

Christianity has three forms. One is the productive element of religion which inspires joy in all religion. The second acts as an intermediary in the form of the belief in the capacity of all earthly things to be the bread and wine of Eternal Life. The third is the belief in Christ, in the Virgin and the Saints. Choose whichever you like, choose all three, and you will thereby become Christians and members of one single, eternal, ineffably happy community.

The ancient Catholic faith, the last of these forms, was applied Christianity come to life. Its omnipresence in life, its love for art, its profound humanity, the inviolability of its marriages, its philanthropic communicativeness, its delight in poverty, obedience and loyalty, contain the basic features of its constitution and make it unmistakable as the true religion.

It has been purified by the river of time and in undivided union with the two other forms of Christianity will eternally bless the earth.

Its accidental form has been almost entirely destroyed, the old papacy lies in its grave and Rome has become a ruin for the second time. Shall not Protestantism finally cease to exist and give way to a new, more lasting Church? The older continents are waiting for Europe's reconciliation and resurrection before they join and become fellow-citizens of the kingdom of heaven. Shall there not soon again exist in Europe a multitude with truly sacred minds, shall not all those who have religious kinship be filled with yearning to see heaven on earth? And shall they not assemble eagerly to chant sacred songs?

Christendom must again become alive and effective, and form for itself a visible Church without consideration to national frontiers, a Church which, eager to become the mediator between the old and new world, receives into its bosom all souls thirsting for a spiritual life.

It must once more pour out the ancient cornucopia of blessing over the nations. Christendom will arise from the sacred heart of a venerable European Council, and the business of religious awakening will be performed according to an all-embracing Divine plan. No one will then be able to protest further against Christian and secular compulsion, for the essence of the Church will be true freedom, and all necessary reforms will be carried out under its guidance as peaceful and formal processes of the state. When? How soon? This we must not ask. Have patience; it will and must come, this sacred age of eternal peace, when the new Jerusalem is the capital of the world; and until that time, be serene and brave amidst the dangers of this present age, companions of my faith, proclaim the divine gospel by word and deed, and remain faithful until death to the true, infinite belief.

'Christendom or Europe' (1799), trans. in *The Political Thought of the German Romantics*, ed. H. S. Reiss (Oxford, Blackwell, 1955), pp. 126–9, 139–41.

William Hazlitt
(1778–1830)

TRULY POPULAR GOVERNMENT

This then is the cause of the people, the good of the people, judged of by common feeling and public opinion. Mr Burke contemptuously defines the people to be 'any faction that at the time can get the power of the sword into its hands'. No: that may be a description of the Government, but it is not of the people. The people is the hand, heart and head of the whole community acting to one purpose, and with a mutual and thorough consent. The hand of the people so employed to execute what the heart feels, and the head thinks, must be employed more beneficially for the cause of the people, than in executing any measures which the cold hearts, and contriving heads of any faction, with distinct privileges and interests, may dictate to betray their cause. The will of the people necessarily tends to the general good as its end; and it must attain that end, and can only attain it, in proportion as it is guided – First, by popular feeling, as arising out of the immediate wants and wishes of the great mass of the people, – secondly, by public opinion, as arising out of the impartial reason and enlightened intellect of the community. What is it that determines the opinion of any number of persons in things they actually feel in their practical and home results? Their common interest. What is it that determines their opinion in things of general inquiry, beyond their immediate experience or interest? Abstract reason. In matters of feeling and common sense, of which each individual is the best judge, the majority are in the right; in things requiring a greater strength of mind to comprehend them, the greatest power of understanding will prevail, if it has but fair play. These two, taken together, as the test of the practical measures or general principles of Government, must be right, cannot be wrong. It is an absurdity to suppose that there can be any better criterion of national grievances, or the proper remedies for them, than the aggregate amount of the actual, dear-bought experience, the honest feelings and heart-felt wishes of a whole people, informed and directed by the greatest power of understanding in the community, unbiased by any sinister motive. Any other standard of public good or ill must, in proportion as it deviates from this, be vitiated in principle, and fatal in its effects. *Vox populi vox Dei*, is the rule of all good Government: for in that voice, truly collected and freely expressed (not when it is made the servile echo of a corrupt Court, or a designing Minister), we have all the sincerity and all the wisdom of the community. If we could suppose society to be transformed into one great animal (like Hobbes's *Leviathan*), each member of which had an intimate connection with the head or Government, so that every individual in it could be made known and have its due weight, the State would have the same consciousness of its own wants and feelings, and the same interest in providing for them, as an individual has with respect to his own welfare. Can any one doubt that such a state of society in which the greatest knowledge of its interests was thus combined with the greatest sympathy with its wants, would realize the idea of a perfect commonwealth? But such a Government would be the precise idea of a truly popular or *representative* Government. The opposite extreme is the purely hereditary and despotic form of Government, where the people are an inert, torpid mass, without the power, scarcely with the will, to make its wants or wishes known: and where the feelings of those who are at the head of the State, centre in their own exclusive interests, pride, passions, prejudices; and all their thoughts are employed in defeating the happiness and undermining the liberties of a country.

'What is the People?' (1818), in *The Collected Works of William Hazlitt*, ed. A. R. Waller and A. Glover (London, Dent, 1902), pp. 291–2.

Percy Bysshe Shelley
(1792–1822)

A MILLION FREE AND
HAPPY MEN

There is no doubt but the world is going wrong, or rather that it is very capable of being much improved. What I mean by this improvement is, the inducement of a more equal and general diffusion of happiness and liberty. – Many people are very rich and many are very poor. Which do you think are happiest? – I can tell you that neither are happy, so far as their station is concerned. Nature never intended that there should be such a thing as a poor man or a rich one. Being put in an unnatural situation, they can neither of them be happy, so far as their situation is concerned. The poor man is born to obey the rich man, though they both come into the world equally helpless, and equally naked. But the poor man does the rich no service by obeying him – the rich man does the poor no good by commanding him. It would be much better if they could be prevailed upon to live equally like brothers – they would ultimately both be happier. But this can be done neither today nor tomorrow, much as such a change is to be desired, it is quite impossible. Violence and folly in this, as in the other case, would only put off the period of its event. Mildness, sobriety and reason, are the effectual methods of forwarding the ends of liberty and happiness.

Although we may see many things put in train, during our lifetime, we cannot hope to see the work of virtue and reason finished now; we can only lay the foundation for our posterity. Government is an evil, it is only the thoughtlessness and vices of men that make it a necessary evil. When all men are good and wise, Government will of itself decay, so long as men continue foolish and vicious, so long will Government, even such a Government as that of England, continue necessary in order to prevent the crimes of bad men. Society is produced by the wants, Government by the wickedness, and a state of just and happy equality by the improvement and reason of man. It is in vain to hope for any liberty and happiness, without reason and virtue – for where there is no virtue there will be crime, and where there is crime there must be Government. Before the restraints of Government are lessened, it is fit that we should lessen the necessity for them. Before Government is done away with, we must reform ourselves. It is this work which I would earnestly recommend to you, O Irishmen, REFORM YOURSELVES – and I do not recommend it to you particularly because I think that you most need it, but because I think that your hearts are warm and your feelings high, and you will perceive the necessity of doing it more than those of a colder and more distant nature.

I look with an eye of hope and pleasure on the present state of things, gloomy and incapable of improvement as they may appear to others. It delights me to see that men begin to think and to act for the good of others. Extensively as folly and selfishness has predominated in this age, it gives me hope and pleasure, at least, to see that many know what is right. Ignorance and vice commonly go together: he that would do good must be wise – a man cannot be truly wise who is not truly virtuous. Prudence and wisdom are very different things. The prudent man is he, who carefully consults for his own good: the wise man is he, who carefully consults for the good of others.

I look upon Catholic Emancipation, and the restoration of the liberties and happiness of Ireland, so far as they are compatible with the English Constitution, as great and important events. I hope to see them soon. But if all ended here, it would give me little pleasure – I should still see thousands miserable and wicked, things would still be wrong. I regard then, the accomplishment of these things as the road to a greater reform – that reform after which virtue and wisdom shall have conquered pain and vice. When no government will be wanted, but that of your neighbour's opinion. – I look to these things with hope and pleasure, because I consider that they will certainly happen, and because men will not then be wicked and miserable. But I do not consider that they will or can immediately happen; their arrival will be gradual, and it all depends upon yourselves how soon or how late these great changes will happen. If all of you, tomorrow were virtuous and wise, Government which today is a safeguard, would then become a tyranny. But I cannot expect a rapid change. Many are obstinate and determined in their vice, whose selfishness makes them think only of their own good, when in fact, the best way even to bring that about, is to make others happy. I do not wish to see things changed now, because it cannot be done without violence, and we may assure ourselves that none of us are fit for any change however good, if we condescend to employ force in a cause which we think right. Force makes the side that employs it directly wrong, and as much as we may pity we cannot approve the headstrong and intolerant zeal of its adherents.

Can you conceive, O Irishmen! a happy state of society – conceive men of every way of thinking living together like brothers. The descendant of the greatest Prince would there, be entitled to no more respect than the son of a peasant. There would be no pomp and no parade, but that which the rich now keep to themselves, would then be distributed among the people. None would be in magnificence, but the superfluities then taken from the rich would be sufficient when spread abroad, to make every one comfortable. – No lover would then be false to his mistress, no mistress would desert her lover. No friend would play false, no rents, no debts, no taxes, no frauds of any kind would disturb the general happiness: good as they would be, wise as they would be, they would be daily getting better and wiser. No beggars would exist, nor any of those wretched women, who are now reduced to a state of the most horrible misery and vice, by men whose wealth makes them villainous and hardened. No thieves or murderers, because poverty would never drive men to take away comforts from another, when he had enough for himself. Vice and misery, pomp and poverty, power and obedience, would then be banished altogether. – It is for such a state as this, Irishmen, that I exhort you to prepare. – 'A camel shall as soon pass through the eye of a needle, as a rich man enter the Kingdom of Heaven.' This is not to be understood literally, Jesus Christ appears to me only to have meant that riches have generally the effect of hardening and vitiating the heart, so has poverty. I think those people then are very silly, and cannot see one inch beyond their noses, who say that human nature is depraved; when at the same time wealth and poverty, those two great sources of crime, fall to the lot of a great majority of people; and when they see that people in moderate circumstances are always most wise and good. – People say that poverty is no evil – they have never felt it, or they would not think so. That wealth is necessary to encourage the arts – but are not the arts very inferior things to virtue and happiness – the man would be very dead to all generous feelings who would rather see pretty pictures and statues, than a million free and happy men.

'An Address to the Irish People' (1812), in *Prose Works of Percy Bysshe Shelley*, ed. H. B. Forman (London, Reeves & Turner, 1880), vol. I, pp. 338–42.

I wandering went

Among the haunts and dwellings of mankind,
And first was disappointed not to see
Such mighty change as I had felt within
Expressed in outward things; but soon I looked,
And behold, thrones were kingless, and men walked
One with the other even as spirits do,
None fawned, none trampled; hate, disdain or fear,
Self-love or self-contempt, on human brows
No more inscribed, as o'er the gate of hell,
'All hope abandon ye who enter here;'
None frowned, none trembled, none with eager fear
Gazed on another's eye of cold command,
Until the subject of a tyrant's will
Became, worse fate, the abject of his own,
Which spurred him, like an outspent horse, to death.
None wrought his lips in truth-entangling lines
Which smiled the lie his tongue disdained to speak;
None, with firm sneer, trod out in his own heart
The sparks of love and hope till there remained
Those bitter ashes, a soul self-consumed,
And the wretch crept a vampire among men,
Infecting all with his own hideous ill;
None talked that common, false, cold, hollow talk
Which makes the heart deny the *yes* it breathes,
Yet question that unmeant hypocrisy
With such a self-mistrust as has no name.
And women, too, frank, beautiful and kind
As the free heaven which rains fresh light and dew
On the wide earth, past; gentle radiant forms,

From custom's evil taint exempt and pure;
Speaking the wisdom once they could not think,
Looking emotions once they feared to feel,
And changed to all which once they dared not be,
Yet being now, made earth like heaven; nor pride,
Nor jealousy, nor envy, nor ill shame,
The bitterest of those drops of treasured gall,
Spoilt the sweet taste of the nepenthe, love.
Thrones, altars, judgement-seats and prisons; wherein,
And beside which, by wretched men were borne
Sceptres, tiaras, swords, and chains, and tomes
Of reasoned wrong, glozed on by ignorance,
Were like those monstrous and barbaric shapes,
The ghosts of a no-more-remembered fame,
Which, from their unworn obelisks, look forth
In triumph o'er the palaces and tombs
Of those who were their conquerors: mouldering round,
These imaged to the pride of kings and priests
A dark yet mighty faith, a power as wide
As is the world it wasted, and are now
But an astonishment:

The painted veil, by those who were, called life,
Which mimicked, as with colours idly spread,
All men believed or hoped, is torn aside;
The loathsome mask has fallen, the man remains
Sceptreless, free, uncircumscribed, but man
Equal, unclassed, tribeless and nationless,
Exempt from awe, worship, degree, the king
Over himself; just, gentle, wise: but man
Passionless? – no, yet free from guilt or pain,
Which were, for his will made or suffered them,
Nor yet exempt, though ruling them like slaves,
From chance, and death, and mutability,
The clogs of that which else might oversoar
The loftiest star of unascended heaven,
Pinnacled dim in the intense inane.

Prometheus Unbound (1820), Act III, Scene IV, lines 126–76, 190–204.

PART II

Thomas Carlyle
(1795–1881)

ARISTOCRACY AND PRIESTHOOD

If the convulsive struggles of the last Half-Century have taught poor struggling convulsed Europe any truth, it may perhaps be this as the essence of innumerable others: That Europe requires a real Aristocracy, a real Priesthood, or it cannot continue to exist. Huge French Revolutions, Napoleonisms, then Bourbonisms with their corollary of Three Days, finishing in very unfinal Louis-Philippisms: all this ought to be didactic! All this may have taught us, that False Aristocracies are insupportable; that No-Aristocracies, Liberty-and-Equalities are impossible; that true Aristocracies are at once indispensable and not easily attained.

Aristocracy and Priesthood, a Governing Class and a Teaching Class: these two, sometimes separate, and endeavouring to harmonize themselves, sometimes conjoined as one, and the King a Pontiff-King: – there did no Society exist without these two vital elements, there will none exist. It lies in the very nature of man: you will visit no remotest village in the most republican country of the world, where virtually or actually you do not find these two powers at work. Man, little as he may suppose it, is necessitated to obey superiors. He is a social being in virtue of this necessity; nay he could not be gregarious otherwise. He obeys those whom he esteems better than himself, wiser, braver; and will forever obey such; and even be ready and delighted to do it.

The Wiser, Braver: these, a Virtual Aristocracy everywhere and every-when, do in all Societies that reach any articulate shape, develop themselves into a ruling class, an Actual Aristocracy, with settled modes of operating, what are called laws and even *private-laws* or privileges, and so forth; very notable to look upon in this world. – Aristocracy and Priesthood, we say, are sometimes united. For indeed the Wiser and the Braver are properly but one class; no wise man but needed first of all to be a brave man, or he never had been wise. The noble Priest was always a noble *Aristos* to begin with, and something more to end with. Your Luther, your Knox, your Anselm, Becket, Abbot Samson, Samuel Johnson, if they had not been brave enough, by what possibility could they ever have been wise? – If, from accident or forethought, this your Actual Aristocracy have got discriminated into Two Classes, there can be no doubt but the Priest Class is the more dignified: supreme over the other, as governing head is over active hand. And yet in practice again, it is likeliest the reverse will be found arranged; – a sign that the arrangement is already vitiated; that a split is introduced into it, which will widen and widen till the whole be rent asunder.

In England, in Europe generally, we may say that these two Virtualities have unfolded themselves into Actualities, in by far the noblest and richest manner any region of the world ever saw. A spiritual Guideship, a practical Governorship, fruit of the grand conscious endeavours, say rather of the immeasurable unconscious instincts and necessities of men, have established themselves; very strange to behold. Everywhere, while so much has been forgotten, you find the King's Palace, and the Viceking's Castle, Mansion, Manorhouse; till there is not an inch of ground from sea to sea but has both its King and Viceking, long due series of Vicekings, its Squire, Earl, Duke or whatever the title of him, – to whom you have given the land, that he may govern you in it.

More touching still, there is not a hamlet where poor peasants congregate, but, by one means and another, a Church-Apparatus has been got together, – roofed edifice, with revenues and belfries; pulpit, reading-desk, with Books and Methods: possibility, in short, and strict prescription, That a man stand there and speak of spiritual things to men. It is beautiful; – even in its great obscuration and decadence, it is among the beautifulest, most touching objects one sees on the Earth. This Speaking Man has indeed, in these times, wandered terribly from the point; has, alas, as it were, totally lost sight of the point: yet, at bottom, whom have we to compare with him? Of all public functionaries boarded and lodged on the Industry of Modern Europe, is there one worthier of the board he has? A man even professing, and never so languidly making still some endeavour, to save the souls of men: contrast him with a man professing to do little but shoot the partridges of men! I wish he could find the point again, this Speaking One; and stick to it with tenacity, with deadly energy; for there is need of him yet! The Speaking Function, this of Truth coming to us with a living voice, nay in a living shape, and as a concrete practical exemplar: this, with all our Writing and Printing Functions, has a perennial place. Could he but find the point again, – take the old spectacles off his nose, and looking up discover, almost in contact with him, what the *real* Satanas, and soul-devouring, world-devouring *Devil*, now is! Original Sin and suchlike are bad enough, I doubt not: but distilled Gin, dark Ignorance, Stupidity, dark Corn-Law, Bastille and Company, what are they! *Will* he discover our new real Satan, whom he has to fight; or go on droning through his old nose-spectacles about old extinct Satans; and never see the real one, till he *feel* him at his own throat and ours? That is a question, for the world! Let us not intermeddle with it here.

Sorrowful, phantasmal as this same Double Aristocracy of Teachers and Governors now looks, it is worth all men's while to know that the purport of it is and remains noble and most real. Dryasdust, looking merely at the surface, is greatly in error as to those ancient Kings. William Conqueror, William Rufus or Redbeard, Stephen Curthose himself, much more Henry Beauclerc and our brave Plantagenet Henry: the life of these men was not a vulturous Fighting; it was a valorous Governing, – to which occasionally Fighting did, and alas must yet, though far seldomer now, superadd itself as an accident, a distressing impedimental adjunct. The fighting too was indispensable, for ascertaining who had the might over whom, the right over whom. By much hard fighting, as we once said, 'the unrealities, beaten into dust, flew gradually off; and left the plain reality and fact, 'Thou stronger than I; thou wiser than I; thou king, and subject I', in a somewhat clearer condition.

Truly we cannot enough admire, in those Abbot-Samson and William-Conqueror times, the arrangement they had made of their Governing Classes. Highly interesting to observe how the sincere insight, on their part, into what did, of primary necessity, behove to be accomplished, had led them to the way of accomplishing it, and in the course of time to get it accomplished! No imaginary Aristocracy would serve their turn; and accordingly they attained a real one. The Bravest men, who, it is ever to be repeated and remembered, are also on the whole the Wisest, Strongest, everyway Best, had here, with a respectable degree of accuracy, been got selected; seated each on his piece of territory, which was lent him, then gradually given him, that he might govern it. These Vicekings, each on his portion of the common soil of England, with a Head King over all, were a 'Virtuality perfected into an Actuality' really to an astonishing extent.

For those were rugged stalwart ages; full of earnestness, of a rude

God's-truth: – nay, at any rate, their *quilting* was so unspeakably *thinner* than ours; Fact came swiftly on them, if at any time they had yielded to Phantasm! 'The Knaves and Dastards' had to be 'arrested' in some measure; or the world, almost within year and day, found that it could not live. The Knaves and Dastards accordingly were got arrested. Dastards upon the very throne had to be got arrested, and taken off the throne, – by such methods as there were; by the roughest method, if there chanced to be no smoother one! Doubtless there was much harshness of operation, much severity; as indeed government and surgery are often somewhat severe. Gurth, born thrall of Cedric, it is like, got cuffs as often as pork-parings, if he misdemeaned himself; but Gurth did belong to Cedric: no human creature then went about connected with nobody; left to go his way into Bastilles or worse, under *Laissez-faire*; reduced to prove his relationship by dying of typhus-fever! – Days come when there is no King in Israel, but every man is his own king, doing that which is right in his own eyes; – and tarbarrels are burnt to 'Liberty', 'Tenpound Franchise' and the like, with considerable effect in various ways! –

That Feudal Aristocracy, I say, was no imaginary one. To a respectable degree, its *Jarls*, what we now call Earls, were *Strong-Ones* in fact as well as etymology; its Dukes *Leaders*; its Lords *Law-wards*. They did all the Soldiering and Police of the country, all the Judging, Law-making, even the Church-Extension; whatsoever in the way of Governing, of Guiding and Protecting could be done. It was a Land Aristocracy; it managed the Governing of this English People, and had the reaping of the Soil of England in return. It is, in many senses, the Law of Nature, this same Law of Feudalism; – no right Aristocracy but a Land one! The curious are invited to meditate upon it in these days. Soldiering, Police and Judging, Church-Extension, nay real Government and Guidance, all this was actually *done* by the Holders of the Land in return for their Land. How much of it is now done by them; done by anybody? Good Heavens, '*Laissez-faire*, Do ye nothing, eat your wages and sleep,' is everywhere the passionate half-wise cry of this time; and they will not so much as do nothing, but must do mere Corn-Laws! We raise Fifty-two millions, from the general mass of us, to get our Governing done – or, alas, to get ourselves persuaded that it is done: and the 'peculiar burden of the Land' is to pay, not all this, but to pay, as I learn, one twenty-fourth part of all this. Our first Chartist Parliament, or Oliver *Redivivus*, you would say, will know where to lay the new taxes of England! – Or, alas, taxes? If we made the Holders of the Land pay every shilling still of the expense of Governing the Land, what were all that? The Land, by mere hired Governors, cannot be got governed. You cannot hire men to govern the Land: it is by a mission not contracted for in the Stock-Exchange, but felt in their own hearts as coming out of Heaven, that men can govern a Land. The mission of a Land Aristocracy is a *sacred* one, in both the senses of that old word. The footing it stands on, at present, might give rise to thoughts other than of Corn-Laws!—

But truly a 'Splendour of God,' as in William Conqueror's rough oath, did dwell in those old rude veracious ages; did inform, more and more, with a heavenly nobleness, all departments of their work and life. Phantasms could not yet walk abroad in mere Cloth Tailorage; they were at least Phantasms 'on the rim of the horizon', pencilled there by an eternal Lightbeam from within. A most 'practical' Hero-worship went on, unconsciously or half-consciously everywhere. A Monk Samson, with a maximum of two shillings in his pocket, could, without ballot-box, be made a Viceking of, being seen to be worthy. The difference between a good man and a bad man was as yet felt to be, what it forever is, an immeasurable one. Who *durst* have elected a Pandarus Dogdraught, in those days, to any office, Carlton Club, Senatorship or place whatsoever? It was felt that the arch Satanas and no other had a clear right of property in Pandarus; that it were better for you to have no hand in Pandarus, to keep out of Pandarus his neighbourhood! Which is, to this hour, the mere fact; though for the present, alas, the forgotten fact. I think they were comparatively blessed times those, in their way! 'Violence', 'war', 'disorder': well, what is war, and death itself, to such a perpetual life-in-death, and 'peace, peace, where there is no peace'! Unless some Hero-worship, in its new appropriate form, can return, this world does not promise to be very habitable long.

Past and Present (1843) (London, Chapman & Hall, 1888), pp. 207–12.

Auguste Comte
(1798–1857)

THE NORMAL STATE OF
THE FINAL ECONOMY

The idea of social subordination is common to the old and the new philosophy, opposite as are their points of view, and transitory as is the one view in comparison with the other. The old philosophy, explaining everything by the human type, saw everywhere a hierarchy regulated in imitation of the social classification. The new philosophy, studying Man in connection with the universe at large, finds this classification to be simply a protraction of the biological hierarchy. But science and theology, considering Man each in its own way, – the one as the first of animals, and the other as the lowest of angels, – lead to a very similar conclusion. The office of positive philosophy in this case is to substantiate the common notion of social subordination by connecting it with the principle which forms all hierarchies.

The highest rank is held, according to that principle, by the speculative class. When the separation of the two powers first took place under monotheism, the legal superiority of the clergy to all other orders was by no means owing only or chiefly to their religious character. It was more on account of their speculative character; and the continued growth of the tendency, amidst the decay of religious influences, shows that it is more disinterested than is commonly supposed, and testifies to the disposition of human reason to place the highest value on the most general conceptions. When the speculative class shall have overcome its dispersive tendencies, and returned to unity of principle amidst its diversity of employments, it will obtain the eminent position for which it is destined, and of which its present situation can scarcely afford any idea. While the speculative class is thus superior in dignity, the active class will be superior in express and immediate power, the division answering to the two opposite ways of classifying men, by capacity and by power. The same principle determines the next subdivision of each class, before pointed out in another connection. The speculative class divides itself, according to the direction taken by the contemplative spirit, into the scientific or philosophical (which we know to be ultimately one), and the aesthetic or poetic. Alike as these two classes are in their distinction from the active, they so differ from each other as to require division on the same principle as runs throughout. Whatever may be the ultimate importance and eminent function of the fine arts, the aesthetic point of view can never compare in generality and abstractness with the scientific or philosophical. The one is concerned with the fundamental conceptions which must direct the universal action of human reason; whereas the other is concerned only with the faculties of expression, which must ever hold a secondary place. As for the other leading class, the active or practical, which comprehends the vast majority, its more complete and marked development has already settled the point of its divisions; so that, in regard to them, the theory has only to rationalize the distinctions sanctioned by spontaneous usage. Industrial action is divided into production and transmission of products; the second of which is obviously superior to the first in regard to the abstractness of the work and the generality of the relations. Further division seems to be indicated according as production relates to the mere formation of materials or their working up; and as the transmission is of the products themselves, or of their representative signs, the generality being greater in the second particulars than in the first. Thus we find the industrial hierarchy formed, the bankers being in the first rank; then the merchants; then the manufacturers; and finally the agriculturists; the labours of the latter being more concrete, and their relations more special, than those of the other three classes. It would be out of place to proceed here to further subdivisions. They will be determined by the same principle when the progress of reorganization is sufficiently advanced; and I may observe that when that time comes the most concrete producers, the labourers, whose collisions with their employers are now the most dangerous feature of our industrial state, will be convinced that the position of the capitalist is owing, not to any abuse of strength or wealth, but to the more abstract and general character of his function. The action and responsibility of the operative are less extensive than those of the employer; and the subordination of the one to the other is therefore as little arbitrary and mutable as any other social gradation.

When the gradation is once established, it will be preserved from question and confusion, not only by the clearness of its principle, but by the consciousness in each order that its own subordination to the one above it is the condition of its superiority to those below it; and the lowest of all is not without its own special privileges. The abuses attending all inequality will be restrained, not only by the fundamental education common to all, but by the more extended and severe moral obligations which press upon members of society, in proportion to the generality of their functions. Again, in proportion as social occupations are particular and concrete, their utility is direct, incontestable and assured, and the existence of the workers is more independent, and their responsibility more restricted, – corresponding as their labours do to the most indispensable wants. Thus, if the higher ranks are dignified by a more eminent and difficult co-operation, the lower have a more certain and urgent function: and the last could provisionally exist by themselves, without perverting their essential character; whereas the others could not. This difference is not only a guarantee of social harmony, but it is favourable to private happiness, which, when the primary wants are securely provided for, depends mainly on the small amount of habitual solicitude: and thus, the lowest classes really are privileged in that freedom from care, and that thoughtlessness, which would be a serious fault in the higher classes, but are natural to them.

It can hardly be necessary to point out that there will be perfect freedom in the formation of the respective classes of the positive hierarchy. The direct effect of a universal education is to place every one in the situation best adapted to his abilities, whatever his birth may have been. This is a liberty which depends more on general manners than on political institutions; and it depends upon two conditions, – that access to every social career should remain open to the capable; and that there should be some means of excluding the unworthy. When order is once completely established, such changes will become exceptional; because it is natural for professions to be hereditary. Few have a determinate vocation, and few social employments require such a vocation; so that the disposition to domestic imitation will have its way; whereas, the quality of the universal education and the state of social manners will be safeguards against this hereditary tendency assuming any oppressive form. There is no room for apprehension of any restoration of the system of castes. Caste can have none but a theological foundation; and we have long passed out of the last social phase that is compatible with it; and its remaining traces are, as I have shown, fast disappearing from amidst the advanced civilization of Western Europe.

It remains for me to point out the connection between such an organization and the just claims of the lower classes: and for this purpose I must ascertain the influence of such a connection, both upon the mass of the people and upon the speculative class.

Any spiritual power must be, by its very nature, popular; for its function is to set up morality to guide the social movement, and its closest relations therefore must be with the most numerous classes, who most need its protection. The Catholic Church was obviously doomed to decay when it forsook its task of enlightening and protecting the people, and inclined to aristocratic interests: and in the same way, the inherent nullity of Protestantism appeared in the impotence of its puny authorities to protect the lower classes: and in the same way again, we recognize the empiricism and selfishness which spoil the speculative elements of our modern society in the strange aristocratic tendencies of so many *savans* and artists, who forget their own humble origin, and disdain to apply to the instruction and protection of the people the influence they have acquired, – preferring indeed to use it in confirmation of their own oppressive pretensions. There must be, in the normal state of the final economy, a strong sympathy between the speculative class and the multitude, from their analogous relation to the possessors of the chief temporal power, from their somewhat similar practical situation, and from their equivalent habits of material improvidence. Yet more important is the popular efficacy of the speculative authority, on account both of its educational function and of its regular intervention as moderator in social conflicts, through its habitual elevation of views and generosity of disposition. Without at all quitting its attitude of impartiality, its chief care will always be directed towards the humbler classes, who, on the one hand, are much the most in need of a public education such as their private means cannot attain; and, on the other hand, are much more exposed to constant injury. Even now, vast benefit would ensue if, in preparation for the system to come, positive knowledge and philosophy were sedulously brought within reach of the people. In the educational direction, the intellectual expansion would be much greater than is now easily believed: and the advantage in the other respect, in protecting them from collision with the governing classes, would be no less evident. The positive philosophy would teach them the real value of the political institutions from which they are apt to hope so much, and convince them of the superiority of moral over political solutions. All evils and all pretexts derived from social disturbance would thus be obviated: quacks and dreamers would lose their vocation; and no excuse would be left for delay in social reform. When it is seen why wealth must chiefly abound among the industrial leaders, the positive philosophy will show that it is of small importance to popular interests in what hands capital is deposited, if its employment is duly useful to society at large: and that condition depends much more on moral than on political methods. No jealous legal provision against the selfish use of wealth, and no mischievous intervention, paralysing social activity by political pro-hibition, can be nearly so effectual as general reprobation, grounded on an ascertained principle, under the reign of positive morality. The new philosophical action would either obviate or repress all the dangers which attend the institution of property, and correct popular tendencies by a wise analysis of social difficulties, and a salutary conversion of questions of right into questions of duty. – In its impartiality it will make the superior classes participate in the lesson, proving to them the great moral obliga-tions inherent in their position; so that, for instance, in this matter of property, the rich will morally consider themselves the depositories of the wealth of society, the use of which will not involve any political responsi-bility (except in extreme cases), but should lie under a moral supervision, necessarily open to all, from the indisputableness of its principle, and of which the spiritual authority is the natural organ. Since the abolition of personal servitude, the lowest class has never been really incorporated with the social system: the power of capital, once a means of emancipation, and then of independence, has become exorbitant in daily transactions, however just is its influence through its generality and superior responsi-bility. In short, this philosophy will show that industrial relations, instead of being left to a dangerous empiricism and an oppressive antagonism, must be systematized according to moral laws. The duty to the lower classes will not consist in alms-giving, which can never be more than a secondary resource, nor made reconcilable with any high social destina-tion, in the present advanced state of human condition and dignity. The obligation will be to procure for all, suitable education and employment, – the only conditions that the lower classes can justly demand. Without entering on the perplexed subject of wages, it is enough to say that their settlement will be largely influenced by the same agency. We need not inquire whether any political institutions will in course of time embody social securities of this kind: it is enough that the principle will remain eminently moral, in as far as it will be efficacious and harmonizing.

The Positive Philosophy of Auguste Comte (1830–42), trans. Harriet Martineau (London, Trubner, n.d.), vol. II, pp. 480–3, 485–7.

Alexis de Tocqueville
(1805–1859)

RECONCILING ONESELF TO DEMOCRACY

To return to the main subject of your letters, I will tell you, my dear friend, that the impression made upon you by my book,[1] although it is stronger in one sense than I would wish, does not surprise or alarm me. Here is the political aim of the work:

I wanted to show what from our time constituted a democratic people, and, by means of this rigorously exact portrait, I sought to produce a double effect on the minds of my contemporaries.

To those who have constructed for themselves an ideal democracy, a glittering dream, which they believe can be easily realized, I sought to show that they had painted the picture in false colours; that the democratic government which they extol, if it procures real benefits for the men who may support it, has none of the elevated characteristics attributed to it by their imagination; that this government can, in any case, only maintain itself on the basis of certain conditions of enlightenment, of private morality and of beliefs, which we have by no means reached, and which one must work hard to obtain before deriving political consequences from them.

To those for whom the word democracy is synonymous with turmoil, anarchy, extortion and murders, I tried to show that democracy could lead to society being governed in a manner which respects men's fortunes, recognizes their rights, preserves their liberty and honours their beliefs; that if a democratic government developed, to a less degree than some other type, certain noble faculties of the human personality, it had its noble and great sides; and that perhaps, after all, it was the will of God to distribute a middling degree of happiness among all men, rather than concentrating a great quantity of happiness in some and allowing a small

[1] *Democracy in America.*

148

number to approach perfection. I sought to prove to them that, whatever their opinion about this matter, it was too late to discuss it; that society was advancing and sweeping them each day along with it towards the equalization of conditions; that it was now only a question of choosing between evils that were henceforth inevitable; that the question was certainly not one of knowing whether one could obtain aristocracy or democracy, but rather whether one would have a democratic society advancing without poetry and without grandeur, but with order and morality; or else a democratic society that was disordered and corrupt, abandoned to frenzied passions or bent under a yoke heavier than all those that have weighed upon men since the fall of the Roman Empire.

I wished to diminish the ardour of the former, and, without discouraging them, to show them the sole path to be taken.

I sought to diminish the terrors of the latter and make their will yield to the idea of an inevitable future, in such a way that, the former being less impetuous and the latter offering less resistance, society might advance more peacefully towards the necessary accomplishment of its destiny. That is the governing idea of the work, an idea which links together all the others in a single web, and which you ought to have seen more clearly than you have. Indeed, there have hitherto been very few who have understood it. I please many men of opposed opinions, not because they understand me, but because they find in my work, considering it from only one side, arguments favourable to their passion of the moment. But I have confidence in the future and I hope that a day will come when all will see clearly that which only some perceive today . . .

'Lettre à Eugène Stoffels' (1835), in *Œuvres et Correspondance Inédites*, ed. Gustave de Beaumont (Paris, 1861), vol. I, pp. 427-9. (Translated by Steven Lukes.)

John Stuart Mill
(1806–1873)

THE MAXIMUM SCOPE FOR INDIVIDUAL INITIATIVE

Though a better organization of governments would greatly diminish the force of the objection to the mere multiplication of their duties, it would still remain true that in all the more advanced communities the great majority of things are worse done by the intervention of government, than the individuals most interested in the matter would do them, or cause them to be done, if left to themselves. The grounds of this truth are expressed with tolerable exactness in the popular dictum, that people understand their own business and their own interests better, and care for them more, than the government does, or can be expected to do. This maxim holds true throughout the greatest part of the business of life, and wherever it is true we ought to condemn every kind of government intervention that conflicts with it. The inferiority of government agency, for example, in any of the common operations of industry or commerce, is proved by the fact, that it is hardly ever able to maintain itself in equal competition with individual agency, where the individuals possess the requisite degree of industrial enterprise, and can command the necessary assemblage of means. All the facilities which a government enjoys of access to information; all the means which it possesses of remunerating, and therefore of commanding, the best available talent in the market – are not an equivalent for the one great disadvantage of an inferior interest in the result.

It must be remembered, besides, that even if a government were superior in intelligence and knowledge to any single individual in the nation, it must be inferior to all the individuals of the nation taken together. It can neither possess in itself, nor enlist in its service, more than a portion of the acquirements and capacities which the country contains, applicable to any given purpose. There must be many persons equally qualified for the work with those whom the government employs, even if it selects its instruments with no reference to any consideration but their fitness. Now these are the very persons into whose hands, in the cases of most common occurrence, a system of individual agency naturally tends to throw the work, because they are capable of doing it better or on cheaper terms than any other persons. So far as this is the case, it is evident that government, by excluding or even by superseding individual agency, either substitutes a less qualified instrumentality for one better qualified, or at any rate substitutes its own mode of accomplishing the work, for all the variety of modes which would be tried by a number of equally qualified persons aiming at the same end; a competition by many degrees more propitious to the progress of improvement than any uniformity of system.

I have reserved for the last place one of the strongest of the reasons against the extension of government agency. Even if the government could comprehend within itself, in each department, all the most eminent intellectual capacity and active talent of the nation, it would not be the less desirable that the conduct of a large portion of the affairs of the society should be left in the hands of the persons immediately interested in them. The business of life is an essential part of the practical education of a people; without which, book and school instruction, though most necessary and salutary, does not suffice to qualify them for conduct, and for the adaptation of means to ends. Instruction is only one of the desiderata of mental improvement; another, almost as indispensable, is a vigorous exercise of the active energies; labour, contrivance, judgement, self-control: and the natural stimulus to these is the difficulties of life. This doctrine is not to be confounded with the complacent optimism, which represents the evils of life as desirable things, because they call forth qualities adapted to combat with evils. It is only because the difficulties exist, that the qualities which combat with them are of any value. As practical beings it is our business to free human life from as many as possible of its difficulties, and not to keep up a stock of them as hunters preserve game for the exercise of pursuing it. But since the need of active talent and practical judgement in the affairs of life can only be diminished, and not, even on the most favourable supposition, done away with, it is important that those endowments should be cultivated not merely in a select few, but in all, and that the cultivation should be more varied and complete than most persons are able to find in the narrow sphere of their merely individual interests. A people among whom there is no habit of spontaneous action for a collective interest – who look habitually to their government to command or prompt them in all matters of joint concern – who expect to have everything done for them, except what can be made an affair of mere habit and routine – have their faculties only half developed; their education is defective in one of its most important branches.

Not only is the cultivation of the active faculties by exercise, diffused through the whole community, in itself one of the most valuable of national possessions: it is rendered, not less, but more necessary, when a high degree of that indispensable culture is systematically kept up in the chiefs and functionaries of the state. There cannot be a combination of circumstances more dangerous to human welfare, than that in which intelligence and talent are maintained at a high standard within a governing corporation, but starved and discouraged outside the pale. Such a system, more completely than any other, embodies the idea of despotism, by arming with intellectual superiority as an additional weapon those who have already the legal power. It approaches as nearly as the organic difference between human beings and other animals admits, to the government of sheep by their shepherd without anything like so strong an interest as the shepherd has in the thriving condition of the flock. The only security against political slavery is the check maintained over governors by the diffusion of intelligence, activity and public spirit among the governed. Experience proves the extreme difficulty of permanently keeping up a sufficiently high standard of those qualities; a difficulty which increases, as the advance of civilization and security removes one after another of the hardships, embarrassments and dangers against which individuals had formerly no resource but in their own strength, skill and courage. It is therefore of supreme importance that all classes of the community, down to the lowest, should have much to do for themselves; that as great a demand should be made upon their intelligence and virtue as it is in any respect equal to; that the government should not only leave as far as possible to their own faculties the conduct of whatever concerns themselves alone, but should suffer them, or rather encourage them, to manage as many as possible of their joint concerns by voluntary co-operation; since this discussion and management of collective interests is the great school of that public spirit, and the great source of that intelligence of public affairs, which are always regarded as the distinctive character of the public of free countries.

A democratic constitution, not supported by democratic institutions in detail, but confined to the central government, not only is not political freedom, but often creates a spirit precisely the reverse, carrying down to the lowest grade in society the desire and ambition of political domination. In some countries the desire of the people is for not being tyrannized over, but in others it is merely for an equal chance to everybody of tyrannizing. Unhappily this last state of the desires is fully as natural to mankind as the former, and in many of the conditions even of civilized humanity is far more largely exemplified. In proportion as the people are accustomed to manage their affairs by their own active intervention, instead of leaving them to the government, their desires will turn to repelling tyranny, rather than to tyrannizing: while in proportion as all real initiative and direction resides in the government, and individuals habitually feel and act as under its perpetual tutelage, popular institutions develop in them not the desire of freedom, but an unmeasured appetite for place and power; diverting the intelligence and activity of the country from its principal business to a wretched competition for the selfish prizes and the petty vanities of office.

The preceding are the principal reasons, of a general character, in favour of restricting to the narrowest compass the intervention of a public authority in the business of the community: and few will dispute the more than sufficiency of these reasons, to throw, in every instance, the burden of making out a strong case, not on those who resist, but on those who recommend, government interference. *Laisser-faire*, in short, should be the general practice: every departure from it, unless required by some great good, is a certain evil.

Principles of Political Economy (1848), new ed. (London, Longmans, 1909), pp. 947–50.

Such being the reasons which make it imperative that human beings should be free to form opinions, and to express their opinions without reserve; and such the baneful consequences to the intellectual, and through that to the moral nature of man, unless this liberty is either conceded, or asserted in spite of prohibition; let us next examine whether the same reasons do not require that men should be free to act upon their opinions – to carry these out in their lives, without hindrance, either physical or moral, from their fellow-men, so long as it is at their own risk and peril. This last proviso is of course indispensable. No one pretends that actions should be as free as opinions. On the contrary, even opinions lose their immunity when the circumstances in which they are expressed are such as to constitute their expression a positive instigation to some mischievous act. An opinion that corn-dealers are starvers of the poor, or that private property is robbery, ought to be unmolested when simply circulated through the press, but may justly incur punishment when delivered orally to an excited mob assembled before the house of a corn-dealer, or when handed about among the same mob in the form of a placard. Acts, of whatever kind, which, without justifiable cause, do harm to others, may be, and in the more important cases absolutely require to be, controlled by the unfavourable sentiments, and, when needful, by the active interference of mankind. The liberty of the individual must be thus far limited; he must not make himself a nuisance to other people. But if he refrains from molesting others in what concerns them, and merely acts according to his own inclination and judgement in things which concern himself, the same reasons which show that opinion should be free, prove also that he should be allowed, without molestation, to carry his opinions into practice at his own cost. That mankind are not infallible; that their truths, for the most part, are only half-truths; that unity of opinion, unless resulting from the fullest and freest comparison of opposite opinions, is not desirable, and diversity not an evil, but a good, until mankind are much more capable than at present of recognizing all sides of the truth, are principles applicable to men's modes of action, not less than to their opinions. As it is useful that while mankind are imperfect there should be different opinions, so it is that there should be different experiments of living; that free scope should be given to varieties of character, short of injury to others; and that the worth of different modes of life should be proved practically, when any one thinks fit to try them. It is desirable, in short, that in things which do not primarily concern others, individuality should assert itself. Where, not the person's own character, but the traditions or customs of other people are the rule of conduct, there is wanting one of the principal ingredients of human happiness, and quite the chief ingredient of individual and social progress.

In maintaining this principle, the greatest difficulty to be encountered does not lie in the appreciation of means towards an acknowledged end, but in the indifference of persons in general to the end itself. If it were felt that the free development of individuality is one of the leading essentials of well-being; that it is not only a co-ordinate element with all that is designated by the terms civilization, instruction, education, culture, but is itself a necessary part and condition of all those things; there would be no danger that liberty should be undervalued, and the adjustment of the boundaries between it and social control would present no extraordinary difficulty. But the evil is, that individual spontaneity is hardly recognized by the common modes of thinking as having any intrinsic worth, or deserving any regard on its own account. The majority, being satisfied with the ways of mankind as they now are (for it is they who make them what they are), cannot comprehend why those ways should not be good enough for everybody; and what is more, spontaneity forms no part of the ideal of the majority of moral and social reformers, but is rather looked on with jealousy, as a troublesome and perhaps rebellious obstruction to the general acceptance of what these reformers, in their own judgement, think would be best for mankind. Few persons, out of Germany, even comprehend the meaning of the doctrine which Wilhelm von Humboldt, so eminent both as a *savant* and as a politician, made the text of a treatise – that 'the end of man, or that which is prescribed by the eternal or immutable dictates of reason, and not suggested by vague and transient desires, is the highest and most harmonious development of his powers to a complete and consistent whole'; that, therefore, the object 'towards which every human being must ceaselessly direct his efforts, and on which especially those who design to influence their fellow-men must ever keep their eyes, is the individuality of power and development'; that for this there are two requisites, 'freedom and variety of situations'; and that from the union of these arise 'individual vigour and manifold diversity', which combine themselves in 'originality'.[1]

It is not by wearing down into uniformity all that is individual in themselves, but by cultivating it, and calling it forth, within the limits imposed by the rights and interests of others, that human beings become a noble and beautiful object of contemplation; and as the works partake the character of those who do them, by the same process human life also becomes rich, diversified and animating, furnishing more abundant aliment to high thoughts and elevating feelings, and strengthening the tie which binds every individual to the race, by making the race infinitely better worth belonging to. In proportion to the development of his individuality, each person becomes more valuable to himself, and is

[1] *The Sphere and Duties of Government*, from the German of Baron Wilhelm von Humboldt, pp. 11–13.

therefore capable of being more valuable to others. There is a greater fulness of life about his own existence, and when there is more life in the units there is more in the mass which is composed of them. As much compression as is necessary to prevent the stronger specimens of human nature from encroaching on the rights of others cannot be dispensed with; but for this there is ample compensation even in the point of view of human development. The means of development which the individual loses by being prevented from gratifying his inclinations to the injury of others, are chiefly obtained at the expense of the development of other people. And even to himself there is a full equivalent in the better development of the social part of his nature, rendered possible by the restraint put upon the selfish part. To be held to rigid rules of justice for the sake of others, develops the feelings and capacities which have the good of others for their object. But to be restrained in things not affecting their good, by their mere displeasure, develops nothing valuable, except such force of character as may unfold itself in resisting the restraint. If acquiesced in, it dulls and blunts the whole nature. To give any fair play to the nature of each, it is essential that different persons should be allowed to lead different lives. In proportion as this latitude has been exercised in any age, has that age been noteworthy to posterity. Even despotism does not produce its worst effects, so long as individuality exists under it; and whatever crushes individuality is despotism, by whatever name it may be called, and whether it professes to be enforcing the will of God or the injunctions of men.

'On Liberty' (1859), in *On Liberty, and Considerations on Representative Government*, ed. R. B. McCallum (Oxford, Blackwell, 1946), pp. 49–51, 55–6.

We may take, as a first instance, the administration of justice; with the more propriety, since there is no part of public business in which the mere machinery, the rules and contrivances for conducting the details of the operation, are of such vital consequence. Yet even these yield in importance to the qualities of the human agents employed. Of what efficacy are rules of procedure in securing the ends of justice, if the moral condition of the people is such that the witnesses generally lie, and the judges and their subordinates take bribes? Again, how can institutions provide a good municipal administration if there exists such indifference to the subject that those who would administer honestly and capably cannot be induced to serve, and the duties are left to those who undertake them because they have some private interest to be promoted? Of what avail is the most broadly popular representative system if the electors do not care to choose the best member of parliament, but choose him who will spend most money to be elected? How can a representative assembly work for good if its members can be bought, or if their excitability of temperament, uncorrected by public discipline or private self-control, makes them incapable of calm deliberation, and they resort to manual violence on the floor of the House, or shoot at one another with rifles? How, again, can government, or any joint concern, be carried on in a tolerable manner by people so envious that, if one among them seems likely to succeed in anything, those who ought to co-operate with him form a tacit combination to make him fail? Whenever the general disposition of the people is such that each individual regards those only of his interests which are selfish, and does not dwell on, or concern himself for, his share of the general interest, in such a state of things good government is impossible. The influence of defects of intelligence in obstructing all the elements of good government requires no illustration. Government consists of acts done by human beings; and if the agents, or those who choose the agents, or those to whom the agents are responsible, or the lookers-on whose opinion ought to influence and check all these, are mere masses of ignorance, stupidity and baleful prejudice, every operation of government will go wrong; while, in proportion as the men rise above this standard, so will the government improve in quality; up to the point of excellence, attainable but nowhere attained, where the officers of government, themselves persons of superior virtue and intellect, are surrounded by the atmosphere of a virtuous and enlightened public opinion.

The first element of good government, therefore, being the virtue and intelligence of the human beings composing the community, the most important point of excellence which any form of government can possess is to promote the virtue and intelligence of the people themselves. The first question in respect to any political institutions is, how far they tend to foster in the members of the community the various desirable qualities, moral and intellectual; or rather (following Bentham's more complete classification) moral, intellectual and active. The government which does this the best has every likelihood of being the best in all other respect, since it is on these qualities, so far as they exist in the people, that all possibility of goodness in the practical operations of the government depends.

We may consider, then, as one criterion of the goodness of a government, the degree in which it tends to increase the sum of good qualities in the governed, collectively and individually; since, besides that their well-being is the sole object of government, their good qualities supply the moving force which works the machinery.

Now there can be no kind of doubt that the passive type of character is favoured by the government of one or a few, and the active self-helping type by that of the Many. Irresponsible rulers need the quiescence of the ruled more than they need any activity but that which they can compel. Submissiveness to the prescriptions of men as necessities of nature is the lesson inculcated by all governments upon those who are wholly without participation in them. The will of superiors, and the law as the will of superiors, must be passively yielded to. But no men are mere instruments or materials in the hands of their rulers who have will or spirit or a spring of internal activity in the rest of their proceedings; and any manifestation of these qualities, instead of receiving encouragement from despots, has to get itself forgiven by them. Even when irresponsible rulers are not sufficiently conscious of danger from the mental activity of their subjects to be desirous of repressing it, the position itself is a repression. Endeavour is even more effectually restrained by the certainty of its impotence than by any positive discouragement. Between subjection to the will of others, and the virtues of self-help and self-government, there is a natural incompatibility. This is more or less complete, according as the bondage is strained or relaxed. Rulers differ very much in the length to which they carry the control of the free agency of their subjects, or the suppression of it by managing their business for them. But the difference is in degree, not in principle; and the best despots often go to the greatest lengths in chaining up the free agency of their subjects. A bad despot, when his own personal indulgences have been provided for, may sometimes be willing to let the people alone; but a good despot insists on doing them good, by making them do their own business in a better way than they themselves know of. The regulations which restricted to fixed processes all the leading branches of French manufactures were the work of the great Colbert.

Very different is the state of the human faculties where a human being feels himself under no other external restraint than the necessities of nature, or mandates of society which he has his share in imposing, and which it is open to him, if he thinks them wrong, publicly to dissent from, and exert himself actively to get altered. No doubt, under a government partially popular, this freedom may be exercised even by those who are not partakers in the full privileges of citizenship. But it is a great additional stimulus to anyone's self-help and self-reliance when he starts from even ground, and has not to feel that his success depends on the impression he can make upon the sentiments and dispositions of a body of whom he is not one. It is a great discouragement to an individual, and a still greater one to a class, to be left out of the constitution; to be reduced to plead from outside the door to the arbiters of their destiny, not taken into consultation within. The maximum of the invigorating effect of freedom upon the character is only obtained when the person acted on either is, or is looking forward to becoming, a citizen as fully privileged as any other. What is still more important than even this matter of feeling is the practical discipline which the character obtains from the occasional demand made upon the citizens to exercise, for a time and in their turn, some social function. It is not sufficiently considered how little there is in most men's ordinary life to give any largeness either to their conceptions or to their sentiments. Their work is a routine; not a labour of love, but of self-interest in the most elementary form, the satisfaction of daily wants; neither the thing done, nor the process of doing it, introduces the mind to thoughts or feelings extending beyond individuals; if instructive books are within their reach, there is no stimulus to read them; and in most cases the individual has no access to any person of cultivation much superior to his own. Giving him something to do for the public, supplies, in a measure, all these deficiencies. If circumstances allow the amount of public duty assigned him to be considerable, it makes him an educated man. Notwithstanding the defects of the social system and moral ideas of antiquity, the practice of the dicastery and the ecclesia raised the intellectual standard of an average Athenian citizen far beyond anything of which there is yet an example in any other mass of men, ancient or modern. The proofs of this are apparent in every page of our great historian of Greece; but we need scarcely look further than to the high quality of the addresses which their great orators deemed best calculated to act with effect on their understanding and will. A benefit of the same kind, though far less in degree, is produced on Englishmen of the lower middle class by their liability to be placed on juries and to serve parish offices; which, though it does not occur to so many, nor is so continuous, nor introduces them to so great a variety of elevated considerations, as to admit of comparison with the public education which every citizen of Athens obtained from her democratic institutions, must make them nevertheless very different beings, in range of ideas and development of faculties, from those who have done nothing in their lives but drive a quill, or sell goods over a counter. Still more salutary is the moral part of the instruction afforded by the participation of the private citizen, if even rarely, in public functions. He is called upon, while so engaged, to weigh interests not his own; to be guided, in case of conflicting claims, by another rule than his private partialities; to apply, at every turn, principles and maxims which have for their reason of existence the common good: and he usually finds associated with him in the same work minds more familiarized than his own with these ideas and operations, whose study it will be to supply reasons to his understanding, and stimulation to his feeling for the general interest. He is made to feel himself one of the public, and whatever is for their benefit to be for his benefit. Where this school of public spirit does not exist, scarcely any sense is entertained that private persons, in no eminent social situation, owe any duties to society, except to obey the laws and submit to the government. There is no unselfish sentiment of identification with the public. Every thought or feeling, either of interest or of duty, is absorbed in the individual and in the family. The man never thinks of any collective interest, of any objects to be pursued jointly with others, but only in competition with them, and in some measure at their expense. A neighbour, not being an ally or an associate, since he is never engaged in any common undertaking for joint benefit, is therefore only a rival. Thus even private morality suffers, while public is actually extinct. Were this the universal and only possible state of things, the utmost aspirations of the lawgiver or the moralist could only stretch to make the bulk of the community a flock of sheep innocently nibbling the grass side by side.

From these accumulated considerations it is evident that the only government which can fully satisfy all the exigencies of the social state is one in which the whole people participate; that any participation, even in the smallest public function, is useful; that the participation should everywhere be as great as the general degree of improvement of the community will allow; and that nothing less can be ultimately desirable than the admission of all to a share in the sovereign power of the State. But since all cannot, in a community exceeding a single small town, participate personally in any but some very minor portions of the public business, it follows that the ideal type of a perfect government must be representative.

'Considerations on Representative Government' (1861), in ibid., pp. 126–7, 148–51.

Pierre-Joseph Proudhon
(1809–1865)

SOCIETY WITHOUT GOVERNMENT

Humanity has had to live, and civilization to develop, for six thousand years, under this inexorable system, of which the first term is *Despair* and the last *Death*. What secret power has sustained it? What force has enabled it to survive? What principles, what ideas, renewed the blood that flowed forth under the poniard of authority, ecclesiastical and secular?

This mystery is now explained.

Beneath the governmental machinery, in the shadow of political institutions, out of the sight of statesmen and priests, society is producing its own organism, slowly and silently; and constructing a new order, the expression of its vitality and autonomy, and the denial of the old politics, as well as of the old religion.

This organization, which is as essential to society as it is incompatible with the present system, has the following principles:

1. The indefinite perfectibility of the individual and of the race;
2. The honorableness of work;
3. The equality of fortunes;
4. The identity of interests;
5. The end of antagonisms;
6. The universality of comfort;
7. The sovereignty of reason;
8. The absolute liberty of the man and of the citizen.

I mention below its principal forms of activity:

a. Division of labour, through which classification of the People by INDUSTRIES replaces classification by *caste*;

b. Collective power, the principle of WORKMEN'S ASSOCIATIONS, in place of *armies*;

c. Commerce, the concrete form of CONTRACT, which takes the place of *Law*;

d. Equality in exchange;

e. Competition;

f. Credit, which turns upon INTERESTS, as the governmental hierarchy turns upon *Obedience*;

g. The equilibrium of values and of properties.

The old system, standing on Authority and Faith, was essentially based upon *Divine Right*. The principle of the sovereignty of the People, introduced later, did not change its nature; and it is a mistake today, in the face of the conclusions of science, to maintain a distinction which does not touch underlying principles, between absolute monarchy and constitutional monarchy, or between the latter and the democratic republic. The sovereignty of the People has been, if I may say so, for a century past, but a skirmishing line for Liberty. It was either an error, or a clever scheme of our fathers to make the sovereign people in the image of the king-man: as the Revolution becomes better understood, this mythology vanishes, all traces of government disappear and follow the principle of government itself to dissolution.

The new system, based upon the spontaneous practice of industry, in accordance with individual and social reason, is the system of *Human Right*. Opposed to arbitrary command, essentially objective, it permits neither parties nor sects; it is complete in itself, and allows neither restriction nor separation.

There is no fusion possible between the political and economic systems, between the system of laws and the system of contracts; one or the other must be chosen. The ox, while it remain an ox, cannot be an eagle, nor can the bat be at the same time a snail. In the same way, while Society maintains in the slightest degree its political form, it cannot become organized according to economic law. How harmonize local initiative with the preponderance of a central authority, or universal suffrage with the hierarchy of officials; the principle that no one owes obedience to a law to which he has not himself consented, with the right of majorities?

If a writer who understood these contradictions should undertake to reconcile them, it would prove him, not a bold thinker, but a wretched charlatan.

This absolute incompatibility of the two systems, so often proved, still does not convince writers who, while admitting the dangers of authority, nevertheless hold to it, as the sole means of maintaining order, and see nothing beside it but empty desolation. Like the sick man in the comedy, who is told that the first thing he must do is to discharge his doctors, if he wants to get well, they persist in asking how can a man get along without a doctor, or a society without a government. They will make the government as republican, as benevolent, as equal as possible; they will set up all possible guarantees against it; they will belittle it, almost attack it, in support of the majesty of the citizens. They tell us: You are the government! You shall govern yourselves, without president, without representatives, without delegates. What have you then to complain about? But to live without government, to abolish all authority, absolutely and unreservedly, to set up pure *anarchy*, seems to them ridiculous and inconceivable, a plot against the Republic and against the nation. What will these people who talk of abolishing government put in place of it? they ask.

We have no trouble in answering.

It is industrial organization that we will put in place of government, as we have just shown.

In place of laws, we will put contracts. – No more laws voted by a majority, nor even unanimously; each citizen, each town, each industrial union, makes its own laws.

In place of political powers, we will put economic forces.

In place of the ancient classes of nobles, burghers and peasants, or of business men and working men, we will put the general titles and special departments of industry: Agriculture, Manufacture, Commerce, etc.

In place of public force, we will put collective force.

In place of standing armies, we will put industrial associations.

In place of police, we will put identity of interests.

In place of political centralization, we will put economic centralization.

Do you see now how there can be order without functionaries, a profound and wholly intellectual unity?

You, who cannot conceive of unity without a whole apparatus of legislators, prosecutors, attorneys-general, custom house officers, policemen, you have never known what real unity is! What you call unity and centralization is nothing but perpetual chaos, serving as a basis for endless tyranny; it is the advancing of the chaotic condition of social forces as an argument for despotism – a despotism which is really the cause of the chaos.

Well, in our turn, let us ask, what need have we of government when we have made an agreement? Does not the National Bank, with its various branches, achieve centralization and unity? Does not the agreement among farm labourers for compensation, marketing and reimbursement for farm properties create unity? From another point of view, do not the industrial associations for carrying on the large-scale industries bring about unity? And the constitution of value, that contract of contracts, as we have called it, is not that the most perfect and indissoluble unity?

And if we must show you an example in our own history in order to convince you, does not that fairest monument of the Convention, the system of weights and measures, form, for fifty years past, the corner-stone of that economic unity which is destined to replace political unity?

Never ask again then what we will put in place of government, nor what will become of society without government, for I assure you that in the future it will be easier to conceive of society without government, than of society with government.

Society, just now, is like the butterfly just out of the cocoon, which shakes its gilded wings in the sunlight before taking flight. Tell it to crawl back into the silken covering, to shun the flowers and to hide itself from the light!

But a revolution is not made with formulas. Prejudice must be attacked at the foundation, overthrown, hurled into dust, its injurious effects explained, its ridiculous and odious nature shown forth. Mankind believes only in its own tests, happy if these tests do not addle its brains and drain its blood. Let us try then by clear criticism to make the test of government so conclusive, that the absurdity of the institution will strike all minds, and Anarchy, dreaded as a scourge, will be accepted as a benefit.

General Idea of the Revolution in the Nineteenth Century (1851), trans. J. B. Robinson (London, Freedom Press, 1923), pp. 243–7.

Alexander Herzen
(1812–1870)

THE PERPETUALLY
RECEDING GOAL

'. . . Cheek by jowl with the contented, those whom the present scheme
of things satisfies, are, on the one hand, the poor – uncultivated, backward and hungry, struggling hopelessly against need, exhausted by work
which cannot give them enough to eat – and, on the other, those like us,
who have incautiously run on ahead, surveyors setting up the landmarks
of a new world of which we shall never even see the foundation. If
anything has been left of all the hopes of life which has slipped through
our fingers (it certainly has), then that is the faith in the future.
Sometime, long after our death, the house for which we have cleared
the site, will be built and in it life will be good and comfortable – for
others.'

'After all, there is no reason to assume that the new world will be
built according to our plan.'

The young man gave a discontented shake of his head and looked for
a moment at the sea. The calm was still absolute; a low, heavy cloud passed
so slowly overhead that the smoke of the vessel mingled with it as it
rose. The sea was black, the air sultry.

'You treat me', he said after a silence, 'as a highwayman treats his
victim. You have robbed me of everything I own and still unsatisfied, you
strip me of my last tatters which shield me from the cold and reach out
for my very hair. You compelled me to doubt very much but I still had
the future and now you have deprived me of that, too. You rob me of my
hopes – like Macbeth you kill my visions.'

'And I was under the impression that I was more like a surgeon who
removes a fungus.'

'Indeed, that is still more apt: the surgeon removes the sick part of the
body, without replacing it with a healthy part.'

'And, incidentally, saves a life, delivering the patient from a harrowing, chronic disease.'

'I know only too well what this delivery of yours means. You fling open the doors of the dungeons and wish to turn out the captive into the steppes, assuring him that he is free; you demolish the Bastille but put up nothing in its place – what is left is just bare ground.'

'That would be wonderful if it were as you say. Unfortunately the remains and the rubble interfere at every step.'

'But what do they interfere with? What is our true vocation, where is our banner? What do we believe in? What do we reject?'

'We believe in everything, but don't believe in ourselves. You seek to find a banner? I seek to lose it. You want a guidebook, while I think that on reaching a certain age one should be ashamed to use it. You have just said that we have set up the landmarks of a new world. . . .'

'And they are pulled up by the spirit of negation and analysis. You have a much more sombre view of the world than I, and the consolation you offer only serves to give more frightful expression to the present ordeal. If the future does not belong to us then our entire civilization is a fraud, the day-dream of a fifteen-year-old girl at which she herself will laugh when she is twenty-five. Our labour is in vain, our efforts ridiculous, our hopes resemble those of *le paysan du Danube*. But then, perhaps, that is what you mean; we should abandon our civilization and, rejecting it, turn back to those laggards?'

'No, it is impossible to renounce progress. What can be done to make me forget what I know? Our civilization is the finest flower of life today – how could one forego one's own progress? But what has that to do with the realization of our ideals; why must the future follow the programme worked out by us?'

'That means, then, that our thoughts have brought us to unrealizable hopes, to absurd expectations. With these hopes aboard, the last fruit of our labours, our ship is caught by the waves and is sinking. The future does not belong to us; we will have naught to do with the present and there is no harbour. We are on board this ship for better or for worse. All that remains to us is to watch, with folded arms, for the water to flood it. He whom this prospect bores and who has more courage, can throw himself into the sea.'

'Rousseau and his disciples imagined that if their ideas of fraternity were not realized, it was because of physical obstacles – because the word was enchained or the action was unfree – and they, consistent to the end, assaulted all that thwarted their ideas. The task was formidable, enormous, but they were victorious. And once victorious, they thought, the time had at last arrived. . . . But this *at last* led them to the guillotine and that was absolutely the best that could have happened to them. Elated with battle and labour, their faith intact, they died, swept away by a stormy blast. They were certain that when the storm subsided, their ideal would be realized – without them, but still realized. At last this lull came. How fortunate that all these enthusiasts had long been in their graves! They did not have to face the fact that their cause had not advanced an inch; that their ideals had remained ideals; that it was not enough to raze the Bastille to make free people of the prisoners. You compare us with them, forgetting that we know what has happened in the fifty years that have passed since their death, that we saw all the hopes of the theoretical minds derided, heard the daemon of history laugh at the expense of their science, ideas, theories. We saw the republic give way to Napoleon, and the Revolution of 1830 conquered by the stock exchange. Having witnessed all that has passed, we cannot harbour the hopes of our predecessors. Having made a deeper study of revolutionary questions we demand today what they demanded, but in a greater and wider degree, yet even their demands remain as inapplicable as before. So, on the one hand, there is the logical consistency of thought and its triumph; on the other hand, its absolute impotence against the world, both deaf and dumb, and inability to grasp the idea of salvation as it is expounded to it – either because this idea is badly expressed or else because it is of purely theoretical, bookish significance – as was, for example, Roman philosophy which never reached more than a small circle of educated people.'

'. . . You are misled by categories which have a poor grasp on life. Consider it well: what is this goal – is it a programme, or a commandment? Who has given it? To whom has it been announced? Is it or is it not obligatory? If it is obligatory then what are we – puppets or people? Indeed, are we morally free beings or simply cogs in a wheel? I find it easier to view life and, consequently, history too, as the end rather than a means to the end.'

'In other words, we are the goal of nature and history.'

'Partly – *plus* the present of all that exists. That embraces everything: the heritage of all past efforts and the germs of all that is to be; the inspiration of the artist, and the energy of the citizen, and the enjoyment of the youth who, at this very moment, is making his way to the secluded arbour where his sweetheart is waiting for him, timid, and full of the moment, without a thought for the future, or of a goal, and the frisky fish splashing about in the moonlight, and the harmony of the whole solar system – in a word, I can make so bold as to round it off, like feudal titles, with the three etc., etc., etc.'

'You are absolutely right in so far as nature is concerned, but it seems to me that you have forgotten that through all those changes and entanglements of history runs a red thread which joins them into one whole. This thread is progress – or, perhaps, you do not recognize progress either?'

'Progress is an inalienable attribute of conscious, uninterrupted development; it is the active record and the physiological perfection of people by social life.'

'Is it possible that you do not see the goal here?'

'On the contrary, here I see the consequence. If progress is the goal, then what is it we are working for? What is this Moloch who, as the toilers approach him, recedes instead of rewarding them; who, to console the exhausted and doomed crowds greeting him with *morituri te salutant*, can only reply with the ironic promise that after their death life on earth will be splendid. Can it be that you, too, doom the people of today to the sad destiny of the caryatids supporting the balcony on which others will dance some day? Or assign them to the role of those unfortunate workers who, knee-deep in mud, are to drag along the bark with the mysterious golden fleece in her hold and the meek inscription 'Future Progress' on her flags. The exhausted drop in their tracks, while others pick up the harness with renewed strength, yet the road, as you have said, remains as long as it was at the start, for there is no end to progress. This in itself should make people cautious: the aim, endlessly far, is not an aim but a snare. The goal must be nearer – at least wages or the enjoyment of labour. Every epoch, every generation, every life has had and will still have their plenitude. As it advances new demands arise, new ordeals, new means and some faculties develop at the expense of others; finally, the cerebral matter itself improves. . . . Why do you smile? Yes, indeed, the cerebrum improves. Everything natural shocks and astonishes you, idealists, just as once knights were astounded to hear that villains also demanded human rights. When Goethe was in Italy he compared the skull of the ancient ox with that of one of our days and discovered that the contemporary ox had thinner bones, and a larger cavity for the cerebral hemispheres. The ancient ox was, evidently, stronger than ours, but the

latter attained greater cerebral development during his peaceful submission to man. What makes you think that man is less capable of development than the ox? This growth of the species is not, as you suppose, the
goal but an inherent attribute of a continuous line of generations. The
goal of every generation is the generation itself. So far from using the
generation as a means for attaining a future result, nature is not, indeed,
concerned about the future at all. It is prepared, like Cleopatra, to dissolve a pearl in wine if only for the momentary pleasure it gives. At
heart nature is a bayadère and a bacchante.'

'From the Other Shore' (1850), in *Selected Philosophical Works* (Moscow,
1956), pp. 354–5, 357–8, 362–3.

Mikhail Bakunin
(1814–1876)

THE MOST ABSOLUTE LIBERTY

... Socialism is *justice*. When we speak of justice, we do not mean that which is given us in legal codes and by Roman jurisprudence, based largely on acts of violence accomplished by force, consecrated by time and by the blessings of some church, whether christian or pagan, and as such accepted as absolute principles, from which all else follows as nothing but an entirely logical deduction[1] – we speak of the justice that is based solely upon the consciences of men, which you will find in every man's conscience, even in that of children, and which is expressed in terms of a simple *equation*.

This justice, which is so universal and which none the less, due to the incursions of force and of religious influences, has never as yet prevailed, in the political, the legal or the economic worlds, must serve as a basis for the new world. Without it there will be no liberty, no republic, no prosperity, no peace! It must therefore preside over all our resolutions, so that we can effectively co-operate in the establishment of peace.

This justice commands us to take into our hands the cause of the people, until now so horribly mistreated, and to claim on its behalf political liberty, and economic and social emancipation.

We do not propose to you, gentlemen, such and such a socialist system. What we ask of you is to proclaim anew that great principle of the French Revolution: that every man should have the material and moral means

[1] In this connection, the science of law presents a perfect similarity with theology. These two sciences both take their starting-points—the first from a real but iniquitous fact, namely appropriation by force, or conquest; the second from a fictional and absurd fact, namely divine revelation, conceived as an absolute principle—and, basing themselves on this absurdity or this iniquity, both have recourse to the most rigorous logic in order to build, in the one case, a theological system and, in the other, a legal system.

of developing all his humanity, a principle expressed, we believe, in the following task:

To organize society in such a way that every individual, man or woman, embarking on life, finds himself with virtually equal means for the development of his various faculties and for their employment through his work; to organize a society which, rendering any individual, whoever he is, unable to exploit the labour of others, does not allow anyone to share in the enjoyment of social wealth, which is in fact nothing but the product of labour, except in so far as he has directly contributed to producing it by his own labour.

The complete accomplishment of this task will certainly be the work of centuries. But history has set it and henceforth we could not put it aside, without condemning ourselves to total impotence.

We hasten to add that we energetically reject all attempts at social organization which, not committed to the most complete liberty of individuals and of associations, would require the establishment of a regulative authority of whatever kind; and in the name of that liberty which we recognize as the unique basis and sole legitimate origin of every organization, economic or political, we will always protest against everything which resembles, either closely or distantly, communism or State socialism.

The sole thing which, in our view, the State can and should do is to modify, at first gradually, the right of inheritance, so as to arrive as soon as possible at its complete abolition. The right of inheritance, being a pure creation of the State, one of the essential conditions of the very existence of the authoritarian and divine State, can and must be abolished by liberty in the State – which amounts to saying that the State itself must be dissolved within a society organized freely according to justice. This right will, we maintain, necessarily be abolished because, so long as *inheritance* exists, there will be *hereditary* economic inequality, not the natural inequality of individuals but the artificial inequality of classes – and because the latter is necessarily always expressed in the hereditary inequality of men's mental development and culture, and will continue to be the source and the consecration of all political and social inequalities. Equality at the point of departure, at the beginning of life for everyone, in so far as this equality will depend on the economic and political organization of society, and in order that everyone, abstracting from natural differences, should properly only be the child of his work – that is the task of justice. In our view, the public provision of education and instruction of all children of both sexes, including their maintenance from birth to the age of majority, should be the sole legacy of all those who die. We may add, as Slavs and Russians, that with us the social idea, based on the general and traditional instinct of our peoples, is that the land, property of the whole people, must only be owned by those who cultivate it with their hands.

We are convinced, Gentlemen, that this principle is just, that it is an essential and inevitable condition of every serious social reform and that, in consequence, western Europe in its turn will not fail to accept it and recognize it, despite all the difficulties which its realization will encounter in certain countries, such as France for instance, where the majority of peasants already enjoy the ownership of their land, but where on the other hand the great majority of those same peasants will soon come to possess nothing, because of the subdivision which is the inevitable result of the politico-economic system that currently prevails in that country. We advance no proposition on this subject, as in general we abstain from all assertions relating to specific problems of social science and politics, convinced that all these questions must become the subject of a serious and deep discussion in our journal. We therefore confine ourselves today to offering you the following declaration:

'*Convinced that the serious realization of liberty, justice and peace in the world will be impossible so long as the vast majority of peoples remain dispossessed of property, deprived of education, and condemned to political and social ineffectiveness and to a state of de facto if not de jure slavery, by poverty as well as by the need imposed on them to work without respite or leisure, producing all the riches in which the world glories today, while receiving in return so small a part that it scarcely suffices to secure tomorrow's bread;*

'*Convinced that for all these peoples, hitherto so horribly mistreated by the centuries, the question of bread is the question of intellectual emancipation, of liberty and of humanity;*

'*That liberty without socialism is privilege and injustice; and that socialism without liberty is slavery and brutality:*

'*The League loudly proclaims the necessity of a radical social and economic reform having as its aim the deliverance of the labour of the people from the yoke of capital and property-owners, and based on the strictest justice – not legal, not theological, not metaphysical, but simply human – on positive science and on the most absolute liberty.*'

'Fédéralisme, Socialisme et Antithéologisme' (?1865–7), in M. Bakounin, *Œuvres* (Paris, P. V. Stock, 1895), pp. 54–9. (Translated by Steven Lukes.)

Karl Marx
(1818–1883)

UNALIENATED SOCIETY

Supposing that we had produced in a human manner; each of us would in his production have doubly affirmed himself and his fellow man. I would have (1) objectified in my production my individuality and its peculiarity and thus both in my activity enjoyed an individual expression of my life and also in looking at the object have had the individual pleasure of realizing that my personality was objective, visible to the senses and thus a power raised beyond all doubt. (2) In your enjoyment or use of my product I would have had the direct enjoyment of realizing that I had both satisfied a human need by my work and also objectified the human essence and therefore fashioned for another human being the object that met his need. (3) I would have been for you the mediator between you and the species and thus been acknowledged and felt by you as a completion of your own essence and a necessary part of yourself and have thus realized that I am confirmed both in your thought and in your love. (4) In my expression of my life I would have fashioned your expression of your life, and thus in my own activity have realized my own essence, my human, my communal essence.

In that case our products would be like so many mirrors, out of which our essence shone.

Thus in this relationship what occurred on my side would also occur on yours.

If we consider the different stages as they occur in our supposition:

My work would be a free expression of my life, and therefore a free enjoyment of my life. Presupposing private property, my work is an alienation of my life, because I work in order to live, to furnish myself with the means of living. My work is not my life.

Secondly: In work the peculiarity of my individuality would have been affirmed since it is my individual life. Work would thus be genuine, active property. Presupposing private property, my individuality is so far externalized that I hate my activity: it is a torment to me and only the appearance of an activity and thus also merely a forced activity that is laid upon me through an exterior, arbitrary need, not an inner and necessary one.

My labour can only appear in my object as what it is. It cannot appear as what it essentially is not. Therefore it appears still as merely the expression of my loss of self and my powerlessness that is objective, observable, visible and therefore beyond all doubt.

> 'Notes on James Mill' (1844), in Marx–Engels, *Historisch-Kritische Gesamtausgabe* (Berlin, Marx–Engels Verlag, 1927–9), vol. I, III, pp. 546ff. (Translated by David McLellan.)

Political emancipation is a reduction of man, on the one hand to a member of civil society, an *independent* and *egoistic* individual, and on the other hand, to a *citizen*, to a moral person.

Human emancipation will only be complete when the real, individual man has absorbed into himself the abstract citizen; when as an individual man, in his everyday life, in his work and in his relationships, he has become a *species-being*; and when he has recognized and organized his own powers (*forces propres*) as *social* powers so that he no longer separates this social power from himself as *political* power.

The relation of man to woman is the *most natural* relation of human being to human being. It indicates, therefore, how far man's *natural* behaviour has become *human*, and how far his *human* essence has become a *natural* essence for him, how far his *human nature* has become *nature* for him. It also shows how far man's needs have become *human* needs, and consequently how far the other person, as a person, has become one of his needs, and to what extent he is in his individual existence at the same time a social being. The first positive annulment of private property, crude communism, is, therefore, only a *phenomenal form* of the infamy of private property representing itself as positive community.

Communism (*a*) still political in nature, democratic or despotic; (*b*) with the abolition of the state, yet still incomplete and influenced by private property, that is, by the alienation of man. In both forms communism is already aware of being the reintegration of man, his return to himself, the supersession of man's self-alienation. But since it has not yet grasped the positive nature of private property, or the *human* nature of needs, it is still captured and contaminated by private property. It has well understood the concept, but not the essence.

Communism is the *positive* abolition of *private property*, of *human self-alienation* and thus the real *appropriation* of *human* nature through and for man. It is, therefore, the return of man himself as a *social*, i.e. really human, being, a complete and conscious return which assimilates all the wealth of previous development. Communism as a fully developed naturalism is humanism and as a fully developed humanism is naturalism. It is the *definitive* resolution of the antagonism between man and nature, and between man and man. It is the true solution of the conflict between existence and essence, between objectification and self-affirmation, between freedom and necessity, between individual and species. It is the solution of the riddle of history and knows itself to be this solution.

When communist *artisans* form associations, teaching and propaganda are their first aims. But their association itself creates a new need – the need for society – and what appeared to be a means has become an end. The most striking results of this practical development are to be seen when French socialist workers meet together. Smoking, eating and drinking are no longer simply means of bringing people together. Society, association, entertainment which also has society as its aim, is sufficient for them; the brotherhood of man is no empty phrase but a reality, and the nobility of man shines forth upon us from their toil-worn bodies.

Money, then, appears as a *disruptive* power for the individual and for the social bonds, which claim to be self-subsistent *entities*. It changes fidelity into infidelity, love into hate, hate into love, virtue into vice, vice into virtue, servant into master, stupidity into intelligence and intelligence into stupidity.

Let us assume *man* to be *man*, and his relation to the world to be a human one. Then love can only be exchanged for love, trust for trust, etc. If you wish to enjoy art you must be an artistically cultivated person; if you wish to influence other people you must be a person who really has a stimulating and encouraging effect upon others. Every one of your relations to man and to nature must be a *specific expression*, corresponding to the object of your will, of your *real individual* life. If you love without evoking love in return, i.e. if you are not able, by the *manifestation* of yourself as a loving person, to make yourself a *beloved person*, then your love is impotent and a misfortune.

Early Writings (1844), ed. T. B. Bottomore (London, Watts, 1963), pp. 31, 154–5, 176, 193–4.

... the division of labour offers us the first example of how, as long as man remains in natural society, that is, as long as a cleavage exists between the particular and the common interest, as long, therefore, as activity is not voluntarily, but naturally, divided, man's own deed becomes an alien power opposed to him, which enslaves him instead of being controlled by him. For as soon as the distribution of labour comes into being, each man has a particular, exclusive sphere of activity, which is forced upon him and from which he cannot escape. He is a hunter, a fisherman, a shepherd or a critical critic, and must remain so if he does not want to lose his means of livelihood; while in communist society, where nobody has one exclusive sphere of activity but each can become accomplished in any branch he wishes, society regulates the general production and thus makes it possible for me to do one thing today and another tomorrow, to hunt in the morning, fish in the afternoon, rear cattle in the evening, criticize after dinner, just as I have a mind, without ever becoming hunter, fisherman, shepherd or critic. This fixation of social activity, this consolidation of what we ourselves produce into an objective power above us, growing out of our control, thwarting our expectations, bringing to naught our calculations, is one of the chief factors in historical development up till now.

The transformation, through the division of labour, of personal powers (relationships) into material powers, cannot be dispelled by dismissing the general idea of it from one's mind, but can only be abolished by the individuals again subjecting these material powers to themselves and abolishing the division of labour. This is not possible without the community. Only in community [with others has each] individual the means of cultivating his gifts in all directions; only in the community, therefore, is personal freedom possible. In the previous substitutes for the community, in the State, etc., personal freedom has existed only for the individuals who developed within the relationships of the ruling class, and only in so far as they were individuals of this class. The illusory community, in which individuals have up till now combined, always took on an independent existence in relation to them, and was at the same time, since it was the combination of one class over against another, not only a completely illusory community, but a new fetter as well. In the real community the individuals obtain their freedom in and through their association.

The exclusive concentration of artistic talent in particular individuals, and its suppression in the broad mass which is bound up with this, is a consequence of division of labour. If, even in certain social conditions, everyone was an excellent painter, that would not at all exclude the possibility of each of them being also an original painter, so that here too the difference between 'human' and 'unique' labour amounts to sheer nonsense. In any case, with a communist organization of society, there disappears the subordination of the artist to local and national narrowness, which arises entirely from division of labour, and also the subordination of the artist to some definite art, thanks to which he is exclusively a painter, sculptor, etc., the very name of his activity adequately expressing the narrowness of his professional development and his dependence on division of labour. In a communist society there are no painters but at most people who engage in painting among other activities.

The German Ideology (1845) (Moscow, Progress Publishers, 1964), pp. 44–5, 91–2, 431–2.

The standpoint of the old materialism is civil society; the standpoint of the new is human society, or social humanity.

Tenth *Thesis on Feuerbach* (1845), in ibid., p. 647.

The distinguishing feature of Communism is not the abolition of property generally, but the abolition of bourgeois property. But modern bourgeois private property is the final and most complete expression of the system of producing and appropriating products, that is based on class antagonisms, on the exploitation of the many by the few.

In this sense, the theory of the Communists may be summed up in the single sentence: Abolition of private property.

In bourgeois society, living labour is but a means to increase accumulated labour. In Communist society, accumulated labour is but a means to widen, to enrich, to promote the existence of the labourer.

In bourgeois society, therefore, the past dominates the present; in Communist society, the present dominates the past. In bourgeois society capital is independent and has individuality, while the living person is dependent and has no individuality.

And the abolition of this state of things is called by the bourgeois, abolition of individuality and freedom! And rightly so. The abolition of bourgeois individuality, bourgeois independence and bourgeois freedom is undoubtedly aimed at.

By freedom is meant, under the present bourgeois conditions of production, free trade, free selling and buying.

Communism deprives no man of the power to appropriate the products of society; all that it does is to deprive him of the power to subjugate the labour of others by means of such appropriation.

Abolition of the family! Even the most radical flare up at this infamous proposal of the Communists.

On what foundation is the present family, the bourgeois family, based? On capital, on private gain. In its completely developed form this family exists only among the bourgeoisie. But this state of things finds its complement in the practical absence of the family among the proletarians, and in public prostitution.

The bourgeois family will vanish as a matter of course when its complement vanishes, and both will vanish with the vanishing of capital.

Do you charge us with wanting to stop the exploitation of children by their parents? To this crime we plead guilty.

But, you will say, we destroy the most hallowed of relations, when we replace home education by social.

And your education! Is not that also social, and determined by the social conditions under which you educate, by the intervention, direct or indirect, of society, by means of schools, etc.? The Communists have not invented the intervention of society in education; they do but seek to alter the character of that intervention, and to rescue education from the influence of the ruling class.

Bourgeois marriage is in reality a system of wives in common and thus, at the most, what the Communists might possibly be reproached with, is that they desire to introduce, in substitution for a hypocritically concealed, an openly legalized community of women. For the rest, it is self-evident that the abolition of the present system of production must bring with it the abolition of the community of women springing from that system, i.e., of prostitution both public and private.

The Communists are further reproached with desiring to abolish countries and nationality.

The working men have no country. We cannot take from them what they have not got. Since the proletariat must first of all acquire political supremacy, must rise to be the leading class of the nation, must constitute itself *the* nation, it is, so far, itself national, though not in the bourgeois sense of the word.

National differences and antagonisms between peoples are daily more and more vanishing, owing to the development of the bourgeoisie, to freedom of commerce, to the world-market, to uniformity in the mode of production and in the conditions of life corresponding thereto.

The supremacy of the proletariat will cause them to vanish still faster. United action, of the leading civilized countries at least, is one of the first conditions for the emancipation of the proletariat.

In proportion as the exploitation of one individual by another is put an end to, the exploitation of one nation by another will also be put an end to. In proportion as the antagonism between classes within the nation vanishes, the hostility of one nation to another will come to an end.

The Communist revolution is the most radical rupture with traditional property relations; no wonder that its development involves the most radical rupture with traditional ideas.

When, in the course of development, class distinctions have disappeared, and all production has been concentrated in the hands of a vast association of the whole nation, the public power will lose its political character. Political power, properly so called, is merely the organized power of one class for oppressing another. If the proletariat during its contest with the bourgeoisie is compelled, by the force of circumstances, to organize itself as a class, if, by means of a revolution, it makes itself the ruling class, and, as such, sweeps away by force the old conditions of production, then it will, along with these conditions, have swept away the conditions for the existence of class antagonisms and of classes generally, and will thereby have abolished its own supremacy as a class.

In place of the old bourgeois society, with its classes and class antagonisms, we shall have an association, in which the free development of each is the condition for the free development of all.

'Communist Manifesto' (1848), in Marx–Engels, *Selected Works* (Moscow, Foreign Languages Publishing House, 1962), vol. I, pp. 47–54.

We have seen how this absolute contradiction between the technical necessities of Modern Industry, and the social character inherent in its capitalistic form, dispels all fixity and security in the situation of the labourer; how it constantly threatens, by taking away the instruments of labour, to snatch from his hands his means of subsistence,[1] and, by suppressing his detail-function, to make him superfluous. We have seen, too, how this antagonism vents its rage in the creation of that monstrosity, an industrial reserve army, kept in misery in order to be always at the disposal of capital; in the incessant human sacrifices from among the working-class, in the most reckless squandering of labour-power, and in the devastation caused by a social anarchy which turns every economical progress into a social calamity. This is the negative side. But if, on the one hand, variation of work at present imposes itself after the manner of an overpowering natural law, and with the blindly destructive action of a natural law that meets with resistance[2] at all points, Modern Industry,

[1] 'You take my life
    When you do take the means whereby I live.' SHAKESPEARE.
[2] A French workman, on his return from San-Francisco, writes as follows: 'I never could have believed, that I was capable of working at the various occupations I was employed on in California. I was firmly convinced that I was fit for nothing but letter-press printing. . . . Once in the midst of this world of adventurers, who change their occupation as often as they do their shirt, egad, I did as the others. As mining did not turn out remunerative enough, I left it for the town, where in succession I became typographer, slater, plumber, etc. In consequence of thus finding out that I am fit for any sort of work, I feel less of a mollusk and more of a man.' (A. Courbon, *De l'enseignement professionnel*, 2ème ed., p. 50.)

on the other hand, through its catastrophes imposes the necessity of recognizing, as a fundamental law of production, variation of work, consequently fitness of the labourer for varied work, consequently the greatest possible development of his varied aptitudes. It becomes a question of life and death for society to adapt the mode of production to the normal functioning of this law. Modern Industry, indeed, compels society, under penalty of death, to replace the detail-worker of today, crippled by life-long repetition of one and the same trivial operation, and thus reduced to the mere fragment of a man, by the fully developed individual, fit for a variety of labours, ready to face any change of production, and to whom the different social functions he performs, are but so many modes of giving free scope to his own natural and acquired powers.

One step already spontaneously taken towards effecting this revolution is the establishment of technical and agricultural schools, and of 'écoles d'enseignement professionnel', in which the children of the working-men receive some little instruction in technology and in the practical handling of the various implements of labour. Though the Factory Act, that first and meagre concession wrung from capital, is limited to combining elementary education with work in the factory, there can be no doubt that when the working class comes into power, as inevitably it must, technical instruction, both theoretical and practical, will take its proper place in the working-class schools. There is also no doubt that such revolutionary ferments, the final result of which is the abolition of the old division of labour, are diametrically opposed to the capitalistic form of production, and to the economic status of the labourer corresponding to that form. But the historical development of the antagonisms, immanent in a given form of production, is the only way in which that form of production can be dissolved and a new form established.

However terrible and disgusting the dissolution, under the capitalist system, of the old family ties may appear, nevertheless, modern industry, by assigning as it does an important part in the process of production, outside the domestic sphere, to women, to young persons and to children of both sexes, creates a new economical foundation for a higher form of the family and of the relations between the sexes. It is, of course, just as absurd to hold the Teutonic-christian form of the family to be absolute and final as it would be to apply that character to the ancient Roman, the ancient Greek or the Eastern forms which, moreover, taken together form a series in historic development. Moreover, it is obvious that the fact of the collective working group being composed of individuals of both sexes and all ages, must necessarily, under suitable conditions, become a source of humane development; although in its spontaneously developed, brutal, capitalistic form, where the labourer exists for the process of production, and not the process of production for the labourer, that fact is a pestiferous source of corruption and slavery.

In fact, the realm of freedom actually begins only where labour which is determined by necessity and mundane considerations ceases; thus, in the very nature of things it lies beyond the sphere of actual material production. Just as the savage must wrestle with Nature to satisfy his wants, to maintain and reproduce life, so must civilized man, and he must do so in all social formations and under all possible modes of production. With his development this realm of physical necessity expands as a result of his wants; but, at the same time, the forces of production which satisfy these wants also increase. Freedom in this field can only consist in socialized man, the associated producers, rationally regulating their interchange with Nature, bringing it under their common control, instead of being ruled by it as by the blind forces of Nature; and achieving this with the least expenditure of energy and under conditions most favourable to, and worthy of, their human nature. But it nonetheless still remains a realm of necessity. Beyond it begins that development of human energy which is an end in itself, the true realm of freedom, which, however, can blossom forth only with this realm of necessity as its basis. The shortening of the working-day is its basic prerequisite.

> *Capital* (1867–79), vol. I (1867) (London, Glaisher, 1912), pp. 493–4, 496, and vol. III (first published 1893–4) (Moscow, Foreign Languages Publishing House, 1962), pp. 799–800.

The direct antithesis to the empire was the Commune. The cry of 'social republic', with which the revolution of February was ushered in by the Paris proletariat, did but express a vague aspiration after a Republic that was not only to supersede the monarchical form of class rule, but class rule itself. The Commune was the positive form of that Republic.

Paris, the central seat of the old governmental power, and, at the same time, the social stronghold of the French working class, had risen in arms against the attempt of Thiers, and the Rurals to restore and perpetuate that old governmental power bequeathed to them by the empire. Paris could resist only because, in consequence of the siege, it had got rid of the army, and replaced it by a National Guard, the bulk of which consisted of working men. This fact was now to be transformed into an institution. The first decree of the Commune, therefore, was the suppression of the standing army, and the substitution for it of the armed people.

The Commune was formed of the municipal councillors, chosen by universal suffrage in the various wards of the town, responsible and revocable at short terms. The majority of its members were naturally working men, or acknowledged representatives of the working class. The Commune was to be a working, not a parliamentary, body, executive and legislative at the same time. Instead of continuing to be the agent of the Central Government, the police was at once stripped of its political attributes, and turned into the responsible and at all times revocable agent of the Commune. So were the officials of all other branches of the Administration. From the members of the Commune downwards, the public service had to be done at *workmen's wages*. The vested interests and the representation allowances of the high dignitaries of State disappeared along with the high dignitaries themselves. Public functions ceased to be the private property of the tools of the Central Government. Not only municipal administration, but the whole initiative hitherto exercised by the State was laid into the hands of the Commune.

Having once got rid of the standing army and the police, the physical force elements of the old Government, the Commune was anxious to break the spiritual force of repression, the 'parson-power', by the disestablishment and disendowment of all churches as proprietary bodies. The priests were sent back to the recesses of private life, there to feed upon the alms of the faithful in imitation of their predecessors, the Apostles. The whole of the educational institutions were opened to the people gratuitously, and at the same time cleared of all interference of Church and State. Thus, not only was education made accessible to all, but science itself freed from the fetters which class prejudice and governmental force had imposed upon it.

The judicial functionaries were to be divested of that sham independence which had but served to mask their abject subserviency to all succeeding governments to which, in turn, they had taken, and broken, the oaths of allegiance. Like the rest of public servants, magistrates and judges were to be elective, responsible and revocable.

The Paris Commune was, of course, to serve as a model to all the great industrial centres of France. The communal *régime* once established in Paris and the secondary centres, the old centralized Government would in the provinces, too, have to give way to the self-government of the producers. In a rough sketch of national organization which the Commune had no time to develop, it states clearly that the Commune was to be the political form of even the smallest country hamlet, and that in the rural districts the standing army was to be replaced by a national militia, with an extremely short term of service. The rural communes of every district were to administer their common affairs by an assembly of delegates in the central town, and these district assemblies were again to send deputies to the National Delegation in Paris, each delegate to be at any time revocable and bound by the *mandat impératif* (formal instructions) of his constituents. The few but important functions which still would remain for a central government were not to be suppressed, as has been intentionally mis-stated, but were to be discharged by Communal, and therefore strictly responsible agents. The unity of the nation was not to be broken, but, on the contrary, to be organized by the Communal Constitution and to become a reality by the destruction of the State power which claimed to be the embodiment of that unity independent of, and superior to, the nation itself, from which it was but a parasitic excrescence. While the merely repressive organs of the old governmental power were to be amputated, its legitimate functions were to be wrested from an authority usurping pre-eminence over society itself, and restored to the responsible agents of society. Instead of deciding once in three or six years which member of the ruling class was to misrepresent the people in Parliament, universal suffrage was to serve the people, constituted in Communes, as individual suffrage serves every other employer in the search for the workmen and managers in his business. And it is well known that companies, like individuals, in matters of real business generally know how to put the right man in the right place, and, if they for once make a mistake, to redress it promptly. On the other hand, nothing could be more foreign to the spirit of the Commune than to supersede universal suffrage by hierarchic investiture.

It is generally the fate of completely new historical creations to be mistaken for the counterpart of older and even defunct forms of social life, to which they may bear a certain likeness. Thus, this new Commune, which breaks the modern State power, has been mistaken for a reproduction of the medieval Communes, which first preceded, and afterwards became the substratum of, that very State power. The Communal Constitution has been mistaken for an attempt to break up into a federation of small States, as dreamt of by Montesquieu and the Girondins, that unity of great nations which, if originally brought about by political force, has now become a powerful coefficient of social production. The antagonism of the Commune against the State power has been mistaken for an exaggerated form of the ancient struggle against over-centralization. Peculiar historical circumstances may have prevented the classical development, as in France, of the bourgeois form of government, and may have allowed, as in England, to complete the great central State organs by corrupt vestries, jobbing councillors and ferocious poor-law guardians in the towns, and virtually hereditary magistrates in the counties. The Communal Constitution would have restored to the social body all the forces hitherto absorbed by the State parasite feeding upon, and clogging the free movement of, society. By this one act it would have initiated the regeneration of France. The provincial French middle class saw in the Commune an attempt to restore the sway their order had held over the country under Louis Philippe, and which, under Louis Napoleon, was supplanted by the pretended rule of the country over the towns. In reality, the Communal Constitution brought the rural producers under the intellectual lead of the central towns of their districts, and these secured to them, in the working men, the natural trustees of their interests. The very existence of the Commune involved, as a matter of course, local municipal liberty, but no longer as a check upon the, now superseded, State power. It could only enter into the head of a Bismarck, who, when not engaged on his intrigues of blood and iron, always likes to resume his old trade, so befitting his mental calibre, of contributor to *Kladderadatsch*[1] (the Berlin *Punch*), it could only enter into such a head, to ascribe to the Paris Commune aspirations after that caricature of the old French municipal organization of 1791, the Prussian municipal constitution which degrades the town governments to mere secondary wheels in the police-machinery of the Prussian State. The Commune made that catchword of bourgeois revolutions, cheap government, a reality, by destroying the two greatest sources of expenditure – the standing army and State functionarism. Its very existence presupposed the non-existence of monarchy, which, in Europe at least, is the normal incumbrance and indispensable cloak of class-rule. It supplied the Republic with the basis of really democratic institutions. But neither cheap

[1] *Kladderadatsch:* German satirical journal which began to appear in Berlin in 1848.

Government nor the 'true Republic' was its ultimate aim; they were its mere concomitants.

The multiplicity of interpretations to which the Commune has been subjected, and the multiplicity of interests which construed it in their favour, show that it was a thoroughly expansive political form, while all previous forms of government had been emphatically repressive. Its true secret was this. It was essentially a working-class government, the produce of the struggle of the producing against the appropriating class, the political form at last discovered under which to work out the economic emancipation of labour.

Except on this last condition, the Communal Constitution would have been an impossibility and a delusion. The political rule of the producer cannot coexist with the perpetuation of his social slavery. The Commune was therefore to serve as a lever for uprooting the economical foundations upon which rests the existence of classes, and therefore of class-rule. With labour emancipated, every man becomes a working man, and productive labour ceases to be a class attribute.

It is a strange fact. In spite of all the tall talk and all the immense literature, for the last sixty years, about Emancipation of Labour, no sooner do the working men anywhere take the subject into their own hands with a will, than uprises at once all the apologetic phraseology of the mouthpieces of present society with its two poles of Capital and Wages Slavery (the landlord now is but the sleeping partner of the capitalist), as if capitalist society was still in its purest state of virgin innocence, with its antagonisms still undeveloped, with its delusions still unexploded, with its prostitute realities not yet laid bare. The Commune, they exclaim, intends to abolish property, the basis of all civilization! Yes, gentlemen, the Commune intended to abolish that class-property which makes the labour of the many the wealth of the few. It aimed at the expropriation of the expropriators. It wanted to make individual property a truth by transforming the means of production, land and capital, now chiefly the means of enslaving and exploiting labour, into mere instruments of free and associated labour. – But this is Communism, 'impossible' Communism! Why, those members of the ruling classes who are intelligent enough to perceive the impossibility of continuing the present system – and they are many – have become the obtrusive and full-mouthed apostles of co-operative production. If co-operative production is not to remain a sham and a snare; if it is to supersede the Capitalist system; if united co-operative societies are to regulate national production upon a common plan, thus taking it under their own control, and putting an end to the constant anarchy and periodical convulsions which are the fatality of Capitalist production – what else, gentlemen, would it be but Communism, 'possible' Communism?

The working class did not expect miracles from the Commune. They have no ready-made utopias to introduce *par décret du peuple*. They know that in order to work out their own emancipation, and along with it that higher form to which present society is irresistibly tending by its own economical agencies, they will have to pass through long struggles, through a series of historic processes, transforming circumstances and men. They have no ideals to realize, but to set free the elements of the new society with which old collapsing bourgeois society itself is pregnant.

'The Civil War in France' (1871), in Marx–Engels, *Selected Works* (Moscow, Foreign Languages Publishing House, 1962), vol. I, pp. 518–23.

In a higher phase of communist society, after the enslaving subordination of the individual to the division of labour, and therewith also the antithesis between mental and physical labour, has vanished; after labour has become not only a means of life but life's prime want; after the productive forces have also increased with the all-round development of the individual, and all the springs of co-operative wealth flow more abundantly – only then can the narrow horizon of bourgeois right be crossed in its entirety and society inscribe on its banners: From each according to his ability, to each according to his needs!

'Critique of the Gotha Programme' (1875), in ibid., vol. II, p. 24.

Friedrich Engels
(1820–1895)

THE ASCENT TO THE KINGDOM
OF FREEDOM

Whilst the capitalist mode of production more and more completely transforms the great majority of the population into proletarians, it creates the power which, under penalty of its own destruction, is forced to accomplish this revolution. Whilst it forces on more and more the transformation of the vast means of production, already socialized, into state property, it shows itself the way to accomplishing this revolution. *The proletariat seizes political power and turns the means of production into state property.*

But, in doing this, it abolishes itself as proletariat, abolishes all class distinctions and class antagonisms, abolishes also the state as state. Society thus far, based upon class antagonisms, had need of the state. That is, of an organization of the particular class which was *pro tempore* the exploiting class, an organization for the purpose of preventing any interference from without with the existing conditions of production, and, therefore, especially, for the purpose of forcibly keeping the exploited classes in the condition of oppression corresponding with the given mode of production (slavery, serfdom, wage-labour). The state was the official representative of society as a whole; the gathering of it together into a visible embodiment. But it was this only in so far as it was the state of that class which itself represented, for the time being, society as a whole: in ancient times, the state of slaveowning citizens; in the Middle Ages, the feudal lords; in our own time, the bourgeoisie. When at last it becomes the real representative of the whole of society, it renders itself unneccessary. As soon as there is no longer any social class to be held in subjection; as soon as class-rule and the individual struggle for existence based upon our present anarchy in production, with the collisions and excesses arising from these, are removed, nothing more remains to be repressed, and a special repressive force, a state, is no longer necessary. The first act by virtue of which the state really constitutes itself the representative of the whole of society – the taking possession of the means of production in the name of society – this is, at the same time, its last independent act as a state. State interference in social relations becomes, in one domain after another, superfluous, and then dies out of itself; the government of persons is replaced by the administration of things, and by the conduct of processes of production. The state is not 'abolished'. *It dies out*. This gives the measure of the value of the phrase '*a free state*', both as to its justifiable use at times by agitators, and as to its ultimate scientific insufficiency; and also of the demands of the so-called anarchists for the abolition of the state out of hand.

Since the historical appearance of the capitalist mode of production, the appropriation by society of all the means of production has often been dreamed of, more or less vaguely, by individuals, as well as by sects, as the ideal of the future. But it could become possible, could become a historical necessity, only when the actual conditions for its realization were there. Like every other social advance, it becomes practicable, not by men understanding that the existence of classes is in contradiction to justice, equality, etc., not by the mere willingness to abolish these classes, but by virtue of certain new economic conditions. The separation of society into an exploiting and an exploited class, a ruling and an oppressed class, was the necessary consequence of the deficient and restricted development of production in former times. So long as the total social labour only yields a produce which but slightly exceeds that barely necessary for the existence of all; so long, therefore, as labour engages all or almost all the time of the great majority of the members of society – so long, of necessity, this society is divided into classes. Side by side with the great majority, exclusively bond slaves to labour, arises a class freed from directly productive labour, which looks after the general affairs of society: the direction of labour, state business, law, science, art, etc. It is, therefore, the law of division of labour that lies at the basis of the division into classes. But this does not prevent this division into classes from being carried out by means of violence and robbery, trickery and fraud. It does not prevent the ruling class, once having the upper hand, from consolidating its power at the expense of the working class, from turning its social leadership into an intensified exploitation of the masses.

But if, upon this showing, division into classes has a certain historical justification, it has this only for a given period, only under given social conditions. It was based upon the insufficiency of production. It will be swept away by the complete development of modern productive forces.

And, in fact, the abolition of classes in society presupposes a degree of historical evolution at which the existence, not simply of this or that particular ruling class, but of any ruling class at all, and, therefore, the existence of class distinction itself has become an obsolete anachronism. It presupposes, therefore, the development of production carried out to a degree at which appropriation of the means of production and of the products, and, with this, of political domination, of the monopoly of culture, and of intellectual leadership by a particular class of society, had become not only superfluous but economically, politically, intellectually, a hindrance to development.

This point is now reached. Their political and intellectual bankruptcy is scarcely any longer a secret to the bourgeoisie themselves. Their economic bankruptcy recurs regularly every ten years. In every crisis, society is suffocated beneath the weight of its own productive forces and products, which it cannot use, and stands helpless, face to face with the absurd contradiction that the producers have nothing to consume, because consumers are wanting. The expansive force of the means of production bursts the bonds that the capitalist mode of production had imposed upon them. Their deliverance from these bonds is the one precondition for an unbroken, constantly accelerated development of the productive forces, and therewith for a practically unlimited increase of production itself. Nor is this all. The socialized appropriation of the means of production does away, not only with the present artificial restrictions upon production, but also with the positive waste and devastation of productive forces and products that are at the present time the inevitable concomitants of production, and that reach their height in the crises. Further, it sets free for the community at large a mass of means of production and of products, by doing away with the senseless extravagance of the ruling classes of today and their political representatives. The possibility of securing for every member of society, by means of socialized production, an existence not only fully sufficient materially, and becoming day by day more full, but an existence guaranteeing to all the free development and exercise of their physical and mental faculties – this possibility is now for the first time here, but *it is here*.

With the seizing of the means of production by society, production of commodities is done away with, and, simultaneously, the mastery of the product over the producer. Anarchy in social production is replaced by systematic, definite organization. The struggle for individual existence disappears. Then for the first time man, in a certain sense, is finally marked off from the rest of the animal kingdom, and emerges from mere animal conditions of existence into really human ones. The whole sphere of the conditions of life which environ man, and which have hitherto ruled man, now comes under the dominion and control of man, who for the first time becomes the real, conscious lord of Nature, because he has now become master of his own social organization. The laws of his own social action, hitherto standing face to face with man as laws of Nature foreign to, and dominating him, will then be used with full understanding, and so mastered by him. Man's own social organization, hitherto confronting him as a necessity imposed by Nature and history, now becomes the result of his own free action. The extraneous objective forces that have hitherto governed history pass under the control of man himself. Only from that time will man himself, more and more consciously, make his own history – only from that time will the social causes set in movement by him have, in the main and in a constantly growing measure, the results intended by him. It is the ascent of man from the kingdom of necessity to the kingdom of freedom.

'Socialism: Utopian and Scientific' (1880), trans. in Marx–Engels, *Selected Works* (Moscow, Foreign Languages Publishing House, 1962), vol. II, pp. 150–3.

Herbert Spencer
(1820–1903)

PERFECT INDIVIDUATION AND MUTUAL DEPENDENCE

To possess a greater variety of senses, of instincts, of powers, of qualities – to be more complex in character and attributes, is to be more completely distinguishable from all other created things; or to exhibit a more marked individuality. For, manifestly, as there are some properties which all entities, organic and inorganic, have in common, namely, weight, mobility, inertia, etc.; and as there are additional properties which all organic entities have in common, namely, powers of growth and multiplication; and as there are yet further properties which the higher organic entities have in common, namely sight, hearing, etc.; then those still higher organic entities possessing characteristics not shared in by the rest, thereby differ from a larger number of entities than the rest, and differ in more points – that is, are more separate, more individual. Observe, again, that the greater power of self-preservation shown by beings of superior type may also be generalized under this same term – a 'tendency to individuation'. The lower the organism, the more is it at the mercy of external circumstances. It is continually liable to be destroyed by the elements, by want of food, by enemies; and eventually is so destroyed in nearly all cases. That is, it lacks power to preserve its individuality; and loses this, either by returning to the form of inorganic matter, or by absorption into some other individuality. Conversely, where there is strength, sagacity, swiftness (all of them indicative of superior structure), there is corresponding ability to maintain life – to prevent the individuality from being so easily dissolved; and therefore the individuation is more complete.

In man we see the highest manifestation of this tendency. By virtue of his complexity of structure, he is furthest removed from the inorganic world in which there is least individuality. Again, his intelligence and adaptability commonly enable him to maintain life to old age – to complete the cycle of his existence; that is, to fill out the limits of this individuality to the full. Again, he is self-conscious; that is, he recognizes his own individuality. And, as lately shown, even the change observable in human affairs, is still toward a greater development of individuality – may still be described as 'a tendency to individuation'.

But note lastly, and note chiefly, as being the fact to which the foregoing sketch is introductory, that what we call the moral law – the law of equal freedom, is the law under which individuation becomes perfect; and that ability to recognize and act up to this law, is the final endowment of humanity – an endowment now in process of evolution. The increasing assertion of personal rights, is an increasing demand that the external conditions needful to a complete unfolding of the individuality shall be respected. Not only is there now a consciousness of individuality, and an intelligence whereby individuality may be preserved; but there is a perception that the sphere of action requisite for due development of the individuality may be claimed; and a correlative desire to claim it. And when the change at present going on is complete – when each possesses an active instinct of freedom, together with an active sympathy – then will all the still existing limitations to individuality, be they governmental restraints, or be they the aggressions of men on one another, cease. Then, none will be hindered from duly unfolding their natures; for whilst every one maintains his own claims, he will respect the like claims of others. Then, there will no longer be legislative restrictions and legislative burdens; for by the same process these will have become both needless and impossible. Then, for the first time in the history of the world, will there exist beings whose individualities can be expanded to the full in all directions. And thus, as before said, in the ultimate man perfect morality, perfect individuation and perfect life will be simultaneously realized.

Yet must this highest individuation be joined with the greatest mutual dependence. Paradoxical though the assertion looks, the progress is at once toward complete separateness and complete union. But the separateness is of a kind consistent with the most complex combinations for fulfilling social wants; and the union is of a kind that does not hinder entire development of each personality. Civilization is evolving a state of things and a kind of character, in which two apparently conflicting requirements are reconciled. To achieve the creative purpose – the greatest sum of happiness, there must on the one hand exist an amount of population maintainable only by the best possible system of production; that is, by the most elaborate subdivision of labour; that is, by the extremest mutual dependence: whilst on the other hand, each individual must have the opportunity to do whatever his desires prompt. Clearly these two conditions can be harmonized only by that adaptation humanity is under-going – that process during which all desires inconsistent with the most perfect social organization are dying out, and other desires corresponding to such an organization are being developed. How this will eventuate in producing at once perfect individuation and perfect mutual dependence, may not be at once obvious. But probably an illustration will sufficiently elucidate the matter. Here are certain domestic affections, which can be gratified only by the establishment of relationships with other beings. In the absence of those beings, and the consequent dormancy of the feelings with which they are regarded, life is incomplete – the individuality is shorn of its fair proportions. Now as the normal unfolding of the conjugal and parental elements of the individuality depends on having a family, so, when civilization becomes complete, will the normal unfolding of all other elements of the individuality depend upon the existence of the civilized state. Just that kind of individuality will be acquired which finds in the most highly-organized community the fittest sphere for its manifes-tation – which finds in each social arrangement a condition answering to some faculty in itself – which could not, in fact, expand at all, if otherwise circumstanced. The ultimate man will be one whose private requirements coincide with public ones. He will be that manner of man, who, in spon-taneously fulfilling his own nature, incidentally performs the functions of a social unit; and yet is only enabled so to fulfil his own nature, by all others doing the like.

Social Statics (1850) (London, Williams & Norgate, 1868), pp. 480–3.

SALVATION WILL COME FROM THE PEOPLE

Know, learned professor, that social and civic ideals, as such, in so far as they are not organically connected with moral ideals, but exist by themselves like a separate half cut off from the whole by your learned knife; in so far, finally, as they may be taken from the outside and successfully transplanted to any other place, in so far as they are a separate 'institution' – such ideals, I say, neither have nor have had nor ever could have any existence at all! For what is a social ideal and how shall we understand the word? Surely its essence lies in men's aspiration to find a formula of political organization for themselves, a possible organization which shall be faultless and satisfactory to all – is it not so? But people do not know the formula. Though they have been searching for it through the six thousand years of history, they cannot find it. The ant knows the formula of the ant-hill, the bee of the hive – though they do not know it after the manner of human knowledge, they know it in their own way and desire nothing beyond – but man does not know his formula. If this be so, whence could the ideal of civic organization appear in human society? Examine the question historically and you will immediately see whence it comes. You will see that it is nothing else than the product of the moral self-perfection of the individual units. Thence it takes its rise, and it has been so from time immemorial and it will be so for ever and ever. In the origin of any people or any nation, the moral idea has always preceded the birth of the nation, because it was the moral idea which created the nation. This moral idea always issued forth from mystical ideas, from the conviction that man is eternal, that he is more than an earth-born animal, that he is united to other worlds and to eternity. Those convictions have always and everywhere been formulated into a religion, into a confession of a new idea, and always so soon as a new religion began, a new nationality was also created immediately. Consider the Jews and the Moslems. The Jewish nationality was formed only after the law of Moses, though it began with the law of Abraham, and the Moslem nationalities appeared only after the Koran. In order to preserve the spiritual treasures they had received men instantly began to draw towards each other, and only then, jealously and avidly, working 'beside one another, for one another, and with one another', as you so eloquently express it, only then did men begin to seek how they should organize themselves so as to preserve without loss the treasures they had received, how they should find a civic formula of common life that would really help them to exhibit in its full glory to the whole world the moral treasure which they had received.

And observe that so soon as the spiritual ideal – after times and centuries had passed – had begun to be shaken and weakened in a particular nationality, the nationality itself also began to decline, and at the same time her civic organization began to fall and all the civic ideals which had formed in her began to be obscured. According to the mould in which a nation's religion was being cast, the social forms of the people were also engendered and formulated. Therefore civic ideals are always directly and organically connected with moral ideas, and generally the former are created by the latter alone. They never appear *of themselves*, for when they appear they have one aim alone, the satisfaction of the moral aspirations of the particular people to the exact degree to which those moral aspirations are being formed. Therefore 'self-perfection in the spirit of religion' in the life of nations is the foundation of everything, since self-perfection is *the confession of the religion which they have received*, and 'civic ideals' never appear nor can they be engendered without the aspiration to self-perfection. You will perhaps reply that you yourself said that 'personal self-perfection is the beginning of everything' and that you severed nothing at all with your knife. But this is the very thing that you severed; you cut the living organism into two halves. Self-perfection is not only 'the beginning of everything', it is the continuation and the issue as well. It, and it alone, includes, creates and preserves the organism of nationality. For its sake does the civic formula of a nation live, since it was created only in order to preserve it as the treasure primarily received. But when a nationality begins to lose the desire within itself for a common self-perfection of its individuals *in the spirit which gave it birth*, then all the 'civic institutions' gradually perish, because there is nothing left to be preserved. Thus it is quite impossible to say what you say in the following phrase:

'That is why the social perfection of a people very greatly depends upon the degree of perfection of their political institutions, which educate in man the civic, if not the Christian virtues.'

'The civic, if not the Christian virtues'! Can you not see here the learned knife which divides the indivisible, which cuts the whole and living organism into two separate, dead halves, the moral and the civic? You will say that the most lofty moral idea may be contained in 'political institutions' and the title of 'citizen', that in mature and developed nations the 'civic idea' always takes the place of the original religious idea, which degenerates into the former, and to which the civic idea succeeds by right. Yes, there are many who assert this thing; but we have not yet seen this dream in realization. When the moral and religious idea of a nationality is spent, there is always revealed a panic and cowardly desire for a union, whose sole purpose is 'to save men's bellies' – there are no other purposes left for a civic union. At the present moment the French bourgeoisie is actually uniting itself with this purpose 'of saving their bellies' from the fourth estate which is already battering at its doors. But 'the saving of bellies' is the last and most impotent idea of all those which unite mankind. This is already the beginning of the end, the omen of annihilation. They are uniting themselves and keeping a sharp eye open for the first moment of danger when they will scatter like lightning. And what can save 'the institution' as such, taken by itself? If these are brothers, there will be brotherhood. If there are no brothers, you will not achieve brotherhood by any 'institution'. What is the sense of erecting an 'institution' and carving upon it *Liberté, Égalité, Fraternité*? You will get no good from an 'institution' and you will be driven, necessarily and infallibly you will be driven, to add to the three *constituant* words the fourth also: *ou la mort. Fraternité ou la mort*: and brother will begin to chop off the head of brother in order to attain brotherhood by means of a 'civic institution'. This is only an example, but it is a good one.

You, M. Gradovsky, like Aleko, look for salvation in things and in eternal phenomena. Grant that we have fools and rogues in Russia. We have only to transplant some institution from Europe and – according to you – 'everything will be saved'. The mechanical transportation of European forms into Russia (which will be shattered in Europe tomorrow), which are foreign to our people and contrary to the popular will, is we know well the all-important word of Russian Europeanism. And by the way, M. Gradovsky, when you censure our lack of organization, blaming Russia and pointing to Europe with admiration, you say:

'And in the meanwhile we cannot get rid of the inconsistencies and contradictions of which Europe got rid long ago.'

Has Europe got rid of them? Where did you learn this? She is on the eve of ruin, your Europe, of a general, universal and terrible castrophe. The ant-hill which has long been in course of formation within her, without a Church and without Christ (for the Church, having muddied her ideal, was long ago embodied in the State), with a moral principle shattered to its foundations, having lost all that it had of universal and of absolute – that ant-hill, I say, is wholly undermined. The fourth estate is coming; it knocks and batters at the door, and if the door be not opened, it will be broken down. The fourth estate does not want the ideals of old; it denounces all that has been up till now. It will not make little compromises, little concessions; you will not save the building by little supports. Something will come which none imagine. All these parliamentarisms, all the social theories nowadays professed, banks, science, Jews – all will be annihilated in a single instant and leave no trace, except perhaps the Jews, who will even then devise a method of action by which the work of destruction may be profitable to them. All these things are near, 'at the gate'. You laugh? Blessed are they that laugh. God grant you years that you may yourself behold it. You will be surprised in that day. You will laugh and say: 'How well you love Europe if you prophesy this of her!' Am I glad? I have only the feeling that the reckoning is made. The final account, the payment of the bill, may come to pass much sooner than the quickest imagination can conceive. The symptoms are terrible. Alone, the inveterately unnatural political situation of the powers of Europe may serve for a beginning to anything! How could they be natural, if their formation was unnatural and the abnormality has accumulated for centuries? One small portion of mankind shall not possess the rest as a slave; yet it was solely for this purpose that *all* the civic institutions of Europe (long since un-Christian, which are now perfectly pagan) have hitherto been formed. This unnaturalness and these 'insoluble' political questions (which are, by the way, familiar to everybody) must infallibly lead to one huge, final, disintegrating, political war, in which all Powers will have a share, and which will break out in our century, perhaps even in the coming decade. And do you think that society *now* can endure a long political war? The capitalists are cowardly and timorous, the Jews also; all the factories and banks will be closed as soon as the war begins to be protracted or threatens to be a long one, and millions of hungry mouths, of miserable proletarians, will be thrown into the street. Do you rely upon the wisdom of statesmen and upon their refusal to undertake a war? When was it possible to place any reliance upon that wisdom? Do you put your trust in Parliaments, and believe that they will foresee the results and refuse the money for the war? But when have Parliaments foreseen results and refused money to the slightest insistence of a man in power? But the proletarian is in the street. Do you think he will wait and starve in patience as he used? After he has tasted political socialism, after the International, after the Socialist Congresses and the Paris Commune? No, it will not now be as it used to be. They will hurl themselves upon Europe and all the old things will crumble for ever. The waves will be broken by our shore alone, since only then will it be palpably and evidently revealed how greatly different is our national organism from the European. Then, even you, *messieurs les doctrinaires*, will perhaps bethink yourselves and begin to search in our people for 'national principles' at which you only laugh now.

And now, gentlemen, now you point us to Europe and appeal to us to transplant those very institutions which will crumble there tomorrow, as absurdities which have had their day and in which a great many clever people even there no longer believe, which maintain themselves and exist only by the force of inertia. Who but an abstract doctrinaire could seriously take the comedy of the union of the bourgeoisie, which we see in Europe, as the normal formula of the union of men upon the earth? We are told that they got rid of contradictions long ago – and this after twenty constitutions in less than a century, and after well-nigh a dozen revolutions? Oh, perhaps, it will only be then that we shall be freed for a while from Europe, and ourselves engage, without European tutelage, in the pursuit of our own social ideals which inevitably spring from Christ and personal self-perfection, M. Gradovsky.

You will ask: 'What social and political ideals of our own can we have to save Europe?' Why, social ideals better than the European, stronger than the European, stronger than yours and even – oh, horror – more liberal than yours! Yes, more liberal because they spring directly from the organism of our people and are not a servile and bloodless importation from the west. I cannot of course say much upon this subject, if only because this paper is already too long. But in this connection, remember what was the ancient Christian Church and what it aspires to be. It began immediately after the death of Christ, with a handful of people, and instantly, almost in the very first days after the death of Christ, it attempted to discover its 'civic formula', which was wholly based upon the moral expectation of satisfying the spirit by the principles of personal self-perfection. Then arose the Christian communities – Churches; then speedily began to be created a new and hitherto unheard-of nationality, a nationality of universal brotherhood and humanity, in the shape of the catholic ecumenical Church. But the Church was persecuted, and the ideal grew beneath the earth, and above it, on the face of the earth, an immense building was also being formed, a huge ant-hill, the old Roman empire, which was also the ideal and the outcome of the moral aspirations of the whole ancient world. But the ant-hill did not fortify itself; it was undermined by the Church. Then occurred the collision of the two most opposite ideas that could exist in the world. The Man-God met the God-Man, the Apollo Belvedere met the Christ. A compromise arose: the Empire accepted Christianity, and the Church accepted Roman law and the Roman state. A small part of the Church went into the desert and began to continue its former work. Christian communities once more appeared, then monasteries; and there were only attempts that have lasted even unto our day. The large remaining part of the Church was subsequently divided, it is well known, into two halves. In the western half the State ultimately completely overcame the Church. The Church was destroyed and finally transformed into the State. The Papacy appeared – the continuation of the ancient Roman Empire in a new incarnation. In the eastern half the State was subdued and destroyed by the sword of Mahomet, and there remained Christ alone, already separated from the Church. And the State, which had accepted and exalted Christ anew, suffered such terrible and unending sufferings at the hands of its enemies, from the Tartar kingdoms, from disorganization, from serfdom, from Europe and Europeanism, and endures so much until this day, that a real social formula in the sense of the spirit of love and Christian self-perfection has not yet been evolved in it. You, M. Gradovsky, mercilessly reproach Russia with her disorganization. But who was it that hindered her from organizing herself well during the whole of the last two centuries and especially during the last fifty years? Just such people as yourself, M. Gradovsky, Russian Europeans who were always with us for the two centuries and now have settled upon us particularly. Who is the enemy of Russia's organic and independent development upon her own national principles? Who sneers and will not admit even the existence of those principles and does not even want to see them? Who wanted to remake our people, by fantastically 'raising them up to himself' – simply in order to manufacture little Europeans, like themselves, by occasionally breaking off from the mass of the people a single individual and corrupting him into a European, if only by virtue of the revers of his uniform? By that I do not mean that a European is corrupt; I say only that to remake a Russian into a European in the way in which the Liberals do, is often real corruption. Yet in this lies the whole ideal of their programme of activity, in just paring off single individuals from the general mass. What absurdity! Did they really want to tear off and remake in exactly this way all the eighty millions of our people? Do you seriously believe that all our people, as a whole, in its great mass, will consent to become such an impersonality as these gentlemen, these Russian Europeans?

'The Journal of an Author' (1880), in *The Dream of a Queer Fellow and the Pushkin Speech*, trans. S. Koteliansky and J. Middleton Murry (London, Allen & Unwin, 1960), pp. 83–90.

The spirit of isolation is coming upon the people too. Money-lenders and devourers of the commune are rising up. Already the merchant grows more and more eager for rank, and strives to show himself cultured though he has not a trace of culture, and to this end meanly despises his old traditions, and is even ashamed of the faith of his fathers. He visits princes, though he is only a peasant corrupted. The peasants are rotting in drunkenness and cannot shake off the habit. And what cruelty to their wives, to their children even! All from drunkenness! I've seen in the factories children of nine years old, frail, rickety, bent and already depraved. The stuffy workshop, the din of machinery, work all day long, the vile language and the drink, the drink – is that what a little child's heart needs? He needs sunshine, childish play, good examples all about him, and at least a little love. There must be no more of this, monks, no more torturing of children, rise up and preach that, make haste, make haste!

But God will save Russia, for though the peasants are corrupted and cannot renounce their filthy sin, yet they know it is cursed by God and that they do wrong in sinning. So that our people still believe in righteousness, have faith in God and weep tears of devotion.

It is different with the upper classes. They, following science, want to base justice on reason alone, but not with Christ, as before; and they have already proclaimed that there is no crime, that there is no sin. And that's consistent, for if you have no God what is the meaning of crime? In

Europe the people are already rising up against the rich with violence, and the leaders of the people are everywhere leading them to bloodshed, and teaching them that their wrath is righteous. But their 'wrath is accursed, for it is cruel'. But God will save Russia as He has saved her many times. Salvation will come from the people, from their faith and their meekness.

Fathers and teachers, watch over the people's faith and this will not be a dream. I've been struck all my life in our great people by their dignity, their true and seemly dignity. I've seen it myself, I can testify to it, I've seen it and marvelled at it, I've seen it in spite of the degraded sins and poverty-stricken appearance of our peasantry. They are not servile, and even after two centuries of serfdom they are free in manner and bearing, yet without insolence, and not revengeful and not envious. 'You are rich and noble, you are clever and talented, well, be so, God bless you. I respect you, but I know that I too am a man. By the very fact that I respect you without envy I prove my dignity as a man.'

In truth if they don't say this (for they don't know how to say this yet), that is how they act. I have seen it myself, I have known it myself and, would you believe it, the poorer our Russian peasant is, the more noticeable is that serene goodness, for the rich among them are for the most part corrupted already, and much of that is due to our carelessness and indifference. But God will save His people, for Russia is great in her humility. I dream of seeing, and seem to see clearly already, our future. It will come to pass, that even the most corrupt of our rich will end by being ashamed of his riches before the poor, and the poor, seeing his humility, will understand and give way before him, will respond joyfully and kindly to his honourable shame. Believe me that it will end in that; things are moving to that. Equality is to be found only in the spiritual dignity of man, and that will only be understood among us. If we were brothers, there would be fraternity, but before that, they will never agree about the division of wealth. We preserve the image of Christ, and it will shine forth like a precious diamond to the whole world. So may it be, so may it be!

The Brothers Karamazov (1878–80), trans. C. Garnett, Everyman ed. (London, Dent, 1960), vol. I, pp. 326–8.

A SOCIETY OF EQUALS

Life itself consists, say the philosophers, in the effort *to affirm one's own essence*; meaning by this, to develop one's own existence fully and freely, to have ample light and air, to be neither cramped nor overshadowed. Democracy is trying to *affirm its own essence*; to live, to enjoy, to possess the world, as aristocracy has tried, and successfully tried, before it. Ever since Europe emerged from barbarism, ever since the condition of the common people began a little to improve, ever since their minds began to stir, this effort of democracy has been gaining strength; and the more their condition improves, the more strength this effort gains. So potent is the charm of life and expansion upon the living; the moment men are aware of them, they begin to desire them, and the more they have of them, the more they crave.

This movement of democracy, like other operations of nature, merits properly neither blame nor praise. Its partisans are apt to give it credit which it does not deserve, while its enemies are apt to upbraid it unjustly. Its friends celebrate it as the author of all freedom. But political freedom may very well be established by aristocratic founders; and, certainly, the political freedom of England owes more to the grasping English barons than to democracy. Social freedom, – equality, – that is rather the field of the conquest of democracy. And here what I must call the injustice of its enemies comes in. For its seeking after equality, democracy is often, in this country above all, vehemently and scornfully blamed; its temper contrasted with that worthier temper which can magnanimously endure social distinctions; its operations all referred, as of course, to the stirrings of a base and malignant envy. No doubt there is a gross and vulgar spirit of envy, prompting the hearts of many of those who cry for equality. No doubt there are ignoble natures which prefer equality to liberty. But what we have to ask is, when the life of democracy is admitted as something natural and inevitable, whether this or that product of democracy is a necessary growth from its parent stock, or merely an excrescence upon it. If it be the latter, certainly it may be due to the meanest and most culpable passions. But if it be the former, then this product, however base and blameworthy the passions which it may sometimes be made to serve, can in itself be no more reprehensible than the vital impulse of democracy is in itself reprehensible; and this impulse is, as has been shown, identical with the ceaseless vital effort of human nature itself.

Now, can it be denied, that a certain approach to equality, at any rate a certain reduction of signal inequalities, is a natural, instinctive demand of that impulse which drives society as a whole, – no longer individuals and limited classes only, but the mass of a community, – to develop itself with the utmost possible fulness and freedom? Can it be denied, that to live in a society of equals tends in general to make a man's spirits expand, and his faculties work easily and actively; while, to live in a society of superiors, although it may occasionally be a very good discipline, yet in general tends to tame the spirits and to make the play of the faculties less secure and active? Can it be denied, that to be heavily overshadowed, to be profoundly insignificant, has, on the whole, a depressing and benumbing effect on the character? I know that some individuals react against the strongest impediments, and owe success and greatness to the efforts which they are thus forced to make. But the question is not about individuals. The question is about the common bulk of mankind, persons without extraordinary gifts or exceptional energy, and who will ever require, in order to make the best of themselves, encouragement and directly favouring circumstances. Can any one deny, that for these the spectacle, when they would rise, of a condition of splendour, grandeur and culture, which they cannot possibly reach, has the effect of making them flag in spirit, and of disposing them to sink despondingly back into their own condition? Can any one deny, that the knowledge how poor and insignificant the best condition of improvement and culture attainable by them must be esteemed by a class incomparably richer-endowed, tends to cheapen this modest possible amelioration in the account of those classes also for whom it would be relatively a real progress, and to disenchant their imaginations with it? It seems to me impossible to deny this. And therefore a philosophic observer,[1] with no love for democracy, but rather with

[1] M. de Tocqueville. See his *Démocratie en Amérique* (ed. of 1835), vol. I, p. 11. '*Le peuple est plus grossier dans les pays aristocratiques que partout ailleurs. Dans ces lieux, où se*

a terror of it, has been constrained to remark, that 'the common people is more uncivilized in aristocratic countries than in any others'; because there 'the lowly and the poor feel themselves, as it were, overwhelmed with the weight of their own inferiority.' He has been constrained to remark,[1] that 'there is such a thing as a manly and legitimate passion for equality, prompting men to desire to be, *all* of them, in the enjoyment of power and consideration!' And, in France, that very equality, which is by us so impetuously decried, while it has by no means improved (it is said) the upper classes of French society, has undoubtedly given to the lower classes, to the body of the common people, a self-respect, an enlargement of spirit, a consciousness of counting for something in their country's action, which has raised them in the scale of humanity. The common people, in France, seems to me the soundest part of the French nation. They seem to me more free from the two opposite degradations of multitudes, brutality and servility, to have a more developed human life, more of what distinguishes elsewhere the cultured classes from the vulgar, than the common people in any other country with which I am acquainted.

I do not say that grandeur and prosperity may not be attained by a nation divided into the most widely distinct classes, and presenting the most signal inequalities of rank and fortune. I do not say that great national virtues may not be developed in it. I do not even say that a popular order, accepting this demarcation of classes as an eternal providential arrangement, not questioning the natural right of a superior order to lead it, content within its own sphere, admiring the grandeur and high-mindedness of its ruling class, and catching on its own spirit some reflex of what it thus admires, may not be a happier body, as to the eye of the imagination it is certainly a more beautiful body, than a popular order, pushing, excited and presumptuous; a popular order, jealous of recognizing fixed superiorities, petulantly claiming to be as good as its betters, and tastelessly attiring itself with the fashions and designations which have become unalterably associated with a wealthy and refined class, and which, tricking out those who have neither wealth nor refinement, are ridiculous. But a popular order of that old-fashioned stamp exists now only for the imagination. It is not the force with which modern society has to reckon. Such a body may be a sturdy, honest and sound-hearted lower class; but it is not

---

recontrent des hommes si forts et si riches, les faibles et les pauvres se sentent comme accablés de leur bassesse; ne découvrant aucun point par lequel ils puissent regagner l'égalité, ils désespèrent entièrement d'eux-mêmes, et se laissent tomber au-dessous de la dignité humaine.'
[1] *Démocratie en Amérique*, vol. I, p. 60.

a democratic people. It is not that power, which at the present day in all nations is to be found existing; in some, has obtained the mastery; in others, is yet in a state of expectation and preparation.

'Democracy' (1861), in *The Portable Matthew Arnold*, ed. L. Trilling (New York, Viking, 1949), pp. 441–5.

THE NATION AS A COMMUNITY

A nation is a soul, a spiritual principle. Two things, which are really only one, go to make up this soul or spiritual principle. One of these things lies in the past, the other in the present. The one is the possession in common of a rich heritage of memories; and the other is actual agreement, the desire to live together and the will to continue to make the most of the joint inheritance. Man, gentlemen, cannot be improvised. The nation, like the individual, is the fruit of a long past spent in toil, sacrifice and devotion. Ancestor-worship is of all forms the most justifiable, since our ancestors have made us what we are. A heroic past, great men and glory – I mean real glory – these should be the capital of our company when we come to found a national idea. To share the glories of the past, and a common will in the present; to have done great deeds together, and to desire to do more – these are the essential conditions of a people's being. Love is in proportion to the sacrifices one has made and the evils one has borne. We love the house that we have built and that we hand down to our successors. The Spartan song 'We are what ye were, and we shall be what ye are', is, in its simplicity, the abridged version of every national anthem.

In the past, a heritage of glory and of grief to be shared; in the future, one common plan to be realized; to have suffered, rejoiced and hoped together; these are things of greater value than identity of custom-houses and frontiers in accordance with strategic notions. These are things which are understood, in spite of differences in race and language. I said just now 'to have suffered together', for indeed common suffering unites more strongly than common rejoicing. Among national memories, sorrows have greater value than victories; for they impose duties and demand common effort.

Thus we see that a nation is a great solid unit, formed by the realization of sacrifices in the past, as well as of those one is prepared to make in the future. A nation implies a past; while, as regards the present, it is all contained in one tangible fact, viz., the agreement and clearly expressed desire to continue a life in common. The existence of a nation is (if you will forgive me the metaphor) a daily plebiscite, just as that of the individual is a continual affirmation of life. I am quite aware that this is less metaphysical than the doctrine of divine right, and smacks less of brute force than alleged historic right. According to the notions that I am expounding, a nation has no more right than a king, to say to a province: 'You belong to me; so I will take you'. A province means to us its inhabitants; and if any one has a right to be consulted in the matter, it is the inhabitant. It is never to the true interest of a nation to annex or keep a country against its will. The people's wish is after all the only justifiable criterion, to which we must always come back.

We have excluded from politics the abstract principles of metaphysics and theology; and what remains? There remains man, with his desires and his needs. But you will tell me that the consequences of a system that puts these ancient fabrics at the mercy of the wishes of usually unenlightened minds, will be the secession and ultimate disintegration of nations. It is obvious that in such matters no principles should be pushed too far, and that truths of this nature are applicable only as a whole and in a very general sort of way. Human wishes change indeed: but what in this world does not? Nations are not eternal. They have had beginnings and will have ends; and will probably be replaced by a confederation of Europe. But such is not the law of the age in which we live. Nowadays it is a good, and even a necessary, thing that nations should exist. Their existence is the guarantee of liberty, which would be lost, if the world had but one law and one master.

By their various, and often contrasting, attainments, the nations serve the common task of humanity; and all play some instrument in that grand orchestral concert of mankind, which is, after all, the highest ideal reality that we attain. Taken separately, they all have their weak points; and I often tell myself that a man who should have the vices that are held to be virtues in nations, a man battening on empty glory, and so jealous, selfish and quarrelsome as to be ready to draw his sword at the slightest provocation, would be the most intolerable creature. But such discordant details vanish when all is taken together. What sufferings poor humanity has endured and what trials await it yet! May it be guided by the spirit of wisdom and preserved from the countless dangers that beset the path!

And now, gentlemen, let me sum it all up. Man is the slave neither of his race, nor his language, nor his religion, nor of the windings of his rivers and mountain ranges. That moral consciousness which we call a nation is created by a great assemblage of men with warm hearts and healthy minds: and as long as this moral consciousness can prove its strength by the sacrifices demanded from the individual for the benefit of the community, it is justifiable and has the right to exist. If doubts arise concerning its frontiers, let the population in dispute be consulted: for surely they have a right to a say in the matter. This will bring a smile to the lips of the transcendental politicians, those infallible beings who spend their lives in self-deception and who, from the summit of their superior principles, cast a pitying eye upon our commonplaces. 'Consult the population! Stuff and nonsense! This is only another of these feeble French ideas that aim at replacing diplomacy and war by methods of infantile simplicity.' Well, gentlemen, let us wait a while. Let the kingdom of the transcendentalists endure for its season; and let us learn to submit to the scorn of the mighty. It may be, that after many fruitless fumblings, the world will come back to our modest empirical solutions. The art of being right in the future is, at certain times, the art of resigning oneself to being old-fashioned.

'What is a Nation?' (1882), trans. in *Modern Political Doctrines*, ed. A. Zimmern (London, O.U.P., 1939), pp. 202–5.

Leo Tolstoy
(1828–1910)

A NATURAL SOCIETY BASED ON LABOUR

After breakfast Levin was not in the same place in the string of mowers as before, but found himself between the old man who had accosted him quizzically, and now invited him to be his neighbour, and a young peasant who had only been married in the autumn and who was mowing this summer for the first time.

The old man, holding himself erect, went in front, moving with long, regular strides, his feet turned out and swinging his scythe as precisely and evenly, and apparently as effortlessly, as a man swings his arms in walking. As if it were child's play, he laid the grass in a high, level ridge. It seemed as if the sharp blade swished of its own accord through the juicy grass.

Behind Levin came the lad Mishka. His pleasant, boyish face, with a twist of fresh grass bound round his hair, worked all the time with effort; but whenever anyone looked at him he smiled. He would clearly sooner die than own it was hard work for him.

Levin kept between them. In the very heat of the day the mowing did not seem such hard work. The perspiration with which he was drenched cooled him, while the sun, that burned his back, his head and his arms, bare to the elbow, gave a vigour and dogged energy to his labour; and more and more often now came those moments of oblivion, when it was possible not to think of what one was doing. The scythe cut of itself. Those were happy moments. Still more delightful were the moments when they reached the river at the end of the rows and the old man would rub his scythe with a thick knot of wet grass, rinse the steel blade in the fresh water of the stream, ladle out a little in a tin dipper and offer Levin a drink.

'What do you say to my home-brew, eh? Good, eh?' he would say with a wink.

And truly Levin had never tasted any drink so good as this warm water with bits of grass floating in it and a rusty flavour from the tin dipper. And immediately after this came the blissful, slow saunter, with his hand on the scythe, during which he could wipe away the streaming sweat, fill his lungs with air and look about at the long line of mowers and at what was happening around in the forest and the country.

The longer Levin mowed, the oftener he experienced those moments of oblivion when it was not his arms which swung the scythe but the scythe seemed to mow of itself, a body full of life and consciousness of its own, and as though by magic, without a thought being given to it, the work did itself regularly and carefully. These were the most blessed moments.

It was only hard work when he had to interrupt this unconscious motion and think; when he had to mow round a hillock or a tuft of sorrel. The old man did this easily. When he came to a hillock he would change his action and go round the hillock with short strokes first with the point and then with the heel of the scythe. And while he did this he noted everything he came to; sometimes he would pick a wild berry and eat it, or offer it to Levin; sometimes he threw a twig out of the way with the point of the steel, or examined a quail's nest, from which the hen-bird flew up from right under the scythe; or caught a snake that crossed his path, lifting it on the scythe as though on a fork, showed it to Levin, and flung it away.

For both Levin and the young lad on the other side of him such changes of position were difficult. Repeating over and over again the same strained movement, they found themselves in the grip of feverish activity and were quite incapable of altering the motion of their bodies and at the same time observing what was before them.

Levin did not notice how time was passing. Had he been asked how long he had been working he would have answered, 'Half an hour' – and it was getting on for dinner-time. As they were walking back over the cut grass, the old man drew Levin's attention to the little girls and boys approaching from different sides, along the road and through the long grass – hardly visible above it – carrying the haymakers' pitchers of rye-beer stoppered with rags, and bundles of bread which dragged their little arms down.

'Look'ee, little lady-birds crawling along!' he said, pointing to them and glancing at the sun from under his hand.

They completed two more rows; the old man stopped.

'Come, master, dinner-time!' he said briskly. And on reaching the stream the mowers moved off across the cut grass towards their pile of coats, where the children who had brought their dinners sat waiting for them.

The men who had driven from a distance gathered in the shadow of their carts; those who lived nearer went under a willow bush, over which they threw grass.

Levin sat down beside them; he did not want to go away.

All constraint in the presence of the master had disappeared long ago. The peasants began preparing for dinner. Some had a wash, the young lads bathed in the stream, others arranged places for their after-dinner rest, untied their bundles of bread and unstoppered their pitchers of rye-beer.

The old man crumbled up some bread in a cup, pounded it with the handle of a spoon, poured water on it from the dipper, broke up some more bread and, having sprinkled it with salt, turned to the east to say his prayer.

'Come, master, have some of my dinner,' he said, squatting on his knees in front of the cup.

The bread and water was so delicious that Levin changed his mind about going home. He shared the old man's meal and chatted to him about his family affairs, taking the keenest interest in them, and told him about his own affairs and all the circumstances that could be of interest to the old peasant. He felt much nearer to him than to his brother, and could not help smiling at the affection he felt for this man. When the old chap got up again, said his prayer and lay down under a bush, putting some grass under his head for a pillow, Levin did the same and, in spite of the clinging flies that were so persistent in the sunshine and the insects that tickled his hot face and body, he fell asleep at once, and only woke when the sun had gone the other side of the bush and reached him. The old man had been awake some time and sat whetting the scythes of the younger lads.

Levin looked about him and hardly recognized the place, everything was so altered. A wide expanse of meadow was already mown and the sweet-smelling hay shone with a peculiar fresh glitter in the slanting rays of the evening sun. And the bushes by the river had been cut down, and the river itself, not visible before, its curves now gleaming like steel, and the peasants getting up and moving about, the steep wall of yet uncut grass, and the hawks hovering over the stripped meadow – all was completely new. Rousing himself, Levin began calculating how much had been done and how much more could still be done that day.

The forty-two men had got through a considerable amount. They had cut the whole of the big meadow, which used to take thirty men two days in the time of serf labour. Only the corners remained to be done, where the rows were short. But Levin wanted to get as much mowing done that day as possible, and was vexed with the sun for sinking so quickly. He did not feel the least bit tired and was only eager to go on and finish as much as he could.

'What do you think – could we do Mashkin hill today too?' he said to the old man.

'If God wills. The sun's getting low, though. Would there be a drop of vodka for the lads?'

About tea-time, when they were sitting down again and those who smoked were lighting their pipes, the old man told the men that there would be vodka if they mowed Mashkin hill.

'What, not mow that? Come on, Titus! We'll do it in no time! We can eat our fill after dark. Come on!' cried voices, and the mowers went back to work, eating up their bread as they went.

'Now then, lads, keep going!' said Titus, and ran on ahead almost at a trot.

'Get along, get along!' said the old man, hurrying after him and easily catching him up. 'I'll mow you down, you watch!'

And young and old mowed away, as if they were racing each other. Yet, however fast they worked, they did not spoil the grass and the swaths fell as neatly and exactly as before. The little patch left in the corner was whisked off in five minutes. The last of the mowers had scarcely finished their swaths before those in front had slung their coats over their shoulders and were crossing the road towards Mashkin hill.

The sun was already sinking into the trees when they entered the woody little ravine of Mashkin hill, their dippers rattling as they walked. The grass in the middle of the hollow was waist-high, tender, soft and feathery, speckled here and there among the trees with wild pansies.

After a brief consultation – whether they should take the rows lengthwise or diagonally – Prohor Yermilin, also a renowned mower, a huge, black-haired peasant, went on ahead. He went up to the top, turned back again and started mowing, and they all proceeded to fall into line behind him, going downhill through the hollow and uphill right to the edge of the trees. The sun sank behind the forest. The dew was falling by now. The mowers were in the sun only on the ridge; below, where the mist was rising, and on the opposite side, they were in the fresh, dewy shade. The work progressed briskly.

The grass cut with a juicy sound and fell in high, fragrant rows. On the short rows the mowers bunched together, their tin dippers rattling, their scythes ringing when they touched, the whetstones whistling upon the blades, and their good-humoured voices resounding as they urged each other on.

Levin still kept between the young peasant and the old man. The old man, who had put on his sheepskin jacket, was just as jolly, chaffing and free in his movements as before. In the wood their scythes were continually cutting birch-mushrooms, grown plump in the succulent grass. But the old man bent down every time he came across a mushroom, picked it up and put it inside his smock. 'Another little treat for my old woman,' he said as he did so.

It was easy enough to mow the wet, soft grass but going up and down the steep slopes of the ravine was hard work. But this did not trouble the old man. Swinging his scythe just as usual, taking short, firm steps with feet shod in large plaited shoes, he climbed slowly up the slope, and though his whole frame and the breeches below his smock shook with effort, he did not miss one blade of grass or let a single mushroom escape him, and never ceased joking with the other peasants and Levin. Levin followed him and often thought he must fall, as he climbed up a steep cliff that would have been difficult going even without the scythe in his hand. But he managed to clamber up and do what he had to do. Some external force seemed to propel him on.

> *Anna Karenin* (1875–6), trans. Rosemary Edmunds (London, Penguin, 1954), pt. III, ch. V, pp. 272–7.

It is only to our perverted ideas, that it seems, when the master sends his clerk to be a peasant, or government sentences one of its ministers to deportation, that they are punished and have been dealt with hardly. In reality they have had a great good done to them; that is, they have exchanged their heavy special work for a pleasant alternation of labour.

In a natural society all is different. I know a commune where the people earn their living themselves. One of the members of this community was more educated than the rest; and they require him to deliver lectures, for which he has to prepare himself during the day, that he may be able to deliver them in the evening. He does it joyfully, feeling that he is useful to others, and that he can do it well. But he grows tired of the exclusive mental labour, and his health suffers accordingly. The members of the community therefore pity him, and ask him to come and labour in the field again.

For men who consider labour to be the essential thing and the joy of life, the ground, the basis, of it will always be the struggle with nature, – not only in agricultural labour, but also in that of handicraft, mental work and intercourse with men.

The divergence from one or many of these kinds of labour, and specialities of labour, will be performed only when a man of special gifts, being fond of this work, and knowing that he performs it better than anybody else, will sacrifice his own advantage in order to fulfil the demands which others put directly to him.

Only with such a view of labour and the natural division of labour resulting from it, will that curse disappear which in our imagination we have put upon labour; and every labour will always be a joy, because man will do either an unquestionably useful, pleasant and easy work, or will be conscious that he makes a sacrifice by performing a more difficult special labour for the good of others.

But the division of labour is, it is said, more advantageous. Advantageous for whom? Is it more advantageous to make with all speed as many boots and cotton-prints as possible? But who will make these boots and cotton-prints? Men who from generation to generation have been making only pin-heads? How, then, can it be more advantageous for people? If the object were to make as many cotton-prints and pins as possible, it would be so; but the question is, how to make people happy?

The happiness of men consists in life. And life is in labour.

How, then, can the necessity of painful, oppressing work be advantageous for men? If the question were only for the advantage of some men without any consideration of the welfare of all, then it might be most advantageous for some men to eat others. They say it is savoury!

The thing most advantageous for all men is what I wish for myself, – the greatest welfare and the satisfying of all my wants which are ingrafted in me, those of body as well as those of soul, of conscience and of reason.

The hatred and contempt of the oppressed people are increasing and the physical and moral strength of the richer classes are decreasing: the deceit which supports all is wearing out, and the rich classes have nothing wherewith to comfort themselves in this mortal danger. To return to the old order of things is impossible, to restore the old prestige is impossible. It only remains for those who are not willing to change the course of their lives, and to turn over a new leaf, – to hope that, during their lives, they may fare well enough, after which the people may do as they like. So think the blind crowd of the rich; but the danger ever increases, and the awful catastrophe comes nearer and nearer.

There are three reasons which should prove to rich people the necessity of turning over a new leaf: First, desire for their own personal welfare and that of their families, which is not secured by the way in which rich people are living; secondly, the inability to satisfy the voice of conscience, which is obviously impossible in the present condition of things; and thirdly, the threatening and constantly increasing danger to life, which cannot be met by any outward means. All these together ought to induce rich people to change their mode of life. This change alone would satisfy the desire of welfare and conscience, and would remove the danger. There is but one means of making such change – to leave off deceiving ourselves, to repent, and to acknowledge labour to be, not a curse, but the joyful business of life.

To this it is replied, 'What will come out of the fact of my physical labour during ten, eight or five hours, while thousands of peasants would gladly do it for the money which I have?'

The first good result would be, that you will become livelier, healthier, sounder, kinder; and you will learn that real life from which you have hidden yourself, or which was hidden from you.

The second good result will be, that, if you have a conscience, it will not only cease to suffer as it now suffers when looking at the labour of men, – the importance of which we always, from our ignorance, either increase or diminish, – but you will constantly experience a joyful acknowledgement that with each day you are satisfying more and more the demands of your conscience, and are leaving behind you that awful state in which so much evil is accumulated in our lives that we feel that we cannot possibly do any good in the world; you will experience the joy of free life, with the possibility of doing good to others; you will open for yourself a way into regions of the world of morality which have hitherto been shut to you.

The third good result will be this, that instead of constant fear of revenge upon your evil deeds, you will feel that you are saving others from this revenge, and are principally saving the oppressed from the cruel feeling of rancour and resentment.

But it is generally said, that it would be ridiculous if we, men of our stamp, with deep philosophical, scientific, political, artistic, ecclesiastical, social questions before us, we, state ministers, senators, academists, professors, artists, singers, we, whose quarter-hours are valued so highly by men, should spend our time in doing – what? Cleaning our boots, washing our shirts, digging, planting potatoes, or feeding our chickens and cows, and so on, – in business which not only our house-porter, or our cook, but thousands of men besides who value our time, would be very glad to do for us.

But why do we dress, wash and comb our hair ourselves? Why do we walk, hand chairs to ladies, to our guests, open and shut the door, help people into carriages and perform hundreds of actions which were formerly performed for us by our slaves?

Because we consider that such may be done by ourselves; that they are compatible with human dignity; that is, human duty. The same holds good with physical labour. Man's dignity, his sacred duty, is to use his hands, his feet, for the purpose for which they were given him, to spend the swallowed food in work, which produces the food, and not to be wasted by disuse, not merely that he may wash and clean them and use them only for the purpose of stuffing food and cigarettes into his mouth.

Such is the meaning of physical labour for every man in every society. But in our class, with the divergence from this law of nature came the misery of a whole circle of men; and for us, physical labour receives another meaning, – the meaning of a preaching and a propaganda which divert the terrible evil which threatens mankind.

What Shall We Do? (1886), A New Translation ed. A.C.F. and I.F.M. (London, The Free Age Press, 1904), pp. 217–18, 221–2.

William Morris
(1834–1896)

FROM CLASS TO PERSONAL
RELATIONS

Kelmscott House,
Upper Mall,
Hammersmith.
April 2nd, 1888.

Dear Sir,

Socialism is a theory of life, taking for its starting point the evolution of Society; or, let us say, of man as a social being.

Since man has certain material *necessities* as an animal, Society is founded on man's attempts to satisfy those necessities; and Socialism, or social consciousness, points out to him the way of doing so which will interfere least with the development of his specially human capacities, and the satisfaction of what, for lack of better words, I will call his spiritual and mental necessities.

The foundation of Socialism, therefore, is economical. Man as a social animal tends to the acquirement of power over nature, and to the beneficent use of that power, which again implies a condition of society in which every one is able to satisfy his needs in return for the due exercise of his capacities for the benefit of the race. But this economical aim which, to put it in another way, is the fair apportionment of labour and the results of labour, must be accompanied by an ethical or religious sense of the responsibility of each man to each and all of his fellows.

Socialism aims, therefore, at realizing equality of condition as its economical goal, and the habitual love of humanity as its rule of ethics.

Properly speaking, in a condition of equality politics would no longer exist; but, to use the word as distinguishing the social habits that have not to do directly with production, the political position of Socialism is to substitute the relation of persons to persons for the relation of things to persons. A man, I mean, would no longer take his position as the dweller in such and such a place, or the filler of such and such an office, or (as now) the owner of such and such property, but as being such and such a man. In such a state of Society laws of repression would be minimized, and the whole body of law which now deals with things and their domination over persons would cease to exist. In a condition of personal equality, also, there could no longer be rivalry between those inhabiting different places. Nationality, except as a geographical or ethnological expression, would have no meaning.

Equality as to livelihood, mutual respect and responsibility, and complete freedom within those limits – which would, it must be remembered, be accepted voluntarily and indeed habitually, are what Socialism looks forward to.

But there would be few, if any, Socialists who would not admit that between this condition of things and our present Society there must be a transitional condition, during which we must waive the complete realization of our ideal.

This transitional condition is what we Socialists of today believe will be gradually brought about in our own times. It will be brought about partly, we think, by the further development of democracy, and partly by the conscious attempts of the Socialists themselves.

The democracy have yet to get rid of certain survivals and superstitions. They will also be forced to deal with the circumstances produced by the gradual decline of the commercial system which has created democracy; as, for instance, the lack of employment for a large part of the population; their lack of leisure; their wretched housing and so forth. The democracy by such action will improve the position of the working classes, or at least they will put them into such a position as will increase their discontent by making them conscious of possible remedies for their inferior position. But as constitutional democrats they can go no further than this; they must take the present relations between wage-earners and capitalists as a basis for improvement, and on that basis improvement must be very limited. It is the Socialists only who can claim a measure which will realize a new basis of society; that measure is *the abolition of private ownership in the means of production*. The land, factories, machinery, means of transit and whatever wealth of any sort is used for the reproduction of wealth, and which therefore is necessary to labour and can only be *used* by it, must be *owned* by the nation only, to be *used* by the workers (who will then include all honest men) according to their capacity.[1]

This claim for the abolition of the monopoly in the means of production is made by all Socialists of every shade; it forms the political platform of the party, and nothing short of this is a definite Socialist claim. It is true that some of us (myself amongst others) look further than this, as the first part of my paper indicates; but we are all prepared to accept whatever consequences may follow the realization of this claim; and for my part I believe that whatever struggle or violence there may be in the realization of Socialism will all take place in the carrying out of this initial step; that after that the class struggle, now thousands of years old, having come to an end, no new class will arise to dominate the workers; and that whatever steps may be necessary to bring us to the fulness of the fellowship, which, as you justly say, is the aim of Socialism, there will be no serious contest over them; they will come of themselves until the habit of Socialism will be thoroughly formed, and no one will have to use the word any more, as it will embrace the whole of human life. What further fulness of the consciousness of life may follow on that none can say. Only this remains to be said, that Socialism does not recognize any finality in the progress and aspirations of humanity; and that we clearly understand that the furthest we can now conceive of is only a stage of the great journey of evolution that joins the future and the past to the present.

This seems to me to be a fair sketch of what Socialists wish to see brought about. I have not attempted to go into details as to the means and so forth, because I supposed what you wanted was just the root principles, and the necessary actions resulting from them.

Yours truly.

WILLIAM MORRIS.

KELMSCOTT HOUSE,
UPPER MALL,
HAMMERSMITH.
April 10th, 1888.

DEAR SIR,

I think that what lies at the root of the due answer to your objections is, that our *present* representative system is the reflection of our *class* society.

---

[1] I ask you to keep well in mind the distinction between the *ownership* of wealth which implies no corresponding duties, and the *possession of it for use* which implies full responsibility towards other people.

The fact of the antagonism of classes underlies all our government, and causes political parties, who are continually making exhibitions of themselves to the disgust of all sensible men; making party questions out of matters of universal public convenience, and delaying reforms of the most obvious nature long after the whole country has cried out for them. This is, I think, a necessary result of government, or, if you please, of political government; and what causes that government is, as I have said, the contest of classes which our competitive system forces on us.

Under these conditions the business of a statesman is to balance the greed and fears of the proprietary class against the necessities and demands of the working class. This is a sorry business, and leads to all kinds of trickery and evasion; so that it is more than doubtful whether a statesman can be a moderately honest man.

Now the contest of classes being abolished all this would fall to the ground. The relations of men to each other would become personal; wealth would be looked upon as an instrument of life, and not as a reason for living, and therefore dominant over men's lives. Whatever laws existed would be much fewer, very simple and easily understood by all; they would mostly concern the protection of the person. In dealing with property, its fetish quality having disappeared, its *use* only would have to be considered; e.g. shall we (the public) work this coal mine or shut it up? Is it necessary for us to lay down this park in wheat, or can we afford to keep it as a place of recreation? Will it be desirable to improve this shoemaking machine, or can we go on with it as it is? Will it be necessary to call for special volunteers to cultivate yonder fen, or will the action of the law of compensation be inducement enough for its cultivation? – and so forth.

Of course it is clear that such considerations can only be held when all such things as this are public property.

The instances you give of public management (you might have added the Poor Laws in spite of the cruelty and stupidity of their administration forced on them by our economical position) show this at least, that whatever theories of individualist property holding there may be, they cannot be thoroughly carried out in practice.

But to return to our 'government' of the future, which would be rather an administration of *things* than a government of *persons*. Without dogmatizing on the matter, I will venture to give you my own views on the subject, as I know that they are those held by many Socialists. Nations, as political entities, would cease to exist; civilization would mean the federalization of a variety of communities great and small, at one end of which would be the township and the local guild, in which administration would be carried on perhaps in direct assemblies in *more majorum*, and at the other some central body whose function would be almost entirely the guardianship of the *principles* of society, and would, when necessary, enforce their practice; e.g. it would not allow slavery in any form to be practised in any community. But even this shadow of centralization would disappear at last when men gained the habit of looking reasonably at these matters. It would, in fact, be chiefly needed as a safeguard against the heredity of bad habits, and the atavism which would give us bad specimens now and again. Between these two poles there would be various federations which would grow together or dissolve as convenience of place, climate, language, etc., dictated, and would dissolve peaceably when occasion prompted. Of course public intercourse between the members of the federation would have to be carried on by means of delegation, but the delegates would not pretend to represent any one or anything but the business with which they are delegated; e.g. 'We are a shoemaking community chiefly, you cotton spinners; are we making too many shoes? Shall we turn, some of us, to gardening for a month or two, or shall we go on?' – and so forth.

Absolute facts and information would be the main business of public assemblies.

Of course every competent citizen would have to take part in public business; and also no one would receive any special dignity, still less any domination for filling any post; he would do his work there because he could do it best, i.e. easiest. To my mind the essential thing to this view (which can be filled in in detail as much as you please, but always with a tolerable certainty that the actual details won't be like the imagined ones) is the township, or parish, or ward, or local guild, small enough to manage its own affairs directly. And I don't doubt that gradually all public business would be so much simplified that it would come to little more than a correspondence. 'Such are the facts with us; compare them with the facts with you. You know how to act' – so that we should tend to the abolition of *all* government, and even of all regulations that were not really habitual; and voluntary association would become a necessary habit, and the only bond of society.

I admit that this is a long way ahead: the contest of classes is still going on, and we cannot help taking part in it.

State Socialism will have to intervene between our present breakdown and communism; but I do not think it will last long when it is fully developed, especially as I think there are signs that it will come in the municipal rather than the imperial form; which I think a very good thing.

To conclude, I must remind you that however gradually the change comes from monopoly to freedom, it will only be when the first stage which recognizes the principle, at least, is complete that our present inequalities can be, I won't say abolished, but even much palliated. The present system is based on the assumed necessity of a proprietary class and a proletariat. As long as this lasts, whatever advantages you give to the latter must result in the aggrandizement of the former, except so far as the proletariat are struggling towards revolution by rebellion of various kinds; the lowest form of which is the ordinary stealing, lying and cheating of the criminal class, and the highest, conscious political action directed against the dominant class; workmen's combinations for strikes and such like lying between two extremes, and being, like the others, a necessary form of the class struggle, but a temporary one; the link between the pure hopelessness of the slave, and the self-sacrificing, dignified hope of the rebel, who feels his rights of citizenship, and is determined to claim them for his class, whatever may happen to himself personally.

As to when the change will come about, that is not our business. It is clearly hope of its advent that *forces* us into agitation. For my part I think that though it may be long before the revolution will be complete, it is already amongst us; and that a very few years will see a great change in the attitude of political parties towards Socialism. I am certain that they will be forced into Socialistic experiments, which may be partial failures, but which will always leave their mark; and that this will go on till it will be only one conscious step over the border, and monopoly will be no more.

I have thus troubled you with another long letter, but as I believe you are anxious for information I also think you can excuse it.

Yours faithfully,

WILLIAM MORRIS.

Letters on Socialism (1888) (London, privately printed, 1894), Letters I and III, pp. 3–10, 15–23.

T. H. Green
(1836–1882)

POSITIVE FREEDOM

We shall probably all agree that freedom, rightly understood, is the greatest of blessings; that its attainment is the true end of all our effort as citizens. But when we thus speak of freedom, we should consider carefully what we mean by it. We do not mean merely freedom from restraint or compulsion. We do not mean merely freedom to do as we like irrespectively of what it is that we like. We do not mean a freedom that can be enjoyed by one man or one set of men at the cost of a loss of freedom to others. When we speak of freedom as something to be so highly prized, we mean a positive power or capacity of doing or enjoying something worth doing or enjoying, and that, too, something that we do or enjoy in common with others. We mean by it a power which each man exercises through the help or security given him by his fellow-men, and which he in turn helps to secure for them. When we measure the progress of a society by its growth in freedom, we measure it by the increasing development and exercise on the whole of those powers of contributing to social good with which we believe the members of the society to be endowed; in short, by the greater power on the part of the citizens as a body to make the most and best of themselves. Thus, though of course there can be no freedom among men who act not willingly but under compulsion, yet on the other hand the mere removal of compulsion, the mere enabling a man to do as he likes, is in itself no contribution to true freedom. In one sense no man is so well able to do as he likes as the wandering savage. He has no master. There is no one to say him nay. Yet we do not count him really free, because the freedom of savagery is not strength, but weakness. The actual powers of the noblest savage do not admit of comparison with those of the humblest citizen of a law-abiding state. He is not the slave of man, but he is the slave of nature.

Of compulsion by natural necessity he has plenty of experience, though of restraint by society none at all. Nor can he deliver himself from that compulsion except by submitting to this restraint. So to submit is the first step in true freedom, because the first step towards the full exercise of the faculties with which man is endowed. But we rightly refuse to recognize the highest development on the part of an exceptional individual or exceptional class, as an advance towards the true freedom of man, if it is founded on a refusal of the same opportunity to other men. The powers of the human mind have probably never attained such force and keenness, the proof of what society can do for the individual has never been so strikingly exhibited, as among the small groups of men who possessed civil privileges in the small republics of antiquity. The whole framework of our political ideas, to say nothing of our philosophy, is derived from them. But in them this extraordinary efflorescence of the privileged class was accompanied by the slavery of the multitude. That slavery was the condition on which it depended, and for that reason it was doomed to decay. There is no clearer ordinance of that supreme reason, often dark to us, which governs the course of man's affairs, than that no body of men should in the long run be able to strengthen itself at the cost of others' weakness. The civilization and freedom of the ancient world were short-lived because they were partial and exceptional. If the ideal of true freedom is the maximum of power for all members of human society alike to make the best of themselves, we are right in refusing to ascribe the glory of freedom to a state in which the apparent elevation of the few is founded on the degradation of the many, and in ranking modern society, founded as it is on free industry, with all its confusion and ignorant licence and waste of effort, above the most splendid of ancient republics.

If I have given a true account of that freedom which forms the goal of social effort, we shall see that freedom of contract, freedom in all the forms of doing what one will with one's own, is valuable only as a means to an end. That end is what I call freedom in the positive sense: in other words, the liberation of the powers of all men equally for contributions to a common good. No one has a right to do what he will with his own in such a way as to contravene this end. It is only through the guarantee which society gives him that he has property at all, or, strictly speaking, any right to his possessions. This guarantee is founded on a sense of common interest. Every one has an interest in securing to every one else the free use and enjoyment and disposal of his possessions, so long as that freedom on the part of one does not interfere with a like freedom on the part of others, because such freedom contributes to that equal development of the faculties of all which is the highest good for all. This is the true and the only justification of rights of property. Rights of property, however, have been and are claimed which cannot be thus justified. We are all now agreed that men cannot rightly be the property of men. The institution of property being only justifiable as a means to the free exercise of the social capabilities of all, there can be no true right to property of a kind which debars one class of men from such free exercise altogether. We condemn slavery no less when it arises out of a voluntary agreement on the part of the enslaved person. A contract by which any one agreed for a certain consideration to become the slave of another we should reckon a void contract. Here, then, is a limitation upon freedom of contract which we all recognize as rightful. No contract is valid in which human persons, willingly or unwillingly, are dealt with as commodities, because such contracts of necessity defeat the end for which alone society enforces contracts at all.

'Lecture on Liberal Legislation and Freedom of Contract' (1881), in *Works*, 6th imp. (London, Longmans Green, 1911), vol. III, pp. 370–3.

PART III

Peter A. Kropotkin
(1842–1921)

HARMONY WITHOUT GOVERNMENT

ANARCHISM, the name given to a principle or theory of life and conduct under which society is conceived without government (from Gr. ἀν- and ἀρχή, without authority) – harmony in such a society being obtained, not by submission to law or by obedience to any authority, but by free agreements concluded between the various groups, territorial and professional, freely constituted for the sake of production and consumption, as also for the satisfaction of the infinite variety of needs and aspirations of a civilized being. In a society developed on these lines, the voluntary associations which already now begin to cover all the fields of human activity would take a still greater extension so as to substitute themselves for the State in all its functions. They would represent an interwoven network, composed of an infinite variety of groups and federations of all sizes and degrees, local, regional, national and international – temporary or more or less permanent – for all possible purposes: production, consumption and exchange, communications, sanitary arrangements, education, mutual protection, defence of the territory, and so on; and, on the other side, for the satisfaction of an ever-increasing number of scientific, artistic, literary and sociable needs. Moreover, such a society would represent nothing immutable. On the contrary – as is seen in organic life at large – harmony would (it is contended) result from an ever-changing adjustment and readjustment of equilibrium between the multitude of forces and influences, and this adjustment would be the easier to obtain as none of the forces would enjoy a special protection from the State.

If, it is contended, society were organized on these principles, man would not be limited in the free exercise of his powers in productive work by a capitalist monopoly, maintained by the State; nor would he be limited in the exercise of his will by a fear of punishment, or by obedience towards individuals or metaphysical entities, which both lead to depression of initiative and servility of mind. He would be guided in his actions by his own understanding, which necessarily would bear the impression of a free action and reaction between his own self and the ethical conceptions of his surroundings. Man would thus be enabled to obtain the full development of all his faculties, intellectual, artistic and moral, without being hampered by overwork for the monopolists, or by the servility and inertia of mind of the great number. He would thus be able to reach full *individualization*, which is not possible either under the present system of *individualism*, or under any system of State Socialism in the so-called *Volkstaat* (popular State).

The Anarchist writers consider, moreover, that their conception is not a Utopia, constructed on the *a priori* method, after a few desiderata have been taken as postulates. It is derived, they maintain, from an *analysis of tendencies* that are at work already, even though State Socialism may find a temporary favour with the reformers. The progress of modern technics, which wonderfully simplifies the production of all the necessaries of life; the growing spirit of independence, and the rapid spread of free initiative and free understanding in all branches of activity – including those which formerly were considered as the proper attribution of Church and State – are steadily reinforcing the no-government tendency.

Anarchists and the State. – As to economical conceptions, the Anarchists, in common with all Socialists, of whom they constitute the left wing, maintain that the now prevailing system of private ownership in land, and our capitalist production for the sake of profits, represent a monopoly which runs against both the principles of justice and the dictates of utility. They are the main obstacle which prevents the successes of modern technics from being brought into the service of all, so as to produce general well-being. The Anarchists consider the wage-system and capitalist production altogether as an obstacle to progress. But they point out also that the State was, and continues to be, the chief instrument for permitting the few to monopolize the land, and the capitalists to appropriate for themselves a quite disproportionate share of the yearly accumulated surplus of production. Consequently, while combating the present monopolization of land, and capitalism altogether, the anarchists combat with the same energy the State, as the main support of that system, not this or that special form, but the State altogether, whether it be a monarchy or even a republic governed by means of the *referendum*.

The State organization, having always been, both in ancient and modern history (Macedonian empire, Roman empire, modern European States grown up on the ruins of the autonomous cities), the instrument for establishing monopolies in favour of the ruling minorities, cannot be made to work for the destruction of these monopolies. The Anarchists consider, therefore, that to hand over to the State all the main sources of economical life – the land, the mines, the railways, banking, insurance and so on – as also the management of all the main branches of industry, in addition to all the functions already accumulated in its hands (education, State-supported religions, defence of the territory, etc.), would mean to create a new instrument of tyranny. State capitalism would only increase the powers of bureaucracy and capitalism. True progress lies in the direction of decentralization, both *territorial* and *functional*, in the development of the spirit of local and personal initiative, and of free federation from the simple to the compound, in lieu of the present hierarchy from the centre to the periphery.

In common with most Socialists, the Anarchists recognize that, like all evolution in nature, the slow evolution of society is followed from time to time by periods of accelerated evolution which are called revolutions; and they think that the era of revolutions is not yet closed. Periods of rapid changes will follow the periods of slow evolution, and these periods must be taken advantage of – not for increasing and widening the powers of the State, but for reducing them, through the organization in every township or commune of the local groups of producers and consumers, as also the regional, and eventually the international, federations of these groups.

In virtue of the above principles the anarchists refuse to be party to the present State organization and to support it by infusing fresh blood into it. They do not seek to constitute, and invite the working men not to constitute, political parties in the parliaments. Accordingly, since the foundation of the first International Working Men's Association in 1864, they have endeavoured to promote their ideas directly amongst the labour organizations and to induce those unions to a direct struggle against capital, distrusting parliamentary legislation.

Scientific Anarchist-Communism. – As one of the anarchist-Communist direction, the present writer for many years endeavoured to develop the following ideas: to show the intimate, logical connection which exists between the modern philosophy of natural sciences and anarchism; to put anarchism on a scientific basis by the study of the tendencies that are apparent now in society and may indicate its further evolution; and to work out the basis of anarchist ethics. As regards the substance of anarchism itself, it was Kropotkin's aim to prove that Communism – at least partial – has more chances of being established than collectivism, especially in communes taking the lead, and that free, or anarchist-Communism is the only form of Communism that has any chance of being accepted in civilized societies; Communism and anarchy are therefore two terms of evolution which complete each other, the one rendering the other possible and acceptable. He has tried, moreover, to indicate how, during a revolutionary period, a large city – if its inhabitants have accepted the idea – could organize itself on the lines of free Communism; the city guaranteeing to every inhabitant dwelling, food and clothing to an extent corresponding to the comfort now available to the middle classes only, in exchange for a half-day's or a five-hours' work; and how all those things which would be considered as luxuries might be obtained by every one if he joins for the other half of the day all sorts of free associations pursuing all possible aims – educational, literary, scientific, artistic, sports and so on. In order to prove the first of these assertions he has analysed the possibilities of agriculture and industrial work, both being combined with brain work. And in order to elucidate the main factors of human evolution he has analysed the part played in history by the popular constructive agencies of mutual aid and the historical role of the State.

'Anarchism' (1910), reprinted in *Encyclopaedia Britannica*, 14th ed. (London and New York, 1926), vol. I, pp. 873–4, 877.

Vilfredo Pareto
(1848–1923)

INEVITABLE OLIGARCHY

The concepts various individuals have of what is good for them and good for others are essentially heterogeneous, and there is no way of reducing them to unity.

That fact is denied by people who think they know the absolute. They reduce all human opinions to their own opinion, eliminating the others by those processes of derivation of which we have given many examples; but the elimination is valid only for themselves and their followers, other people remaining of the differing opinions.

Social reformers as a rule also fail to notice, or at least they disregard, the fact that individuals entertain different opinions with regard to utility, and that they do so because they get the data they require from their own sentiments. They say, and believe, that they are solving an objective problem: 'What is the *best* form for a society?' Actually they are solving a subjective problem: 'What form of society best fits my sentiments?' The reformer, of course, is certain that his sentiments have to be shared by all honest men and that they are not merely excellent in themselves but are also in the highest degree beneficial to society. Unfortunately that belief in no way alters the realities.[1]

All governments use force, and all assert that they are founded on reason. In the fact, whether universal suffrage prevails or not, it is always an oligarchy that governs, finding ways to give to the 'will of the people'

[1] From the strictly objective standpoint the term 'best' as used in their theorem needs defining – it is essential, that is, to state exactly what the term is supposed to stand for. That is like determining exactly which one of the numberless states X one elects to consider. The ambiguity in the term is a favourite one with reformers and the many other people of their kind. It arises in the mistaken notion that there is one state X only. As a matter of fact there are an infinite number of states X.

that expression which the few desire, from the 'royal law' that bestowed the *imperium* on the Roman Emperors down to the votes of a legislative majority elected in one way or another, from the plebiscite that gave the empire to Napoleon III down to the universal suffrage that is shrewdly bought, steered and manipulated by our 'speculators'. Who is this new god called Universal Suffrage? He is no more exactly definable, no less shrouded in mystery, no less beyond the pale of reality, than the hosts of other divinities; nor are there fewer and less patent contradictions in his theology than in theirs. Worshippers of Universal Suffrage are not led by their god. It is they who lead him – and by the nose, determining the forms in which he must manifest himself. Oftentimes, proclaiming the sanctity of 'majority rule', they resist 'majority rule' by obstructionist tactics, even though they form but small minorities, and burning incense to the goddess Reason, they in no wise disdain, in certain cases, alliances with Chicanery, Fraud and Corruption.

Substantially such derivations express the sentiments felt by people who have climbed into the saddle and are willing to stay there – along with the far more general sentiment that social stability is a good thing. If, the moment a group, large or small, ceased to be satisfied with certain norms established in the community of which it is a part, it flew to arms to abolish them, organized society would fall to pieces. Social stability is so beneficial a thing that to maintain it it is well worth while to enlist the aid of fantastic ideals and this or that theology – among the others, the theology of universal suffrage – and be resigned to putting up with certain actual disadvantages. Before it becomes advisable to disturb the public peace, such disadvantages must have grown very very serious; and since human beings are effectively guided not by the sceptical reasonings of science but by 'living faiths' expressed in ideals, theories such as the divine right of kings, the legitimacy of oligarchies, of 'the people', of 'majorities', of legislative assemblies and other such things, may be useful within certain limits, and have in fact proved to be, however absurd they may be from the scientific standpoint.

Theories designed to justify the use of force by the governed are almost always combined with theories condemning the use of force by the public authority. A few dreamers reject the use of force in general, on whatever side; but their theories either have no influence at all or else serve merely to weaken resistance on the part of people in power, so clearing the field for violence on the part of the governed. In view of that we may confine ourselves to considering such theories, in general, in the combined form.

No great number of theories are required to rouse to resistance and to the use of force people who are, or think they are, oppressed. The derivations therefore are chiefly designed to incline people who would otherwise be neutral in the struggle to condemn resistance on the part of the governing powers, and so to make their resistance less vigorous; or at a venture, to persuade the rulers themselves in that sense, a thing, for that matter, that is not likely to have any great success in our day save with those whose spinal columns have utterly rotted from the bane of humanitarianism. A few centuries ago some results might have been achieved in our Western countries by working with religious derivations upon sincere Christians; and, in other countries, by working upon firm believers with derivations of the religion prevailing in the given case. Since humanitarianism is a religion, like the Christian, the Moslem, or any other, we may say, in general, that one may sometimes secure the aid of neutrals and weaken resistance on the part of people in power by using derivations of the religion, whatever it may be, in which they sincerely believe. But since derivations readily lend themselves to proving the pro and the contra, that device is often of scant effect even when it is not a mere mask for interests.

Government and its forms. Among the complex phenomena that are observable in a society, of very great importance is the system of government. That is closely bound up with the character of the governing class, and both stand in a relationship of interdependence with all other social phenomena.

Oftentimes, as usual, too much importance has been attached to forms at the expense, somewhat, of substance; and the thing chiefly considered has been the form that the political régime assumed. However, in France, especially during the reign of Napoleon III, and more particularly among economists, a tendency developed to ascribe little or no importance to forms of government, and not only that, to substance as well. That was going to another extreme, and exclusively 'political' theories of society were met with exclusively 'economic' theories, among them the theory of economic determinism – the usual mistake of disregarding mutual correlations in social phenomena.

Those who attach supreme significance to forms of government find it very important to answer the question, 'What is the best form of government?' But that question has little or no meaning unless the society to which the government is to be applied is specified and unless some explanation is given of the term 'best', which alludes in a very indefinite way to the various individual and social utilities. Although that has now and then been sensed, consideration of governmental forms has given rise to countless derivations leading up to this or that political myth, both derivations and myths being worth exactly zero from the logico-experimental standpoint, but both of them – or, rather the sentiments that they manifest – having, it may be, effects of great consequence in the way of influencing human conduct. It cannot be doubted that the sentiments manifested by the monarchical, republican, oligarchic, democratic and still other faiths, have played and continue to play no mean part in social phenomena, as is the case with the sentiments underlying other religions. The 'divine rights' of the prince, of the aristocracy, of the people, the proletariat, the majority – or any other divine right that might be imagined – have not the slightest experimental validity. We must therefore consider them extrinsically only, as facts, as manifestations of sentiments, operating, like other traits in the human beings that go to make up a given society, to determine its mode of being, its form. To say that no one of these 'rights' has any experimental foundation does not, of course, in any way impugn the utility to society with which it may be credited. Such an inference would be justified if the statement were a derivation, since in such reasonings it is generally taken for granted that anything that is not rational is harmful. But the question of utility is left untouched when the statement is rigorously logico-experimental, since then it contains no such implicit premise.[1]

The Mind and Society: A Treatise on General Sociology (1916), ed. A. Livingstone (New York, Dover Publications, 1963), vol. II, pp. 1476–8, 1526–8, 1566–8. (Republication of 1935 ed.)

[1] The study of forms of government belongs to *special* sociology. Here we are concerned with them only incidentally in connection with our quest for the substance underlying derivations and for the relationship between types of ruling-class composition and other social phenomena.

Eduard Bernstein
(1850–1932)

SOCIALISM AS ORGANIZING
LIBERALISM

What is the principle of democracy?

The answer to this appears very simple. At first one would think it settled by the definition 'government by the people'. But even a little consideration tells us that by that only quite a superficial, purely formal definition is given, whilst nearly all who use the word democracy today understand by it more than a mere form of government. We shall come much nearer to the definition if we express ourselves negatively, and define democracy as an absence of class government, as the indication of a social condition where a political privilege belongs to no one class as opposed to the whole community. By that the explanation is already given as to why a monopolist corporation is in principle anti-democratic. This negative definition has, besides, the advantage that it gives less room than the phrase 'government by the people' to the idea of the oppression of the individual by the majority which is absolutely repugnant to the modern mind. Today we find the oppression of the minority by the majority 'undemocratic', although it was originally held to be quite consistent with government by the people. The idea of democracy includes, in the conception of the present day, a notion of justice – an equality of rights for all members of the community, and in that principle the rule of the majority, to which in every concrete case the rule of the people extends, finds its limits. The more it is adopted and governs the general consciousness, the more will democracy be equal in meaning to the highest possible degree of freedom for all.

Democracy is in principle the suppression of class government, though it is not yet the actual suppression of classes. They speak of the conservative character of the democracy, and to a certain degree rightly. Absolutism, or semi-absolutism, deceives its supporters as well as its opponents as to the extent of their power. Therefore in countries where it obtains, or where its traditions still exist, we have flitting plans, exaggerated language, zigzag politics, fear of revolution, hope in oppression. In a democracy the parties, and the classes standing behind them, soon learn to know the limits of their power, and to undertake each time only as much as they can reasonably hope to carry through under the existing circumstances. Even if they make their demands rather higher than they seriously mean in order to give way in the unavoidable compromise – and democracy is the high school of compromise – they must still be moderate. The right to vote in a democracy makes its members virtually partners in the community, and this virtual partnership must in the end lead to real partnership. With a working class undeveloped in numbers and culture the general right to vote may long appear as the right to choose 'the butcher'; with the growing number and knowledge of the workers it is changed, however, into the implement by which to transform the representatives of the people from masters into real servants of the people.

The aim of all socialist measures, even of those which appear outwardly as coercive measures, is the development and the securing of a free personality. Their more exact examination always shows that the coercion included will raise the sum total of liberty in society, and will give more freedom over a more extended area than it takes away. The legal day of a maximum number of hours' work, for example, is actually a fixing of a minimum of freedom, a prohibition to sell freedom longer than for a certain number of hours daily, and, in principle, therefore, stands on the same ground as the prohibition agreed to by all liberals against selling oneself into personal slavery. It is thus no accident that the first country where a maximum hours' day was carried out was Switzerland, the most democratically progressive country in Europe, and democracy is only the political form of liberalism. Being in its origin a counter-movement to the oppression of nations under institutions imposed from without or having a justification only in tradition, liberalism first sought its realization as the principle of the sovereignty of the age and of the people, both of which principles formed the everlasting discussion of the philosophers of the rights of the state in the seventeenth and eighteenth centuries, until Rousseau set them up in his *Contrat Social* as the fundamental conditions of the legitimacy of every constitution, and the French Revolution proclaimed them – in the Democratic Constitution of 1793 permeated with Rousseau's spirit[1] – as inalienable rights of men.

The Constitution of 1793 was the logical expression of the liberal ideas of the epoch, and a cursory glance over its contents shows how little it was, or is, an obstacle to socialism. Babeuf, and the believers in absolute equality, saw in it an excellent starting point for the realization of their communistic strivings, and accordingly wrote 'The Restoration of the Constitution of 1793' at the head of their demands.

There is actually no really liberal thought which does not also belong to the elements of the ideas of socialism. Even the principle of economic personal responsibility which belongs apparently so entirely to the Manchester School cannot, in my judgement, be denied in theory by socialism nor be made inoperative under any conceivable circumstances. Without responsibility there is no freedom; we may think as we like theoretically about man's freedom of action, we must practically start from it as the foundation of the moral law, for only under this condition is social morality possible. And similarly, in our states which reckon with millions, a healthy social life is, in the age of traffic, impossible if the economic personal responsibility of all those capable of work is not assumed. The recognition of individual responsibility is the return of the individual to society for services rendered or offered him by society.

Perhaps I may be allowed to quote some passages from my article on 'The Social-Political Meaning of Space and Numbers'.

'Changes in the economic personal responsibility of those capable of work can, then, as far as we can see, only be made relatively. Labour statistics can be developed very much more, the exchange or adjustment of labour be very much perfected, the change of work be made easier and a right of the workers developed which renders possible an infinitely greater security of existence and facility for the choice of a calling than are given today. The most advanced organs of economic self-help – the great trade unions – already point out in this respect the way which evolution will presumably take. . . . If already strong trade unions secure to those of their members fit to work a certain right of occupation, when they impress the employers that it is very inadvisable to dismiss a member of the union without very valid reasons recognized also by the union, if they in giving information to members seeking occupation supply their

[1] Sovereignty 'rests with the people. It is indivisible, imprescriptible, inalienable' (Article 25). 'A people has at any time the right to revise, reform and alter its constitution. No generation can bind the next to its laws' (Article 28).

wants in order of application, there is in all this an indication of the development of a democratic right to work.' Other beginnings of it are found today in the form of industrial courts, trades councils and similar creations in which democratic self-government has taken shape, though still often imperfectly. On the other side, doubtless, the extension of the public services, particularly of the system of education and of reciprocal arrangements (insurances, etc.) helps very much towards divesting economic personal responsibility of its hardness. But a right to work, in the sense that the state guarantees to everyone occupation in his calling, is quite improbable in a visible time, and also not even desirable. What its pleaders want can only be attained with advantage to the community in the way described by the combination of various organs, and likewise the common duty to work can only be realized in this way without a deadening bureaucracy. In such great and complicated organisms as our modern civilized states and their industrial centres an absolute right to work would simply result in disorganization; it is 'only conceivable as a source of the most odious arbitrariness and everlasting quarrelling'.

Liberalism had historically the task of breaking the chains which the fettered economy and the corresponding organizations of law of the middle ages had imposed on the further development of society. That it at first strictly maintained the form of bourgeois liberalism did not stop it from actually expressing a very much wider-reaching general principle of society whose completion will be socialism.

Socialism will create no new bondage of any kind whatever. The individual is to be free, not in the metaphysical sense, as the anarchists dreamed – i.e., free from all duties towards the community – but free from every economic compulsion in his action and choice of a calling. Such freedom is only possible for all by means of organization. In this sense one might call socialism 'organizing liberalism' for when one examines more closely the organizations that socialism wants and how it wants them, he will find that what distinguishes them above all from the feudalistic organizations, outwardly like them, is just their liberalism, their democratic constitution, their accessibility. Therefore the trade union, striving after an arrangement similar to a guild, is, in the eyes of the socialist, the product of self-defence against the tendency of capitalism to overstock the labour market; but, at the same time, just on account of its tendency towards a guild, and to the degree in which that obtains, is it an unsocialistic corporate body.

The work here indicated is no very simple problem; it rather conceals within itself a whole series of dangers. Political equality alone has never hitherto sufficed to secure the healthy development of communities whose centre of gravity was in the giant towns. It is, as France and the United States show, no unfailing remedy against the rank growth of all kinds of social parasitism and corruption. If solidity did not reach so far down in the constitution of the French nation, and if the country were not so well favoured geographically, France would have long since been ruined by the land plague of the official class which has gained a footing there. In any case this plague forms one of the causes why, in spite of the great keenness of the French mind, the industrial development of France remains more backward than that of the neighbouring countries. If democracy is not to excel centralized absolutism in the breeding of bureaucracies, it must be built up on an elaborately organized self-government with a corresponding economic, personal responsibility of all the units of administration as well as of the adult citizens of the state. Nothing is more injurious to its healthy development than enforced uniformity and a too abundant amount of protectionism or subventionism.

To create the organizations described – or, so far as they are already begun, to develop them further – is the indispensable preliminary to what we call socialism of production.

Evolutionary Socialism: A Criticism and Affirmation (1899), trans. E. C. Harvey (London, Independent Labour Party, 1909), pp. 141–4, 149–55.

Oscar Wilde
(1854–1900)

ATTAINING INDIVIDUALISM
THROUGH SOCIALISM

It is clear, then, that no Authoritarian Socialism will do. For while under the present system a very large number of people can lead lives of a certain amount of freedom and expression and happiness, under an industrial-barrack system, or a system of economic tyranny, nobody would be able to have any such freedom at all. It is to be regretted that a portion of our community should be practically in slavery, but to propose to solve the problem by enslaving the entire community is childish. Every man must be left quite free to choose his own work. No form of compulsion must be exercised over him. If there is, his work will not be good for him, will not be good in itself and will not be good for others. And by work I simply mean activity of any kind.

I hardly think that any Socialist, nowadays, would seriously propose that an inspector should call every morning at each house to see that each citizen rose up and did manual labour for eight hours. Humanity has got beyond that stage, and reserves such a form of life for the people whom, in a very arbitrary manner, it chooses to call criminals. But I confess that many of the socialistic views that I have come across seem to me to be tainted with ideas of authority, if not of actual compulsion. Of course, authority and compulsion are out of the question. All association must be quite voluntary. It is only in voluntary associations that man is fine.

But it may be asked how Individualism, which is now more or less dependent on the existence of private property for its development, will benefit by the abolition of such private property. The answer is very simple. It is true that, under existing conditions, a few men who have had private means of their own, such as Byron, Shelley, Browning, Victor Hugo, Baudelaire and others, have been able to realize their personality, more or less completely. Not one of these men ever did a single day's work for hire. They were relieved from poverty. They had an immense advantage. The question is whether it would be for the good of Individualism that such an advantage should be taken away. Let us suppose that it is taken away. What happens then to Individualism? How will it benefit?

It will benefit in this way. Under the new conditions Individualism will be far freer, far finer and far more intensified than it is now. I am not talking of the great imaginatively realized Individualism of such poets as I have mentioned, but of the great actual Individualism latent and potential in mankind generally. For the recognition of private property has really harmed Individualism, and obscured it, by confusing a man with what he possesses. It has led Individualism entirely astray. It has made gain, not growth, its aim. So that man thought that the important thing was to have, and did not know that the important thing is to be. The true perfection of man lies, not in what man has, but in what man is. Private property has crushed true Individualism, and set up an Individualism that is false. It has debarred one part of the community from being individual by starving them. It has debarred the other part of the community from being individual by putting them on the wrong road, and encumbering them. Indeed, so completely has man's personality been absorbed by his possessions that the English law has always treated offences against a man's property with far more severity than offences against his person, and property is still the test of complete citizenship. The industry necessary for the making of money is also very demoralizing. In a community like ours, where property confers immense distinction, social position, honour, respect, titles and other pleasant things of the kind, man, being naturally ambitious, makes it his aim to accumulate this property, and goes on wearily and tediously accumulating it long after he has got far more than he wants, or can use, or enjoy, or perhaps even know of. Man will kill himself by overwork in order to secure property, and really, considering the enormous advantages that property brings, one is hardly surprised. One's regret is that society should be constructed on such a basis that man has been forced into a groove in which he cannot freely develop what is wonderful, and fascinating, and delightful in him – in which, in fact, he misses the true pleasure and joy of living. He is also, under existing conditions, very insecure. An enormously wealthy merchant may be – often is – at every moment of his life at the mercy of things that are not under his control. If the wind blows an extra point or so, or the weather suddenly changes, or some trivial thing happens, his ship may go down, his speculations may go wrong and he finds himself a poor man, with his social position quite gone. Now, nothing should be able to harm a man except himself. Nothing should be able to rob a man at all. What a man really has, is what is in him. What is outside of him should be a matter of no importance.

With the abolition of private property, then, we shall have true, beautiful, healthy Individualism. Nobody will waste his life in accumulating things, and the symbols for things. One will live. To live is the rarest thing in the world. Most people exist, that is all.

It is a question whether we have ever seen the full expression of a personality, except on the imaginative plane of art. In action, we never have.

It will be a marvellous thing – the true personality of man – when we see it. It will grow naturally and simply, flowerlike, or as a tree grows. It will not be at discord. It will never argue or dispute. It will not prove things. It will know everything. And yet it will not busy itself about knowledge. It will have wisdom. Its value will not be measured by material things. It will have nothing. And yet it will have everything, and whatever one takes from it, it will still have, so rich will it be. It will not be always meddling with others, or asking them to be like itself. It will love them because they will be different. And yet while it will not meddle with others, it will help all, as a beautiful thing helps us, by being what it is. The personality of man will be very wonderful. It will be as wonderful as the personality of a child.

Individualism, then, is what through Socialism we are to attain. As a natural result the State must give up all idea of government. It must give it up because, as a wise man once said many centuries before Christ, there is such a thing as leaving mankind alone; there is no such thing as governing mankind. All modes of government are failures. Despotism is unjust to everybody, including the despot, who was probably made for better things. Oligarchies are unjust to the many, and ochlocracies are unjust to the few. High hopes were once formed of democracy; but democracy means simply the bludgeoning of the people by the people for the people. It has been found out. I must say that it was high time, for all authority is quite degrading. It degrades those who exercise it, and degrades those over whom it is exercised. When it is violently, grossly and cruelly used, it produces a good effect, by creating, or at any rate bringing out, the spirit of revolt and Individualism that is to kill it.

When it is used with a certain amount of kindness, and accompanied by prizes and rewards, it is dreadfully demoralizing. People, in that case, are less conscious of the horrible pressure that is being put on them, and so go through their lives in a sort of coarse comfort, like petted animals, without ever realizing that they are probably thinking other people's thoughts, living by other people's standards, wearing practically what one may call other people's second-hand clothes and never being themselves for a single moment. 'He who would be free', says a fine thinker, 'must not conform.' And authority, by bribing people to conform, produces a very gross kind of overfed barbarism amongst us.

Now as the State is not to govern, it may be asked what the State is to do. The State is to be a voluntary association that will organize labour, and be the manufacturer and distributor of necessary commodities. The State is to make what is useful. The individual is to make what is beautiful. And as I have mentioned the word labour, I cannot help saying that a great deal of nonsense is being written and talked nowadays about the dignity of manual labour. There is nothing necessarily dignified about manual labour at all, and most of it is absolutely degrading. It is mentally and morally injurious to man to do anything in which he does not find pleasure, and many forms of labour are quite pleasureless activities, and should be regarded as such. To sweep a slushy crossing for eight hours on a day when the east wind is blowing is a disgusting occupation. To sweep it with mental, moral or physical dignity seems to me to be impossible. To sweep it with joy would be appalling. Man is made for something better than disturbing dirt. All work of that kind should be done by a machine.

And I have no doubt that it will be so. Up to the present, man has been, to a certain extent, the slave of machinery, and there is something tragic in the fact that as soon as man had invented a machine to do his work he began to starve. This, however, is, of course, the result of our property system and our system of competition. One man owns a machine which does the work of five hundred men. Five hundred men are, in consequence, thrown out of employment, and, having no work to do, become hungry and take to thieving. The one man secures the produce of the machine and keeps it, and has five hundred times as much as he should have, and probably, which is of much more importance, a great deal more than he really wants. Were that machine the property of all, everybody would benefit by it. It would be an immense advantage to the community. All unintellectual labour, all monotonous, dull labour, all labour that deals with dreadful things, and involves unpleasant conditions, must be done by machinery. Machinery must work for us in coal mines, and do all sanitary services, and be the stoker of steamers, and clean the streets, and run messages on wet days, and do anything that is tedious or distressing. At present machinery competes against man. Under proper conditions machinery will serve man. There is no doubt at all that this is the future of machinery; and just as trees grow while the country gentleman is asleep, so while Humanity will be amusing itself, or enjoying cultivated leisure – which, and not labour, is the aim of man – or making beautiful things, or reading beautiful things, or simply contemplating the world with admiration and delight, machinery will be doing all the necessary and unpleasant work. The fact is, that civilization requires slaves. The Greeks were quite right there. Unless there are slaves to do the ugly, horrible, uninteresting work, culture and contemplation become almost impossible. Human slavery is wrong, insecure and demoralizing. On mechanical slavery, on the slavery of the machine, the future of the world depends. And when scientific men are no longer called upon to go down to a depressing East End and distribute bad cocoa and worse blankets to starving people, they will have delightful leisure in which to devise wonderful and marvellous things for their own joy and the joy of everyone else. There will be great storages of force for every city, and for every house if required, and this force man will convert into heat, light or motion, according to his needs. Is this Utopian? A map of the world that does not include Utopia is not worth even glancing at, for it leaves out the one country at which Humanity is always landing. And when Humanity lands there, it looks out and, seeing a better country, sets sail. Progress is the realization of Utopias.

'The Soul of Man under Socialism' (1891), in *Selected Essays and Poems* (London, Penguin, 1954), pp. 23–6, 26–7, 30–1, 32–4.

Sigmund Freud
(1856–1939)

CULTURE AND AGGRESSION: A PERMANENT TENSION

The existence of this inclination to aggression, which we can detect in ourselves and justly assume to be present in others, is the factor which disturbs our relations with our neighbour and which forces civilization into such a high expenditure (of energy). In consequence of this primary mutual hostility of human beings, civilized society is perpetually threatened with disintegration. The interest of work in common would not hold it together; instinctual passions are stronger than reasonable interests. Civilization has to use its utmost efforts in order to set limits to man's aggressive instincts and to hold the manifestations of them in check by psychical reaction-formations. Hence, therefore, the use of methods intended to incite people into identifications and aim-inhibited relationships of love, hence the restriction upon sexual life, and hence too the ideal's commandment to love one's neighbour as oneself – a commandment which is really justified by the fact that nothing else runs so strongly counter to the original nature of man. In spite of every effort, these endeavours of civilization have not so far achieved very much. It hopes to prevent the crudest excesses of brutal violence by itself assuming the right to use violence against criminals, but the law is not able to lay hold of the more cautious and refined manifestations of human aggressiveness. The time comes when each one of us has to give up as illusions the expectations which, in his youth, he pinned upon his fellow-men, and when he may learn how much difficulty and pain has been added to his life by their ill-will. At the same time, it would be unfair to reproach civilization with trying to eliminate strife and competition from human activity. These things are undoubtedly indispensable. But opposition is not necessarily enmity; it is merely misused and made an *occasion* for enmity.

The communists believe that they have found the path to deliverance from our evils. According to them, man is wholly good and is well-disposed to his neighbour; but the institution of private property has corrupted his nature. The ownership of private wealth gives the individual power, and with it the temptation to ill-treat his neighbour; while the man who is excluded from possession is bound to rebel in hostility against his oppressor. If private property were abolished, all wealth held in common, and everyone allowed to share in the enjoyment of it, ill-will and hostility would disappear among men. Since everyone's needs would be satisfied, no one would have any reason to regard another as his enemy; all would willingly undertake the work that was necessary. I have no concern with any economic criticisms of the communist system; I cannot enquire into whether the abolition of private property is expedient or advantageous.[1] But I am able to recognize that the psychological premises on which the system is based are an untenable illusion. In abolishing private property we deprive the human love of aggression of one of its instruments, certainly a strong one, though certainly not the strongest; but we have in no way altered the differences in power and influence which are misused by aggressiveness, nor have we altered anything in its nature. Aggressiveness was not created by property. It reigned almost without limit in primitive times, when property was still very scanty, and it already shows itself in the nursery almost before property has given up its primal, anal form; it forms the basis of every relation of affection and love among people (with the single exception, perhaps, of the mother's relation to her male child). If we do away with personal rights over material wealth, there still remains prerogative in the field of sexual relationships, which is bound to become the source of the strongest dislike and the most violent hostility among men who in other respects are on an equal footing. If we were to remove this factor, too, by allowing complete freedom of sexual life and thus abolishing the family, the germ-cell of civilization, we cannot, it is true, easily foresee what new paths the development of civilization could take; but one thing

[1] Anyone who has tasted the miseries of poverty in his own youth and has experienced the indifference and arrogance of the well-to-do, should be safe from the suspicion of having no understanding or good will towards endeavours to fight against the inequality of wealth among men and all that it leads to. To be sure, if an attempt is made to base this fight upon an abstract demand, in the name of justice, for equality for all men, there is a very obvious objection to be made – that nature, by endowing individuals with extremely unequal physical attributes and mental capacities, has introduced injustices against which there is no remedy.

we can expect, and that is that this indestructible feature of human nature will follow it there.

The cultural super-ego has developed its ideals and set up its demands. Among the latter, those which deal with the relations of human beings to one another are comprised under the heading of ethics. People have at all times set the greatest value on ethics, as though they expected that it in particular would produce especially important results. And it does in fact deal with a subject which can easily be recognized as the sorest spot in every civilization. Ethics is thus to be regarded as a therapeutic attempt – as an endeavour to achieve, by means of a command of the super-ego, something which has so far not been achieved by means of any other cultural activities. As we already know, the problem before us is how to get rid of the greatest hindrance to civilization – namely, the constitutional inclination of human beings to be aggressive towards one another; and for that very reason we are especially interested in what is probably the most recent of the cultural commands of the super-ego, the commandment to love one's neighbour as oneself. In our research into, and therapy of, a neurosis, we are led to make two reproaches against the super-ego of the individual. In the severity of its commands and prohibitions it troubles itself too little about the happiness of the ego, in that it takes insufficient account of the resistances against obeying them – of the instinctual strength of the id (in the first place), and of the difficulties presented by the real external environment (in the second). Consequently we are very often obliged, for therapeutic purposes, to oppose the super-ego, and we endeavour to lower its demands. Exactly the same objections can be made against the ethical demands of the cultural super-ego. It, too, does not trouble itself enough about the facts of the mental constitution of human beings. It issues a command and does not ask whether it is possible for people to obey it. On the contrary, it assumes that a man's ego is psychologically capable of anything that is required of it, that his ego has unlimited mastery over his id. This is a mistake; and even in what are known as normal people the id cannot be controlled beyond certain limits. If more is demanded of a man, a revolt will be produced in him or a neurosis, or he will be made unhappy. The commandment, 'Love thy neighbour as thyself', is the strongest defence against human aggressiveness and an excellent example of the unpsychological proceedings of the cultural super-ego. The commandment is impossible to fulfil; such an enormous inflation of love can only lower its value, not get rid of the difficulty. Civilization pays no attention to all this; it merely admonishes us that the harder it is to obey the precept the more meritorious it is to do so. But anyone who follows such a precept in present-day civilization only puts himself at a disadvantage *vis-à-vis* the person who disregards it. What a potent obstacle to civilization aggressiveness must be, if the defence against it can cause as much unhappiness as aggressiveness itself! 'Natural' ethics, as it is called, has nothing to offer here except the narcissistic satisfaction of being able to think oneself better than others. At this point the ethics based on religion introduces its promises of a better after-life. But so long as virtue is not rewarded here on earth, ethics will, I fancy, preach in vain. I too think it quite certain that a real change in the relations of human beings to possessions would be of more help in this direction than any ethical commands; but the recognition of this fact among socialists has been obscured and made useless for practical purposes by a fresh idealistic misconception of human nature.

I believe the line of thought which seeks to trace in the phenomena of cultural development the part played by a super-ego promises still further discoveries. I hasten to come to a close. But there is one question which I can hardly evade. If the development of civilization has such a far-reaching similarity to the development of the individual and if it employs the same methods, may we not be justified in reaching the diagnosis that, under the influence of cultural urges, some civilizations, or some epochs of civilization – possibly the whole of mankind – have become 'neurotic'? An analytic dissection of such neuroses might lead to therapeutic recommendations which could lay claim to great practical interest. I would not say that an attempt of this kind to carry psycho-analysis over to the cultural community was absurd or doomed to be fruitless. But we should have to be very cautious and not forget that, after all, we are only dealing with analogies and that it is dangerous, not only with men but also with concepts, to tear them from the sphere in which they have originated and been evolved. Moreover, the diagnosis of communal neuroses is faced with a special difficulty. In an individual neurosis we take as our starting-point the contrast that distinguishes the patient from his environment, which is assumed to be 'normal'. For a group all of whose members are affected by one and the same disorder no such background could exist; it would have to be found elsewhere. And as regards the therapeutic application of our knowledge, what would be the use of the most correct analysis of social neuroses, since no one possesses authority to impose such a therapy upon the group? But in spite of all these difficulties, we may expect that one day someone will venture to embark upon a pathology of cultural communities.

For a wide variety of reasons, it is very far from my intention to express an opinion upon the value of human civilization. I have endeavoured to guard myself against the enthusiastic prejudice which holds that our civilization is the most precious thing that we possess or could acquire and that its path will necessarily lead to heights of unimagined perfection. I can at least listen without indignation to the critic who is of the opinion that when one surveys the aims of cultural endeavour and the means it employs, one is bound to come to the conclusion that the whole effort is not worth the trouble, and that the outcome of it can only be a state of affairs which the individual will be unable to tolerate. My impartiality is made all the easier to me by my knowing very little about all these things. One thing only do I know for certain and that is that man's judgements of value follow directly his wishes for happiness – that, accordingly, they are an attempt to support his illusions with arguments. I should find it very understandable if someone were to point out the obligatory nature of the course of human civilization and were to say, for instance, that the tendencies to a restriction of sexual life or to the institution of a humanitarian ideal at the expense of natural selection were developmental trends which cannot be averted or turned aside and to which it is best for us to yield as though they were necessities of nature. I know, too, the objection that can be made against this, to the effect that in the history of mankind, trends such as these, which were considered unsurmountable, have often been thrown aside and replaced by other trends. Thus I have not the courage to rise up before my fellow-men as a prophet, and I bow to their reproach that I can offer them no consolation: for at bottom that is what they are all demanding – the wildest revolutionaries no less passionately than the most virtuous believers.

The fateful question for the human species seems to me to be whether and to what extent their cultural development will succeed in mastering the disturbance of their communal life by the human instinct of aggression and self-destruction. It may be that in this respect precisely the present time deserves a special interest. Men have gained control over the forces of nature to such an extent that with their help they would have no difficulty in exterminating one another to the last man. They know this, and hence comes a large part of their current unrest, their unhappiness and their mood of anxiety. And now it is to be expected that the other of the two 'Heavenly Powers', eternal Eros, will make an effort to assert himself in the struggle with his equally immortal adversary. But who can foresee with what success and with what result?[1]

'Civilization and its Discontents' (1930), in *The Standard Edition of the Complete Psychological Works of Sigmund Freud*, rev. and ed. James Strachey (London, The Hogarth Press and the Institute of Psycho-Analysis, 1961), vol. XXI, pp. 112–14, 142–5.

[1] The final sentence was added in 1931 – when the menace of Hitler was already beginning to be apparent.

Émile Durkheim
(1858–1917)

MORALIZING ECONOMIC LIFE AND EMANCIPATING THE INDIVIDUAL

So it is a strangely superficial notion – this view of the classical economists, to whom all collective discipline is a kind of rather tyrannous
militarization. In reality, when it is normal and what it ought to be, it is
something very different. It is at once the epitome and the governing
condition of a whole life in common which individuals have no less at
heart than their own lives. And when we wish to see the guilds
reorganized on a pattern we will presently try to define, it is not simply
to have new codes superimposed on those existing; it is mainly so that
economic activity should be permeated by ideas and needs other than
individual ideas and needs, in fine, so that it should be socialized. It is, too,
with the aim that the professions should become so many moral *milieux*
and that these (comprising always the various organs of industrial and
commercial life) should constantly foster the morality of the professions.
As to the rules, although necessary and inevitable, they are but the outward expression of these fundamental principles. It is not a matter of
co-ordinating any changes outwardly and mechanically, but of bringing
men's minds into mutual understanding.

Moreover, it is not on economic grounds that the guild or corporative
system seems to me essential but for moral reasons. It is only through the
corporative system that the moral standard of economic life can be raised.
We can give some idea of the present situation by saying that the greater
part of the social functions (and this greater part means today the economic
– so wide is their range) are almost devoid of any moral influence, at any
rate in what is their own field. To be sure, the rules of common morality
apply to them, but they are rules made for a life in common and not
for this specific kind of life. Further, they are rules governing those relations of the specific kind of life which are not peculiar to industry and

253

commerce: they do not apply to the others. And why, indeed, in the case
of those others, should there be no need to submit to a moral influence?
What is to become of public morality if there is so little trace of the
principle of duty in this whole sphere that is so important in the social life?
There are professional ethics for the priest, the soldier, the lawyer, the
magistrate and so on. Why should there not be one for trade and industry?
Why should there not be obligations of the employee towards the employer and vice versa; or of business men one towards the other, so as to
lessen or regulate the competition they set up and to prevent it from
turning into a conflict sometimes – as today – almost as cruel as actual
warfare? All these rights and obligations cannot, however, be the same
in all branches of industry: they have to vary according to the conditions
in each. The obligations in the agricultural industry are not those obtain-
ing in the unhealthy industries, nor of course do those in commerce
correspond to those in what we call industry, and so on. A comparison
may serve to let us realize where we stand on these points. In the human
body all visceral functions are controlled by a particular part of the
nervous system other than the brain: this consists of the sympathetic
nerve and the vagus or pneumo-gastric nerves. Well, in our society, too,
there is a brain which controls the function of inter-relationship; but the
visceral functions, the functions of the vegetative life or what corresponds
to them, are subject to no regulative action. Let us imagine what would
happen to the functions of heart, lungs, stomach and so on, if they were
free like this of all discipline. . . . Just such a spectacle is presented by
nations where there are no regulative organs of economic life. To be
sure, the social brain, that is, the State, tries hard to take their place and
carry out their functions. But it is unfitted for it and its intervention, when
not simply powerless, causes troubles of another kind.

This is why I believe that no reform has greater urgency. I will not
say it would achieve everything, but it is the preliminary condition that
makes all the others possible. Let us suppose that by a miracle the whole
system of property is entirely transformed overnight and that on the
collective formula the means of production are taken out of the hands
of individuals and made over absolutely to collective ownership. All the
problems around us that we are debating today will still persist in their
entirety. There will always be an economic mechanism and various
agencies to combine in making it work. The rights and obligations of these
various agencies therefore have to be determined and in the different
branches of industry at that. So a corpus of rules has to be laid down,

fixing the stint of work, the pay of the members of staff and their obligations to one another, towards the community, and so on. This means,
then, that we should still be faced with a blank page to work on. Supposing the means – the machinery of labour – had been taken out of these
hands or those and placed in others, we should still not know how the
machinery worked or what the economic life should be, nor what to do
in the face of this change in conditions. The state of anarchy would still
persist; for, let me repeat, this state of anarchy comes about not from this
machinery being in these hands and not in those, but because the activity
deriving from it is not regulated. And it will not be regulated, nor its
moral standard raised, by any witchcraft. This control by rule and raising
of moral standards can be established neither by the scientist in his study
nor by the statesman; it has to be the task of the groups concerned. Since
these groups do not exist at the present time, it is of the greatest urgency
that they be created. The other problems can only be usefully tackled
after that.

Let us imagine – spread over the whole country – the various industries
grouped in separate categories based on similarity and natural affinity.
An administrative council, a kind of miniature parliament, nominated by
election, would preside over each group. We go on to imagine this council
or parliament as having the power, on a scale to be fixed, to regulate
whatever concerns the business: relations of employers and employed –
conditions of labour – wages and salaries – relations of competitors one
with another, and so on . . . and there we have the guild restored, but
in an entirely novel form. The establishment of this central organ
appointed for the management of the group in general, would in no way
exclude the forming of subsidiary and regional organs under its direction
and subordinate to it. The general rules to be laid down by it might be
made specific and adapted to apply to various parts of the area by industrial boards. These would be more regional in character just as today
under Parliament there are councils for the *département* or municipality.
In this way, economic life would be organized, regulated and defined,
without losing any of its diversity. Such organization would do no more
than introduce into the economic order the reforms already made in all
other spheres of the national life. Customs, morals, political administration, all of which formerly had a local character and varied from place to
place, have gradually moved towards uniformity and to a loss of diversity.
The former autonomous organs, the tribunals, the feudal and communal

powers, have become with time auxiliary organs, subordinate to the central organism that took shape. Is it not to be expected that the economic order will be transformed with the same trend and by the same process? What existed at the outset was a local structure, an affair of the community: what has to take its place is not a complete absence of organization, a state of anarchy; rather it would be a structure that was comprehensive and national, uniform and at the same time complex, in which the local groupings of the past would still survive, but simply as agencies to ensure communication and diversity.

Finally, it seems certain that this whole framework should be attached to the central organ, that is, to the State. Occupational legislation could hardly be other than an application in particular of the law in general, just as professional ethics can only be a special form of common morality.

We should now set forth how the State, without pursuing a mystic aim of any kind, goes on expanding its functions. If indeed we work on the premise that the rights of the individual are not *ipso facto* his at birth; that they are not inscribed in the nature of things with such certainty as warrants the State in endorsing them and promulgating them; that, on the contrary, the rights have to be won from the opposing forces that deny them; that the State alone is qualified to play this part – then it cannot keep to the functions of supreme arbiter and of administrator of an entirely prohibitive justice, as the utilitarian or Kantian individualism would have it. No, the State must deploy energies equal to those for which it has to provide a counter-balance. It must even permeate all those secondary groups of family, trade and professional association, Church, regional areas and so on . . . which tend, as we have seen, to absorb the personality of their members. It must do this, in order to prevent this absorption and free these individuals, and so as to remind these partial societies that they are not alone and that there is a right that stands above their own rights. The State must therefore enter into their lives, it must supervise and keep a check on the way they operate and to do this it must spread its roots in all directions. For this task, it cannot just withdraw into the tribunals, it must be present in all spheres of social life and make itself felt. Wherever these particular collective forces exist, there the power of the State must be, to neutralize them: for if they were left alone and to their own devices, they would draw the individual within their exclusive domination. Now, societies are becoming ever greater in scale and ever more complex: they are made up of circles of increasing diversity, and of manifold agencies, and these already possess in themselves a value to be reckoned. Therefore if it is to fulfil its function, the State, too, must branch out and evolve to the same degree.

Let us see why and how the main function of the State is to liberate the individual personalities. It is solely because, in holding its constituent societies in check, it prevents them from exerting the repressive influences over the individual that they would otherwise exert. So there is nothing inherently tyrannical about State intervention in the different fields of collective life; on the contrary, it has the object and the effect of alleviating tyrannies that do exist. It will be argued, might not the State in turn become despotic? Undoubtedly, provided there were nothing to counter that trend. In that case, as the sole existing collective force, it produces the effects that any collective force not neutralized by any counter-force of the same kind would have on individuals. The State itself then becomes a leveller and repressive. And its repressiveness becomes even harder to endure than that of small groups, because it is more artificial. The State, in our large-scale societies, is so removed from individual interests that it cannot take into account the special or local and other conditions in which they exist. Therefore when it does attempt to regulate them, it succeeds only at the cost of doing violence to them and distorting them. It is, too, not sufficiently in touch with individuals in the mass to be able to mould them inwardly, so that they readily accept its pressure on them. The individual eludes the State to some extent – the State can only be effective in the context of a large-scale society – and individual diversity may not come to light. Hence, all kinds of resistance and distressing conflicts arise. The small groups do not have this drawback. They are close enough to the things that provide their *raison d'être* to be able to adapt their actions exactly and they surround the individuals closely enough to shape them in their own image. The inference to be drawn from this comment, however, is simply that if that collective force, the State, is to be the liberator of the individual, it has itself need of some counterbalance; it must be restrained by other collective forces, that is, by those secondary groups we shall discuss later on. . . . It is not a good thing for the groups to stand alone, nevertheless they have to exist. And it is out of this conflict of social forces that individual liberties are born. Here again we see the significance of these groups. Their usefulness is not merely to regulate and govern the interests they are meant to serve.

They have a wider purpose; they form one of the conditions essential to the emancipation of the individual.

> *Professional Ethics and Civic Morals* (1898–1900), trans. C. Brookfield (London, Routledge, 1957), pp. 29–31, 37–8, 39, 62–3, 65–6.

Gaetano Mosca
(1858–1941)

REVIVING THE GOLDEN MEAN

... in any form of political organization, authority is either transmitted from above downward in the political or social scale, or from below upward. Either the choice of the lower official is left to the one above him, till we reach the supreme head, who chooses his immediate collaborators – the case of the typical absolute monarchy; or else the authority of the governor derives from the governed, as was the case in ancient Greece and in republican Rome.

The two systems may be fused and balanced in various ways, as happens in representative governments today. The present form of government in the United States would be a good example. There the president is chosen by the citizens as a whole, and he in turn appoints all the principal officials of the executive branch of the federal government and the magistrates of the Supreme Court.

The type of political organization in which authority is transmitted from the top of the political ladder to officials below Plato calls 'monarchical'. It might more accurately be styled 'autocratic', because a monarch, in the broad sense of the term, is just the head of a state, and there is always such a head, whatever the political system. It is more difficult to choose the word that is exactly suited to Plato's second type. Following his example, one might call it 'democratic'. We consider it more satisfactory to call it 'liberal', for by 'democracy' today we commonly mean a form of government in which all citizens have an equal share in the creation of the sovereign power. That has not always been the case in the past in systems in which 'the people' chose their governors, because 'the people' often meant a restricted aristocracy. One need only recall what happened under the constitutions of Greece and Rome. Some of them were unquestionably 'liberal'. In many medieval communes only men who were enrolled in the major trade guilds were fully-fledged citizens. The designation 'liberal' seems to us all the more appropriate in that it has become the custom to regard as 'free' peoples those whose rulers, according to law at least, must be chosen by all, or even by a part of the governed, and whose law must be an emanation of the general will. In autocratic systems, the law either has something immutable and sacred about it or else it is an expression of the autocrat's will or, rather, of the will of those who act in his name.

Conversely, the term 'democratic' seems more suitable for the tendency which aims to replenish the ruling class with elements deriving from the lower classes, and which is always at work, openly or latently and with greater or lesser intensity, in all political organisms. 'Aristocratic' we would call the opposite tendency, which also is constant and varies in intensity, and which aims to stabilize social control and political power in the descendants of the class that happens to hold possession of it at the given historical moment.

All these great thinkers or statesmen, then, would seem to have had one common feeling: that the soundness of political institutions depends upon an appropriate fusing and balancing of the differing but constant principles and tendencies which are at work in all political organisms. It would be premature in the present state of political science to attempt to formulate a law, but some such hypothesis as the following might be ventured: that violent political upheavals, such as occurred at the fall of the Roman Empire and are today occurring in Russia, entailing unutterable suffering for large portions of humanity and interrupting the progress of civilization for long years and perhaps centuries, arise primarily from the virtually absolute predominance of one of the two principles, or one of the two tendencies, that we have been studying; whereas the stability of states, the infrequency of such catastrophes, depends on a proper balancing of the two principles, the two tendencies.

This hypothesis could be corroborated by historical experiences in considerable numbers. But it rests primarily upon the assumption that only the opposition – one might almost say only the competition – of these contrary principles and tendencies can prevent an overaccentuation of the vices that are congenital to each of them.

This conclusion would correspond very closely to the old doctrine of the golden mean, which judged mixed governments best. In fact, we would only be reviving that doctrine, though on the basis of the more exact and profound knowledge that our times have attained as to the natural laws that influence and control the political organization of society. To be sure, there would still be the difficulty of determining just where the golden mean lies, and that difficulty would be so great that each of us could feel quite free to locate it as best suits his passions and interests.

But one practical method has occurred to us for helping well-meaning persons, whose exclusive aim is the general welfare and prosperity quite apart from any personal interest, or any systematic preconception. It would be to watch for – so to say – atmospheric changes in the times and in the peoples who live about us.

When, for instance, a glacial calm prevails, when we can feel no breath of political discussion blowing, when everybody is raising hymns of praise to some great restorer of order and peace, then we may rest assured that the autocratic principle is prevailing too strongly over the liberal, and vice versa when everybody is cursing tyrants and championing liberty. So too, when the novelists and poets are vaunting the glories of great families and uttering imprecations upon the common herd, we may safely consider that the aristocratic tendency is becoming too strong; and when a wild wind of social equality is howling and all men are voicing their tenderness for the interests of the humble, it is evident that the democratic tendency is strongly on the upgrade and approaching the danger point. To put the matter in two words, it is just a question of following a rule that is the opposite of the one that climbers have consciously or unconsciously followed at all times in all countries. If we do that, the little nucleus of sound minds and choice spirits that keep mankind from going to the dogs every other generation may on occasion be able to render a service to its contemporaries, and especially to the children of its contemporaries. For in political life, the mistakes of one generation are almost always paid for by the generation that follows.

'Elementi di Scienza Politica' (1923, vol. II), trans. as chs. 12–17 of *The Ruling Class*, ed. A. Livingstone, paperback ed. (New York, McGraw-Hill, 1939), pp. 394–5, 428–9.

Georg Simmel
(1858–1918)

HIERARCHY WITHOUT OPPRESSION

Historical development, however, shows sporadic beginnings of a social form whose fundamental perfection could reconcile the continuation of super-subordination with the values of freedom. It is on behalf of this form that socialism and anarchism fight for the abolition of super-subordination. After all, the motivation of the endeavor lies exclusively in the feeling-states of individuals, in the consciousness of degradation and oppression, in the descent of the whole ego to the lowness of the social stratum and, on the other hand, in the personal haughtiness into which self-feelings are transformed by externally leading positions. If some kind of social organization could avoid these psychological consequences of social inequality, social inequality could continue to exist without difficulties. Very often, one overlooks the purely technical character of socialism, the fact that it is a *means* for bringing about certain subjective reactions, that its ultimate source lies in men and in their life-feelings which are to be released by it. To be sure, the means – in accord with our psychological constitution – often becomes the end. The rational organization of society and the elimination of command and subjection appear as values not questioned beyond themselves, values claiming realization irrespective of those personal, eudaemonistic results. And yet, in these lies that real psychological power which socialism has at its disposal to inject into the movement of history. As a mere *means*, however, socialism succumbs to the fate of every means, namely, of never being, in principle, the *only* one. Since different causes may have the same effect, it is never impossible that the same purpose may be reached by different means. In so far as socialism is considered an institution depending on the will of people, it is only the first proposal for eliminating those eudaemonistic imperfections which derive from historical inequality. For this reason, it is so closely associated with the need for abolishing these inequalities that it appears synonymous with it.

But if it were possible to dissolve the association between super-subordination and the feeling of personal devaluation and oppression, there is no logical reason why the all-decisive feeling of dignity and of a life which is its own master, should stand and fall only with socialism. Maybe this aim will be achieved if the individual feeling of life grows more psychologically independent of external activity in general and, in particular, of the position which the individual occupies within the sphere of this external activity. It could be imagined that, in the course of civilization, work on behalf of production becomes more and more a mere technique, more and more losing its consequences for the personality and its intimate concerns. As a matter of fact, we do find as the sociological type which underlies various developments, an approximation to this separation of personality and work. While originally the two were fused, division of labor and production for the market, that is, for completely unknown and indifferent consumers, have later permitted the personality increasingly to withdraw from work and to become based upon itself. No matter how unconditional the expected obedience may be, at this later stage it at least no longer penetrates into the layers that are decisive for life-feeling and personality-value. Obedience is merely a technical necessity, a form of organization which remains in the separate sphere of external matters, in the same way as manual labor itself.

This differentiation of objective and subjective life-elements, whereby subordination is preserved as a technical-organizational value which has no personally and internally depressing and degrading consequences, is, of course, no panacea for all the difficulties and sufferings that are everywhere produced by domination and obedience. In the present context, the differentiation is merely the principal expression of a tendency which is only partially effective and which in actuality never yields an undistorted and conclusive result. Voluntary military service, however, is one of its purest examples in our time. The intellectually and socially highest person may subordinate himself to a non-commissioned officer and actually tolerate a treatment which, if it really concerned his ego and feeling of honor, would move him to the most desperate reactions. But he is aware that he must bow before an objective technique, not as an individual personality, but only as an impersonal link requiring such discipline. This awareness, at least in many cases, prevents a feeling of degradation and oppression from arising. In the field of economics, it is particularly the transition from job work to machine work and from compensation in kind to compensation in wage which promote this objectification of super-subordination – as compared with the situation of the journeyman where the supervision and domination of the master extend to all aspects of the journeyman's life, quite beyond the prerogative which accrues to the master from the journeyman's role as a worker.

The same goal of development might be served by a further important type of sociological formation. It will be recalled that Proudhon wished to eliminate super-subordination by dissolving all dominating structures which, as the vehicles of social forces, have become differentiated out of individual interaction, and by once more founding all order and cohesion upon the direct interaction of free, co-ordinate individuals. But this co-ordination can perhaps be reached even if superordination and sub-ordination continue to exist – provided they are reciprocal. We would then have an ideal organization, in which A is superordinate to B in one respect or at one time, but in which, in another respect or at another time, B is superordinate to A. This arrangement would preserve the organizational value of super-subordination, while removing its oppressiveness, onesidedness and injustice. As a matter of fact, there are a great many phenomena of social life in which this form-type is realized, even though only in an embryonic, mutilated and covert way. A small-scale example might be the production association of workers for an enterprise for which they elect a master and foreman. While they are subordinate to him in regard to the technique of the enterprise, they yet are his superordinates with respect to its general direction and results. All groups in which the leader changes either through frequent elections or according to a rule of succession – down to the presidents of social clubs – transform the synchronous combination of superordination and subordination into their temporal alternation. In doing so, they gain the technical advantages of super-subordination while avoiding its personal disadvantages. All outspoken democracies try to attain this by means of brief office terms or by the prohibition of re-election, or both. In this fashion, the ideal of everybody having his turn is realized as far as possible. Simultaneous superordination and subordination is one of the most powerful forms of interaction. In its correct distribution over numerous fields, it can constitute a very strong bond between individuals, merely by the close interaction entailed by it.

> 'Sociology: Studies of the Forms of Societalization' (1908, 3rd ed. 1923), in *The Sociology of Georg Simmel,* ed. and trans. K. H. Wolff (Glencoe, Free Press, n.d.), pp. 282–5.

Sidney Webb (1859–1947)
and Beatrice Webb (1858–1943)

MEASUREMENT AND PUBLICITY

The disastrous assumption on which the Capitalist System was based –
an assumption as immoral as it was fortunately untrue – that man in
society is and should be inspired, in the exercise of his function, by
the passion for riches, was a morbid obsession into which Western Europe
passed less than three centuries ago, and out of which it is now emerging.
The assumption was never accepted by the learned professions, nor, in
Great Britain, by the typical civil servants. It never even penetrated to the
bulk of the manual workers, who were saved from the assumption by the
fact that, as a class, they had only the smallest possible opportunity of
acquiring riches. The equivalent in their case was the equally demoralizing
motive of the fear of starvation. We think that the tide has now turned.
The rapid growth of the consumers' Co-operative Movement on the one
hand, and of State and Municipal enterprise on the other, has given the
community a large and constantly growing class of administrators and
technicians who are debarred by economic circumstances and by professional honour from making profit out of each day's transactions. From
these men and women society is accustomed to ask and to receive assiduous
and honest public service in return for their accustomed livelihood. It is
this assumption of honest public service that, with a better organization
of industry, we hope and expect to generalize. And we mean by honest
public service no Utopian altruism. Martyrs and saints, like poets and
inventors, are needed for the progress of the human race to ever higher
planes of feeling and intellect. But no Socialist expects, or even desires,
a race of self-sacrificing saints who deny to themselves that enjoyment of
life which they seek to maximize in the lives of other people, any more
than he expects or desires that all men shall be artistic geniuses or scientific
discoverers. What the establishment of a genuine Co-operative Common-

wealth requires in the way of an advance in morality is no more than that those who have the gift for industrial organization should be as public-spirited in their work, and as modest in their claims to a livelihood, as is already normally the case among scientific workers, teachers in schools and colleges, the whole army of civil servants of every degree and kind, municipal officers of every grade, the administrators of the Co-operative Movement and the officials of the Trade Union world. And this substitution of the motive of public service for the motive of self-enrichment will be fostered by the change already beginning in public opinion, which will make 'living by owning' as shameful as the pauperism of the wastrel; and will, moreover, regard the exceptionally gifted man who insists on extorting from the community the full rent of his ability as a mean fellow – as mean as the surgeon who refuses to operate except for the highest fee that he can extract. Equally influential will be the social approval and public honour given, not to success in amassing riches, but to dis-interested and zealous public service. Is it cynical to suggest that, for one pioneer in a higher morality there are hundreds of worthy citizens whose lack of moral imagination will lead them to accept a higher morality as a new convention, to which they automatically conform? New and better conventions in morality, which are at all times within the capacity of the community, are, in fact, the normal way of standardizing and generalizing the moral discoveries of the race, just as the new scientific school-books serve to standardize and generalize our widening knowledge. Men are, in their manners and morals, to a far larger extent than is yet realized, what their fellows expect them to be. It is in this sense that Socialist institutions within a community, exacting from the average man a higher level of morality than that of the Capitalist System – like a genuine League of Nations among communities themselves – bring about an actual change of heart, and are thus the effective instruments of religion.

It is, indeed, not any failure in public spirit that presents, at least in an Anglo-Saxon race, the greatest obstacle to social amelioration. More diffi-cult, in our view, will it be to induce the whole body of citizens – the wealthy and the college-trained no less than the manual workers – to realize the imperative need for a rapid development of science in its widest sense, alike in the discovery of new knowledge and in the universal dis-semination of scientific methods of thinking. This is necessary if we are to get a greater output. Not the least of the shortcomings of the Capitalist System has been its calamitous failure to produce, in the aggregate, anything like enough commodities and services even to keep the community in health and efficiency, let alone enough to constitute a decent mental and physical environment for the whole people. In the Great War, indeed, this failure in production was so glaringly revealed that a capitalist government had, perforce, hastily to improvise a different organization, in order merely to survive.[1] More science in the organization of production (not of material commodities only) is therefore indispensable. If we wish to divide among the whole community a larger quantity and a higher quality of commodities and services than the painfully exiguous yield of the Capitalist System of today, the necessary increase in output has to be secured. And goodwill alone will not secure it. Even the replacement of the desire for riches by the motive of public service, as the dominant stimulus of personal effort, will not give us the needful larger and better production, without the application of much more science to the work than the Capitalist System has yet known how to harness. The need is, of course, not for physical science only. It was one of the disastrous mistakes of the Victorian era that physical science seemed to be the only science worth cultivating. There is no reason to fear that mechanics, physics and chemistry will be neglected, even if discoverers have no chance of accumulating personal riches. There is, indeed, good ground for expecting discovery in physical science to go forward by leaps and bounds, in a way that may presently transform all our dealings with forms of force and kinds of substance. But what is no less needed than this greater knowledge of things, is the greater knowledge of men: of the conditions of the successful working of social institutions. That on which the world today most needs light is how to render more effective every form of social organization: how to make more socially

---

[1] Now that the war is over, we find again put forward the (surely ironical?) defence of private property in the instruments of production, that, however inadequate may be its provision for the mass of the workers, it, at least, affords to a small minority of landlords and capitalists the ease and plenty on which alone such of them as are active administrators can put forth their full powers! Apart from the disquieting fact that the community, in thus feeding luxuriously a whole class, has no guarantee that any one of the class will devote himself to the public service – apart also from the still more disquieting doubt whether the possession of riches can be relied on as a stimulus to productive effort – the validity of this defence of the Capitalist System depends, perhaps, on whether it is any longer possible to compel the great majority of the people, whom the system does not seem to fatten, and who are no longer either so ignorant or so powerless as they were, to continue to work upon such terms. A refusal might lead, at least temporarily, to a dead level of economic disaster. Unfortunately the disaster to the rich that an economic upheaval might produce would not bring wealth to the poor, and might, conceivably, not be even a stage on the road to a decent social order.

fertile the relations among men. And this nascent science and art of democratic institutions, in which, for all that has so far been done, a hundredfold yet remains to do, must be, in the generation that is to come, as effectively opened up to the masses of manual workers as to the administrators and technicians. Without this community in knowledge there will, very shortly, be no popular consent. There is no need so imperative today as increased economic and political science. There is no peril so dangerous as the failure to get community of education among all classes.

It is, perhaps, in this respect that Parliamentary institutions have most lamentably fallen short. They have had no regard for knowledge. If they are now so rapidly losing public respect, and the support of popular consent, it is because Members of Parliament and Cabinet Ministers show themselves not only so ignorant of their job, but also so complacently unaware that they have anything to learn; and therefore quite unconscious of the need for making the electorate any better educated than they are themselves.

But our present failures are to be ascribed, not merely to deficiencies in knowledge, but also to the impossibility, with our existing institutions, of bringing into play such knowledge as is available. The House of Commons and the Cabinet, as they exist today, are as incapable of organizing the industrial and social life of Great Britain, so as to make a decent social order, as the Capitalist System has proved itself to be. It is for this reason that thoughtful Socialists lay so much stress on quite a different conception of Government. They are insistent, for the new social order, not only on a varied and highly developed organization of knowledge, and of an 'Adult Education' far transcending the present imagination of the Board of Education, but also on such a transformation of administrative institutions, from the House of Commons to the Trade Union, as will provide an environment of free initiative and personal activity, which are now so much restricted, and without which there can, in the long run, be no full social efficiency. It is with this object that, far from heaping up all government on a centralized authority, they propose the widest possible variety in the forms of socialization – calling in aid a far-reaching reorganization of the vocational world, a vast extension of the consumers' Co-operative Movement, a great development of Local Government and even the splitting into two of the powers of Parliament itself. The same sense of the need for much more detailed knowledge and much more widely disseminated personal interest in production and distribution than the Capitalist System has been able to afford, lies at the back of the proposals for a constantly increasing participation of employees of all kinds and grades in the management of the enterprise. We ourselves lay equal stress on the freedom of the independent professional, and even on the continuance, unabsorbed, of individual producers themselves owning the instruments with which they labour. What we visualize is a community so variously organized, and so highly differentiated in function as to be not only invigorated by a sense of personal freedom, but also constantly swept by the fresh air of experiment, observation and verification. We want to get rid of the 'stuffiness' of private interests which now infects our institutions; and to usher in a reign of 'Measurement and Publicity'. It is to a free Democracy, inspired by the spirit of social service, and illumined by ever-increasing knowledge, that we dedicate this book.

A Constitution for the Socialist Commonwealth of Great Britain (London, Longmans, Green & Co., 1920), pp. 350–6.

Max Weber
(1864–1920)

THE BUREAUCRATIC FUTURE

Imagine the consequences of that comprehensive bureaucratization and rationalization which already today we see approaching. Already now, throughout private enterprise in wholesale manufacture, as well as in all other economic enterprises run on modern lines, *Rechenhaftigkeit*, rational calculation, is manifest at every stage. By it, the performance of each individual worker is mathematically measured, each man becomes a little cog in the machine and, aware of this, his one preoccupation is whether he can become a bigger cog. Take as an extreme example the authoritative power of the State or of the municipality in a monarchical constitution: it is strikingly reminiscent of the ancient kingdom of Egypt, in which the system of the 'minor official' prevailed at all levels. To this day there has never existed a bureaucracy which could compare with that of Egypt. This is known to everyone who knows the social history of ancient times; and it is equally apparent that today we are proceeding towards an evolution which resembles that system in every detail, except that it is built on other foundations, on technically more perfect, more rationalized and therefore much more mechanized foundations. The problem which besets us now is not: how can this evolution be changed? – for that is impossible, but: what will come of it? We willingly admit that there are honourable and talented men at the top of our administration; that in spite of all the exceptions such people have opportunities to rise in the official hierarchy, just as the universities, for instance, claim that, in spite of all the exceptions, they constitute a chance of selection for talent. But horrible as the thought is that the world may one day be peopled with professors (laughter) – we would retire on to a desert island if such a thing were to happen (laughter) – it is still more horrible to think that the world could one day be filled with nothing but those little cogs, little men clinging to little jobs and striving towards bigger ones – a state of affairs which is to be seen once more, as in the Egyptian records, playing an ever-increasing part in the spirit of our present administrative system, and specially of its offspring, the students. This passion for bureaucracy, as we have heard it expressed here, is enough to drive one to despair. It is as if in politics the spectre of timidity – which has in any case always been rather a good standby for the German – were to stand alone at the helm; as if we were deliberately to become men who need 'order' and nothing but order, who become nervous and cowardly if for one moment this order wavers, and helpless if they are torn away from their total incorporation in it. That the world should know no men but these: it is in such an evolution that we are already caught up, and the great question is therefore not how we can promote and hasten it, but what can we oppose to this machinery in order to keep a portion of mankind free from this parcelling-out of the soul, from this supreme mastery of the bureaucratic way of life.

'Max Weber on Bureaucratization in 1909' from Appendix 1 in J. P. Mayer, *Max Weber and German Politics* (London, Faber, 1944), pp. 96–7.

William Butler Yeats
(1865–1939)

TRADITIONAL SANCTITY AND LOVELINESS

There where the course is,
Delight makes all of the one mind,
The riders upon the galloping horses,
The crowd that closes in behind:
We, too, had good attendance once,
Hearers and hearteners of the work;
Aye, horsemen for companions,
Before the merchant and the clerk
Breathed on the world with timid breath.
Sing on: somewhere at some new moon,
We'll learn that sleeping is not death,
Hearing the whole earth change its tune,
Its flesh being wild, and it again
Crying aloud as the racecourse is,
And we find hearteners among men
That ride upon horses.

'At Galway Races' (1910), in *The Collected Poems of W. B. Yeats* (London, Macmillan, 1963), p. 108.

Under my window-ledge the waters race,
Otters below and moor-hens on the top,
Run for a mile undimmed in Heaven's face
Then darkening through 'dark' Raftery's 'cellar' drop,
Run underground, rise in a rocky place

In Coole demesne, and there to finish up
Spread to a lake and drop into a hole.
What's water but the generated soul?

Upon the border of that lake's a wood
Now all dry sticks under a wintry sun,
And in a copse of beeches there I stood,
For Nature's pulled her tragic buskin on
And all the rant's a mirror of my mood:
At sudden thunder of the mounting swan
I turned about and looked where branches break
The glittering reaches of the flooded lake.

Another emblem there! That stormy white
But seems a concentration of the sky;
And, like the soul, it sails into the sight
And in the morning's gone, no man knows why;
And is so lovely that it sets to right
What knowledge or its lack had set awry,
So arrogantly pure, a child might think
It can be murdered with a spot of ink.

Sound of a stick upon the floor, a sound
From somebody that toils from chair to chair;
Beloved books that famous hands have bound,
Old marble heads, old pictures everywhere;
Great rooms where travelled men and children found
Content or joy; a last inheritor
Where none has reigned that lacked a name and fame
Or out of folly into folly came.

A spot whereon the founders lived and died
Seemed once more dear than life; ancestral trees,
Or gardens rich in memory glorified
Marriages, alliances and families,
And every bride's ambition satisfied.
Where fashion or mere fantasy decrees
We shift about – all that great glory spent –
Like some poor Arab tribesman and his tent.

We were the last romantics – chose for theme
Traditional sanctity and loveliness;
Whatever's written in what poets name
The book of the people; whatever most can bless
The mind of man or elevate a rhyme;
But all is changed, that high horse riderless,
Though mounted in that saddle Homer rode
Where the swan drifts upon a darkening flood.

'Coole Park and Ballylee' (1931), in ibid., pp. 275–6.

V. I. Lenin
(1870–1924)

THE HIGHER STAGE OF COMMUNISM

Marx continues:

... In a higher phase of communist society, after the enslaving sub-ordination of the individual to the division of labour and with it also the antithesis between mental and physical labour has vanished, after labour has become not only a livelihood but life's prime want, after the productive forces have increased with the all-round development of the individual, and all the springs of co-operative wealth flow more abundantly – only then can the narrow horizon of bourgeois right be crossed in its entirety and society inscribe on its banners: From each according to his ability, to each according to his needs!

Only now can we fully appreciate the correctness of Engels's remarks mercilessly ridiculing the absurdity of combining the words 'freedom' and 'state'. So long as the state exists there is no freedom. When there is freedom, there will be no state.

The economic basis for the complete withering away of the state is such a high stage of development of communism at which the antithesis between mental and physical labour disappears, at which there conse-quently disappears one of the principal sources of modern *social* inequality – a source, moreover, which cannot on any account be removed immedi-ately by the mere conversion of the means of production into public property, by the mere expropriation of the capitalists.

This expropriation will make it *possible* for the productive forces to develop to a tremendous extent. And when we see how incredibly capital-ism is already *retarding* this development, when we see how much progress could be achieved on the basis of the level of technique already attained, we are entitled to say with the fullest confidence that the expropriation of the capitalists will inevitably result in an enormous development of the productive forces of human society. But how rapidly this development will proceed, how soon it will reach the point of breaking away from the division of labour, of doing away with the antithesis between mental and physical labour, of transforming labour into 'life's prime want' – we do not and *cannot* know.

That is why we are entitled to speak only of the inevitable withering away of the state, emphasizing the protracted nature of this process and its dependence upon the rapidity of development of the *higher phase* of communism, and leaving the question of the time required for, or the concrete forms of, the withering away quite open, because there is *no* material for answering these questions.

The state will be able to wither away completely when society adopts the rule: 'From each according to his ability, to each according to his needs', i.e. when people have become so accustomed to observing the fundamental rules of social intercourse and when their labour has become so productive that they will voluntarily work *according to their ability*. 'The narrow horizon of bourgeois right', which compels one to calculate with the heartlessness of a Shylock whether one has not worked half an hour more than somebody else, whether one is not getting less pay than somebody else – this narrow horizon will then be crossed. There will then be no need for society, in distributing products, to regulate the quantity to be received by each; each will take freely 'according to his needs'.

From the bourgeois point of view, it is easy to declare that such a social order is 'sheer utopia' and to sneer at the socialists for promising everyone the right to receive from society, without any control over the labour of the individual citizen, any quantity of truffles, cars, pianos, etc. Even to this day, most bourgeois 'savants' confine themselves to sneering in this way, thereby betraying both their ignorance and their selfish defence of capitalism.

Ignorance – for it has never entered the head of any socialist to 'promise' that the higher phase of the development of communism will arrive; as for the great socialists' *forecast* that it will arrive, it presupposes not the present productivity of labour and *not the present* ordinary run of people, who, like the seminary students in Pomyalovsky's stories, are capable of damaging the stocks of public wealth 'just for fun', and of demanding the impossible.

Until the 'higher' phase of communism arrives, the socialists demand the *strictest* control by society *and by the state* over the measure of labour and the measure of consumption; but this control must *start* with the expropriation of the capitalists, with the establishment of workers' control over the capitalists, and must be exercised not by a state of bureaucrats, but by a state of *armed workers*.

The selfish defence of capitalism by the bourgeois ideologists (and their hangers-on, like the Tseretelis, Chernovs and Co.) consists in that they *substitute* arguing and talk about the distant future for the vital and burning question of *present-day* politics, namely, the expropriation of the capitalists, the conversion of *all* citizens into workers and other employees of *one* huge 'syndicate' – the whole state – and the complete subordination of the entire work of this syndicate to a genuinely democratic state, *the state of the Soviets of Workers' and Soldiers' Deputies*.

In fact, when a learned professor, followed by the philistine, followed in turn by the Tseretelis and Chernovs, talks of wild utopias, of the demagogic promises of the Bolsheviks, of the impossibility of 'introducing' socialism, it is the higher stage, or phase, of communism he has in mind, which no one has ever promised or even thought to 'introduce', because, generally speaking, it cannot be 'introduced'.

And this brings us to the question of the scientific distinction between socialism and communism which Engels touched on in his above-quoted argument about the incorrectness of the name 'Social-Democrat'. Politically, the distinction between the first, or lower, and the higher phase of communism will in time, probably, be tremendous. But it would be ridiculous to recognize this distinction now, under capitalism, and only individual anarchists, perhaps, could invest it with primary importance (if there still are people among the anarchists who have learned nothing from the 'Plekhanov' conversion of the Kropotkins, of Grave, Cornelissen and other 'stars' of anarchism into social-chauvinists or 'anarcho-trenchists', as Ghe, one of the few anarchists who have still preserved a sense of honour and a conscience, has put it).

But the scientific distinction between socialism and communism is clear. What is usually called socialism was termed by Marx the 'first', or lower, phase of communist society. In so far as the means of production become *common* property, the word 'communism' is also applicable here, providing we do not forget that this is *not* complete communism. The great significance of Marx's explanations is that here, too, he consistently applies materialist dialectics, the theory of development, and regards communism as something which develops *out of* capitalism. Instead of scholastically invented, 'concocted' definitions and fruitless disputes over words (What is socialism? What is communism?), Marx gives an analysis of what might be called the stages of the economic maturity of communism.

In its first phase, or first stage, communism *cannot* as yet be fully mature economically and entirely free from traditions or vestiges of capitalism. Hence the interesting phenomenon that communism in its first phase retains 'the narrow horizon of *bourgeois* right'. Of course, bourgeois right in regard to the distribution of *consumer* goods inevitably presupposes the existence of the *bourgeois state*, for right is nothing without an apparatus capable of *enforcing* the observance of the standards of right.

It follows that under communism there remains for a time not only bourgeois right, but even the bourgeois state, without the bourgeoisie!

This may sound like a paradox or simply a dialectical conundrum, of which Marxism is often accused by people who have not taken the slightest trouble to study its extraordinarily profound content.

But in fact, remnants of the old, surviving in the new, confront us in life at every step, both in nature and in society. And Marx did not arbitrarily insert a scrap of 'bourgeois' right into communism, but indicated what is economically and politically inevitable in a society emerging *out of the womb* of capitalism.

Democracy is of enormous importance to the working class in its struggle against the capitalists for its emancipation. But democracy is by no means a boundary not to be overstepped; it is only one of the stages on the road from feudalism to capitalism, and from capitalism to communism.

Democracy means equality. The great significance of the proletariat's struggle for equality and of equality as a slogan will be clear if we correctly interpret it as meaning the abolition of *classes*. But democracy means only *formal* equality. And as soon as equality is achieved for all members of society *in relation* to ownership of the means of production, that is, equality of labour and wages, humanity will inevitably be confronted with the question of advancing farther, from formal equality to actual equality, i.e. to the operation of the rule 'from each according to his ability, to each according to his needs'. By what stages, by means of what practical measures humanity will proceed to this supreme aim we do not and cannot know. But it is important to realize how infinitely mendacious is the ordinary bourgeois conception of socialism as something lifeless, rigid, fixed once and for all, whereas in reality *only* socialism will be the beginning of a rapid, genuine, truly mass forward movement, embracing first the *majority* and then the whole of the population, in all spheres of public and private life.

Democracy is a form of the state, one of its varieties. Consequently, it, like every state, represents, on the one hand, the organized, systematic use of force against persons; but, on the other hand, it signifies the formal recognition of equality of citizens, the equal right of all to determine the structure of, and to administer, the state. This, in turn, results in the fact that, at a certain stage in the development of democracy, it first welds together the class that wages a revolutionary struggle against capitalism – the proletariat, and enables it to crush, smash to atoms, wipe off the face of the earth the bourgeois, even the republican-bourgeois, state machine, the standing army, the police and the bureaucracy and to substitute for them a *more* democratic state machine, but a state machine nevertheless, in the shape of armed workers who proceed to form a militia involving the entire population.

Here 'quantity turns into quality': *such* a degree of democracy implies overstepping the boundaries of bourgeois society and beginning its socialist reorganization. If really *all* take part in the administration of the state, capitalism cannot retain its hold. The development of capitalism, in turn, creates the *preconditions* that *enable* really 'all' to take part in the administration of the state. Some of these preconditions are: universal literacy, which has already been achieved in a number of the most advanced capitalist countries, then the 'training and disciplining' of millions of workers by the huge, complex, socialized apparatus of the postal service, railways, big factories, large-scale commerce, banking, etc., etc.

Given these *economic* preconditions, it is quite possible, after the overthrow of the capitalists and the bureaucrats, to proceed immediately, overnight, to replace them in the *control* over production and distribution, in the work of *keeping account* of labour and products, by the armed workers, by the whole of the armed population. (The question of control and accounting should not be confused with the question of the scientifically trained staff of engineers, agronomists and so on. These gentlemen are working today in obedience to the wishes of the capitalists, and will work even better tomorrow in obedience to the wishes of the armed workers.)

Accounting and control – that is *mainly* what is needed for the 'smooth working', for the proper functioning, of the *first phase* of communist society. *All* citizens are transformed into hired employees of the state, which consists of the armed workers. *All* citizens become employees and workers of a *single* country-wide state 'syndicate'. All that is required is that they should work equally, do their proper share of work and get equal pay. The accounting and control necessary for this have been *simplified* by capitalism to the utmost and reduced to the extraordinarily simple operations – which any literate person can perform – of supervising and recording, knowledge of the four rules of arithmetic, and issuing appropriate receipts.[1]

When the *majority* of the people begin independently and everywhere to keep such accounts and exercise such control over the capitalist (now converted into employees) and over the intellectual gentry who preserve their capitalist habits, this control will really become universal, general and popular; and there will be no getting away from it, there will be 'nowhere to go'.

The whole of society will have become a single office and a single factory, with equality of labour and pay.

But this 'factory' discipline, which the proletariat, after defeating the capitalists, after overthrowing the exploiters, will extend to the whole of society, is by no means our ideal, or our ultimate goal. It is only a necessary *step* for thoroughly cleaning society of all the infamies and abominations of capitalist exploitation, *and for further* progress.

From the moment all members of society, or at least the vast majority, have learned to administer the state *themselves*, have taken this work into their own hands, have organized control over the insignificant capitalist minority, over the gentry who wish to preserve their capitalist habits and over the workers who have been thoroughly corrupted by capitalism – from this moment the need for government of any kind begins to disappear altogether. The more complete the democracy, the nearer the moment when it becomes unnecessary. The more democratic the 'state' which consists of the armed workers, and which is 'no longer a state in the proper sense of the word', the more rapidly *every form* of state begins to wither away.

For when *all* have learned to administer and actually do independently administer social production, independently keep accounts and exercise control over the parasites, the sons of the wealthy, the swindlers and other 'guardians of capitalist traditions', the escape from this popular accounting and control will inevitably become so incredibly difficult, such a rare exception, and will probably be accompanied by such swift and severe punishment (for the armed workers are practical men and not

---

[1] When the more important functions of the state are reduced to such accounting and control by the workers themselves, it will cease to be a 'political state' and 'public functions will lose their political character and become mere administrative functions'.

sentimental intellectuals, and they will scarcely allow anyone to trifle with them), that the *necessity* of observing the simple, fundamental rules of the community will very soon become a *habit*.

Then the door will be thrown wide open for the transition from the first phase of communist society to its higher phase, and with it to the complete withering away of the state.

'State and Revolution' (1917), in *Selected Works* (London, Lawrence & Wishart, 1969), pp. 332–7.

Rosa Luxemburg
(1870–1919)

THE MOST UNLIMITED, THE BROADEST DEMOCRACY

Lenin says: the bourgeois state is an instrument of oppression of the working class; the socialist state, of the bourgeoisie. To a certain extent, he says, it is only the capitalist state stood on its head. This simplified view misses the most essential thing: bourgeois class rule has no need of the political training and education of the entire mass of the people, at least not beyond certain narrow limits. But for the proletarian dictatorship that is the life element, the very air without which it is not able to exist.

'Thanks to the open and direct struggle for governmental power,' writes Trotsky, 'the laboring masses accumulate in the shortest time a considerable amount of political experience and advance quickly from one stage to another of their development.'

Here Trotsky refutes himself and his own friends. Just because this is so, they have blocked up the fountain of political experience and the source of this rising development by their suppression of public life! Or else we would have to assume that experience and development were necessary up to the seizure of power by the Bolsheviks, and then, having reached their highest peak, became superfluous thereafter. (Lenin's speech: Russia is won for socialism!!!)

In reality, the opposite is true! It is the very giant tasks which the Bolsheviks have undertaken with courage and determination that demand the most intensive political training of the masses and the accumulation of experience.

Freedom only for the supporters of the government, only for the members of one party – however numerous they may be – is no freedom at all. Freedom is always and exclusively freedom for the one who thinks differently. Not because of any fanatical concept of 'justice' but because all that is instructive, wholesome and purifying in political freedom depends on this essential characteristic, and its effectiveness vanishes when 'freedom' becomes a special privilege.

The Bolsheviks themselves will not want, with hand on heart, to deny that, step by step, they have to feel out the ground, try out, experiment, test now one way now another, and that a good many of their measures do not represent priceless pearls of wisdom. Thus it must and will be with all of us when we get to the same point – even if the same difficult circumstances may not prevail everywhere.

The tacit assumption underlying the Lenin–Trotsky theory of the dictatorship is this: that the socialist transformation is something for which a ready-made formula lies completed in the pocket of the revolutionary party, which needs only to be carried out energetically in practise. This is, unfortunately – or perhaps fortunately – not the case. Far from being a sum of ready-made prescriptions which have only to be applied, the practical realization of socialism as an economic, social and juridical system is something which lies completely hidden in the mists of the future. What we possess in our program is nothing but a few main signposts which indicate the general direction in which to look for the necessary measures, and the indications are mainly negative in character at that. Thus we know more or less what we must eliminate at the outset in order to free the road for a socialist economy. But when it comes to the nature of the thousand concrete, practical measures, large and small, necessary to introduce socialist principles into economy, law and all social relationships, there is no key in any socialist party program or textbook. That is not a shortcoming but rather the very thing that makes scientific socialism superior to the utopian varieties. The socialist system of society should only be, and can only be, an historical product, born out of the school of its own experiences, born in the course of its realization, as a result of the developments of living history, which – just like organic nature of which, in the last analysis, it forms a part – has the fine habit of always producing along with any real social need the means to its satisfaction, along with the task simultaneously the solution. However, if such is the case, then it is clear that socialism by its very nature cannot be decreed or introduced by *ukase*. It has as its prerequisite a number of measures of force – against property, etc. The negative, the tearing down, can be decreed; the building up, the positive, cannot. New territory. A thousand problems. Only experience is capable of correcting and opening new ways. Only unobstructed, effervescing life falls into a thousand new forms and improvisations, brings to light creative force, itself corrects all mistaken attempts. The public life of countries with limited freedom is so poverty-stricken, so miserable, so rigid, so unfruitful, precisely because, through the exclusion of democracy, it cuts off the living sources of all spiritual riches and progress. (Proof: the year 1905 and the months from February to October 1917.) There it was political in character; the same thing applies to economic and social life also. The whole mass of the people must take part in it. Otherwise, socialism will be decreed from behind a few official desks by a dozen intellectuals.

Public control is indispensably necessary. Otherwise the exchange of experiences remains only with the closed circle of the officials of the new regime. Corruption becomes inevitable. (Lenin's words, Bulletin No. 29.) Socialism in life demands a complete spiritual transformation in the masses degraded by centuries of bourgeois class rule. Social instincts in place of egotistical ones, mass initiative in place of inertia, idealism which conquers all suffering, etc., etc. No one knows this better, describes it more penetratingly, repeats it more stubbornly than Lenin. But he is completely mistaken in the means he employs. Decree, dictatorial force of the factory overseer, draconic penalties, rule by terror – all these things are but palliatives. The only way to a rebirth is the school of public life itself, the most unlimited, the broadest democracy and public opinion. It is rule by terror which demoralizes.

When all this is eliminated, what really remains? In place of the representative bodies created by general, popular elections, Lenin and Trotsky have laid down the soviets as the only true representation of the laboring masses. But with the repression of political life in the land as a whole, life in the soviets must also become more and more crippled. Without general elections, without unrestricted freedom of press and assembly, without a free struggle of opinion, life dies out in every public institution, becomes a mere semblance of life, in which only the bureaucracy remains as the active element. Public life gradually falls asleep, a few dozen party leaders of inexhaustible energy and boundless experience direct and rule. Among them, in reality only a dozen outstanding heads do the leading and an élite of the working class is invited from time to time to meetings where they are to applaud the speeches of the leaders, and to approve proposed resolutions unanimously – at bottom, then, a clique affair – a dictatorship, to be sure, not the dictatorship of the proletariat, however, but only the dictatorship of a handful of politicians, that is a dictatorship in the bourgeois sense, in the sense of the rule of the Jacobins (the postponement of the Soviet Congress from three-month periods to six-month periods!).

Yes, we can go even further: such conditions must inevitably cause a brutalization of public life: attempted assassinations, shooting of hostages, etc. (Lenin's speech on discipline and corruption.)

'The Russian Revolution' (1918, first pub. posthumously 1922), trans. in *The Russian Revolution and Leninism or Marxism*, introd. B. D. Wolfe (Ann Arbor, Univ. of Michigan Press, 1961), pp. 68–72.

Bertrand Russell
(1872–1970)

SOCIALISM ALONE IS BY NO MEANS SUFFICIENT

I do not think any reasonable person can doubt that the evils of power in the present system are vastly greater than is necessary, nor that they might be immeasurably diminished by a suitable form of Socialism. A few fortunate people, it is true, are now enabled to live freely on rent or interest, and they could hardly have more liberty under another system. But the great bulk, not only of the very poor, but of all sections of wage-earners and even of the professional classes, are the slaves of the need for getting money. Almost all are compelled to work so hard that they have little leisure for enjoyment or for pursuits outside their regular occupation. Those who are able to retire in later middle age are bored, because they have not learnt how to fill their time when they are at liberty, and such interests as they once had apart from work have dried up. Yet these are the exceptionally fortunate: the majority have to work hard till old age, with the fear of destitution always before them, the richer ones dreading that they will be unable to give their children the education or the medical care that they consider desirable, the poorer ones often not far removed from starvation. And almost all who work have no voice in the direction of their work; throughout the hours of labour they are mere machines carrying out the will of a master. Work is usually done under disagreeable conditions, involving pain and physical hardship. The only motive to work is wages: the very idea that work might be a joy, like the work of the artist, is usually scouted as utterly Utopian.

But all these evils are wholly unnecessary. If the civilized portion of mankind could be induced to desire their own happiness more than another's pain, if they could be induced to work constructively for improvements which they would share with all the world rather than destructively to prevent other classes or nations from stealing a march on them, the whole system by which the world's work is done might be reformed root and branch within a generation.

From the point of view of liberty, what system would be the best? In what direction should we wish the forces of progress to move?

From this point of view, neglecting for the moment all other considerations, I have no doubt that the best system would be one not far removed from that advocated by Kropotkin, but rendered more practicable by the adoption of the main principles of Guild Socialism. Since every point can be disputed, I will set down without argument the kind of organization of work that would seem best.

Education should be compulsory up to the age of sixteen, or perhaps longer; after that, it should be continued or not at the option of the pupil, but remain free (for those who desire it) up to at least the age of twenty-one. When education is finished, no one should be *compelled* to work, and those who chose not to work should receive a bare livelihood, and be left completely free; but probably it would be desirable that there should be a strong public opinion in favour of work, so that only comparatively few should choose idleness. One great advantage of making idleness economically possible is that it would afford a powerful motive for making work not disagreeable; and no community where most work is disagreeable can be said to have found a solution of economic problems. I think it is reasonable to assume that few would choose idleness, in view of the fact that even now at least nine out of ten of those who have (say) £100 a year from investments prefer to increase their income by paid work.

Coming now to that great majority who will not choose idleness, I think we may assume that, with the help of science, and by the elimination of the vast amount of unproductive work involved in internal and international competition, the whole community could be kept in comfort by means of four hours' work a day. It is already being urged by experienced employers that their employees can actually produce as much in a six hours' day as they can when they work eight hours. In a world where there is a much higher level of technical instruction than there is now, the same tendency will be accentuated. People will be taught not only, as at present, one trade, or one small portion of a trade, but several trades, so that they can vary their occupation according to the seasons and the fluctuations of demand. Every industry will be self-governing as regards all its internal affairs, and even separate factories will decide for themselves all questions that only concern those who work in them. There will not be capitalist management, as at present, but management by elected representatives, as in politics. Relations between different groups of producers will be settled by the Guild Congress, matters concerning the community as the inhabitants of a certain area will continue to be decided by Parliament, while all disputes between Parliament and the Guild Congress will be decided by a body composed of representatives of both in equal numbers.

Payment will not be made, as at present, only for work actually required and performed, but for willingness to work. This system is already adopted in much of the better paid work: a man occupies a certain position, and retains it even at times when there happens to be very little to do. The dread of unemployment and loss of livelihood will no longer haunt men like a nightmare. Whether all who are willing to work will be paid equally, or whether exceptional skill will still command exceptional pay, is a matter which may be left to each Guild to decide for itself. An opera-singer who received no more pay than a scene-shifter might choose to be a scene-shifter until the system was changed: if so, higher pay would probably be found necessary. But if it were freely voted by the Guild, it could hardly constitute a grievance.

Whatever might be done towards making work agreeable, it is to be presumed that some trades would always remain unpleasant. Men could be attracted into these by higher pay or shorter hours, instead of being driven into them by destitution. The community would then have a strong economic motive for finding ways of diminishing the disagreeableness of these exceptional trades.

There would still have to be money, or something analogous to it, in any community such as we are imagining. The Anarchist plan of a free distribution of the total produce of work in equal shares does not get rid of the need for some standard of exchange value, since one man will choose to take his share in one form and another in another. When the day comes for distributing luxuries, old ladies will not want their quota of cigars, nor young men their just proportion of lap-dog: this will make it necessary to know how many cigars are the equivalent of one lap-dog. Much the simplest way is to pay an income, as at present, and allow relative values to be adjusted according to demand. But if actual coin were paid, a man might hoard it and in time become a capitalist. To prevent this, it would be best to pay notes available only during a certain period, say one year from the date of issue. This would enable a man to save up for his annual holiday, but not to save indefinitely.

There is a very great deal to be said for the Anarchist plan of allowing necessaries, and all commodities that can easily be produced in quantities adequate to any possible demand, to be given away freely to all who ask for them, in any amounts they may require. The question whether this plan should be adopted is, to my mind, a purely technical one: would it be, in fact, possible to adopt it without much waste and consequent diversion of labour to the production of necessaries when it might be more usefully employed otherwise? I have not the means of answering this question, but I think it exceedingly probable that, sooner or later, with the continued improvement in the methods of production, this Anarchist plan will become feasible; and when it does, it certainly ought to be adopted.

Women in domestic work, whether married or unmarried, will receive pay as they would if they were in industry. This will secure the complete economic independence of wives, which is difficult to achieve in any other way, since mothers of young children ought not to be expected to work outside the home.

The expense of children will not fall, as at present, on the parents. They will receive, like adults, their share of necessaries, and their education will be free.[1] There is no longer to be the present competition for scholarships among the abler children: they will not be imbued with the competitive spirit from infancy, or forced to use their brains to an unnatural degree, with consequent listlessness and lack of health in later life. Education will be far more diversified than at present: greater care will be taken to adapt it to the needs of different types of young people. There will be more attempt to encourage initiative among pupils and less desire to fill their minds with a set of beliefs and mental habits regarded as desirable by the State, chiefly because they help to preserve the *status quo*. For the great majority of children it will probably be found desirable to have much more outdoor education in the country. And for older boys and girls whose interests are not intellectual or artistic, technical education, undertaken in a liberal spirit, is far more useful in promoting mental activity than book-learning, which they regard (however falsely) as wholly useless except for purposes of examination. The really useful education is that which follows the direction of the child's own instinctive interests, supplying knowledge for which it is seeking, not dry, detailed information wholly out of relation to its spontaneous desires.

[1] Some may fear that the result would be an undue increase of population, but such fears I believe to be groundless. See chapter IV, on 'Work and Pay', also ch. VI of *Principles of Social Reconstruction* (George Allen & Unwin, Ltd.).

Government and Law will still exist in our community, but both will be reduced to a minimum. There will still be acts which will be forbidden – for example, murder. But very nearly the whole of that part of the criminal law which deals with property will have become obsolete, and many of the motives which now produce murders will be no longer operative. Those who nevertheless still do commit crimes will not be blamed or regarded as wicked: they will be regarded as unfortunate, and kept in some kind of mental hospital until it is thought that they are no longer a danger. By education and freedom and the abolition of private capital, the number of crimes can be made exceedingly small. By the method of individual curative treatment, it will generally be possible to secure that a man's first offence shall also be his last, except in the case of lunatics and the feeble-minded, for whom of course a more prolonged but not less kindly detention may be necessary.

Government may be regarded as consisting of two parts: the one, the decisions of the community or its recognized organs; the other, the enforcing of those decisions upon all who resist them. The first part is not objected to by Anarchists. The second part, in an ordinary civilized State, may remain entirely in the background: those who have resisted a new law while it was being debated will, as a rule, submit to it when it is passed, because resistance is generally useless in a settled and orderly community. But the possibility of governmental force remains, and indeed is the very reason for the submission which makes force unnecessary. If, as Anarchists desire, there were no use of force by Government, the majority could still band themselves together and use force against the minority. The only difference would be that their army or their police force would be *ad hoc*, instead of being permanent and professional. The result of this would be that every one would have to learn how to fight, for fear a well-drilled minority should seize power and establish an old-fashioned oligarchic State. Thus the aim of the Anarchists seems hardly likely to be achieved by the methods which they advocate.

Our discussion has led us to the belief that the communal ownership of land and capital, which constitutes the characteristic doctrine of Socialism and Anarchist Communism, is a necessary step towards the removal of the evils from which the world suffers at present and the creation of such a society as any humane man must wish to see realized. But though a necessary step, Socialism alone is by no means sufficient. There are various forms of Socialism: the form in which the State is the employer and all

who work receive wages from it involves dangers of tyranny and interference with progress which would make it, if possible, even worse than
the present regime. On the other hand, Anarchism, which avoids the
dangers of State Socialism, has dangers and difficulties of its own, which
make it probable that, within any reasonable period of time, it could not
last long even if it were established. Nevertheless it remains an ideal to
which we should wish to approach as nearly as possible, and which, in
some distant age, we hope may be reached completely. Syndicalism shares
many of the defects of Anarchism, and, like it, would prove unstable,
since the need of a central government would make itself felt almost at
once.

The system we have advocated is a form of Guild Socialism, leaning
more, perhaps, towards Anarchism than the official Guildsman would
wholly approve. It is in the matters that politicians usually ignore –
science and art, human relations, and the joy of life – that Anarchism is
strongest, and it is chiefly for the sake of these things that we included
such more or less Anarchist proposals as the 'vagabond's wage'. It is by
its effects outside economics and politics, at least as much as by effects
inside them, that a social system should be judged. And if Socialism ever
comes, it is only likely to prove beneficent if non-economic goods are
valued and consciously pursued.

The world that we must seek is a world in which the creative spirit
is alive, in which life is an adventure full of joy and hope, based rather
upon the impulse to construct than upon the desire to retain what we
possess or to seize what is possessed by others. It must be a world in
which affection has free play, in which love is purged of the instinct for
domination, in which cruelty and envy have been dispelled by happiness
and the unfettered development of all the instincts that build up life and
fill it with mental delights. Such a world is possible; it waits only for men
to wish to create it.

Roads to Freedom: Socialism, Anarchism and Syndicalism (London, Allen &
Unwin, 1918), pp. 191–9, 209–10.

DEMOCRACY: THE UNDISCOVERABLE TREASURE

The formation of oligarchies within the various forms of democracy is the outcome of organic necessity, and consequently affects every organization, be it socialist or even anarchist. Haller long ago noted that in every form of social life relationships of dominion and of dependence are created by Nature herself. The supremacy of the leaders in the democratic and revolutionary parties has to be taken into account in every historic situation present and to come, even though only a few and exceptional minds will be fully conscious of its existence. The mass will never rule except *in abstracto*. Consequently the question we have to discuss is not whether ideal democracy is realizable, but rather to what point and in what degree democracy is desirable, possible and realizable at a given moment. In the problem as thus stated we recognize the fundamental problem of politics as a science. Whoever fails to perceive this must, as Sombart says, either be so blind and fanatical as not to see that the democratic current daily makes undeniable advance, or else must be so inexperienced and devoid of critical faculty as to be unable to understand that all order and all civilization must exhibit aristocratic features. The great error of socialists, an error committed in consequence of their lack of adequate psychological knowledge, is to be found in their combination of pessimism regarding the present, with rosy optimism and immeasurable confidence regarding the future. A realistic view of the mental condition of the masses shows beyond question that even if we admit the possibility of moral improvement in mankind, the human materials with whose use politicians and philosophers cannot dispense in their plans of social reconstruction are not of a character to justify excessive optimism. Within the limits of time for which human provision is possible, optimism will remain the exclusive privilege of utopian thinkers.

The socialist parties, like the trade unions, are living forms of social life. As such they react with the utmost energy against any attempt to analyse their structure or their nature, as if it were a method of vivisection. When science attains to results which conflict with their apriorist idealogy, they revolt with all their power. Yet their defence is extremely feeble. Those among the representatives of such organizations whose scientific earnestness and personal good faith make it impossible for them to deny outright the existence of oligarchical tendencies in every form of democracy, endeavour to explain these tendencies as the outcome of a kind of atavism in the mentality of the masses, characteristic of the youth of the movement. The masses, they assure us, are still infected by the oligarchic virus simply because they have been oppressed during long centuries of slavery, and have never yet enjoyed an autonomous existence. The socialist regime, however, will soon restore them to health, and will furnish them with all the capacity necessary for self-government. Nothing could be more anti-scientific than the supposition that as soon as socialists have gained possession of governmental power it will suffice for the masses to exercise a little control over their leaders to secure that the interests of these leaders shall coincide perfectly with the interests of the led. This idea may be compared with the view of Jules Guesde, no less anti-scientific than anti-Marxist (though Guesde proclaims himself a Marxist), that whereas Christianity has made God into a man, socialism will make man into a god.

The objective immaturity of the mass is not a mere transitory phe-nomenon which will disappear with the progress of democratization *au lendemain du socialisme*. On the contrary, it derives from the very nature of the mass as mass, for this, even when organized, suffers from an incurable incompetence for the solution of the diverse problems which present themselves for solution – because the mass *per se* is amorphous, and there-fore needs division of labour, specialization and guidance. 'L'espèce humaine veut être gouvernée; elle le sera. J'ai honte de mon espèce', wrote Proudhon from his prison in 1850. Man as individual is by nature predestined to be guided, and to be guided all the more in proportion as the functions of life undergo division and subdivision. To an enormously greater degree is guidance necessary for the social group.

From this chain of reasoning and from these scientific convictions it would be erroneous to conclude that we should renounce all endeavours to ascertain the limits which may be imposed upon the powers exercised over the individual by oligarchies (state, dominant class, party, etc.). It would be an error to abandon the desperate enterprise of endeavouring to discover a social order which will render possible the complete realization of the idea of popular sovereignty. In the present work, as the writer said at the outset, it has not been his aim to indicate new paths. But it seemed necessary to lay considerable stress upon the pessimist aspect of democracy which is forced on us by historical study. We had to inquire whether, and within what limits, democracy must remain purely ideal, possessing no other value than that of a moral criterion which renders it possible to appreciate the varying degrees of that oligarchy which is immanent in every social regime. In other words, we have had to inquire if, and in what degree, democracy is an ideal which we can never hope to realize in practice. A further aim of this work was the demolition of some of the facile and superficial democratic illusions which trouble science and lead the masses astray. Finally, the author desired to throw light upon certain sociological tendencies which oppose the reign of democracy, and to a still greater extent oppose the reign of socialism.

The writer does not wish to deny that every revolutionary working-class movement, and every movement sincerely inspired by the democratic spirit, may have a certain value as contributing to the enfeeblement of oligarchic tendencies. The peasant in the fable, when on his death-bed, tells his sons that a treasure is buried in the field. After the old man's death the sons dig everywhere in order to discover the treasure. They do not find it. But their indefatigable labour improves the soil and secures for them a comparative well-being. The treasure in the fable may well symbolize democracy. Democracy is a treasure which no one will ever discover by deliberate search. But in continuing our search, in labouring indefatigably to discover the indiscoverable, we shall perform a work which will have fertile results in the democratic sense. We have seen, indeed, that within the bosom of the democratic working-class party are born the very tendencies to counteract which that party came into existence. Thanks to the diversity and to the unequal worth of the elements of the party, these tendencies often give rise to manifestations which border on tyranny. We have seen that the replacement of the traditional legitimism of the powers-that-be by the brutal plebiscitary rule of Bonapartist parvenus does not furnish these tendencies with any moral or aesthetic superiority. Historical evolution mocks all the prophylactic measures that have been adopted for the prevention of oligarchy. If laws are passed to control the dominion of the leaders, it is the laws which gradually weaken, and not the leaders. Sometimes, however, the democratic principle carries with it, if not a cure, at least a palliative, for the disease of oligarchy. When Victor Considérant formulated his 'democratico-pacifist' socialism, he declared that socialism signified, not the rule of society by the lower classes of the population, but the government and organization of society in the interest of all, through the intermediation of a group of citizens; and he added that the numerical importance of this group must increase *pari passu* with social development. This last observation draws attention to a point of capital importance. It is, in fact, a general characteristic of democracy, and hence also of the labour movement, to stimulate and to strengthen in the individual the intellectual aptitudes for criticism and control. We have seen how the progressive bureaucratization of the democratic organism tends to neutralize the beneficial effects of such criticism and such control. None the less it is true that the labour movement, in virtue of the theoretical postulates it proclaims, is apt to bring into existence (in opposition to the will of the leaders) a certain number of free spirits who, moved by principle, by instinct or by both, desire to revise the base upon which authority is established. Urged on by conviction or by temperament, they are never weary of asking an eternal 'Why?' about every human institution. Now this predisposition towards free inquiry, in which we cannot fail to recognize one of the most precious factors of civilization, will gradually increase in proportion as the economic status of the masses undergoes improvement and becomes more stable, and in proportion as they are admitted more effectively to the advantages of civilization. A wider education involves an increasing capacity for exercising control. Can we not observe every day that among the well-to-do the authority of the leaders over the led, extensive though it be, is never so unrestricted as in the case of the leaders of the poor? Taking in the mass, the poor are powerless and disarmed *vis-à-vis* their leaders. Their intellectual and cultural inferiority makes it impossible for them to see whither the leader is going, or to estimate in advance the significance of his actions. It is, consequently, the great task of social education to raise the intellectual level of the masses, so that they may be enabled, within the limits of what is possible, to counteract the oligarchical tendencies of the working-class movement.

In view of the perennial incompetence of the masses, we have to recognize the existence of two regulative principles:

1. The *ideological* tendency of democracy towards criticism and control;
2. The *effective* counter-tendency of democracy towards the creation of parties ever more complex and ever more differentiated – parties, that

is to say, which are increasingly based upon the competence of the few.

To the idealist, the analysis of the forms of contemporary democracy cannot fail to be a source of bitter deceptions and profound discouragement. Those alone, perhaps, are in a position to pass a fair judgement upon democracy who, without lapsing into dilettantist sentimentalism, recognize that all scientific and human ideals have relative values. If we wish to estimate the value of democracy, we must do so in comparison with its converse, pure aristocracy. The defects inherent in democracy are obvious. It is none the less true that as a form of social life we must choose democracy as the least of evils. The ideal government would doubtless be that of an aristocracy of persons at once morally good and technically efficient. But where shall we discover such an aristocracy? We may find it sometimes, though very rarely, as the outcome of deliberate selection; but we shall never find it where the hereditary principle remains in operation. Thus monarchy in its pristine purity must be considered as imperfection incarnate, as the most incurable of ills; from the moral point of view it is inferior even to the most revolting of demagogic dictatorships, for the corrupt organism of the latter at least contains a healthy principle upon whose working we may continue to base hopes of social resanation. It may be said, therefore, that the more humanity comes to recognize the advantages which democracy, however imperfect, presents over aristocracy, even at its best, the less likely is it that a recognition of the defects of democracy will provoke a return to aristocracy. Apart from certain formal differences and from the qualities which can be acquired only by good education and inheritance (qualities in which aristocracy will always have the advantage over democracy – qualities which democracy either neglects altogether, or, attempting to imitate them, falsifies them to the point of caricature), the defects of democracy will be found to inhere in its inability to get rid of its aristocratic scoriae. On the other hand, nothing but a serene and frank examination of the oligarchical dangers of democracy will enable us to minimize these dangers, even though they can never be entirely avoided.

The democratic currents of history resemble successive waves. They break ever on the same shoal. They are ever renewed. This enduring spectacle is simultaneously encouraging and depressing. When democracies have gained a certain stage of development, they undergo a gradual transformation, adopting the aristocratic spirit, and in many cases also the aristocratic forms, against which at the outset they struggled so fiercely. Now new accusers arise to denounce the traitors; after an era of glorious combats and of inglorious power, they end by fusing with the old dominant class; whereupon once more they are in their turn attacked by fresh opponents who appeal to the name of democracy. It is probable that this cruel game will continue without end.

Political Parties (1911), trans. E. and C. Paul (New York, Dover Publications, 1959), pp. 402–8. (Republication of 1915 English edition.)

PART IV

E. M. Forster
(1879–1970)

THE NEW ECONOMY WITH
THE OLD MORALITY

Temperamentally, I am an individualist. Professionally I am a writer, and my books emphasize the importance of personal relationships and the private life, for I believe in them. What can a man with such an equipment, and with no technical knowledge, say about the Challenge of our Time? Like everyone else, I can see that our world is in a terrible mess, and having been to India last winter I know that starvation and frustration can reach proportions unknown to these islands. Wherever I look, I can see, in the striking phrase of Robert Bridges, 'the almighty cosmic Will fidgeting in a trap'. But who set the trap, and how was it sprung? If I knew, I might be able to unfasten it. I do not know. How can I answer a challenge which I cannot interpret? It is like shouting defiance at a big black cloud. Some of the other speakers share my diffidence here, I think. Professor Bernal[1] does not. He perceives very precisely what the Challenge of our Time is and what is the answer to it. Professor Bernal's perceptions are probably stronger than mine. They are certainly more selective, and many things which interest or upset me do not enter his mind at all – or enter it in the form of cards to be filed for future use.

I belong to the fag-end of Victorian liberalism, and can look back to an age whose challenges were moderate in their tone, and the cloud on whose horizon was no bigger than a man's hand. In many ways it was an admirable age. It practised benevolence and philanthropy, was humane and intellectually curious, upheld free speech, had little colour-prejudice, believed that individuals are and should be different, and entertained a sincere faith in the progress of society. The world was to become better and better, chiefly through the spread of parliamentary institutions. The

[1] Professor Bernal had been one of the previous speakers in this broadcast series.

education I received in those far-off and fantastic days made me soft and I am very glad it did, for I have seen plenty of hardness since, and I know it does not even pay. Think of the end of Mussolini – the hard man, hanging upside-down like a turkey, with his dead mistress swinging beside him. But though the education was humane it was imperfect, inasmuch as we none of us realized our economic position. In came the nice fat dividends, up rose the lofty thoughts, and we did not realize that all the time we were exploiting the poor of our own country and the backward races abroad, and getting bigger profits from our investments than we should. We refused to face this unpalatable truth. I remember being told as a small boy, 'Dear, don't talk about money, it's ugly' – a good example that of Victorian defence mechanism.

All that has changed in the present century. The dividends have shrunk to decent proportions and have in some cases disappeared. The poor have kicked. The backward races are kicking – and more power to their boots. Which means that life has become less comfortable for the Victorian liberal, and that our outlook, which seems to me admirable, has lost the basis of golden sovereigns upon which it originally rose, and now hangs over the abyss. I indulge in these reminiscences because they lead to the point I want to make.

If we are to answer the Challenge of our Time successfully, we must manage to combine the new economy and the old morality. The doctrine of *laisser-faire* will not work in the material world. It has led to the black market and the capitalist jungle. We must have planning and ration books and controls, or millions of people will have nowhere to live and nothing to eat. On the other hand, the doctrine of *laisser-faire* is the only one that seems to work in the world of the spirit; if you plan and control men's minds you stunt them, you get the censorship, the secret police, the road to serfdom, the community of slaves. Our economic planners sometimes laugh at us when we are afraid of totalitarian tyranny resulting from their efforts – or rather they sneer at us, for there is some deep connection between planning and sneering which psychologists should explore. But the danger they brush aside is a real one. They assure us that the new economy will evolve an appropriate morality, and that when all people are properly fed and housed, they will have an outlook which will be right, because they are the people. I cannot swallow that. I have no mystic faith in the people. I have in the individual. He seems to me a divine achievement and I mistrust any view which belittles him. If anyone calls you a wretched little individual – and I've been called that – don't you take it lying down. You are important because everyone else is an individual too – including the person who criticizes you. In asserting your personality you are playing for your side.

That then is the slogan with which I would answer, or partially answer, the Challenge of our Time. We want the New Economy with the Old Morality. We want planning for the body and not for the spirit. But the difficulty is this: where does the body stop and the spirit start? In the Middle Ages a hard and fast line was drawn between them, and according to the medieval theory of the Holy Roman Empire men rendered their bodies to Caesar and their souls to God. But the theory did not work. The Emperor, who represented Caesar, collided in practice with the Pope, who represented Christ. And we find ourselves in a similar dilemma today. Suppose you are planning the world distribution of food. You can't do that without planning world population. You can't do that without regulating the number of births and interfering with family life. You must supervise parenthood. You are meddling with the realms of the spirit, of personal relationship, although you may not have intended to do so. And you are brought back again to that inescapable arbiter, your own temperament. When there is a collision of principles would you favour the individual at the expense of the community as I would? Or would you prefer economic justice for all at the expense of personal freedom?

In a time of upheaval like the present, this collision of principles, this split in one's loyalties, is always occurring. It has just occurred in my own life. I was brought up as a boy in one of the home counties, in a district which I still think the loveliest in England. There is nothing special about it – it is agricultural land, and could not be described in terms of beauty spots. It must always have looked much the same. I have kept in touch with it, going back to it as to an abiding city and still visiting the house which was once my home, for it is occupied by friends. A farm is through the hedge, and when the farmer there was eight years old and I was nine, we used to jump up and down on his grandfather's straw ricks and spoil them. Today he is a grandfather himself, so that I have the sense of five generations continuing in one place. Life went on there as usual until this spring. Then someone who was applying for a permit to lay a water pipe was casually informed that it would not be granted since the whole area had been commandeered. Commandeered for what? Had not the war ended? Appropriate officials of the Ministry of Town and Country Planning now arrived from London and announced that a satellite town for 60,000 people is to be built. The people now living and working there are doomed; it is death in life for them and they move in a nightmare. The best agricultural land has been taken, they assert; the poor land down by the railway has been left; compensation is inadequate. Anyhow, the satellite town has finished them off as completely as it will obliterate the ancient and delicate scenery. Meteorite town would be a better name. It has fallen out of a blue sky.

'Well,' says the voice of planning and progress, 'why this sentimentality? People must have houses.' They must, and I think of working-class friends in north London who have to bring up four children in two rooms, and many are even worse off than that. But I cannot equate the problem. It is a collision of loyalties. I cannot free myself from the conviction that something irreplaceable has been destroyed, and that a little piece of England has died as surely as if a bomb had hit it. I wonder what compensation there is in the world of the spirit, for the destruction of the life here, the life of tradition.

These are personal reminiscences and I am really supposed to be speaking from the standpoint of the creative artist. But you will gather what a writer, who also cares for men and women and for the countryside, must be feeling in the world today. Uncomfortable, of course. Sometimes miserable and indignant. But convinced that a planned change must take place if the world is not to disintegrate, and hopeful that in the new economy there may be a sphere both for human relationships, and for the despised activity known as art. What ought the writer, the artist, to do when faced by the Challenge of our Time? Briefly, he ought to express what he wants and not what he is told to express by the planning authorities. He ought to impose a discipline on himself rather than accept one from outside. And that discipline may be aesthetic, rather than social or moral; he may wish to practise art for art's sake. That phrase has been foolishly used and often raises a giggle. But it is a profound phrase. It indicates that art is a self-contained harmony. Art is valuable not because it is educational (though it may be), not because it is recreative (though it may be), not because everyone enjoys it (for everybody does not), not even because it has to do with beauty. It is valuable because it has to do with order, and creates little worlds of its own, possessing internal harmony, in the bosom of this disordered planet. It is needed at once and now. It is needed before it is appreciated and independent of appreciation. The idea that it should not be permitted until it receives communal acclaim and unless it is for all, is perfectly absurd. It is the activity which brought man out of original darkness and differentiates him from the beasts, and we must continue to practise and respect it through the darkness of today.

I am speaking like an intellectual, but the intellectual, to my mind, is more in touch with humanity than is the confident scientist, who patronizes the past, over-simplifies the present and envisages a future where his leadership will be accepted. Owing to the political needs of the moment, the scientist occupies an abnormal position, which he tends to forget. He is subsidized by the terrified governments who need his aid, pampered and sheltered as long as he is obedient, and prosecuted under Official Secrets Acts when he has been naughty. All this separates him from ordinary men and women and makes him unfit to enter into their feelings. It is high time he came out of his ivory laboratory. We want him to plan for our bodies. We do not want him to plan for our minds, and we cannot accept, so far, his assurance that he will not.

'The Challenge of Our Time' (1946), in *Two Cheers for Democracy* (London, Edward Arnold, 1951), Penguin ed. (London, 1965), pp. 64-9.

R. H. Tawney
(1880–1962)

PRODUCTION WITH A PURPOSE

So the organization of society on the basis of functions, instead of on that of rights, implies three things. It means, first, that proprietary rights shall be maintained when they are accompanied by the performance of service and abolished when they are not. It means, second, that the producers shall stand in a direct relation to the community for whom production is carried on, so that their responsibility to it may be obvious and unmistakable, not lost, as at present, through their immediate subordination to shareholders whose interest is not service but gain. It means, in the third place, that the obligation for the maintenance of the service shall rest upon the professional organizations of those who perform it, and that, subject to the supervision and criticism of the consumer, those organizations shall exercise so much voice in the government of industry as may be needed to secure that the obligation is discharged.

It is obvious, indeed, that no change of system or machinery can avert those causes of social *malaise* which consist in the egotism, greed or quarrelsomeness of human nature. What it can do is to create an environment in which those are not the qualities which are encouraged. It cannot secure that men live up to their principles. What it can do is to establish their social order upon principles to which, if they please, they can live up and not live down. It cannot control their actions. It can offer them an end on which to fix their minds. And, as their minds are, so in the long run and with exceptions, their practical activity will be.

The first condition of the right organization of industry is, then, the intellectual conversion which, in their distrust of principles, Englishmen are disposed to place last or to omit altogether. It is that emphasis should be transferred from the opportunities which it offers to the social functions which it performs; that those concerned should be clear as to its end and should judge it by reference to that end, not by incidental consequences which are foreign to it, however brilliant or alluring those consequences may be. What gives its meaning to any activity which is not purely automatic is its purpose. It is because the purpose of industry, which is the conquest of nature for the service of man, is neither adequately expressed in its organization not present to the minds of those engaged in it, because it is not regarded as a function but as an opportunity for personal gain or advancement or display, that the economic life of modern societies is in a perpetual state of morbid irritation. If the conditions which produce that unnatural tension are to be removed, it can only be effected by the growth of a habit of mind which will approach questions of economic organization from the standpoint of the purpose which it exists to serve, and which will apply to it something of the spirit expressed by Bacon when he said that the work of men ought to be carried on 'for the glory of God and the relief of men's estate'.

Sentimental idealism? But consider the alternative. The alternative is war; and continuous war must, sooner or later, mean something like the destruction of civilization. The havoc which the assertion of the right to unlimited economic expansion has made of the world of States needs no emphasis. Those who have lived from 1914 to 1921 will not ask why mankind has not progressed more swiftly; they will be inclined to wonder that it has progressed at all. For every century or oftener it has torn itself to pieces, usually, since 1648, because it supposed prosperity was to be achieved by the destruction of an economic rival; and, as these words are written, the victors in the war for freedom, in defiance of their engagements and amid general applause from the classes who will suffer most from the heroics of their rulers, are continuing the process of ruining themselves in order to enjoy the satisfaction of more completely ruining the vanquished. The test of the objects of a war is the peace which follows it. Millions of human beings endured for four years the extremes of misery for ends which they believed to be but little tainted with the meaner kinds of self-interest. But the historian of the future will consider, not what they thought, but what their statesmen did. He will read the Treaty of Versailles; and he will be merciful if, in its provisions with regard to coal and shipping and enemy property and colonies and indemnities, he does not find written large the *Macht-Politik* of the Acquisitive Society, the natural, if undesired, consequence of which is war.

There are, however, various degrees both of war and of peace, and it is an illusion to suppose that domestic tranquillity is either the necessary, or the probable, alternative, to military collisions abroad. What is more probable, unless mankind succeeds in basing its social organization upon some moral principles which command general acceptance, is an embittered struggle of classes, interests and groups. The principle upon which our society professed to be based for nearly a hundred years after 1789 – the principle of free competition – has clearly spent its force. In the last few years Great Britain – not to mention America and Germany – has plunged, as far as certain great industries are concerned, into an era of something like monopoly with the same light-hearted recklessness as a century ago it flung itself into an era of individualism. No one who reads the Reports of the Committee on Trusts appointed by the Ministry of Reconstruction and of the Committee set up under the Profiteering Act upon soap, or sewing cotton, or oil, or half-a-dozen other products, can retain the illusion that the consumer is protected by the rivalry of competing producers. The choice before him, to an increasing extent, is not between competition and monopoly, but between a monopoly which is irresponsible and private and a monopoly which is responsible and public. No one who observes how industrial agreements between workers and employers are actually reached can fail to see that they are settled by a trial of strength between two compactly organized armies, who are restrained from collision only by fear of its possible consequences. Fear is a powerful, but a capricious, motive, and it will not always restrain them. When prudence is overborne by rashness, or when the hope of gain outweighs the apprehension of loss, there will be a collision. No man can say where it will end. No man can even say with confidence that it will produce a more tolerable social order. It is idle to urge that any alternative is preferable to government by the greedy materialists who rule mankind at present, for greed and materialism are not the monopoly of a class. If those who have the will to make a better society have not at present the power, it is conceivable that when they have the power, they too, like their predecessors, may not have the will.

So, in the long run, it is the principles which men accept as the basis of their social organization which matter. And the principle which we have tried to put forward is that industry and property and economic activity should be treated as functions, and should be tested, at every point, by their relation to a social purpose. Viewed from that angle, issues which are insoluble when treated on the basis of rights may be found more susceptible of reasonable treatment. For a purpose is, in the first place, a principle of limitation. It determines the end for which, and therefore the limits within which, an activity is to be carried on. It divides what is worth doing from what is not, and settles the scale upon which what is worth doing ought to be done. It is, in the second place, a principle of unity, because it supplies a common end to which efforts can be directed, and submits interests, which would otherwise conflict, to the judgement of an over-ruling object. It is, in the third place, a principle of apportionment or distribution. It assigns to the different parties or groups engaged in a common undertaking the place which they are to occupy in carrying it out. Thus it establishes order, not upon chance or power, but upon a principle, and bases remuneration not upon what men can with good fortune snatch for themselves, nor upon what, if unlucky, they can be induced to accept, but upon what is appropriate to their function, no more and no less, so that those who perform no function receive no payment, and those who contribute to the common end receive honourable payment for honourable service.

The Acquisitive Society (1921) (London, Fontana, 1961), pp. 176–80. (First pub. by G. Bell & Sons.)

J. M. Keynes
(1883–1946)

THE SUCCESSFUL FUNCTIONING OF INDIVIDUAL INITIATIVE

For my own part, I believe that there is social and psychological justification for significant inequalities of incomes and wealth, but not for such large disparities as exist today. There are valuable human activities which require the motive of money-making and the environment of private wealth-ownership for their full fruition. Moreover, dangerous human proclivities can be canalized into comparatively harmless channels by the existence of opportunities for money-making and private wealth, which, if they cannot be satisfied in this way, may find their outlet in cruelty, the reckless pursuit of personal power and authority, and other forms of self-aggrandizement. It is better that a man should tyrannize over his bank balance than over his fellow-citizens; and whilst the former is sometimes denounced as being but a means to the latter, sometimes at least it is an alternative. But it is not necessary for the stimulation of these activities and the satisfaction of these proclivities that the game should be played for such high stakes as at present. Much lower stakes will serve the purpose equally well, as soon as the players are accustomed to them. The task of transmuting human nature must not be confused with the task of managing it. Though in the ideal commonwealth men may have been taught or inspired or bred to take no interest in the stakes, it may still be wise and prudent statesmanship to allow the game to be played, subject to rules and limitations, so long as the average man, or even a significant section of the community, is in fact strongly addicted to the money-making passion.

The State will have to exercise a guiding influence on the propensity to consume partly through its scheme of taxation, partly by fixing the rate of interest and partly, perhaps, in other ways. Furthermore, it seems unlikely that the influence of banking policy on the rate of interest will be sufficient by itself to determine an optimum rate of investment. I conceive, therefore, that a somewhat comprehensive socialization of investment will prove the only means of securing an approximation to full employment; though this need not exclude all manner of compromises and of devices by which public authority will co-operate with private initiative. But beyond this no obvious case is made out for a system of State Socialism which would embrace most of the economic life of the community. It is not the ownership of the instruments of production which it is important for the State to assume. If the State is able to determine the aggregate amount of resources devoted to augmenting the instruments and the basic rate of reward to those who own them, it will have accomplished all that is necessary. Moreover, the necessary measures of socialization can be introduced gradually and without a break in the general traditions of society.

Our criticism of the accepted classical theory of economics has consisted not so much in finding logical flaws in its analysis as in pointing out that its tacit assumptions are seldom or never satisfied, with the result that it cannot solve the economic problems of the actual world. But if our central controls succeed in establishing an aggregate volume of output corresponding to full employment as nearly as is practicable, the classical theory comes into its own again from this point onwards. If we suppose the volume of output to be given, i.e. to be determined by forces outside the classical scheme of thought, then there is no objection to be raised against the classical analysis of the manner in which private self-interest will determine what in particular is produced, in what proportions the factors of production will be combined to produce it, and how the value of the final product will be distributed between them. Again, if we have dealt otherwise with the problem of thrift, there is no objection to be raised against the modern classical theory as to the degree of consilience between private and public advantage in conditions of perfect and imperfect competition respectively. Thus, apart from the necessity of central controls to bring about an adjustment between the propensity to consume and the inducement to invest, there is no more reason to socialize economic life than there was before.

To put the point concretely, I see no reason to suppose that the existing system seriously misemploys the factors of production which are in use. There are, of course, errors of foresight; but these would not be avoided by centralizing decisions. When 9,000,000 men are employed out of

10,000,000 willing and able to work, there is no evidence that the labour of these 9,000,000 men is misdirected. The complaint against the present system is not that these 9,000,000 men ought to be employed on different tasks, but that tasks should be available for the remaining 1,000,000 men. It is in determining the volume, not the direction, of actual employment that the existing system has broken down.

Thus I agree with Gesell that the result of filling in the gaps in the classical theory is not to dispose of the 'Manchester System', but to indicate the nature of the environment which the free play of economic forces requires if it is to realize the full potentialities of production. The central controls necessary to ensure full employment will, of course, involve a large extension of the traditional functions of government. Furthermore, the modern classical theory has itself called attention to various conditions in which the free play of economic forces may need to be curbed or guided. But there will still remain a wide field for the exercise of private initiative and responsibility. Within this field the traditional advantages of individualism will still hold good.

Let us stop for a moment to remind ourselves what these advantages are. They are partly advantages of efficiency – the advantages of decentralization and of the play of self-interest. The advantage to efficiency of the decentralization of decisions and of individual responsibility is even greater, perhaps, than the nineteenth century supposed; and the reaction against the appeal to self-interest may have gone too far. But, above all, individualism, if it can be purged of its defects and its abuses, is the best safeguard of personal liberty in the sense that, compared with any other system, it greatly widens the field for the exercise of personal choice. It is also the best safeguard of the variety of life, which emerges precisely from this extended field of personal choice, and the loss of which is the greatest of all the losses of the homogeneous or totalitarian state. For this variety preserves the traditions which embody the most secure and successful choices of former generations; it colours the present with the diversification of its fancy; and, being the handmaid of experiment as well as of tradition and of fancy, it is the most powerful instrument to better the future.

Whilst, therefore, the enlargement of the functions of government, involved in the task of adjusting to one another the propensity to consume and the inducement to invest, would seem to a nineteenth-century publicist or to a contemporary American financier to be a terrific encroachment on individualism, I defend it, on the contrary, both as the only practicable means of avoiding the destruction of existing economic forms in their entirety and as the condition of the successful functioning of individual initiative.

For if effective demand is deficient, not only is the public scandal of wasted resources intolerable, but the individual enterpriser who seeks to bring these resources into action is operating with the odds loaded against him. The game of hazard which he plays is furnished with many zeros, so that the players *as a whole* will lose if they have the energy and hope to deal all the cards. Hitherto the increment of the world's wealth has fallen short of the aggregate of positive individual savings; and the difference has been made up by the losses of those whose courage and initiative have not been supplemented by exceptional skill or unusual good fortune. But if effective demand is adequate, average skill and average good fortune will be enough.

The authoritarian state systems of today seem to solve the problem of unemployment at the expense of efficiency and of freedom. It is certain that the world will not much longer tolerate the unemployment which, apart from brief intervals of excitement, is associated – and, in my opinion, inevitably associated – with present-day capitalistic individualism. But it may be possible by a right analysis of the problem to cure the disease whilst preserving efficiency and freedom.

A General Theory of Employment, Interest and Money (1936) (London, Macmillan, 1960), pp. 374, 378–81.

Benito Mussolini
(1883–1945)

ORGANIZED, CENTRALIZED, AUTHORITARIAN DEMOCRACY

After Socialism, Fascism attacks the whole complex of democratic ideologies and rejects them both in their theoretical premises and in their applications or practical manifestations. Fascism denies that the majority, through the mere fact of being a majority, can rule human societies; it denies that this majority can govern by means of a periodical consultation; it affirms the irremediable, fruitful and beneficent inequality of men, who cannot be levelled by such a mechanical and extrinsic fact as universal suffrage. By democratic regimes we mean those in which from time to time the people is given the illusion of being sovereign, while true effective sovereignty lies in other, perhaps irresponsible and secret, forces. Democracy is a regime without a king, but with very many kings, perhaps more exclusive, tyrannical and violent than one king even though a tyrant. This explains why Fascism, although before 1922 for reasons of expediency it made a gesture of republicanism, renounced it before the March on Rome, convinced that the question of the political forms of a State is not pre-eminent today, and that studying past and present monarchies, past and present republics it becomes clear that monarchy and republic are not to be judged *sub specie aeternitatis*, but represent forms in which the political evolution, the history, the tradition, the psychology of a given country are manifested. Now Fascism overcomes the antithesis between monarchy and republic which retarded the movements of democracy, burdening the former with every defect and defending the latter as the regime of perfection. Now it has been seen that there are inherently reactionary and absolutistic republics, and monarchies that welcome the most daring political and social innovations.

'Reason, Science', said Renan (who was inspired before Fascism existed) in one of his philosophical Meditations, 'are products of humanity, but to expect reason directly from the people and through the people is a chimera. It is not necessary for the existence of reason that everybody should know it. In any case, if such an initiation should be made, it would not be made by means of base democracy, which apparently must lead to the extinction of every difficult culture, and every higher discipline. The principle that society exists only for the prosperity and the liberty of the individuals who compose it does not seem to conform with the plans of nature, plans in which the species alone is taken into consideration and the individual seems to be sacrificed. It is strongly to be feared lest the last word of democracy thus understood (I hasten to say that it can also be understood in other ways) would be a social state in which a degenerate mass would have no other care than to enjoy the ignoble pleasures of vulgar men.'

Thus far Renan. Fascism rejects in democracy the absurd conventional lie of political equalitarianism clothed in the dress of collective irresponsibility and the myth of happiness and indefinite progress. But if democracy can be understood in other ways, that is, if democracy means not to relegate the people to the periphery of the State, then Fascism could be defined as an 'organized, centralized, authoritarian democracy'.

But the Fascist repudiations of Socialism, Democracy, Liberalism must not make one think that Fascism wishes to make the world return to what it was before 1789, the year which has been indicated as the year of the beginning of the liberal-democratic age. One does not go backwards. The Fascist doctrine has not chosen De Maistre as its prophet. Monarchical absolutism is a thing of the past and so also is every theocracy. So also feudal privileges and division into impenetrable and isolated castes have had their day. The theory of Fascist authority has nothing to do with the police State. A party that governs a nation in a totalitarian way is a new fact in history. References and comparisons are not possible. Fascism takes over from the ruins of Liberal Socialistic democratic doctrines those elements which still have a living value. It preserves those that can be called the established facts of history, it rejects all the rest, that is to say the idea of a doctrine which holds good for all times and all peoples. If it is admitted that the nineteenth century has been the century of Socialism, Liberalism and Democracy, it does not follow that the twentieth must also be the century of Liberalism, Socialism and Democracy. Political doctrines pass; peoples remain. It is to be expected that this century may be that of authority, a century of the 'Right', a Fascist century. If the nineteenth was the century of the individual (Liberalism means individualism) it may be expected that this one may be the century of 'collectivism' and therefore the century of the State. That a new doctrine should use the still vital elements of other doctrines is perfectly logical. No doctrine is born quite new, shining, never before seen. No doctrine can boast of an absolute 'originality'. It is bound, even if only historically, to other doctrines that have been, and to develop into other doctrines that will be. Thus the scientific socialism of Marx is bound to the Utopian Socialism of the Fouriers, the Owens and the Saint-Simons; thus the Liberalism of the nineteenth century is connected with the whole 'Enlightenment' of the eighteenth century. Thus the doctrines of democracy are bound to the *Encyclopédie*. Every doctrine tends to direct the activity of men towards a determined objective; but the activity of man reacts upon the doctrine, transforms it, adapts it to new necessities or transcends it. The doctrine itself, therefore, must be, not words, but an act of life. Hence, the pragmatic veins in Fascism, its will to power, its will to be, its attitude in the face of the fact of 'violence' and of its own courage.

The keystone of Fascist doctrine is the conception of the State, of its essence, of its tasks, of its ends. For Fascism the State is an absolute before which individuals and groups are relative. Individuals and groups are 'thinkable' in so far as they are within the State. The Liberal State does not direct the interplay and the material and spiritual development of the groups, but limits itself to registering the results; the Fascist State has a consciousness of its own, a will of its own, on this account it is called an 'ethical' State. In 1929, at the first quinquennial assembly of the regime, I said: 'For Fascism, the State is not the night-watchman who is concerned only with the personal security of the citizens; nor is it an organization for purely material ends, such as that of guaranteeing a certain degree of prosperity and a relatively peaceful social order, to achieve which a council of administration would be sufficient; nor is it a creation of mere politics with no contact with the material and complex reality of the lives of individuals and the life of peoples. The State, as conceived by Fascism and as it acts, is a spiritual and moral fact because it makes concrete the political, juridical, economic organization of the nation and such an organization is, in its origin and in its development, a manifestation of the spirit. The State is the guarantor of internal and external security, but it is also the guardian and the transmitter of the spirit of the people as it has been elaborated through the centuries in language, custom, faith. The State is not only present, it is also past, and above all future. It is the State which, transcending the brief limit of individual lives, represents the immanent conscience of the nation. The forms in which States express themselves change, but the necessity of the State remains. It is the State which educates citizens for civic virtue, makes them conscious of their mission, calls them to unity; harmonizes their interests in justice; hands on the achievements of thought in the sciences, the arts, in law, in human solidarity; it carries men from the elementary life of the tribe to the highest human expression of power which is Empire; it entrusts to the ages the names of those who died for its integrity or in obedience to its laws; it puts forward as an example and recommends to the generations that are to come the leaders who increased its territory and the men of genius who gave it glory. When the sense of the State declines and the disintegrating and centrifugal tendencies of individuals and groups prevail, national societies move to their decline.'

From 1929 up to the present day these doctrinal positions have been strengthened by the whole economico-political evolution of the world. It is the State alone that grows in size, in power. It is the State alone that can solve the dramatic contradictions of capitalism. What is called the crisis cannot be overcome except by the State, within the State. Where are the shades of the Jules Simons who, at the dawn of liberalism, proclaimed that 'the State must strive to render itself unnecessary and to prepare for its demise'; of the MacCullochs who, in the second half of the last century, affirmed that the State must abstain from too much governing? And faced with the continual, necessary and inevitable interventions of the State in economic affairs what would the Englishman Bentham now say, according to whom industry should have asked of the State only to be left in peace? Or the German Humboldt, according to whom the 'idle' State must be considered the best? It is true that the second generation of liberal economists was less extremist than the first, and already Smith himself opened, even though cautiously, the door to State intervention in economics. But when one says liberalism, one says the individual; when one says Fascism, one says the State. But the Fascist State is unique; it is an original creation. It is not reactionary, but revolutionary in that it anticipates the solutions of certain universal problems. These problems are no longer seen in the same light: in the sphere of politics they are removed from party rivalries, from the supreme power of parliament, from the irresponsibility of assemblies; in the sphere of economics they are removed from the sphere of the syndicates' activities – activities that were ever widening their scope and increasing their power, both on the workers' side and on the employers' –

removed from their struggles and their designs; in the moral sphere they are divorced from ideas of the need for order, discipline and obedience, and lifted into the plane of the moral commandments of the fatherland. Fascism desires the State to be strong, organic and at the same time founded on a wide popular basis. The Fascist State has also claimed for itself the field of economics and, through the corporative, social and educational institutions which it has created, the meaning of the State reaches out to and includes the farthest off-shoots; and within the State, framed in their respective organizations, there revolve all the political, economic and spiritual forces of the nation. A State founded on millions of individuals who recognize it, feel it, are ready to serve it, is not the tyrannical State of the medieval lord. It has nothing in common with the absolutist States that existed either before or after 1789. In the Fascist State the individual is not suppressed, but rather multiplied, just as in a regiment a soldier is not weakened but multiplied by the number of his comrades. The Fascist State organizes the nation, but it leaves sufficient scope to individuals; it has limited useless or harmful liberties and has preserved those that are essential. It cannot be the individual who decides in this matter, but only the State.

The Fascist State does not remain indifferent to the fact of religion in general and to that particular positive religion which is Italian Catholicism. The State has no theology, but it has an ethic. In the Fascist State religion is looked upon as one of the deepest manifestations of the spirit; it is, therefore, not only respected, but defended and protected. The Fascist State does not create a 'God' of its own, as Robespierre once, at the height of the Convention's foolishness, wished to do; nor does it vainly seek, like Bolshevism, to expel religion from the minds of men; Fascism respects the God of the ascetics, of the saints, of the heroes, and also God as seen and prayed to by the simple and primitive heart of the people.

The Fascist State is a will to power and to government. In it the tradition of Rome is an idea that has force. In the doctrine of Fascism Empire is not only a territorial, military or mercantile expression, but spiritual or moral. One can think of an empire, that is to say a nation that directly or indirectly leads other nations, without needing to conquer a single square kilometre of territory. For Fascism the tendency to Empire, that is to say, to the expansion of nations, is a manifestation of vitality; its opposite, staying at home, is a sign of decadence: peoples who rise or re-rise are imperialist, peoples who die are renunciatory. Fascism is the doctrine that is most fitted to represent the aims, the states of mind of a people, like the Italian people, rising again after many centuries of abandonment or slavery to foreigners. But Empire calls for discipline, co-ordination of forces, duty and sacrifice; this explains many aspects of the practical working of the regime and the direction of many of the forces of the State and the necessary severity shown to those who would wish to oppose this spontaneous and destined impulse of the Italy of the twentieth century, to oppose it in the name of the superseded ideologies of the nineteenth, repudiated wherever great experiments of political and social transformation have been courageously attempted: especially where, as now, peoples thirst for authority, for leadership, for order. If every age has its own doctrine, it is apparent from a thousand signs that the doctrine of the present age is Fascism. That it is a doctrine of life is shown by the fact that it has resuscitated a faith. That this faith has conquered minds is proved by the fact that Fascism has had its dead and its martyrs.

Fascism henceforward has in the world the university of all those doctrines which, by fulfilling themselves, have significance in the history of the human spirit.

'The Doctrine of Fascism' (1932), trans. in *The Social and Political Doctrines of Contemporary Europe*, ed. M. Oakeshott (London, Cambridge University Press, 1940), pp. 172–3, 175–9.

D. H. Lawrence
(1885–1930)

EACH MAN SHALL BE
SPONTANEOUSLY HIMSELF

It is obvious that Whitman's Democracy is not merely a political system, or a system of government – or even a social system. It is an attempt to conceive a new way of life, to establish new values. It is a struggle to liberate human beings from the fixed, arbitrary control of ideals into free spontaneity.

No, the ideal of Oneness, the unification of all mankind into the homogeneous whole, is done away with. The great *desire* is that each single individual shall be incommutably himself, spontaneous and single, that he shall not in any way be reduced to a term, a unit of any Whole.

We must discriminate between an ideal and a desire. A desire proceeds from within, from the unknown, spontaneous soul or self. But an ideal is superimposed from above, from the mind; it is a fixed, arbitrary thing, like a machine control. The great lesson is to learn to break all the fixed ideals, to allow the soul's own deep desires to come direct, spontaneous into consciousness. But it is a lesson which will take many aeons to learn.

Our life, our being depends upon the incalculable issue from the central Mystery into indefinable *presence*. This sounds in itself an abstraction. But not so. It is rather the perfect absence of abstraction. The central Mystery is no generalized abstraction. It is each man's primal original soul or self, within him. And *presence* is nothing mystic or ghostly. On the contrary. It is the actual man present before us. The fact that an actual man present before us is an inscrutable and incarnate Mystery, untranslatable, this is the fact upon which any great scheme of social life must be based. It is the fact of *otherness*.

Each human self is single, incommutable and unique. This is its *first* reality. Each self is unique, and therefore incomparable. It is a single wellhead of creation, unquestionable: it cannot be compared with another self, another well-head, because, in its prime or creative reality, it can never be comprehended by any other self.

The living self has one purpose only: to come into its own fullness of being, as a tree comes into full blossom, or a bird into spring beauty, or a tiger into lustre.

But this coming into full, spontaneous being is the most difficult thing of all. Man's nature is balanced between spontaneous creativity and mechanical-material activity. Spontaneous being is subject to no law. But mechanical-material existence is subject to all the laws of the mechanical-physical world. Man has almost half his nature in the material world. His spontaneous nature *just* takes precedence.

The only thing man has to trust to in coming to himself is his desire and his impulse. Both desire and impulse tend to fall into mechanical automatism: to fall from spontaneous reality into dead or material reality. All our education should be a guarding against this fall.

The fall is possible in a twofold manner. Desires tend to automatize into functional appetites, and impulses tend to automatize into fixed aspirations or ideals. These are the two great temptations of man. Falling into the first temptation, the whole human will pivots on some function, some material activity, which then worked the whole being: like an *idée fixe* in the mental consciousness. This automatized, dominant appetite we call a lust: a lust for power, a lust for consuming, a lust for self-abnegation and merging. The second great temptation is the inclination to set up some fixed centre in the mind, and make the whole soul turn upon this centre. This we call idealism. Instead of the will fixing upon some sensational activity, it fixes upon some aspirational activity, and pivots this activity upon an idea or an ideal. The whole soul streams in the energy of aspiration and turns automatically, like a machine, upon the ideal.

These are the two great temptations of the fall of man, the fall from spontaneous, single, pure being, into what we call materialism or automatism or mechanism of the self. All education must tend against this fall; and all our efforts in all our life must be to preserve the soul free and spontaneous. The whole soul of man must *never* be subjected to one motion or emotion, the life-activity must never be degraded into a fixed activity, there must be *no fixed direction*.

There can be no ideal goal for human life. Any ideal goal means mechanization, materialism and nullity. There is no pulling open the buds to see what the blossom will be. Leaves must unroll, buds swell and open, and *then* the blossom. And even after that, when the flower dies and the leaves fall, *still* we shall not know. There will be more leaves, more buds, more blossoms: and again, a blossom is an unfolding of the creative unknown. Impossible, utterly impossible to preconceive the unrevealed blossom. You cannot forestall it from the last blossom. We know the flower of to-day, but the flower of to-morrow is all beyond us. Only in the material-mechanical world can man forsee, foreknow, calculate and establish laws.

So, we more or less grasp the first term of the new Democracy. We see something of what a man will be unto himself.

Next, what will a man be unto his neighbour? – Since every individual is, in his first reality, a single incommutable soul, not to be calculated or defined in terms of any other soul, there can be no establishing of a mathematical ratio. We cannot say that all men are equal. We cannot say $A=B$. Nor can we say that men are unequal. We may not declare that $A=B+C$.

Where each thing is unique in itself, there can be no comparison made. One man is neither equal nor unequal to another man. When I stand in the presence of another man, and I am my own pure self, am I aware of the presence of an equal, or of an inferior, or of a superior? I am not. When I stand with another man, who is himself, and when I am truly myself, then I am only aware of a Presence, and of the strange reality of Otherness. There is me, and there is *another being*. That is the first part of the reality. There is no comparing or estimating. There is only this strange recognition of *present otherness*. I may be glad, angry or sad, because of the presence of the other. But still no comparison enters in. Comparison enters only when one of us departs from his own integral being, and enters the material mechanical world. Then equality and inequality starts at once.

So, we know the first great purpose of Democracy: that each man shall be spontaneously himself – each man himself, each woman herself, without any question of equality or inequality entering in at all; and that no man shall try to determine the being of any other man, or of any other woman.

But, because of the temptation which awaits every individual – the temptation to fall out of being, into automatism and mechanization, every individual must be ready at all times to defend his own being against the mechanization and materialism forced upon him by those people who have fallen or departed from being. It is the long unending fight, the fight for the soul's own freedom of spontaneous being, against the mechanism and materialism of the fallen.

All the foregoing deals really with the integral, whole nature of man. If man would but *keep* whole, integral, everything could be left at that. There would be no need for laws and governments: agreement would be spontaneous. Even the great concerted social activities would be essentially spontaneous.

But in his present state of unspeakable barbarism, man is unable to distinguish his own spontaneous integrity from his mechanical lusts and aspirations. Hence there must still be laws and governments. But laws and governments henceforth, we see it clearly and we must never forget it, relate only to the material world: to property, the possession of property and the means of life, and to the material-mechanical nature of man.

In the past, no doubt, there were great ideals to fulfil: ideals of brotherhood, oneness and equality. Great sections of humanity tended to cohere into particular brotherhoods, expressing their oneness and their equality and their united purpose in a manner peculiar to themselves. For no matter how single an ideal may be, even such a mathematical ideal as equality and oneness, it will find the most diverse and even opposite expressions. So that brotherhood and oneness in Germany never meant the same as brotherhood and oneness in France. Yet each was brotherhood, and each was oneness. Souls, as they work out the same ideal, work it out differently: always differently, until they reach the point where the spontaneous integrity of being finally breaks. And then, when pure mechanization or materialism sets in, the soul is automatically pivoted, and the most diverse of creatures fall into a common mechanical unison. This we see in America. It is not a homogeneous, spontaneous coherence so much as a disintegrated amorphousness which lends itself to perfect mechanical unison.

Men have reached the point where, in further fulfilling their ideals, they break down the living integrity of their being and fall into sheer mechanical materialism. They become automatic units, determined entirely by mechanical law.

This is horribly true of modern democracy – socialism, conservatism, bolshevism, liberalism, republicanism, communism: all alike. The one principle that governs all the *isms* is the same: the principle of the idealized unit, the possessor of property. Man has his highest fulfilment as a possesor of property: so they all say, really. One half says that the uneducated, being the majority, should possess the property; the other half says that the educated, being the enlightened, should possess the property. There is no more to it. No need to write books about it.

This is the last of the ideals. This is the last phase of the ideal of equality, brotherhood and oneness. All ideals work down to the sheer materialism which is their intrinsic reality, at last.

It doesn't matter, now, who has the property. They have all lost all their being over it. Even property, that most substantial of realities, evaporates once man loses his integral nature. It is curious that it is so, but it is undeniable. So that property is now fast evaporating.

Wherein lies the hope. For with it evaporates the last ideal. Sometime, somewhere, man will wake up and realize that property is only there to be used, not to be possessed. He will realize that possession is a kind of illness of the spirit, and a hopeless burden upon the spontaneous self. The little pronouns 'my' and 'our' will lose all their mystic spell.

The question of property will never be settled till people cease to care for property. Then it will settle itself. A man only needs so much as will help him to his own fulfilments. Surely the individual who wants a motor-car merely for the sake of having it and riding in it is as hopeless an automaton as the motor car itself.

When men are no longer obsessed with the desire to possess property, or with the parallel desire to prevent another man's possessing it, then, and only then shall we be glad to turn it over to the State. Our way of State-ownership is merely a farcical exchange of words, not of ways. We only intend our States to be Unlimited Liability Companies instead of Limited Liability Companies.

The Prime Minister of the future will be no more than a sort of steward, the Minister for Commerce will be the great housekeeper, the Minister for Transport the head-coachman: all just chief servants, no more: servants.

When men become their own decent selves again, then we can so easily arrange the material world. The arrangement will come, as it must come, spontaneously, not by previous ordering. Until such time, what is the good of talking about it? All discussion and idealizing of the possession of property whether individual or group or State possession, amounts now to no more than a fatal betrayal of the spontaneous self. All settlement of the property question must arise spontaneously out of the new impulse in man, to free himself from the extraneous load of possession, and walk naked and light. Every attempt at preordaining a new material world only adds another last straw to the load that already has broken so many backs. If we are to keep our backs unbroken, we must deposit all property on the ground, and learn to walk without it. We must stand aside. And when many men stand aside, they stand in a new world; a new world of man has come to pass. This is the Democracy: the new order.

'Democracy' (1936), reprinted in *Phoenix: The Posthumous Papers of D. H. Lawrence*, ed. E. Macdonald (London, Heinemann, 1961).

N. Bukharin (1888–1938)
and E. Preobrazhensky (1886–1937)

SOCIETY ORGANIZED BUT CLASSLESS

It is evident that the new society must be much more solidly constructed than capitalism. As soon as the fundamental contradictions of capitalism have destroyed the capitalist system, upon the ruins of that system there must arise a new society which will be free from the contradictions of the old. That is to say, the communist method of production must present the following characteristics: In the first place it must be an *organized* society; it must be free from anarchy of production, from competition between individual entrepreneurs, from wars and crises. In the second place it must be a *classless* society, not a society in which the two halves are at eternal enmity one with the other; it must not be a society in which one class exploits the other. Now a society in which there are no classes, and in which production is organized, can only be *a society of comrades, a communist society based upon labour*.

Let us examine this society more closely.

The basis of communist society must be the social ownership of the means of production and exchange. Machinery, locomotives, steamships, factory buildings, warehouses, grain elevators, mines, telegraphs and telephones, the land, sheep, horses, and cattle, must all be at the disposal of society. All these means of production must be under the control of society as a whole, and not as at present under the control of individual capitalists or capitalist combines. What do we mean by 'society as a whole'? We mean that ownership and control is not the privilege of a class but of all the persons who make up society. In these circumstances society will be transformed into a huge working organization for co-operative production. There will then be neither disintegration of production nor anarchy of production. In such a social order, production will be organized. No longer will one enterprise compete with another; the factories, workshops, mines and other productive institutions will all be subdivisions, as it were, of one vast people's workshop, which will embrace the entire national economy of production. It is obvious that so comprehensive an organization presupposes a general plan of production. If all the factories and workshops together with the whole of agricultural production are combined to form an immense co-operative enterprise, it is obvious that everything must be precisely calculated. We must know in advance how much labour to assign to the various branches of industry; what products are required and how much of each it is necessary to produce; how and where machines must be provided. These and similar details must be thought out beforehand, with approximate accuracy at least; and the work must be guided in conformity with our calculations. This is how the organization of communist production will be effected. Without a general plan, without a general directive system, and without careful calculation and book-keeping, there can be no organization. But in the communist social order, there is such a plan.

Mere organization does not, however, suffice. The essence of the matter lies in this, that the organization shall be a co-operative organization of *all* the members of society. The communist system, in addition to effecting organization, is further distinguished by the fact that *it puts an end to exploitation*, that *it abolishes the division of society into classes*. We might conceive the organization of production as being effected in the following manner: a small group of capitalists, a capitalist combine, controls everything; production has been organized, so that capitalist no longer competes with capitalist; conjointly they extract surplus value from the workers, who have been practically reduced to slavery. Here we have organization, but we also have the exploitation of one class by another. Here there is a joint ownership of the means of production, but it is joint ownership by one class, an exploiting class. This is something very different from communism, although it is characterized by the organization of production. Such an organization of society would have removed only one of the fundamental contradictions, the anarchy of production. But it would have strengthened the other fundamental contradiction of capitalism, the division of society into two warring halves; the class war would be intensified. Such a society would be organized along one line only; on another line, that of class structure, it would still be rent asunder. Communist society does not merely organize production; in addition, it frees people from oppression by others. It is organized throughout.

The co-operative character of communist production is likewise displayed in every detail of organization. Under communism, for example, there will not be permanent managers of factories, nor will there be persons who do one and the same kind of work throughout their lives. Under capitalism, if a man is a bootmaker, he spends his whole life in making boots (the cobbler sticks to his last); if he is a pastrycook, he spends all his life baking cakes; if he is the manager of a factory, he spends his days in issuing orders and in administrative work; if he is a mere labourer, his whole life is spent in obeying orders. Nothing of this sort happens in communist society. Under communism people receive a many-sided culture, and find themselves at home in various branches of production: today I work in an administrative capacity, I reckon up how many felt boots or how many French rolls must be produced during the following month; tomorrow I shall be working in a soap factory, next month perhaps in a steam laundry and the month after in an electric power station. This will be possible when all the members of society have been suitably educated.

The communist method of production presupposes in addition that production is not for the market, but for use. Under communism, it is no longer the individual manufacturer or the individual peasant who produces; the work of production is effected by the gigantic co-operative as a whole. In consequence of this change, we no longer have *commodities*, but only *products*. These products are not exchanged one for another; they are neither bought nor sold. They are simply stored in the communal warehouses, and are subsequently delivered to those who need them. In such conditions money will no longer be required. 'How can that be?' some of you will ask, 'In that case one person will get too much and another too little. What sense is there in such a method of distribution?' The answer is as follows. At first, doubtless, and perhaps for twenty or thirty years, it will be necessary to have various regulations. Maybe certain products will only be supplied to those persons who have a special entry in their workbook or on their work-card. Subsequently, when communist society has been consolidated and fully developed, no such regulations will be needed. There will be an ample quantity of all products, our present wounds will long since have been healed and everyone will be able to get just as much as he needs. 'But will not people find it to their interest to take more than they need?' Certainly not. Today, for example, no one thinks it worth while when he wants one seat in a tram, to take three tickets and keep two places empty. It will be just the same in the case of all products. A person will take from the communal storehouse precisely as much as he needs, no more. No one will have any interest in taking more than he wants in order to sell the surplus to others, since all these others can satisfy their needs whenever they please. Money will then have no value. Our meaning is that at the outset, in the first days of communist society, products will probably be distributed in accordance with the amount of work done by the applicant; at a later stage, however, they will simply be supplied according to the needs of the comrades.

In a communist society there will be no classes. But if there will be no classes, this implies that *in communist society there will likewise be no State*. We have previously seen that the State is a class organization of the rulers. The State is always directed by one class against the other. A bourgeois State is directed against the proletariat, whereas a proletarian State is directed against the bourgeoisie. In the communist social order there are neither landlords, nor capitalists, nor wage workers; there are simply people – comrades. If there are no classes, then there is no class war, and there are no class organizations. Consequently the State has ceased to exist. Since there is no class war, the State has become superfluous. There is no one to be held in restraint, and there is no one to impose restraint.

But how, they will ask us, can this vast organization be set in motion without any administration? Who is going to work out the plans for social production? Who will distribute labour power? Who is going to keep account of social income and expenditure? In a word, who is going to supervise the whole affair?

It is not difficult to answer these questions. The main direction will be entrusted to various kinds of book-keeping offices or statistical bureaux. There, from day to day, account will be kept of production and all its needs; there also it will be decided whither workers must be sent, whence they must be taken and how much work there is to be done. And inasmuch as, from childhood onwards, all will have been accustomed to social labour, and since all will understand that this work is necessary and that life goes easier when everything is done according to a prearranged plan and when the social order is like a well-oiled machine, all will work in accordance with the indications of these statistical bureaux. There will be no need for special ministers of State, for police and prisons, for laws and decrees – nothing of the sort. Just as in an orchestra all the performers watch the conductor's baton and act accordingly, so here all will consult the statistical reports and will direct their work accordingly.

The State, therefore, has ceased to exist. There are no groups and there is no class standing above all other classes. Moreover, in these statistical bureaux one person will work today, another tomorrow. The bureaucracy, the permanent officialdom, will disappear. The State will die out.

Manifestly this will only happen in the fully developed and strongly established communist system, after the complete and definitive victory of the proletariat; nor will it follow immediately upon that victory. For a long time yet, the working class will have to fight against all its enemies, and in especial against the relics of the past, such as sloth, slackness, criminality, pride. All these will have to be stamped out. Two or three generations of persons will have to grow up under the new conditions before the need will pass for laws and punishments and for the use of repressive measures by the workers' State. Not until then will all the vestiges of the capitalist past disappear. Though in the intervening period the existence of the workers' State is indispensable, subsequently, in the fully developed communist system, when the vestiges of capitalism are extinct, the proletarian State authority will also pass away. The proletariat itself will become mingled with all the other strata of the population, for everyone will by degrees come to participate in the common labour. Within a few decades there will be quite a new world, with new people and new customs.

As soon as victory has been achieved and as soon as all our wounds have been healed, the communist system will rapidly develop the forces of production. This more rapid development of the forces of production will be due to the following causes.

In the first place, there will have ensued the liberation of the vast quantity of human energy which is now absorbed in the class struggle. Just think how great is the waste of nervous energy, strength and labour – upon the political struggle, upon strikes, revolts and their suppression, trials in the law-courts, police activities, the State authority, upon the daily effort of the two hostile classes. The class war now swallows up vast quantities of energy and material means. In the new system this energy will be liberated; people will no longer struggle one with another. The liberated energy will be devoted to the work of production.

Secondly, the energy and the material means which now are destroyed or wasted in competition, crises and wars, will all be saved. If we consider how much is squandered upon wars alone, we shall realize that this amounts to an enormous quantity. How much, again, is lost to society through the struggle of sellers one with another, of buyers one with another and of sellers with buyers. How much futile destruction results from commercial crises. How much needless outlay results from the disorganization and confusion that prevail in production. All these energies, which now run to waste, will be saved in communist society.

The communist method of production will signify an enormous development of productive forces. As a result, no worker in communist society will have to do as much work as of old. The working day will grow continually shorter, and people will be to an increasing extent freed from the chains imposed on them by nature. As soon as man is enabled to spend less time upon feeding and clothing himself, he will be able to devote more time to the work of mental development. Human culture will climb to heights never attained before. It will no longer be a class culture, but will become a genuinely human culture. Concurrently with the disappearance of man's tyranny over man, the tyranny of nature over man will likewise vanish. Men and women will for the first time be able to lead a life worthy of thinking beings instead of a life worthy of brute beasts.

The ABC of Communism (1919), trans. E. and C. Paul (Communist Party of Great Britain, 1922), pp. 69–76, 77. (Reissued by Penguin Books, 1969.)

T. S. Eliot
(1888–1965)

THE IDEA OF A CHRISTIAN SOCIETY

It should be obvious that the form of political organization of a Christian State does not come within the scope of this discussion. To identify any particular form of government with Christianity is a dangerous error: for it confounds the permanent with the transitory, the absolute with the contingent. Forms of government, and of social organization, are in constant process of change, and their operation may be very different from the theory which they are supposed to exemplify. A theory of the State may be, explicitly or implicitly, anti-Christian: it may arrogate rights which only the Church is entitled to claim, or pretend to decide moral questions on which only the Church is qualified to pronounce. On the other hand, a regime may in practice claim either more or less than it professes, and we have to examine its working as well as its constitution. We have no assurance that a democratic regime might not be as inimical to Christianity in practice, as another might be in theory: and the best government must be relative to the character and the stage of intelligence and education of a particular people in a particular place at a particular time. Those who consider that a discussion of the nature of a Christian society should conclude by supporting a particular form of political organization, should ask themselves whether they really believe our form of government to be more important than our Christianity; and those who are convinced that the present form of government of Britain is the one most suitable for any Christian people, should ask themselves whether they are confusing a Christian society with a society in which individual Christianity is tolerated.

I have tried to restrict my ambition of a Christian society to a social minimum: to picture, not a society of saints, but of ordinary men, of men whose Christianity is communal before being individual. It is very easy for speculation on a possible Christian order in the future to tend to come to rest in a kind of apocalyptic vision of a golden age of virtue. But we have to remember that the Kingdom of Christ on earth will never be realized, and also that it is always being realized; we must remember that whatever reform or revolution we carry out, the result will always be a sordid travesty of what human society should be – though the world is never left wholly without glory. In such a society as I imagine, as in any that is not petrified, there will be innumerable seeds of decay. Any human scheme for society is realized only when the great mass of humanity has become adapted to it; but this adaptation becomes also, insensibly, an adaptation of the scheme itself to the mass on which it operates: the over-whelming pressure of mediocrity, sluggish and indomitable as a glacier, will mitigate the most violent, and depress the most exalted revolution, and what is realized is so unlike the end that enthusiasm conceived, that foresight would weaken the effort. A wholly Christian society might be a society for the most part on a low level; it would engage the co-operation of many whose Christianity was spectral or superstitious or feigned, and of many whose motives were primarily worldly and selfish. It would require constant reform.

I should not like it to be thought, however, that I considered the presence of the higher forms of devotional life to be a matter of minor importance for such a society. I have, it is true, insisted upon the communal, rather than the individual aspect: a community of men and women, not individually better than they are now, except for the capital difference of holding the Christian faith. But their holding the Christian faith would give them something else which they lack: a *respect* for the religious life, for the life of prayer and contemplation, and for those who attempt to practise it. In this I am asking no more of the British Christian, than is characteristic of the ordinary Moslem or Hindu. But the ordinary man would need the opportunity to know that the religious life existed, that it was given its due place, would need to recognize the profession of those who have abandoned the world, as he recognizes the professions practised in it. I cannot conceive a Christian society without religious orders, even purely contemplative orders, even enclosed orders. And, incidentally, I should not like the 'Community of Christians' of which I have spoken, to be thought of as merely the nicest, most intelligent and public-spirited of the upper middle class – it is not to be conceived on that analogy.

We may say that religion, as distinguished from modern paganism, implies a life in conformity with nature. It may be observed that the natural life and the supernatural life have a conformity to each other which neither has with the mechanistic life: but so far has our notion of what is natural become distorted, that people who consider it 'unnatural' and therefore repugnant, that a person of either sex should elect a life of celibacy, consider it perfectly 'natural' that families should be limited to one or two children. It would perhaps be more natural, as well as in better conformity with the Will of God, if there were more celibates and if those who were married had larger families. But I am thinking of 'conformity to nature' in a wider sense than this. We are being made aware that the organization of society on the principle of private profit, as well as public destruction, is leading both to the deformation of humanity by unregulated industrialism, and to the exhaustion of natural resources, and that a good deal of our material progress is a progress for which succeeding generations may have to pay dearly. I need only mention, as an instance now very much before the public eye, the results of 'soil-erosion' – the exploitation of the earth, on a vast scale for two generations, for commercial profit: immediate benefits leading to dearth and desert. I would not have it thought that I condemn a society because of its material ruin, for that would be to make its material success a sufficient test of its excellence; I mean only that a wrong attitude towards nature implies, somewhere, a wrong attitude towards God, and that the consequence is an inevitable doom. For a long enough time we have believed in nothing but the values arising in a mechanized, commercialized, urbanized way of life: it would be as well for us to face the permanent conditions upon which God allows us to live upon this planet. And without sentimentalizing the life of the savage, we might practise the humility to observe, in some of the societies upon which we look down as primitive or backward, the operation of a social-religious-artistic complex which we should emulate upon a higher plane. We have been accustomed to regard 'progress' as always integral; and have yet to learn that it is only by an effort and a discipline, greater than society has yet seen the need of imposing upon itself, that material knowledge and power is gained without loss of spiritual knowledge and power. The struggle to recover the sense of relation to nature and to God, the recognition that even the most primitive feelings should be part of our heritage, seems to me to be the explanation and justification of the life of D. H. Lawrence, and the excuse for his aberrations. But we need not only to learn how to look at the world with the eyes of a Mexican Indian – and I hardly think that Lawrence succeeded – and we certainly cannot afford to stop there. We need to know how to see the world as the Christian Fathers saw it; and the purpose of reascending to origins is that we should be able to return ,with greater spiritual knowledge, to our own situation. We need to recover the sense of religious fear, so that it may be overcome by religious hope.

I should not like to leave the reader supposing that I have attempted to contribute one more amateur sketch of an abstract and impracticable future: the blueprint from which the doctrinaire criticizes the piecemeal day to day efforts of political men. These latter efforts have to go on; but unless we can find a pattern in which all problems of life can have their place, we are only likely to go on complicating chaos. So long, for instance, as we consider finance, industry, trade, agriculture merely as competing interests to be reconciled from time to time as best they may, so long as we consider 'education' as a good in itself of which everyone has a right to the utmost, without any ideal of the good life for society or for the individual, we shall move from one uneasy compromise to another. To the quick and simple organization of society for ends which, being only material and worldly, must be as ephemeral as worldly success, there is only one alternative. As political philosophy derives its sanction from ethics, and ethics from the truth of religion, it is only by returning to the eternal source of truth that we can hope for any social organization which will not, to its ultimate destruction, ignore some essential aspects of reality. The term 'democracy', as I have said again and again, does not contain enough positive content to stand alone against the forces that you dislike – it can easily be transformed by them. If you will not have God (and He is a jealous God) you should pay your respects to Hitler or Stalin.

The Idea of a Christian Society (1939) (London, Faber, 1951), pp. 57–8, 59–63.

G. D. H. Cole
(1889–1959)

THE SELF-GOVERNING COMMUNITY

Guildsmen assume that the essential social values are human values, and that Society is to be regarded as a complex of associations held together by the wills of their members, whose well-being is its purpose. They assume further that it is not enough that the forms of government should have the passive or 'implied' consent of the governed, but that the Society will be in health only if it is in the full sense democratic and self-governing, which implies not only that all the citizens should have a 'right' to influence its policy if they so desire, but that the greatest possible opportunity should be afforded for every citizen actually to exercise this right. In other words, the Guild Socialist conception of democracy, which it assumes to be good, involves an active and not merely a passive citizenship on the part of the members. Moreover, and this is perhaps the most vital and significant assumption of all, it regards this democratic principle as applying, not only or mainly to some special sphere of social action known as 'politics', but to any and every form of social action, and, in especial, to industrial and economic fully as much as to political affairs.

In calling these the fundamental assumptions of Guild Socialism, I do not mean to imply that they are altogether beyond the province of argument. They can indeed be sustained by arguments of obvious force; for it seems clear enough that only a community which is self-governing in this complete sense, over the whole length and breadth of its activities, can hope to call out what is best in its members, or to give them that maximum opportunity for personal and social self-expression which is requisite to real freedom. But such arguments as this, by which the assumptions stated above may be sustained and reinforced, really depend for their appeal upon the same considerations, and are, in the last resort, different ways of stating the same fundamental position. The essence of the Guild Socialist attitude lies in the belief that Society ought to be so organized as to afford the greatest possible opportunity for individual and collective self-expression to all its members, and that this involves and implies the extension of positive self-government through all its parts.

No one can reasonably maintain that Society is organized on such a principle today. We do, indeed, possess in theory a very large measure of democracy; but there are at least three sufficient reasons which make this theoretical democracy largely inoperative in practice. In the first place, even the theory of democracy today is still largely of the 'consciousness of consent' type. It assigns to the ordinary citizen little more than a privilege – which is in practice mainly illusory – of choosing his rulers, and does not call upon him, or assign to him the opportunity, himself to rule. Present-day practice has, indeed, pushed the theory of representative government to the length of substituting almost completely, even in theory, the representative for the represented. This is the essential meaning of the doctrine of the 'sovereignty of Parliament'. Secondly, such democracy as is recognized is conceived in a narrowly 'political' sense, as applying to a quite peculiar sphere known as politics, and not in a broader and more comprehensive sense, as applying to all the acts which men do in association or conjunction. The result is that theoretical 'democrats' totally ignore the effects of undemocratic organization and convention in non-political spheres of social action, not only upon the lives which men lead in those spheres, but also in perverting and annihilating in practice the theoretical democracy of modern politics. They ignore the fact that vast inequalities of wealth and status, resulting in vast inequalities of education, power and control of environment, are necessarily fatal to any real democracy, whether in politics or in any other sphere. Thirdly, the theory of representative government is distorted not only by the substitution of the representative for the represented, but also as a consequence of the extended activity of political government falsifying the operation of the representative method. As long as the purposes of political government are comparatively few and limited, and the vast mass of social activities is either not regulated, or regulated by other means, such as the Medieval Gilds, it is perhaps possible for a body of men to choose one to represent them in relation to all the purposes with which a representative political body has to deal.[1] But, as the purposes covered by political government

[1] Thus, government in Great Britain for some time after 1689 was a fairly adequate representation of the aristocracy, whom alone it set out to represent.

expand, and more and more of social life is brought under political regulation, the representation which may once, within its limitations, have been real, turns into misrepresentation, and the person elected for an indefinitely large number of disparate purposes ceases to have any real representative relation to those who elect him.

It appears to the Guild Socialists, as to all real Socialists, obviously futile to expect true democracy to exist in any Society which recognizes vast inequalities of wealth, status and power among its members. Most obvious of all is it that, if, in the sphere of industry, one man is a master and the other a wage-slave, one enjoys riches and gives commands and the other has only an insecure subsistence and obeys orders, no amount of purely electoral machinery on a basis of 'one man one vote' will make the two really equal socially or politically. For the economic power of the rich master, or of the richer financier who is above even the master, will ring round the wage-slave's electoral rights at every point. A Press which can only be conducted with the support of rich capitalists and advertisers, an expensive machinery of elections, a regime in the school which differs for rich and poor and affords a training for power in the one case and for subjection in the other, a regime in industry which carries on the divergent lessons of the schools – these and a hundred other influences combine to make the real political power of one rich man infinitely greater than that of one who is poor. It is a natural and legitimate conclusion that, if we want democracy, that is, if we want every man's voice to count for as much as it is intrinsically worth, irrespective of any extraneous consideration, we must abolish class distinctions by doing away with the huge inequalities of wealth and economic power on which they really depend.

In a democratic Society, the whole body of consumers and the whole body of producers are practically the same people, only ranged in the two cases in different formations. There can be no real divergence of interests between them. It is a problem not, as in present-day Society, of economic warfare, but of reasonable democratic organization on a functional basis.

The Guild Socialist contends, then, that the internal management and control of each industry or service must be placed, as a trust on behalf of the community, in the hands of the workers engaged in it; but he holds no less strongly that full provision must be made for the representation and safeguarding of the consumers' point of view in relation to each service. Similarly, he contends that general questions of industrial administration extending to all industries should, where they mainly concern the whole body of producers, be entrusted to an organization representing all the producers; but he holds equally that the general point of view of all types of consumers must be fully represented and safeguarded in relation to industry as a whole.

Men will never recognize or regard as self-government in any association a system which does not give to them directly as a group the right of framing their common rules to govern their internal affairs, and of choosing, by their own decisions, those who are to hold office and authority in their midst.

This being so, no solution of the problem of industrial government is really a solution at all unless it places the rights and responsibilities of the internal conduct of industry directly upon the organized bodies of producers. On no other condition will men who have risen to a sense of social capacity and power consent to serve or to give of their best. Any other attempted solution will therefore break down before the unwillingness of the workers to produce, and will afford no way of escape from the impasse to which we have already been brought by the denial under capitalism of the human rights of Labour. It is our business, then, to accept unreservedly this claim of the producer, and at the same time to reconcile it with the consumer's claim that his voice shall also count.

Guild Socialism Re-Stated (London, Leonard Parsons, 1920), pp. 12–16, 38–9, 40–1.

Walter Lippmann
(1889–   )

THERE ARE NO BLUEPRINTS

This truth our contemporary authoritarians, whether of the left or of the right, have failed to grasp. They look upon the great sprawling complex of transactions by which mankind lives; seeing that these transactions are in large part still unregulated by law, and that therefore there is much confusion and injustice, they have turned their backs upon the task of regulation by law and have beguiled themselves with the notion that they can plan this economy systematically and administer it rationally. The exact contrary is the truth. The modern economy is perhaps the least systematic of any that has ever existed. It is world-wide, formless, vast, complicated, and, owing to technological progress, in constant change. For that reason it is incapable of being conceived as a system, or of being replaced by another system, or of being managed as an administrative unit.

The hankering for schemes and systems and comprehensive organization is the wistfulness of an immature philosophy which has not come to terms with reality, no less when the conservators of vested interests would stabilize the modern economy in *status quo* by protective laws and monopolistic schemes than when the revolutionist makes blueprints of a world composed of planned national economies 'co-ordinated' by a world-planning authority. Neither takes any more account of reality than if he were studying landscape architecture with a view to making a formal garden out of the Brazilian jungle.

For the greater the society, the higher and more variable the standards of life, the more diversified the energies of its people for invention, enterprise and adaptation, the more certain it is that the social order cannot be planned *ex cathedra* or governed by administrative command. We live in such an immensely diversified civilization that the only intelligible criterion which political thinkers can entertain in regard to it, the only feasible goal which statesmen can set themselves in governing it, is to reconcile the conflicts which spring from this diversity. They cannot hope to comprehend it as a system. For it is not a system. They cannot hope to plan and direct it. For it is not an organization. They can hope only to dispense lawful justice among individuals and associations where their interests conflict, to mitigate the violence of conflict and competition by seeking to make lawful justice more and more equitable.

It requires much virtue to do that well. There must be a strong desire to be just. There must be a growing capacity to be just. There must be discernment and sympathy in estimating the particular claims of divergent interests. There must be moral standards which discourage the quest of privilege and the exercise of arbitrary power. There must be resolution and valor to resist oppression and tyranny. There must be patience and tolerance and kindness in hearing claims, in argument, in negotiation and in reconciliation.

But these are human virtues; though they are high, they are within the attainable limits of human nature as we know it. They actually exist. Men do have these virtues, all but the most hopelessly degenerate, in some degree. We know that they can be increased. When we talk about them we are talking about virtues that have affected the course of actual history, about virtues that some men have practised more than other men, and no man sufficiently, but enough men in great enough degree to have given mankind here and there and for varying periods of time the intimations of a Good Society.

But the virtues that are required for the overhead administration of a civilization are superhuman; they are attributes of Providence and not of mortal men. It is true that there have been benevolent despots and that for a little while in a particular place they have made possible a better life than their subjects were able to achieve without the rule of a firm and authoritative guardian. And no doubt it is still true that a community which does not have the essential discipline of liberty can choose only among alternative disciplines by authority. But if a community must have such a guardian, then it must resign itself to living a simple regimented existence, must entertain no hopes of the high and diversified standard of life which the division of labor and modern technology make possible. For despots cannot be found who could plan, organize and direct a complex economy.

To do that would require a comprehensive understanding of the life and the labor and the purposes of hundreds of millions of persons, the gift of prophesying their behavior and omnipotence to control it. These faculties no man has ever possessed. When in theorizing we unwittingly postulate such faculties, we are resting our hopes on a conception of human nature which has no warrant whatever in any actual experience. The collectivist planners are not talking about the human race but about some other breed conceived in their dreams. They postulate qualities of intelligence and of virtue so unlike those which men possess that it would be just as intelligible to make plans for a society in which human beings were born equipped to fly like the angels, to feed on the fragrance of the summer breezes and endowed with all possible knowledge.

Thus while the liberal philosophy is concerned with the reform of the laws in order to adapt them to the changing needs and standards of the dynamic economy, while the agenda of reform are long and varied, no one must look to liberalism for a harmonious scheme of social reconstruction. The Good Society has no architectural design. There are no blueprints. There is no mold in which human life is to be shaped. Indeed, to expect the blueprint of such a mold is a mode of thinking against which the liberal temper is a constant protest.

To design a personal plan for a new society is a pleasant form of madness; it is in imagination to play at being God and Caesar to the human race. Any such plan must implicitly assume that the visionary or someone else might find the power, or might persuade the masses to give him the power, to shape society to the plan; all such general plans of social reconstruction are merely the rationalization of the will to power. For that reason they are the subjective beginnings of fanaticism and tyranny. In these utopias the best is the enemy of the good, the heart's desire betrays the interests of man. To think in terms of a new scheme for a whole society is to use the idiom of authority, to approach affairs from the underlying premise that they can be shaped and directed by an overhead control, that social relations can be fabricated according to a master plan drawn up by a supreme architect.

The supreme architect, who begins as a visionary, becomes a fanatic, and ends as a despot. For no one can be the supreme architect of society without employing a supreme despot to execute the design. So if men are to seek freedom from the arbitrary dominion of men over men, they must not entertain fantasies of the future in which they play at being the dictators of civilization. It is the bad habit of an undisciplined imagination. The descent from fantasy to fanaticism is easy. Real dictators raised to power by the fanatics who adore them are only too likely to adopt the fantasy to justify their lust for power.

On the other hand, reasonable and civilized people who would like to make the best of the situation before them, but have no ambition for, or expectation of, the power to reshape a whole society, get no help from these architectural designs. The blueprint, be it as grandiose a work of genius as Plato's *Republic*, cannot hope to fit the specific situation. No *a priori* reasoning can anticipate the precise formulae which will reconcile the infinitely varied interests of men. The reconciliation has to be achieved by the treatment of specific issues and the solution will appear only after the claims and the evidence have been examined and fairly judged. Thus in Plato's great scheme each man was assigned his station and his duties; any architectural plan is necessarily based on the same presumption. But Plato's scheme worked only in Plato's imagination, never in the real world. No such scheme can ever work in the real world. For the scheme implies that men will remain content in the station which the visionary has assigned to them. To formulate such plans is not to design a society for real men. It is to re-create men to fit the design. For in real life men rest content in their station only if their interests have been successfully reconciled: failing that, they do not fit the design until they have been dosed with castor oil, put in concentration camps or exiled to Siberia.

That is why the testament of liberty does not contain the project of a new social order. It adumbrates a way of life in which men seek to reconcile their interests by perfecting the rules of justice. No scheme which promises to obliterate the differences of interest can be deduced from it, no architectural design of society in which all human problems have been resolved. There is no plan of the future: there is, on the contrary, the conviction that the future must have the shape that human energies, purged in so far as possible of arbitrariness, will give it. Compared with the elegant and harmonious schemes which are propounded by the theoretical advocates of capitalism, communism, fascism, it must seem intellectually unsatisfying, and I can well imagine that many will feel about the liberal society as Emma Darwin felt when she wrote about the *Descent of Man*, 'I think it will be very interesting, but that I shall dislike it very much as again putting God further off.'[1]

But though it must seem an insufficient ideal both to those who wish to exercise authority and to those who feel the need of leaning upon authority, it is the only practicable ideal of government in the Great

[1] Cited in Donald Culross Peattie, *Green Laurels*, p. 323.

Society. When huge masses of men have become dependent upon one another through the division of labor in countless, infinitely complex transactions, their activities cannot be planned and directed by public officials.

Thus it is true that the liberal state is not to be conceived as an earthly providence administering civilization. That is the essence of the matter. To the liberal mind the notion that men can authoritatively plan and impose a good life upon a great society is ignorant, impertinent and pretentious. It can be entertained only by men who do not realize the infinite variety of human purposes, who do not appreciate the potentialities of human effort or by men who do not choose to respect them.

The liberal state is to be conceived as the protector of equal rights by dispensing justice among individuals. It seeks to protect men against arbitrariness, not arbitrarily to direct them. Its ideal is a fraternal association among free and equal men. To the initiative of individuals, secure in their rights and accountable to others who have equal rights, liberalism entrusts the shaping of the human destiny. It offers no encouragement to those who dream of what they could make of the world if they possessed supreme power. In the testament of liberty these ambitions have been assessed: the record of all the Caesars from Alexander to Adolf is visible. The world has known many societies in which each man had his station, his duties and his ordained destiny, and the record shows that it is beyond the understanding of men to know all human needs, to appreciate all human possibilities, to imagine all human ends, to shape all human relations.

Yet if the ambitions of liberalism are more modest than those of authority, its promise is greater. It relies upon the development of the latent faculties of all men, shaped by their free transactions with one another. Liberalism commits the destiny of civilization, not to a few finite politicians here and there, but to the whole genius of mankind. This is a grander vision than that of those who would be Caesar and would set themselves up as little tin gods over men. It is a hope engendered in the human heart during the long ages in which the slowly emerging impulses of civilization, beset by barbarism, have struggled to be free.

The Good Society (London, Allen & Unwin, 1937), pp. 362-8.

Boris Pasternak
(1890–1960)

THE IMPOSSIBILITY OF
RESHAPING LIFE

'You've changed, you know. You used to speak more calmly about the revolution, you were less harsh about it.'

'The point is, Larissa Fyodorovna, that there are limits to everything. In all this time something definite should have been achieved. But it turns out that those who inspired the revolution aren't at home in anything except change and turmoil: that's their native element; they aren't happy with anything that's less than on a world scale. For them, transitional periods, worlds in the making, are an end in themselves. They aren't trained for anything else, they don't know about anything except that. And do you know why there is this incessant whirl of never-ending preparations? It's because they haven't any real capacities, they are un-gifted. Man is born to live, not to prepare for life. Life itself – the gift of life – is such a breathtakingly serious thing! – Why substitute this childish harlequinade of adolescent fantasies, these schoolboy escapades? But enough of this.'

'Heavens, Liberius Avercievich, I'm not being supercilious. I have the utmost respect for your educational work. I've read the discussion notes you circulate. I know your ideas on the moral improvement of the soldier – they're excellent. All you say about what the soldier's attitude should be towards his comrades, to the weak, the helpless, to women, and about honour and chastity – it's almost the teaching of the Dukhobors.[1] All that kind of Tolstoyism I know by heart. My own adolescence was full of these aspirations towards a better life. How could I laugh at such things?

'But, firstly, the idea of social betterment as it is understood since the October Revolution doesn't fill me with enthusiasm. Secondly, it is so far

[1] Communities which practised principles similar to those of Tolstoy.

345

from being put into practice, and the mere talk about it has cost such a sea of blood, that I am not at all sure if the end justifies the means. And lastly, and above all, when I hear people speak of reshaping life it makes me lose my self-control and I fall into despair.

'Reshaping life! People who can say that have never understood a thing about life – they have never felt its breath, its heart – however much they have seen or done. They look on it as a lump of raw material which needs to be processed by them, to be ennobled by their touch. But life is never a material, a substance to be moulded. If you want to know, life is the principle of self-renewal, it is constantly renewing and remaking and changing and transfiguring itself, it is infinitely beyond your or my theories about it.'

Doctor Zhivago, trans. Max Hayward and Manya Harari (London, Collins and Harvill Press, 1958), pp. 269, 305–6.

Karl Mannheim
(1893–1947)

THE ADVENT OF PLANNED FREEDOM

Processes are at work both in national and international affairs, which can only find fulfilment in a new form of planning. As long as the social forces are left to themselves, conflict breaks out just when they are on the point of reaching a solution. But it is due to human inadequacy, and not merely to the social forces themselves, that men fail at the eleventh hour to build these latent tendencies into a workable system. At a certain stage of social development it is not enough to leave external trends to themselves; we need a new type of man who can see the right thing to do, and new political groups which will do it.

While hitherto the major changes of history have very often been incomprehensible both to individuals and to sectional groups, the evolution of society has now reached a point at which these processes cannot be adjusted without adequate insight on the part of the actors. Moreover, while hitherto no particular group has had the responsibility of creating social integration – for anything that happened was the result of haphazard compromise between conflicting tendencies – today there are indications that if the groups engaged in politics still refuse to look beyond their own immediate interests, society will be doomed. At the present stage of events we need a new kind of foresight, a new technique for managing conflicts, together with a psychology, morality and plan of action in many ways completely different from those which have obtained in the past. It is only by remaking man himself that the reconstruction of society is possible. The reinterpretation of human aims, the transformation of human capacities, the reconstruction of our moral code are not a subject for edifying sermons or visionary utopias. They are vital to us all, and the only question is what can reasonably be done in this direction.

*   *   *

The new conception of freedom creates the desire to control the effects of the social surroundings as far as possible. This is no mere daydream, it is based on the fact that enormous advances in social technique allow us to influence the conduct of social affairs from the key positions, according to a definite plan. Once we have realized this, our outlook on life will change, and we shall feel that while this chaotic tangle of institutions continues we are no longer free. In order to clear up this confusion we must be willing to forego our former liberties, just as we were in passing from the first stage to the second; provided that in doing so we gain control of the entire social environment. In many spheres we have abandoned those forms of freedom which allowed the individual to use his inventive powers as a means to his own ends, without considering the consequences for society as a whole. The sacrifice of this primary form of freedom will lead to our complete enslavement unless we are willing to accept the further implication of it and thus strive to regulate the entire social network: that is, to regulate all social relationships so as to secure the collective freedom of the group in accordance with a democratically recognized plan. From now on men will find a higher form of freedom in allowing many aspects of their individual lives to be determined by the social order laid down by the group, provided that it is an order which they themselves have chosen.

At the stage we have just reached, it seems to be greater slavery to be able to do as we like in an unjust or badly organized society, than to accept the claims of planning in a healthy society which we ourselves have chosen. The realization that fair and democratic planning does not involve the surrender of our freedom is the mainspring of those arguments which show that an unplanned capitalist society is not the basis of the highest form of liberty.

It has rightly been pointed out that the 'liberties' of liberal capitalist society are often only available to the rich, and that the 'have-nots' are forced to submit to the pressure of circumstances. The real representative of this society would be the free workman, who had the right to sell his labour in a 'free' market, or if he preferred, to give up the struggle and starve. What is the use of freedom in teaching and learning to a poor man who has neither the time nor the means to acquire the necessary education? What use is the freedom to choose our own philosophy of life, to form our own opinions, if the sociological mechanisms of our society create insecurity, anxiety, neuroses, which prevent us from making sound and rational decisions?

Those who cling to the forms of freedom which were current at the stage of invention retort: 'What use is the best social order if it is simply imposed on the individual and he cannot escape from it? What use are the wisest of institutions if I am not free to live my own life? I would rather work out my own solution, however inadequate, to a difficult state of affairs, than be forced into the mould of a situation, however skilfully designed.'

This antagonism clearly shows that the question is only insoluble because the concept of freedom of the second stage has been applied to the third. It is just as impossible to want a rational and planned society without foregoing the luxury of arbitrary interference, as it was for the individual at the stage of invention to preserve his desire for an absolute spontaneity of adjustment.

The guarantees of freedom are entirely different at the three stages. At the first stage freedom is really equivalent to freedom to escape. The possibilities of fleeing from a tyrant, of taking one's head out of the noose, of escaping direct pressure, these are the most obvious marks of freedom. At the second stage where an increasing number of isolated institutions fill up the framework of society and where each is allowed, broadly speaking, to go its own way, the most vital guarantee of freedom consists in playing off these institutions against each other. This is reflected in the political theory of checks and balances. At the stage the balance of power seems to be guaranteed by the mutual supervision and control of individual institutions. Where there is no higher authority to which all lesser powers are subject, freedom can only be guaranteed by a balance of more or less subordinate authorities.

At the third stage, that of planning, freedom cannot consist in the mutual control of individual institutions, for this can never lead to planned co-operation. At the highest stage freedom can only exist when it is secured by planning. It cannot consist in restricting the powers of the planner, but in a conception of planning which guarantees the existence of essential forms of freedom through the plan itself. For every restriction imposed by limited authorities would destroy the unity of the plan, so that society would regress to the former stage of competition and mutual control. As we have said, at the stage of planning freedom can only be guaranteed if the planning authority incorporates it in the plan itself. Whether the sovereign authority be an individual or a group or a popular assembly, it must be compelled by democratic control to allow full scope for freedom in its plan. Once all the instruments of influencing human behaviour have been co-ordinated, planning for freedom is the only logical form of freedom which remains.

This must be carefully considered, for it would be easy to adopt the wrong tactics if we continued to think that freedom could be guaranteed by limiting the unity of the plan, instead of insisting that constitutional guarantees of freedom should be included in the plan itself, and that real political safeguards should be established for its maintenance. Where the key points of a society have already been determined, freedom can only be secured by strategic direction from the key points and not by their destruction.

As soon as the problem of freedom – as opposed to *laisser-faire* – is seen to consist in the creation of free zones within the planned structure, the whole question becomes more detailed. Instead of the unified and abstract conception, concrete issues arise. The various historical interpretations of freedom, freedom of movement, freedom of expression, freedom of opinion, freedom of association, freedom from caprice and tolerance are all special obligations which must be met by the new society. For naturally the advent of planned freedom does not mean that all earlier forms of freedom must be abolished. We saw in the former parts of the book that an advance to a higher social level does not exclude the preservation of former types of action, thought and freedom. On the contrary, the planned retention of ancient liberties is a guarantee against exaggerated dogmatism in planning. We have learnt to realize that even when society has passed to a new stage in many spheres of its existence, some of the old forms of adjustment could still continue. Wherever it is possible and the plan is not endangered every effort must be made to maintain the primary form of freedom – freedom for individual adjustment. This was legitimately re-tained at the stage of invention, and in spite of an increasing mechaniza-tion, it helped to preserve vitality and strengthen initiative. Thus one of the guarantees of freedom in a planned society will be the maintenance of the individual capacity for adjustment. In the same way the freedom achieved at the second stage of invention must be retained in a planned society wherever possible. Constitutional provision must be made for the creation of new institutions through the initiative of small groups, in order to supply the needs of local circles rather than those of the central-ized bureaucracy. It is one of the greatest advantages of the Anglo-Saxon tradition that most public institutions, such as hospitals, schools and universities, are not maintained by the state but are forced as a rule to be self-supporting in order to prove the necessity for their existence. This principle of corporate initiative, these conceptions of the responsibilities and risks which must be borne by small groups, are characteristic of the stage of invention and are genuinely sound. They may mitigate exaggerated tendencies towards centralization, for this technique is a safeguard against bureaucracy and helps to keep the planning authorities in touch with actual conditions. Of course once society has reached the stage of planning separatism and local autonomy cannot be allowed to have the last word as at the stage of invention. Although even in the future corporations must take the initiative in suggesting new institutions, centralized control is essential, in order to criticize any tendencies which are likely to clash with the plan as a whole. This criticism might easily lead once more to an arbitrary bureaucracy, which under cover of objective criticism would oppose the natural growth of these institutions.

But this can only happen if there is no power greater than bureaucracy, for the problem of the democratic constitution of a planned society mainly consists in avoiding bureaucratic absolutism.

It all depends on whether we can find ways of transferring democratic, parliamentary control to a planned society. If this control is destroyed in the effort to establish a planned society, planning will be a disaster, not a cure. On the other hand, planning under communal control, incorporating safeguards of the new freedom, is the only solution possible at the present stage of social technique. The chances of achieving this new society, to be sure, are limited. It is not absolutely predetermined. But this is just where our new freedom begins. We have seen that the quality of freedom varies not only with the ages, but within the boundaries of a single society which gives different scopes to liberty of action. Our present society provides for one kind of freedom within the network of established relationships. But it offers us freedom of another degree outside them – in those spheres where our world is still in the making.

Within the framework of established relationships we can only gradually alter small details, burdened as we are by the pressure of that interdependent system which too often gives our acts only the scope of the mason replacing old bricks in a wall that is already built. But there is a space round the wall where new things have to be done, where new activity from key positions is required. Here as much spontaneity is demanded of our actions as in the first stage where primary freedom reigned. Here is scope for the pioneer, for in face of future possibilities each of us must choose what he would strengthen, what he would overthrow. Thus human freedom is not extinguished when we reach the stage of mass society; on the contrary, this is where its genuine vigour is needed. If we are only willing to contemplate that sector of life in which it is required, we shall see that the man of today has far more freedom in the determination of his destiny than the unsociological ethics of the past would have us believe. Why search the past with a romantic longing for a freedom that is lost, when that freedom is now ready to come into its own if we only have the courage to see what must be seen, to say what must be said, to do what must be done? Rightly understood, recent tendencies towards a mass society, and our ever increasing awareness of the determinism of sociological factors do not release us from responsibility for the future; responsibility increases with every advance in the course of history, and has never been greater than it is today.

Man and Society in an Age of Reconstruction (1935) (London, Routledge, 1940), pp. 14–15, 376–81.

PART V

THE REALM OF GREAT HARMONY

The first of July 1949 marks the fact that the Communist Party of China has already lived through twenty-eight years. Like a man, a political party has its childhood, youth, manhood and old age. The Communist Party of China is no longer a child or a lad in his teens but has become an adult. When a man reaches old age, he will die; the same is true of a party. When classes disappear, all instruments of class struggle – parties and the state machinery – will lose their function, cease to be necessary, therefore gradually wither away and end their historical mission; and human society will move to a higher stage. We are the opposite of the political parties of the bourgeoisie. They are afraid to speak of the extinction of classes, state power and parties. We, on the contrary, declare openly that we are striving hard to create the very conditions which will bring about their extinction. The leadership of the Communist Party and the state power of the people's dictatorship are such conditions. Anyone who does not recognize this truth is no communist. Young comrades who have not studied Marxism–Leninism and have only recently joined the Party may not yet understand this truth. They must understand it – only then can they have a correct world outlook. They must understand that the road to the abolition of classes, to the abolition of state power and to the abolition of parties is the road all mankind must take; it is only a question of time and conditions. Communists the world over are wiser than the bourgeoisie, they understand the laws governing the existence and development of things, they understand dialectics and they can see farther. The bourgeoisie does not welcome this truth because it does not want to be overthrown. To be overthrown is painful and is unbearable to contemplate for those overthrown, for example, for the Kuomintang reactionaries whom we are now overthrowing and for Japanese imperialism which we together with other peoples overthrew some time ago. But for the working class, the labouring people and the Communist Party the question is not one of being overthrown, but of working hard to create the conditions in which classes, state power and political parties will die out very naturally and mankind will enter the realm of Great Harmony.[1]

'Don't you want to abolish state power?' Yes, we do, but not right now; we cannot do it yet. Why? Because imperialism still exists, because domestic reaction still exists, because classes still exist in our country. Our present task is to strengthen the people's state apparatus – mainly the people's army, the people's police and the people's courts – in order to consolidate national defence and protect the people's interests. Given this condition, China can develop steadily, under the leadership of the working class and the Communist Party, from an agricultural into an industrial country and from a new-democratic into a socialist and communist society, can abolish classes and realize the Great Harmony. The state apparatus, including the army, the police and the courts, is the instrument by which one class oppresses another. It is an instrument for the oppression of antagonistic classes; it is violence and not 'benevolence'. 'You are not benevolent!' Quite so. We definitely do not apply a policy of benevolence to the reactionaries and towards the reactionary activities of the reactionary classes. Our policy of benevolence is applied only within the ranks of the people, not beyond them to the reactionaries or to the reactionary activities of reactionary classes.

The people's state protects the people. Only when the people have such a state can they educate and remould themselves on a country-wide scale by democratic methods and, with everyone taking part, shake off the influence of domestic and foreign reactionaries (which is still very strong, will survive for a long time and cannot be quickly destroyed), rid themselves of the bad habits and ideas acquired in the old society, not allow themselves to be led astray by the reactionaries, and continue to advance – to advance towards a socialist and communist society.

Here, the method we employ is democratic, the method of persuasion, not of compulsion. When anyone among the people breaks the law, he too should be punished, imprisoned or even sentenced to death; but this

---

[1] Also known as the world of Great Harmony. It refers to a society based on public ownership, free from class exploitation and oppression – a lofty ideal long cherished by the Chinese people. Here the realm of Great Harmony means communist society.

is a matter of a few individual cases, and it differs in principle from the dictatorship exercised over the reactionaries as a class.

As for the members of the reactionary classes and individual reactionaries, so long as they do not rebel, sabotage or create trouble after their political power has been overthrown, land and work will be given to them as well in order to allow them to live and remould themselves through labour into new people. If they are not willing to work, the people's state will compel them to work. Propaganda and educational work will be done among them too and will be done, moreover, with as much care and thoroughness as among the captured army officers in the past. This, too, may be called a 'policy of benevolence' if you like, but it is imposed by us on the members of the enemy classes and cannot be mentioned in the same breath with the work of self-education which we carry on within the ranks of the revolutionary people.

Such remoulding of members of the reactionary classes can be accomplished only by a state of the people's democratic dictatorship under the leadership of the Communist Party. When it is well done, China's major exploiting classes, the landlord class and the bureaucrat-bourgeoisie (the monopoly capitalist class), will be eliminated for good. There remain the national bourgeoisie; at the present stage, we can already do a good deal of suitable educational work with many of them. When the time comes to realize socialism, that is, to nationalize private enterprise, we shall carry the work of educating and remoulding them a step further. The people have a powerful state apparatus in their hands – there is no need to fear rebellion by the national bourgeoisie.

The serious problem is the education of the peasantry. The peasant economy is scattered, and the socialization of agriculture, judging by the Soviet Union's experience, will require a long time and painstaking work. Without socialization of agriculture, there can be no complete, consolidated socialism. The steps to socialize agriculture must be co-ordinated with the development of a powerful industry having state enterprise as its backbone. The state of the people's democratic dictatorship must systematically solve the problems of industrialization.

Of all things in the world, people are the most precious. Under the leadership of the Communist Party, as long as there are people, every kind of miracle can be performed. We are refuters of Acheson's counter-revolutionary theory. We believe that revolution can change everything, and that before long there will arise a new China with a big population and a great wealth of products, where life will be abundant and culture will flourish. All pessimistic views are utterly groundless.

> 'On the People's Democratic Dictatorship' (1949) and 'The Bankruptcy of the Idealist Conception of History' (1949), in *Selected Works of Mao Tse-Tung*, 4 vols. (Peking, Foreign Languages Press, 1967), pp. 411–12, 418–19, 423, 454.

Some naïve ideas seem to suggest that contradictions no longer exist in a socialist society. To deny the existence of contradictions is to deny dialectics. The contradictions in various societies differ in character, as do the forms of their solution, but society at all times develops through continual contradictions. Socialist society also develops through contradictions between the productive forces and the conditions of production. In a socialist or communist society, technical innovations and improvement in the social system inevitably continue to take place; otherwise the development of society would come to a standstill and society could no longer advance. Humanity is still in its youth. The road it has yet to traverse will be no one knows how many times longer than the road it has already travelled. Contradictions between progress and conservatism, between the advanced and the backward, between the positive and the negative, will constantly occur under varying conditions and different circumstances. Things will keep on like this. One contradiction will lead to another, and when old contradictions are solved new ones will arise. It is obviously incorrect to maintain, as some people do, that the contradiction between idealism and materialism can be eliminated in a socialist or communist society. As long as contradictions exist between the subjective and the objective, between the advanced and the backward, and between the productive forces and the conditions of production, the contradiction between materialism and idealism will continue in a socialist or communist society and will manifest itself in various forms. Since man lives in society, he reflects, in different circumstances and to varying degrees, the contradictions existing in each form of society. Therefore, not everybody will be perfect, even when a communist society is established. By then there will still be contradictions among people, and there will still be good people and bad, people whose thinking is relatively correct and others whose thinking is relatively incorrect. Hence there will still be struggle between people, though its nature and form will be different from those in class societies. Viewed in this light, the existence of contradictions between the individual and the collective in a socialist society is nothing strange. . . .

'On the Historical Experience of the Dictatorship of the Proletariat' (Peking, Foreign Languages Press, 1956).

A. A. Berle Jr.
(1895–   )

AN EVOLVING ECONOMIC UTOPIA

It seems that, in diverse ways, we are nibbling at the edges of a vast, dangerous and fascinating piece of thinking. Despite the absence of clear mandate, in broadest outline we are plotting the course by which the twentieth century in America is expected to produce an evolving economic Utopia, and, apparently, the potential actually exists, bringing that dangerous and thrilling adventure within human reach for the first time in recorded history.

We have not, up to the present, been accustomed to think of the modern corporation as an institution at all, let alone a political institution. We have thought of it merely as an enterprise (or perhaps combination of enterprises) within a community. American political thought has been frightened, and corporations themselves have been frightened, at any suggestion that they might emerge as political institutions in their own and separate right. So we have not been accustomed to place over against each other, as necessarily interrelated facts, the pragmatic concept of the corporation and the philosophical concept of the desirable community. Corporate executives rather resent being assimilated to politicians; still more they resent being called to account by philosophers. They belong to one of the few groups in history to which political power came unsought, or at any rate as a by-product rather than a main objective. It is probable that when Mr Harlow Curtice and Mr Alfred P. Sloan, Jr., wrote in General Motors Annual Report for 1953 that 'with the elimination of controls and with the trend away from a centrally managed economy, industry is possessed of the opportunity to make its maximum contribution to the forward march of our country', they did not think they were talking politics at all. Still less, perhaps, would they consider they had assumed in substantial measure the philosophical burden of judging what is and what should be the 'forward march' of a very great country. But they had done just that.

No one, however, has made a blueprint of the community desired by Standard Oil of New Jersey, or by Sears, Roebuck & Company, by the Southern Pacific Railroad, or by Ohio Edison, least of all the corporations themselves. Yet it seems the aggregate of their day-to-day decisions do form life and community. They do play a notable part in the physical bases on which life is lived. They build or shift or direct frameworks of human experience within which great masses of men live. Indirectly they affect an even greater peripheral group. They do enter into those community institutions, now including colleges and schools and philanthropies, which are the proudest product of American life. To the extent, therefore, that corporation managements, knowingly or unknowingly, reflect a philosophy, they have become a powerful force.

This is a vast and in some ways a humorous historical paradox. Our grandfathers quarrelled with corporations because, as the phrase went, they were 'soulless'. But out of the common denominator of the decision-making machinery some sort of consensus of mind is emerging, by compulsion as it were, which for good or ill is acting surprisingly like a collective soul. Great organizations energizing this sort of causative apparatus have their frightening side. When Mary Wollstonecraft Shelley's hero, Frankenstein, endowed his synthetic robot with a human heart, the monster which before had been a useful mechanical servant suddenly became an uncontrollable force. Our ancestors feared that corporations had no conscience. We are treated to the colder, more modern fear that, perhaps, they have one.

Certain safeguards do exist. Perhaps during the next stage of this twentieth-century drama they will be sufficient. The great difference between the American corporate system and any socialist system lies in the fact that in America there are a few hundred powerful units, each of which has a limited capacity to disagree with its fellow giants and to do something different. If Professor Adelman of Massachusetts Institute of Technology is right, concentration, though great, is not increasing rapidly; the writer agrees that it is proceeding slowly, though probably with somewhat greater speed than Adelman's figures disclose.

To begin with, there is a mighty difference between results obtained by the individual action of some hundreds of large units, unencumbered by a central group which proclaims orthodox doctrine and punishes deviation, and results obtained when substantially all determinative units are compelled to a common standard of choice and action by a central committee or by some central dogma. It is said at the moment that the business world places an undue value on conformity; and this is true. But in the not too distant future it may well appear that the men in the corporate world who stand for unpopular doctrine, who insist, for example, on providing scholarships for poets when well-thought-of businessmen only subsidize engineering research, or even men who insist that community formation is for individuals and therefore compel distribution of profits to their shareholders, instead of conscripting part of them for education and charity, may be found to be the true saviours of a free, energetic and competitive society. As yet the picture of a central group of 'interests' capable of enforcing general agreement is a bogeyman set up by demagogues: it does not exist outside of cartoons. The reality – a 'conscience' in business organizations which does control many men – need be neither impractical nor dangerous once the business community has learned to honour difference and deviation as well as agreement and conformity. Happily in America there have always been the men who will not 'go along'. We have reason to hope there will be enough disagreement so that the nuclei of power and of social organization will not only agree but differ as well.

There is also still another and greater hope. Even within the pressures which organizations exert – even in spite of the necessity that men in great enterprises shall work as a team – the individuals themselves are invariably influenced by certain great philosophical premises. These, in our system, are not derived from within business organization. They come from schools and from teachers; from universities and philosophers; from men of deep human instinct who are, by occasional miracle, saints. Their strength comes from instincts and impulses deeper perhaps than any of us understand. If these impulses, as we hope they may, continue to demand the self-realization of individuals, if they continue to call for methods, institutions and remedies making it possible for every man to protect his personality against invasion, then society emerging in the capitalist revolution will continue to be free, just as the democratic system was the work of men of courage, working against the background of feudal dictatorship of seven centuries ago. A director who stoutly says his corporation has no business to tackle the problem of community organization may go farther, and (for example) with equal stoutness refuse to let his publicity people insert propaganda into public schools. The director who, equally stoutly, says his corporation must assure attainable first-rate education may carry his thinking to the point of demanding (as some, to their everlasting honour, have already done) that academic freedom shall be inviolate, and that controversiality shall be reckoned a virtue, not a fault. In fixing attention on the organization which has been our field of study, one must not forget that the organization itself is composed of men. The common resistance point of these individuals ultimately determines how far any organization can go.

In ascending scale is the fact that so long as speech and thought are free, men will always rise capable of transcending the massed effects of any organization or group of organizations. There is solid ground for the expectation that twenty years from now the men of greatest renown in the United States will be the spiritual, philosophical and intellectual leaders for the sufficient reason that they will be needed more than any other type of men. Society still tends both to produce and to honour the kinds of men it needs most.

The Twentieth-Century Capitalist Revolution (London, Macmillan, 1955), pp. 142, 145–6, 149–53.

Herbert Marcuse
(1898–   )

SOCIETY AS A WORK OF ART

If today these integral features, these truly radical features which make a socialist society a definite negation of the existing societies, if this qualitative difference today appears as Utopian, as idealistic, as metaphysical, this is precisely the form in which these radical features must appear if they are really to be a definite negation of the established society: if socialism is indeed the rupture of history, the radical break, the leap into the realm of freedom – a total rupture.

Let us give one illustration of how this awareness, or half-awareness, of the need for such a total rupture was present in some of the great social struggles of our period. Walter Benjamin quotes reports that during the Paris Commune, in all corners of the city of Paris there were people shooting at the clocks on the towers of the churches, palaces and so on, thereby consciously or half-consciously expressing the need that somehow time has to be arrested; that at least the prevailing, the established time continuum has to be arrested, and that a new time has to begin – a very strong emphasis on the qualitative difference and on the totality of the rupture between the new society and the old.

In this sense, I should like to discuss here with you the repressed prerequisites of qualitative change. I say intentionally 'of qualitative change', not 'of revolution', because we know of too many revolutions through which the continuum of repression has been sustained, revolutions which have replaced one system of domination by another. We must become aware of the essentially new features which distinguish a free society as a definite negation of the established societies, and we must begin formulating these features, no matter how metaphysical, no matter how Utopian, I would even say no matter how ridiculous we may appear to the normal people in all camps, on the right as well as on the left.

What is the dialectic of liberation with which we here are concerned? It is the construction of a free society, a construction which depends in the first place on the prevalence of the vital need for abolishing the established systems of servitude; and secondly, and this is decisive, it depends on the vital commitment, the striving, conscious as well as sub- and un-conscious, for the qualitatively different values of a free human existence. Without the emergence of such new needs and satisfactions, the needs and satisfactions of free men, all change in the social institutions, no matter how great, would only replace one system of servitude by another system of servitude. Nor can the emergence – and I should like to empha-size this – nor can the emergence of such new needs and satisfactions be envisaged as a mere by-product, the mere result, of changed social institutions. We have seen this, it is a fact of experience. The development of the new institutions must already be carried out and carried through by men with the new needs. That, by the way, is the basic idea underlying Marx's own concept of the proletariat as the historical agent of revolution. He saw the industrial proletariat as the historical agent of revolution, not only because it was the basic class in the material process of production, not only because it was at that time the majority of the population, but also because this class was 'free' from the repressive and aggressive competitive needs of capitalist society and therefore, at least potentially, the carrier of essentially new needs, goals and satisfactions.

We can formulate this dialectic of liberation also in a more brutal way, as a vicious circle. The transition from voluntary servitude (as it exists to a great extent in the affluent society) to freedom presupposes the abolition of the institutions and mechanism of repression. And the abolition of the institutions and mechanisms of repression already pre-supposes liberation from servitude, prevalence of the need for liberation. As to needs, I think we have to distinguish between the need for changing intolerable condi-tions of existence, and the need for changing the society as a whole. The two are by no means identical, they are by no means in harmony. If the need is for changing intolerable conditions of existence, with at least a reasonable chance that this can be achieved within the established society, with the growth and progress of the established society, then this is merely quantitative change. Qualitative change is a change of the very system as a whole.

We can sum up the fatal situation with which we are confronted. Radical social change is objectively necessary, in the dual sense that it is the only chance to save the possibilities of human freedom and, furthermore, in the sense that the technical and material resources for the realization of freedom are available. But while this objective need is demonstrably there, the subjective need for such a change does not prevail. It does not prevail precisely among those parts of the population that are traditionally considered the agents of historical change. The subjective need is repressed, again on a dual ground: firstly, by virtue of the actual satisfaction of needs, and secondly, by a massive scientific manipulation and administration of needs – that is, by a systematic social control not only of the consciousness, but also of the unconscious of man. This control has been made possible by the very achievements of the greatest liberating sciences of our time, in psychology, mainly psychoanalysis and psychiatry. That they could become and have become at the same time powerful instruments of suppression, one of the most effective engines of suppression, is again one of the terrible aspects of the dialectic of liberation.

This divergence between the objective and the subjective need changes completely, I suggest, the basis, the prospects and the strategy of liberation. This situation presupposes the emergence of new needs, qualitatively different and even opposed to the prevailing aggressive and repressive needs: the emergence of a new type of man, with a vital, biological drive for liberation, and with a consciousness capable of breaking through the material as well as ideological veil of the affluent society. In other words, liberation seems to be predicated upon the opening and the activation of a depth dimension of human existence, this side of and underneath the traditional material base: not an idealistic dimension, over and above the material base, but a dimension even more material than the material base, a dimension underneath the material base. I will illustrate presently what I mean.

The emphasis on this new dimension does not mean replacing politics by psychology, but rather the other way around. It means finally taking account of the fact that society has invaded even the deepest roots of individual existence, even the unconscious of man. *We* must get at the roots of society in the individuals themselves, the individuals who, because of social engineering, constantly reproduce the continuum of repression even through the great revolution.

This change is, I suggest, not an ideological change. It is dictated by the actual development of an industrial society, which has introduced factors which our theory could formerly correctly neglect. It is dictated by the actual development of industrial society, by the tremendous growth of its material and technical productivity, which has surpassed and rendered obsolete the traditional goals and preconditions of liberation.

Here we are faced with the question: is liberation from the affluent society identical with the transition from capitalism to socialism? The answer I suggest is: It is not identical, if socialism is defined merely as the planned development of the productive forces, and the rationalization of resources (although this remains a precondition for all liberation). It is identical with the transition from capitalism to socialism, if socialism is defined in its most Utopian terms: namely, among others, the abolition of labour, the termination of the struggle for existence – that is to say, life as an end in itself and no longer as a means to an end – and the liberation of human sensibility and sensitivity, not as a private factor, but as a force for transformation of human existence and of its environment. To give sensitivity and sensibility their own right is, I think, one of the basic goals of integral socialism. These are the qualitatively different features of a free society. They presuppose, as you may already have seen, a total trans-valuation of values, a new anthropology. They presuppose a type of man who rejects the performance principles governing the established societies; a type of man who has rid himself of the aggressiveness and brutality that are inherent in the organization of established society, and in their hypocritical, puritan morality; a type of man who is biologically incapable of fighting wars and creating suffering; a type of man who has a good conscience of joy and pleasure, and who works, collectively and individually, for a social and natural environment in which such an existence becomes possible.

The dialectic of liberation, as turned from quantity into quality, thus involves, I repeat, a break in the continuum of repression which reaches into the depth dimension of the organism itself. Or, we may say that today qualitative change, liberation, involves organic, instinctual, biological changes at the same time as political and social changes.

The new needs and satisfactions have a very material basis, as I have indicated. They are not thought out but are the logical derivation from the technical, material and intellectual possibilities of advanced, industrial society. They are inherent in, and the expression of, the productivity of advanced industrial society, which has long since made obsolete all kinds of inner-worldly asceticism, the entire work discipline on which Judaeo-Christian morality has been based.

Why is this society surpassing and negating this type of man, the traditional type of man and the forms of his existence, as well as the morality to which it owes much of its origins and foundations? This new, unheard-of and not anticipated productivity allows the concept of a technology of liberation. Here I can only briefly indicate what I have in mind: such amazing and indeed apparently Utopian tendencies as the convergence of technique and art, the convergence of work and play, the convergence of the realm of necessity and the realm of freedom. How? No longer subjected to the dictates of capitalist profitability and of efficiency, no longer to the dictates of scarcity, which today are perpetuated by the capitalist organization of society, socially necessary labour, material production, would and could become (we see the tendency already) increasingly scientific. Technical experimentation, science and technology would and could become a play with the hitherto hidden – methodically hidden and blocked – potentialities of men and things, of society and nature.

This means one of the oldest dreams of all radical theory and practice. It means that the creative imagination, and not only the rationality of the performance principle, would become a productive force applied to the transformation of the social and natural universe. It would mean the emergence of a form of reality which is the work and the medium of the developing sensibility and sensitivity of man.

And now I throw in the terrible concept: it would mean an 'aesthetic' reality – society as a work of art. This is the most Utopian, the most radical possibility of liberation today.

What does this mean, in concrete terms? I said, we are not concerned here with private sensitivity and sensibility, but with sensitivity and sensibility, creative imagination and play, becoming forces of transformation. As such they would guide, for example, the total reconstruction of our cities and of the countryside; the restoration of nature after the elimination of the violence and destruction of capitalist industrialization; the creation of internal and external space for privacy, individual autonomy, tranquillity; the elimination of noise, of captive audiences, of enforced togetherness, of pollution, of ugliness. These are not – and I cannot emphasize this strongly enough – snobbish and romantic demands. Biologists today have emphasized that these are organic needs for the human organism, and that their arrest, their perversion and destruction by capitalist society, actually mutilates the human organism, not only in a figurative way but in a very real and literal sense.

I believe that it is only in such a universe that man can be truly free, and truly human relationships between free beings can be established. I believe that the idea of such a universe guided also Marx's concept of socialism, and that these aesthetic needs and goals must from the beginning be present in the reconstruction of society, and not only at the end or in the far future. Otherwise, the needs and satisfactions which reproduce a repressive society would be carried over into the new society. Repressive men would carry over their repression into the new society.

'Liberation from the Affluent Society', in *The Dialectics of Liberation*, ed. D. Cooper (London, Penguin, 1968), pp. 177–9, 182–6.

Friedrich A. Hayek
(1899–   )

THE FUNCTIONING OF AN INDIVIDUALIST SOCIETY

While the theory of individualism has thus a definite contribution to make to the technique of constructing a suitable legal framework and of improving the institutions which have grown up spontaneously, its emphasis, of course, is on the fact that the part of our social order which can or ought to be made a conscious product of human reason is only a small part of all the forces of society. In other words, that the state, the embodiment of deliberately organized and consciously directed power, ought to be only a small part of the much richer organism which we call 'society', and that the former ought to provide merely a framework within which free (and therefore not 'consciously directed') collaboration of men has the maximum of scope.

This entails certain corollaries on which true individualism once more stands in sharp opposition to the false individualism of the rationalistic type. The first is that the deliberately organized state on the one side, and the individual on the other, far from being regarded as the only realities, while all the intermediate formations and associations are to be deliberately suppressed, as was the aim of the French Revolution, the noncompulsory conventions of social intercourse are considered as essential factors in preserving the orderly working of human society. The second is that the individual, in participating in the social processes, must be ready and willing to adjust himself to changes and to submit to conventions which are not the result of intelligent design, whose justification in the particular instance may not be recognizable, and which to him will often appear unintelligible and irrational.

I need not say much on the first point. That true individualism affirms the value of the family and all the common efforts of the small community and group, that it believes in local autonomy and voluntary associations, and that indeed its case rests largely on the contention that much for which the coercive action of the state is usually invoked can be done better by voluntary collaboration need not be stressed further. There can be no greater contrast to this than the false individualism which wants to dissolve all these smaller groups into atoms which have no cohesion other than the coercive rules imposed by the state, and which tries to make all social ties prescriptive, instead of using the state mainly as a protection of the individual against the arrogation of coercive powers by the smaller groups.

Quite as important for the functioning of an individualist society as these smaller groupings of men are the traditions and conventions which evolve in a free society and which, without being enforceable, establish flexible but normally observed rules that make the behaviour of other people predictable in a high degree. The willingness to submit to such rules, not merely so long as one understands the reason for them but so long as one has no definite reasons to the contrary, is an essential condition for the gradual evolution and improvement of rules of social intercourse; and the readiness ordinarily to submit to the products of a social process which nobody has designed and the reasons for which nobody may understand is also an indispensable condition if it is to be possible to dispense with compulsion.[1] That the existence of common conventions and traditions among a group of people will enable them to work together smoothly and efficiently with much less formal organization and compulsion than a group without such common background, is, of course, a commonplace. But the reverse of this, while less familiar, is probably not less true: that coercion can probably only be kept to a minimum in a society where conventions and tradition have made the behaviour of man to a large extent predictable.[2]

---

[1] The difference between the rationalistic and the true individualistic approach is well shown in the different views expressed by French observers on the apparent irrationality of English social institutions. While Henri de Saint-Simon, e.g., complains that 'cent volumes *in folio*, du caractère plus fin, ne suffiraient pas pour rendre compte de toutes les inconséquences organiques qui existent en Angleterre' (*Œuvres de Saint-Simon et d'Enfantin* (Paris, 1865–78), XXXVIII, 179), De Tocqueville retorts 'que ces bizarreries des Anglais pussent avoir quelques rapports avec leurs libertés, c'est ce qui ne lui tombe point dans l'esprit' (*L'Ancien Régime et la Révolution*, 7th ed. (Paris, 1866), p. 103).

[2] Is it necessary to quote Edmund Burke once more to remind the reader how essential a condition for the possibility of a free society was to him the strength of moral rules? 'Men are qualified for civil liberty', he wrote, 'in exact proportion to their disposition to put moral chains upon their own appetites; in proportion as their love of justice is

This brings me to my second point: the necessity, in any complex society in which the effects of anyone's action reach far beyond his possible range of vision, of the individual submitting to the anonymous and seemingly irrational forces of society – a submission which must include not only the acceptance of rules of behaviour as valid without examining what depends in the particular instance on their being observed but also a readiness to adjust himself to changes which may profoundly affect his fortunes and opportunities and the causes of which may be altogether unintelligible to him. It is against these that modern man tends to revolt unless their necessity can be shown to rest upon 'reason made clear and demonstrable to every individual'. Yet it is just here that the understandable craving for intelligibility produces illusory demands which no system can satisfy. Man in a complex society can have no choice but between adjusting himself to what to him must seem the blind forces of the social process and obeying the orders of a superior. So long as he knows only the hard discipline of the market, he may well think the direction by some other intelligent human brain preferable; but, when he tries it, he soon discovers that the former still leaves him at least some choice, while the latter leaves him none, and that it is better to have a choice between several unpleasant alternatives than being coerced into one.

The unwillingness to tolerate or respect any social forces which are not recognizable as the product of intelligent design, which is so important a cause of the present desire for comprehensive economic planning, is indeed only one aspect of a more general movement. We meet the same tendency in the field of morals and conventions, in the desire to substitute an artificial for the existing languages, and in the whole modern attitude toward processes which govern the growth of knowledge. The belief that only a synthetic system of morals, an artificial language or even an artificial society can be justified in an age of science, as well as the increasing unwillingness to bow before any moral rules whose utility is not rationally demonstrated, or to conform with conventions whose rationale is not known, are all manifestations of the same basic view which wants all social activity to be recognizably part of a single coherent plan. They

above their rapacity; in proportion as their own soundness and sobriety of understanding is above their vanity and presumption; in proportion as they are more disposed to listen to the councils of the wise and good, in preference to the flattery of knaves' ('A Letter to a Member of the National Assembly' (1791), in *Works* (World's Classics ed.), IV, 319).

are the results of that same rationalistic 'individualism' which wants to see in everything the product of conscious individual reason. They are certainly not, however, a result of true individualism and may even make the working of a free and truly individualistic system difficult or impossible. Indeed, the great lesson which the individualist philosophy teaches us on this score is that, while it may not be difficult to destroy the spontaneous formations which are the indispensable bases of a free civilization, it may be beyond our power deliberately to reconstruct such a civilization once these foundations are destroyed.

I cannot better sum up this attitude of true individualism toward democracy than by once more quoting Lord Acton: 'The true democratic principle', he wrote, 'that none shall have power over the people, is taken to mean that none shall be able to restrain or to elude its power. The true democratic principle, that the people shall not be made to do what it does not like, is taken to mean that it shall never be required to tolerate what it does not like. The true democratic principle, that every man's will shall be as unfettered as possible, is taken to mean that the free will of the collective people shall be fettered in nothing.'[1]

When we turn to equality, however, it should be said at once that true individualism is not equalitarian in the modern sense of the word. It can see no reason for trying to make people equal as distinct from treating them equally. While individualism is profoundly opposed to all prescriptive privilege, to all protection, by law or force, of any rights not based on rules equally applicable to all persons, it also denies government the right to limit what the able or fortunate may achieve. It is equally opposed to any rigid limitation of the position individuals may achieve, whether this power is used to perpetuate inequality or to create equality. Its main principle is that no man or group of men should have power to decide what another man's status ought to be, and it regards this as a condition of freedom so essential that it must not be sacrificed to the gratification of our sense of justice or of our envy.

From the point of view of individualism there would not appear to exist even any justification for making all individuals start on the same level by preventing them from profiting by advantages which they have in no way earned, such as being born to parents who are more intelligent or more conscientious than the average. Here individualism is indeed less

---

[1] Lord Acton, 'Sir Erskine May's Democracy in Europe', reprinted in *The History of Freedom*, pp. 93-4.

'individualistic' than socialism, because it recognizes the family as a legitimate unit as much as the individual; and the same is true with respect to other groups, such as linguistic or religious communities, which by their common efforts may succeed for long periods in preserving for their members material or moral standards different from those of the rest of the population. De Tocqueville and Lord Acton speak with one voice on this subject. 'Democracy and socialism', De Tocqueville wrote, 'have nothing in common but one word, equality. But notice the difference: while democracy seeks equality in liberty, socialism seeks equality in restraint and servitude.' And Acton joined him in believing that 'the deepest cause which made the French revolution so disastrous to liberty was its theory of equality' and that 'the finest opportunity ever given to the world was thrown away, because the passion for equality made vain the hope for freedom'.

'Individualism, True and False' (1946), in Hayek, *Individualism and Economic Order* (London, Routledge, 1949), pp. 22–5, 30–1.

Michael Oakeshott

(1901–   )

THE ENJOYMENT OF ORDERLY AND
PEACEABLE BEHAVIOUR

Let us begin at what I believe to be the proper starting-place; not in the
empyrean, but with ourselves as we have come to be. I and my neighbours, my associates, my compatriots, my friends, my enemies and those
who I am indifferent about, are people engaged in a great variety of
activities. We are apt to entertain a multiplicity of opinions on every
conceivable subject and are disposed to change these beliefs as we grow
tired of them or as they prove unserviceable. Each of us is pursuing a
course of his own; and there is no project so unlikely that somebody will
not be found to engage in it, no enterprise so foolish that somebody will
not undertake it. There are those who spend their lives trying to sell copies
of the Anglican Catechism to the Jews. And one half of the world is
engaged in trying to make the other half want what it has hitherto never
felt the lack of. We are all inclined to be passionate about our own concerns, whether it is making things or selling them, whether it is business
or sport, religion or learning, poetry, drink or drugs. Each of us has
preferences of his own. For some, the opportunities of making choices
(which are numerous) are invitations readily accepted; others welcome
them less eagerly or even find them burdensome. Some dream dreams of
new and better worlds: others are more inclined to move in familiar paths
or even to be idle. Some are apt to deplore the rapidity of change, others
delight in it; all recognize it. At times we grow tired and fall asleep: it is
a blessed relief to gaze in a shop window and see nothing we want; we are
grateful for ugliness merely because it repels attention. But, for the most
part, we pursue happiness by seeking the satisfaction of desires which
spring from one another inexhaustibly. We enter into relationships of
interest and of emotion, of competition, partnership, guardianship, love,
friendship, jealousy and hatred, some of which are more durable than

others. We make agreements with one another; we have expectations about one another's conduct; we approve, we are indifferent and we disapprove. This multiplicity of activity and variety of opinion is apt to produce collisions: we pursue courses which cut across those of others, and we do not all approve the same sort of conduct. But, in the main, we get along with one another, sometimes by giving way, sometimes by standing fast, sometimes in a compromise. Our conduct consists of activity assimilated to that of others in small, and for the most part unconsidered and unobtrusive, adjustments.

Why all this should be so, does not matter. It is not necessarily so. A different condition of human circumstance can easily be imagined, and we know that elsewhere and at other times activity is, or has been, far less multifarious and changeful and opinion far less diverse and far less likely to provoke collision; but, by and large, we recognize this to be our condition. It is an acquired condition, though nobody designed or specifically chose it in preference to all others. It is the product, not of 'human nature' let loose, but of human beings impelled by an acquired love of making choices for themselves. And we know as little and as much about where it is leading us as we know about the fashion in hats of twenty years' time or the design of motor cars.

Surveying the scene, some people are provoked by the absence of order and coherence which appears to them to be its dominant feature; its wastefulness, its frustration, its dissipation of human energy, its lack not merely of a premeditated destination but even of any discernible direction of movement. It provides an excitement similar to that of a stock-car race; but it has none of the satisfaction of a well-conducted business enterprise. Such people are apt to exaggerate the current disorder; the absence of plan is so conspicuous that the small adjustments, and even the more massive arrangements, which restrain the chaos seem to them nugatory; they have no feeling for the warmth of untidiness but only for its inconvenience. But what is significant is not the limitations of their powers of observation, but the turn of their thoughts. They feel that there ought be something that ought to be done to convert this so-called chaos into order, for this is no way for rational human beings to be spending their lives. Like Apollo when he saw Daphne with her hair hung carelessly about her neck, they sigh and say to themselves: 'What if it were properly arranged.' Moreover, they tell us that they have seen in a dream the glorious, collisionless manner of living proper to all mankind, and this dream they understand as their warrant for seeking to remove the diversities and occasions of conflict which distinguish our current manner of living. Of course, their dreams are not all exactly alike; but they have this in common: each is a vision of a condition of human circumstance from which the occasion of conflict has been removed, a vision of human activity co-ordinated and set going in a single direction and of every resource being used to the full. And such people appropriately understand the office of government to be the imposition upon its subjects of the condition of human circumstances of their dream. To govern is to turn a private dream into a public and compulsory manner of living. Thus, politics becomes an encounter of dreams and the activity in which government is held to this understanding of its office and provided with the appropriate instruments.

I do not propose to criticize this jump to glory style of politics in which governing is understood as a perpetual take-over bid for the purchase of the resources of human energy in order to concentrate them in a single direction; it is not at all unintelligible, and there is much in our circumstances to provoke it. My purpose is merely to point out that there is another quite different understanding of government, and that it is no less intelligible and in some respects perhaps more appropriate to our circumstances.

The spring of this other disposition in respect of governing and the instruments of government – a conservative disposition – is to be found in the acceptance of the current condition of human circumstances as I have described it: the propensity to make our own choices and to find happiness in doing so, the variety of enterprises each pursued with passion, the diversity of beliefs each held with the conviction of its exclusive truth; the inventiveness, the changefulness and the absence of any large design; the excess, the over-activity and the informal compromise. And the office of government is not to impose other beliefs and activities upon its subjects, not to tutor or to educate them, not to make them better or happier in another way, not to direct them, to galvanize them into action to lead them or to co-ordinate their activities so that no occasion of conflict shall occur; the office of government is merely to rule. This is a specific and limited activity, easily corrupted when it is combined with any other, and, in the circumstances, indispensable. The image of the ruler is the umpire whose business is to administer the rules of the game, or the chairman who governs the debate according to known rules but does not himself participate in it.

Now people of this disposition commonly defend their belief that the proper attitude of government towards the current condition of human circumstance is one of acceptance by appealing to certain general ideas. They contend that there is absolute value in the free play of human choice, that private property (the emblem of choice) is a natural right, that it is only in the enjoyment of diversity of opinion and activity that true belief and good conduct can be expected to disclose themselves. But I do not think that this disposition requires these or any similar beliefs in order to make it intelligible. Something much smaller and less pretentious will do: the observation that this condition of human circumstance is, in fact, current, and that we have learned to enjoy it and how to manage it; that we are not children *in statu pupillari* but adults who do not consider themselves under any obligation to justify their preference for making their own choices; and that it is beyond human experience to suppose that those who rule are endowed with a superior wisdom which discloses to them a better range of beliefs and activities and which gives them authority to impose upon their subjects a quite different manner of life. In short, if the man of this disposition is asked: Why ought governments to accept the current diversity of opinion and activity in preference to imposing upon their subjects a dream of their own? it is enough for him to reply: Why not? Their dreams are no different from those of anyone else; and if it is boring to have to listen to dreams of others being recounted, it is insufferable to be forced to re-enact them. We tolerate monomaniacs, it is our habit to do so; but why should we be *ruled* by them? Is it not (the man of conservative disposition asks) an intelligible task for a government to protect its subjects against the nuisance of those who spend their energy and their wealth in the service of some pet indignation, endeavouring to impose it upon everybody, not by suppressing their activities in favour of others of a similar kind, but by setting a limit to the amount of noise anyone may emit?

Nevertheless, if this acceptance is the spring of the conservative's disposition in respect of government, he does not suppose that the office of government is to do nothing. As he understands it, there is work to be done which can be done only in virtue of a genuine acceptance of current beliefs simply because they are current and current activities simply because they are afoot. And, briefly, the office he attributes to government is to resolve some of the collisions which this variety of beliefs and activities generates; to preserve peace, not by placing an interdict upon choice and upon the diversity that springs from the exercise of preference, not by imposing substantive uniformity, but by enforcing general rules of procedure upon all subjects alike.

Government, then, as the conservative in this matter understands it, does not begin with a vision of another, different and better world, but with the observation of the self-government practised even by men of passion in the conduct of their enterprises; it begins in the informal adjustments of interests to one another which are designed to release those who are apt to collide from the mutual frustration of a collision. Sometimes these adjustments are no more than agreements between two parties to keep out of each other's way; sometimes they are of wider application and more durable character, such as the International Rules for the prevention of collisions at sea. In short, the intimations of government are to be found in ritual, not in religion or philosophy; in the enjoyment of orderly and peaceable behaviour, not in the search for truth or perfection.

To govern, then, as the conservative understands it, is to provide a *vinculum juris* for those manners of conduct which, in the circumstances, are least likely to result in a frustrating collision of interests; to provide redress and means of compensation for those who suffer from others behaving in a contrary manner; sometimes to provide punishment for those who pursue their own interests regardless of the rules; and, of course, to provide a sufficient force to maintain the authority of an arbiter of this kind. Thus, governing is recognized as a specific and limited activity; not the management of an enterprise, but the rule of those engaged in a great diversity of self-chosen enterprises. It is not concerned with concrete persons, but with activities; and with activities only in respect of their propensity to collide with one another. It is not concerned with moral right and wrong, it is not designed to make men good or even better; it is not indispensable on account of 'the natural depravity of mankind' but merely because of their current disposition to be extravagant; its business is to keep its subjects at peace with one another in the activities in which they have chosen to seek their happiness. And if there is any general idea entailed in this view, it is, perhaps, that a government which does not sustain the loyalty of its subjects is worthless; and that while one which (in the old puritan phrase) 'commands for truth' is incapable of doing so (because some of its subjects will believe its 'truth' to be error), one which is indifferent to 'truth' and 'error' alike, and merely pursues peace, presents no obstacle to the necessary loyalty.

'On Being Conservative' (1956), in *Rationalism in Politics* (London, Methuen, 1962), pp. 184–8, 189–90.

Sir Karl Popper
(1902–   )

UTOPIA AND VIOLENCE

My fundamental attitude towards the problem of reason and violence will by now be understood; and I hope I share it with some of my readers and with many other people everywhere. It is on this basis that I now propose to discuss the problem of Utopianism.

I think we can describe Utopianism as a result of a form of rationalism, and I shall try to show that this is a form of rationalism very different from the form in which I and many others believe. So I shall try to show that there exist at least two forms of rationalism, one of which I believe is right and the other wrong; and that the wrong kind of rationalism is the one which leads to Utopianism.

As far as I can see, Utopianism is the result of a way of reasoning which is accepted by many who would be astonished to hear that this apparently quite inescapable and self-evident way of reasoning leads to Utopian results. This specious reasoning can perhaps be presented in the following manner.

An action, it may be argued, is rational if it makes the best use of the available means in order to achieve a certain end. The end, admittedly, may be incapable of being determined rationally. However this may be, we can judge an action rationally, and describe it as rational or adequate, only relative to some given end. Only if we have an end in mind, and only relative to such an end, can we say that we are acting rationally.

Now let us apply this argument to politics. All politics consists of actions; and these actions will be rational only if they pursue some end. The end of a man's political actions may be the increase of his own power or wealth. Or it may perhaps be the improvement of the laws of the state, a change in the structure of the state.

In the latter case political action will be rational only if we first determine the final ends of the political changes which we intend to bring about. It will be rational only relative to certain ideas of what a state ought to be like. Thus it appears that as a preliminary to any rational political action we must first attempt to become as clear as possible about our ultimate political ends; for example the kind of state which we should consider the best; and only afterwards can we begin to determine the means which may best help us to realize this state, or to move slowly towards it, taking it as the aim of a historical process which we may to some extent influence and steer towards the goal selected.

Now it is precisely this view which I call Utopianism. Any rational and non-selfish political action, on this view, must be preceded by a determination of our ultimate ends, not merely of intermediate or partial aims which are only steps towards our ultimate end, and which therefore should be considered as means rather than as ends; therefore rational political action must be based upon a more or less clear and detailed description or blueprint of our ideal state, and also upon a plan or blueprint of the historical path that leads towards this goal.

I consider what I call Utopianism an attractive and, indeed, an all too attractive theory; for I also consider it dangerous and pernicious. It is, I believe, self-defeating, and it leads to violence.

That it is self-defeating is connected with the fact that it is impossible to determine ends scientifically. There is no scientific way of choosing between two ends. Some people, for example, love and venerate violence. For them a life without violence would be shallow and trivial. Many others, of whom I am one, hate violence. This is a quarrel about ends. It cannot be decided by science. This does not mean that the attempt to argue against violence is necessarily a waste of time. It only means that you may not be able to argue with the admirer of violence. He has a way of answering an argument with a bullet if he is not kept under control by the threat of counter-violence. If he is willing to listen to your arguments without shooting you, then he is at least infected by rationalism, and you may, perhaps, win him over. This is why arguing is no waste of time – as long as people listen to you. But you cannot, by means of argument, make people listen to argument; you cannot, by means of argument, convert those who suspect all argument, and who prefer violent decisions to rational decisions. You cannot prove to them that they are wrong. And this is only a particular case, which can be generalized. No decision about aims can be established by *purely* rational or scientific means. Nevertheless argument may prove extremely helpful in reaching a decision about aims.

Applying all this to the problem of Utopianism, we must first be quite clear that the problem of constructing a Utopian blueprint cannot possibly be solved by science alone. Its aims, at least, must be given before the social scientist can begin to sketch his blueprint. We find the same situation in the natural sciences. No amount of physics will tell a scientist that it is the right thing for him to construct a plough, or an aeroplane, or an atomic bomb. Ends must be adopted by him, or given to him; and what he does *qua* scientist is only to construct means by which these ends can be realized.

In emphasizing the difficulty of deciding, by way of rational argument, between different Utopian ideals, I do not wish to create the impression that there is a realm – such as the realm of ends – which goes altogether beyond the power of rational criticism (even though I certainly wish to say that the realm of ends goes largely beyond the power of *scientific* argument). For I myself try to argue about this realm; and by pointing out the difficulty of deciding between competing Utopian blueprints, I try to argue rationally against choosing ideal ends of this kind. Similarly, my attempt to point out that this difficulty is likely to produce violence is meant as a rational argument, although it will appeal only to those who hate violence.

That the Utopian method, which chooses an ideal state of society as the aim which all our political actions should serve, is likely to produce violence can be shown thus. Since we cannot determine the ultimate ends of political actions scientifically, or by purely rational methods, differences of opinion concerning what the ideal state should be like cannot always be smoothed out by the method of argument. They will at least partly have the character of religious differences. And there can be no tolerance between these different Utopian religions. Utopian aims are designed to serve as a basis for rational political action and discussion, and such action appears to be possible only if the aim is definitely decided upon. Thus the Utopianist must win over, or else crush, his Utopianist competitors who do not share his own Utopian aims and who do not profess his own Utopianist religion.

But he has to do more. He has to be very thorough in eliminating and stamping out all heretical competing views. For the way to the Utopian goal is long. Thus the rationality of his political action demands constancy of aim for a long time ahead; and this can only be achieved if he not merely crushes competing Utopian religions, but as far as possible stamps out all memory of them.

The use of violent methods for the suppression of competing aims becomes even more urgent. For the period of Utopian construction is liable to be one of social change. In such a time ideas are liable to change also. Thus what may have appeared to many as desirable at the time when the Utopian blueprint was decided upon may appear less desirable at a later date. If this is so, the whole approach is in danger of breaking down. For if we change our ultimate political aims while attempting to move towards them we may soon discover that we are moving in circles. The whole method of first establishing an ultimate political aim and then preparing to move towards it must be futile if the aim may be changed during the process of its realization. It may easily turn out that the steps so far taken lead in fact away from the new aim. And if we then change direction in accordance with our new aim we expose ourselves to the same risk. In spite of all the sacrifices which we may have made in order to make sure that we are acting rationally, we may get exactly nowhere – although not exactly to that 'nowhere' which is meant by the word 'Utopia'.

Again, the only way to avoid such changes of our aims seems to be to use violence, which includes propaganda, the suppression of criticism and the annihilation of all opposition. With it goes the affirmation of the wisdom and foresight of the Utopian planners, of the Utopian engineers who design and execute the Utopian blueprint. The Utopian engineers must in this way become omniscient as well as omnipotent. They become gods. Thou shalt have no other Gods before them.

Utopian rationalism is a self-defeating rationalism. However benevolent its ends, it does not bring happiness, but only the familiar misery of being condemned to live under a tyrannical government.

It is important to understand this criticism fully. I do not criticize political ideals as such, nor do I assert that a political ideal can never be realized. This would not be a valid criticism. Many ideals have been realized which were once dogmatically declared to be unrealizable, for example, the establishment of workable and untyrannical institutions for securing civil peace, that is, for the suppression of crime within the state. Again, I see no reason why an international judicature and an international police force should be less successful in suppressing international crime, that is, national aggression and the ill-treatment of minorities or perhaps majorities. I do not object to the attempt to realize such ideals.

Wherein, then, lies the difference between those benevolent Utopian plans to which I object because they lead to violence, and those other important and far-reaching political reforms which I am inclined to recommend?

If I were to give a simple formula or recipe for distinguishing between what I consider to be admissible plans for social reform and inadmissible Utopian blueprints, I might say:

Work for the elimination of concrete evils rather than for the realization of abstract goods. Do not aim at establishing happiness by political means. Rather aim at the elimination of concrete miseries. Or, in more practical terms: fight for the elimination of poverty by direct means – for example, by making sure that everybody has a minimum income. Or fight against epidemics and disease by erecting hospitals and schools of medicine. Fight illiteracy as you fight criminality. But do all this by direct means. Choose what you consider the most urgent evil of the society in which you live, and try patiently to convince people that we can get rid of it.

But do not try to realize these aims indirectly by designing and working for a distant ideal of a society which is wholly good. However deeply you may feel indebted to its inspiring vision, do not think that you are obliged to work for its realization, or that it is your omission to open the eyes of others to its beauty. Do not allow your dreams of a beautiful world to lure you away from the claims of men who suffer here and now. Our fellow men have a claim to our help; no generation must be sacrificed for the sake of future generations, for the sake of an ideal of happiness that may never be realized. In brief, it is my thesis that human misery is the most urgent problem of a rational public policy and that happiness is not such a problem. The attainment of happiness should be left to our private endeavours.

It is a fact, and not a very strange fact, that it is not so very difficult to reach agreement by discussion on what are the most intolerable evils of our society, and on what are the most urgent social reforms. Such an agreement can be reached much more easily than an agreement concerning some ideal form of social life. For the evils are with us here and now. They can be experienced, and are being experienced every day, by many people who have been and are being made miserable by poverty, unemployment, national oppression, war and disease. Those of us who do not suffer from these miseries meet every day others who can describe them to us. This is what makes the evils concrete. This is why we can get somewhere in arguing about them; why we can profit here from the attitude of reasonableness. We can learn by listening to concrete claims, by patiently trying to assess them as impartially as we can and by considering ways of meeting them without creating worse evils.

With ideal goods it is different. These we know only from our dreams and from the dreams of our poets and prophets. They cannot be discussed, only proclaimed from the housetops. They do not call for the rational attitude of the impartial judge, but for the emotional attitude of the impassioned preacher.

The Utopianist attitude, therefore, is opposed to the attitude of reasonableness. Utopianism, even though it may often appear in a rationalist disguise, cannot be more than a pseudo-rationalism.

What, then, is wrong with the apparently rational argument which I outlined when presenting the Utopianist case? I believe that it is quite true that we can judge the rationality of an action only in relation to some aims or ends. But this does not necessarily mean that the rationality of a political action can be judged only in relation to an *historical* end. And it surely does not mean that we must consider every social or political situation merely from the point of view of some preconceived historical ideal, from the point of view of an alleged ultimate aim of the development of history. On the contrary, if among our aims and ends there is anything conceived in terms of human happiness and misery, then we are bound to judge our actions in terms not only of possible contributions to the happiness of man in a distant future, but also of their more immediate effects. We must not argue that a certain social situation is a mere means to an end on the grounds that it is merely a transient historical situation. For all situations are transient. Similarly we must not argue that the misery of one generation may be considered as a mere means to the end of securing the lasting happiness of some later generation or generations; and this argument is improved neither by a high degree of promised happiness nor by a large number of generations profiting by it. All generations are transient. All have an equal right to be considered, but our immediate duties are undoubtedly to the present generation and to the next. Besides, we should never attempt to balance anybody's misery against somebody else's happiness.

With this the apparently rational arguments of Utopianism dissolve into nothing. The fascination which the future exerts upon the Utopianist has nothing to do with rational foresight. Considered in this light the violence which Utopianism breeds looks very much like the running amok of an evolutionist metaphysics, of an hysterical philosophy of history, eager to sacrifice the present for the splendours of the future, and unaware that its principle would lead to sacrificing each particular future period for one which comes after it; and likewise unaware of the trivial truth that the ultimate future of man – whatever fate may have in store for him – can be nothing more splendid than his ultimate extinction.

The appeal of Utopianism arises from the failure to realize that we cannot make heaven on earth. What I believe we can do instead is to make life a little less terrible and a little less unjust in each generation. A good deal can be achieved in this way. Much has been achieved in the last hundred years. More could be achieved by our own generation. There are many pressing problems which we might solve, at least partially, such as helping the weak and the sick, and those who suffer under oppression and injustice; stamping out unemployment; equalizing opportunities; and preventing international crime, such as blackmail and war instigated by men like gods, by omnipotent and omniscient leaders. All this we might achieve if only we could give up dreaming about distant ideals and fighting over our Utopian blueprints for a new world and a new man. Those of us who believe in man as he is, and who have therefore not given up the hope of defeating violence and unreason, must demand instead that every man should be given the right to arrange his life himself so far as this is compatible with the equal rights of others.

'Utopia and Violence' (1947), in *Conjectures and Refutations*, 3rd ed. (London, Routledge, 1969), pp. 357–63.

George Orwell
(1903–1950)

BREATHING THE AIR OF EQUALITY

I had come to Spain with some notion of writing newspaper articles, but I had joined the militia almost immediately, because at that time and in that atmosphere it seemed the only conceivable thing to do. The Anarchists were still in virtual control of Catalonia and the revolution was still in full swing. To anyone who had been there since the beginning it probably seemed even in December or January that the revolutionary period was ending; but when one came straight from England the aspect of Barcelona was something startling and overwhelming. It was the first time that I had ever been in a town where the working class was in the saddle. Practically every building of any size had been seized by the workers and was draped with red flags or with the red and black flag of the Anarchists; every wall was scrawled with the hammer and sickle and with the initials of the revolutionary parties; almost every church had been gutted and its images burnt. Churches here and there were being systematically demolished by gangs of workmen. Every shop and café had an inscription saying that it had been collectivized; even the bootblacks had been collectivized and their boxes painted red and black. Waiters and shopwalkers looked you in the face and treated you as an equal. Servile and even ceremonial forms of speech had temporarily disappeared. Nobody said '*Señor*' or '*Don*' or even '*Usted*'; everyone called everyone else 'Comrade' and 'Thou', and said '*Salud!*' instead of '*Buenos días*'. Tipping was forbidden by law; almost my first experience was receiving a lecture from a hotel manager for trying to tip a lift-boy. There were no private motorcars, they had all been commandeered, and all the trams and taxis and much of the other transport were painted red and black. The revolutionary posters were everywhere, flaming from the walls in clean reds and blues that made the few remaining advertisements look like daubs of mud.

Down the Ramblas, the wide central artery of the town where crowds of people streamed constantly to and fro, the loudspeakers were bellowing revolutionary songs all day and far into the night. And it was the aspect of the crowds that was the queerest thing of all. In outward appearance it was a town in which the wealthy classes had practically ceased to exist. Except for a small number of women and foreigners there were no 'well-dressed' people at all. Practically everyone wore rough working-class clothes, or blue overalls, or some variant of the militia uniform. All this was queer and moving. There was much in it that I did not understand, in some ways I did not even like it, but I recognized it immediately as a state of affairs worth fighting for. Also I believed that things were as they appeared, that this was really a workers' State and that the entire bourgeoisie had either fled, been killed, or voluntarily come over to the workers' side; I did not realize that great numbers of well-to-do bourgeois were simply lying low and disguising themselves as proletarians for the time being.

Together with all this there was something of the evil atmosphere of war. The town had a gaunt untidy look, roads and buildings were in poor repair, the streets at night were dimly lit for fear of air-raids, the shops were mostly shabby and half-empty. Meat was scarce and milk practically unobtainable, there was a shortage of coal, sugar and petrol, and a really serious shortage of bread. Even at this period the bread-queues were often hundreds of yards long. Yet so far as one could judge the people were contented and hopeful. There was no unemployment, and the price of living was still extremely low; you saw very few conspicuously destitute people, and no beggars except the gipsies. Above all, there was a belief in the revolution and the future, a feeling of having suddenly emerged into an era of equality and freedom. Human beings were trying to behave as human beings and not as cogs in the capitalist machine. In the barbers' shops were Anarchist notices (the barbers were mostly Anarchists) solemnly explaining that barbers were no longer slaves. In the streets were coloured posters appealing to prostitutes to stop being prostitutes. To anyone from the hard-boiled, sneering civilization of the English-speaking races there was something rather pathetic in the literalness with which these idealistic Spaniards took the hackneyed phrases of revolution. At that time revolutionary ballads of the naïvest kind, all about proletarian brotherhood and the wickedness of Mussolini, were being sold on the streets for a few centimes each. I have often seen an illiterate militiaman buy one of these ballads, laboriously spell out the words and then, when he had got the hang of it, begin singing it to an appropriate tune.

All this time I was at the Lenin Barracks, ostensibly in training for the front.

I [had] left Barcelona in early January and I did not go on leave till late April; and all this time – indeed, till later – in the strip of Aragon controlled by Anarchist and p.o.u.m. troops, the same conditions persisted, at least outwardly. The revolutionary atmosphere remained as I had first known it. General and private, peasant and militiaman, still met as equals; everyone drew the same pay, wore the same clothes, ate the same food and called everyone else 'thou' and 'comrade'; there was no boss-class, no menial-class, no beggars, no prostitutes, no lawyers, no priests, no boot-licking, no cap-touching. I was breathing the air of equality, and I was simple enough to imagine that it existed all over Spain. I did not realize that more or less by chance I was isolated among the most revolutionary section of the Spanish working class.

Homage to Catalonia (Secker & Warburg, 1938), Penguin ed. (1962), pp. 8–10, 66.

W. H. Auden
(1907–   )

ARCADIA NOT UTOPIA

If the hill overlooking our city has always been known as Adam's Grave, only at dusk can you see the recumbent giant, his head turned to the west, his right arm resting for ever on Eve's haunch,

Can you learn, from the way he looks up at the scandalous pair, what a citizen really thinks of his citizenship.

Just as now you can hear in a drunkard's caterwaul his rebel sorrows crying for a parental discipline, in lustful eyes perceive a disconsolate soul,

Scanning with desperation all passing limbs for some vestige of her faceless angel who in that long ago when wishing was a help mounted her once and vanished:

For Sun and Moon supply their conforming masks, but in this hour of civil twilight all must wear their own faces.

And it is now that our two paths cross.

Both simultaneously recognize his Anti-type: that I am an Arcadian, that he is a Utopian.

He notes, with contempt, my Aquarian belly: I note, with alarm, his Scorpion's mouth.

He would like to see me cleaning latrines: I would like to see him removed to some other planet.

Neither speaks. What experience could we possibly share?

Glancing at a lampshade in a store window, I observe it is too hideous for anyone in their senses to buy: He observes it is too expensive for a peasant to buy.

Passing a slum child with rickets, I look the other way: He looks the other way if he passes a chubby one.

I hope our senators will behave like saints, provided they don't reform me: He hopes they will behave like *baritoni cattivi*, and, when lights burn late in the Citadel,

I (who have never seen the inside of a police station) am shocked and think: 'Were the city as free as they say, after sundown all her bureaus would be huge black stones':

He (who has been beaten up several times) is not shocked at all but thinks: 'One fine night our boys will be working up there.'

You can see, then, why, between my Eden and his New Jerusalem, no treaty is negotiable.

In my Eden a person who dislikes Bellini has the good manners not to get born: In his New Jerusalem a person who dislikes work will be very sorry he was born.

In my Eden we have a few beam-engines, saddle-tank locomotives, overshot waterwheels and other beautiful pieces of obsolete machinery to play with: In his New Jerusalem even chefs will be cucumber-cool machine minders.

In my Eden our only source of political news is gossip: In his New Jerusalem there will be a special daily in simplified spelling for non-verbal types.

In my Eden each observes his compulsive rituals and superstitious tabus but we have no morals: In his New Jerusalem the temples will be empty but all will practise the rational virtues.

One reason for his contempt is that I have only to close my eyes, cross the iron footbridge to the tow-path, take the barge through the short brick tunnel and there I stand in Eden again, welcomed back by the krumhorns, doppions, sordumes of jolly miners and a bob major from the Cathedral (romanesque) of St Sophie (*Die Kalte*):

One reason for my alarm is that, when he closes his eyes, he arrives, not in New Jerusalem, but on some august day of outrage when hellikins cavort through ruined drawing-rooms and fish-wives intervene in the Chamber or

Some autumn night of delations and noyades when the unrepentant thieves (including me) are sequestered and those he hates shall hate themselves instead.

So with a passing glance we take the other's posture; already our steps recede, heading, incorrigible each, towards his kind of meal and evening.

Was it (as it must look to any god of cross-roads) simply a fortuitous intersection of life-paths, loyal to different fibs.

Or else a rendezvous between accomplices who, in spite of themselves, cannot resist meeting.

To remind the other (do both, at bottom, desire truth?) of that half of their secret which he would most like to forget, forcing us both, for a fraction of a second, to remember our victim (but for him I could forget the blood, but for me he could forget the innocence).

On whose immolation (call him Abel, Remus, whom you will, it is one Sin Offering) arcadias, utopias, our dear old bag of a democracy, are alike founded:

For without a cement of blood (it must be human, it must be innocent) no secular wall will safely stand.

'Vespers' from *Collected Shorter Poems, 1927–1957* (London, Faber, 1955).

EDEN

Landscape
Limestone uplands like the Pennines plus a small region of igneous rocks with at least one extinct volcano. A precipitous and indented seacoast.

Climate
British.

Ethnic origin of inhabitants
Highly varied as in the United States, but with a slight nordic predominance.

Language
Of mixed origins like English, but highly inflected.

Weights and Measures
Irregular and complicated. No decimal system.

Religion
Roman Catholic in an easygoing Mediterranean sort of way. Lots of local saints.

Size of Capital
Plato's ideal figure, 5040, about right.

Form of Government
Absolute monarchy, elected for life by lot.

Sources of Natural Power
Wind, water, peat, coal. No oil.

Economic activities
Lead mining, coal mining, chemical factories, paper mills, sheep farm-ing, truck farming, greenhouse horticulture.

Means of transport
Horses and horse-drawn vehicles, narrow-gauge railways, canal barges, balloons. No automobiles or airplanes.

Architecture
State: Baroque. Ecclesiastical: Romanesque or Byzantine. Domestic: Eighteenth-Century British or American Colonial.

Domestic Furniture and Equipment
Victorian except for kitchens and bathrooms which are as full of modern gadgets as possible.

Formal Dress
The fashions of Paris in the 1830's and '40's.

Sources of Public Information
Gossip. Technical and learned periodicals but no newspapers.

Public Statues
Confined to famous defunct chefs.

Public Entertainments
Religious Processions, Brass Bands, Opera, Classical Ballet. No movies, radio or television.

'Reading' in *The Dyer's Hand and other Essays* (London, Faber, 1962).

Claude Lévi-Strauss
(1908–   )

SOCIETY PLACED OUTSIDE HISTORY

So-called primitive societies, of course, exist in history; their past is as old as ours, since it goes back to the origin of the species. Over thousands of years they have undergone all sorts of transformations; they have known wars, migrations, adventure. But they have specialized in ways different from those which we have chosen. Perhaps they have, in certain respects, remained closer to very ancient conditions of life, but this does not preclude the possibility that in other respects they are farther from those conditions than we are.

Although they exist in history, these societies seem to have elaborated or retained a particular wisdom which incites them to resist desperately any structural modifications which would afford history a point of entry into their lives. Those which have best protected their distinctive character appear to be societies predominantly concerned with persevering in their existence. The way in which they exploit the environment guarantees both a modest standard of living and the conservation of natural resources. Their marriage rules, though varied, reveal to the eye of the demographer a common function, namely to set the fertility rate very low and to keep it constant. Finally, a political life based on consent, and admitting of no decisions other than those unanimously arrived at, seems conceived to preclude the possibility of calling on that driving force of collective life which takes advantage of the contrast between power and opposition, majority and minority, exploiter and exploited.

In a word, these societies, which we might define as 'cold' in that their internal environment neighbours on the zero of historical temperature, are, by their limited total manpower and their mechanical mode of functioning, distinguished from the 'hot' societies which appeared in different parts of the world following the Neolithic revolution. In these, differentiations between castes and between classes are urged unceasingly in order to extract social change and energy from them.

The value of this distinction is mainly theoretical: it is unlikely that any society can be found which would correspond exactly to one or the other type. And in another sense also the distinction remains relative, if it is true, as I believe, that social anthropology responds to a double motivation. First: retrospective, since the various types of primitive life are on the point of disappearing and we must hasten to cull our lessons from them. Second: prospective, to the extent that, being conscious of an evolution whose tempo is constantly accelerating, we experience ourselves already as the 'primitives' of our great-grandchildren, so that we seek to validate ourselves by drawing closer to those who were – and still are, for a brief moment – like a part of us which persists in its existence.

On the other hand, neither do those societies which I have called 'hot' manifest this character to an absolute degree. When, on the morrow of the Neolithic revolution, the great city-states of the Mediterranean Basin and of the Far East perpetrated slavery, they constructed a type of society in which the differential statuses of men – some dominant, others dominated – could be used to produce culture at a rate until then inconceivable and unthought of. By the same logic, the industrial revolution of the nineteenth century represents less an evolution oriented in the same direction, than a rough sketch of a different solution: though for a long time it remained based on the same abuses and injustices, yet it made possible the transfer to *culture* of that dynamic function which the proto-historic revolution had assigned to *society*.

If – Heaven forbid! – it were expected of the anthropologist that he predict the future of humanity, he would undoubtedly not conceive of it as a continuation or a projection of present types, but rather on the model of an integration, progressively unifying the appropriate characteristics of the 'cold' societies and the 'hot' ones. His thought would renew connections with the old Cartesian dream of putting machines, like automatons, at the service of man. It would follow this lead through the social philosophy of the eighteenth century and up to Saint-Simon. The latter, in announcing the passage 'from government of men to the administration of things', anticipated in the same breath the anthropological distinction between culture and society. He thus looked forward to an event of which advances in information theory and electronics give us at least a glimpse: the conversion of a type of civilization which inaugurated historical development at the price of the transformation of men into machines into an ideal civilization which would succeed in turning machines into men. Then, culture having entirely taken over the burden of manufacturing progress, society would be freed from the millennial curse which has compelled it to enslave men in order that there be progress. Henceforth, history would make itself by itself. Society, placed outside and above history, would be able to exhibit once again that regular and, as it were, crystalline structure which the best-preserved of primitive societies teach us is not antagonistic to the human condition. In this perspective, utopian as it might seem, social anthropology, would find its highest justification, since the forms of life and thought which it studies would no longer have a purely historical or comparative interest. They would correspond to a permanent hope for mankind over which social anthropology, particularly in the most troubled times, would have a mission to keep watch.

Our science would not have been able to stand as a sentinel in this way – and would not even have conceived of the importance and the necessity of it – if, on the remote borders of the earth, men had not obstinately resisted history, and if they had not remained as living testimonials of that which we want to preserve.

The Scope of Anthropology (1960), trans. S. D. and R. A. Paul (London, Cape, 1967), pp. 46–50.

David Riesman
(1909–   )

THE AMERICAN ATHENS

Americans of the more mobile classes have not only adapted themselves to a fluid society, but have also begun to adapt the society to their own needs. They have achieved an extraordinary ability to make judgements about, and friends with, a great variety of humankind. Whereas more traditional societies have an etiquette to govern the relation between people of different age, class and sex groups, these Americans have abandoned etiquette for a more individualized and personalized approach. And while we are familiar with the negative aspects of this development – its enforced joviality of the 'greeter' and gladhander, its enforced politeness of the Helen Hokinson type – we may in our self-contempt be less ready to see its great adventurousness: the liberation of people and their movements from the chain mail of etiquette.

In the arts of consumption as well as in the arts of production, Americans have moved so fast that, in architecture and design, in moving pictures, and in poetry and criticism, we are living in what I believe to be one of the great cultures of history. It is not fashionable to say this. Yet we may ask, as Crane Brinton does in *Ideas and Men*: What is there in Pericles' famous praise of Athens that does not apply to us, in some or even in extended measure?

Sensitive Americans – and they are more in number than each individually is apt to think – have become exceedingly allergic to anything that smacks of chauvinism; this very symposium is in part a testimony to this development. *Vis-à-vis* Europe, we have lost the defensive aggression of Mark Twain, though his was a needed corrective; *vis-à-vis* Asia, we were until recently taken in by the image of the peaceable, unaggressive, technologically unseduced Chinese. It now seems likely that we shall fall for the idea that the Russians have more to offer the Far East than we; and that they have unequivocally convinced the peasants that this is so. While this attitude stems in part from our disenchantment with machine civilization and our failure to use machinery as a means to greater, more creative leisure, it would appear ludicrous to that part of the world which needs machines before it can realize the possibility of becoming disenchanted with them!

One of the interesting semantic expressions of our own disenchantment is that of bewailing our society as 'impersonal'. What would the member of the village group or small town not give at times for an impersonal setting where he was not constantly part of a web of gossip and surveillance? Furthermore, this use of the term 'impersonal' is a way of deprecating our great human achievement of turning over productive routines to machinery and to formal organization. One result of this attitude is clear enough: the sphere of work tends to come increasingly under the supervision of the engineers whose concern is less to reduce the time and strain of the worker, than to render the workaday world 'meaningful' in terms of shared emotions reminiscent of the guilds, or perhaps of our nostalgic image of the guilds.

A contrary attitude would assume that we should be grateful to find, in our work, areas of freedom from people, where the necessary minimum of productive activity could be accomplished without the strain and waste of time involved in continuous concern for the morale of the working group. If men were not compelled to be sociable at work, they could enjoy sociability in their leisure much more than they often do now. In fact, while men in the nineteenth century may have underestimated their satisfactions from solitary occupations, hobbies and other pursuits, we tend today to reverse these extremes and to forget that men can enjoy, let us say, the physical rhythms of work or the private fantasies of leisure even when they are for long periods deprived of social comradeship at work and play. What is necessary is some sort of balance which will find room for quite idiosyncratic individual desires to be, variously, alone and with others. The flexibility of modern industrial organization, no longer bound geographically to rail lines and power sites, the steady decrease of hours of compulsory work which our abundance allows, and our increasing sensitivity to the psychic as well as physical hazards of the different occupations – these developments permit us to move towards the reorganization of work so that it can offer a greater variety of physical and social challenges and stimulations. But work should never be allowed to become an end in itself simply out of a need to keep ourselves busy.

Apart from the everpresent threat of war – not seldom used as a rationalization to sop up our 'excessive' comforts, leisures and painfully-attained easy-goingnesses – most of our social critics cannot imagine a society being held together without putting organized work in the forefront of its goals and agendas. Their efforts to restore the participative significance of work, allegedly enjoyed in earlier social stages, show the same poverty of imagination as their belief in the inevitable need for the parochial group as the only conceivable building block of society. When we turn to formal politics, we see that the same fundamentally reactionary ideology leads to a demand for national unity and a distrust of the chaos of democratic politics and of the war among the so-called 'special interests'.

The notion that there must be 'agreement on fundamentals' in order that democratic politics may go on is an illusion. Carl J. Friedrich, in *The New Image of the Common Man*, provides a discriminatory critique. While it is true that people must be prepared to accept the fact of a vote or election going against them, and to accept certain legal and juridical minima of the same sort, this is not what is meant when agreement on fundamentals is asked as the price of national unity and survival. What is meant is actually a surrender of special interest claims, whether these grow out of ethnic loyalties, church affiliation, regional, occupational or other ties. What is meant is agreement that democracy itself (defined to mean more, much more, than the legal minimum) is a good thing; agreement on equality of races; agreement to put American needs ahead of any foreign loyalty. Yet the fact is that our democracy, like that of Switzerland, has survived without securing such agreements. In our country, this has been attained by a party system that serves as broker among the special interest groups: the parties do not ask for agreement on fundamentals – certainly, not on ideological fundamentals – but for much more mundane and workable concessions. At the same time, our expanding economy (and concomitantly expanding state services) has made these concessions possible without bankruptcy and, on the whole, with a steady reduction in hardship and injustice.

Those who would like to see the parties 'stand for something', and those who have framed their own image of the future in terms of some Armaggedon of proletarian revolution or overthrow of the 'interests', feel unhappy and misgoverned under such a system. To them it seems simply a lack of system. Thus, we are in part the victims of ideals of polity which turn our virtues into vices and which have confused the Western world since Plato's *Republic*, if not before. What we need are new ideals, framed with the future rather than the past in mind – ideals closer to the potentialities actually realizable under the impetus of industrialization.

One of the elements in such a new ideal would seem to be a relaxation of the demand for political dutifulness now made by many citizens who are worried about apathy. Apathy has many meanings. Its expression today may be one of the ways the individual – in the Soviet zone or Franco's Spain, no less than here – hides from ideological pressures, hides from 'groupism'. Lacking an active counterfaith in individualism, or any way of meeting up with others who share his resentments, he falls back on apathy as a mask behind which he can protect the remnants of his privacy. If it were widely recognized that not all people in a democracy need concern themselves continuously with public affairs (or with the union, or with the P.T.A., or what not), but that all should have a 'right of veto' of which to make sparing, residual exercise, they might more readily agree to comply with the minimal demands for information and participation that such a veto would need for its effectiveness. And with politics no longer regarded as a continuous duty, people might feel less resistance to participation.

If the international (and hence domestic) outlook continues to be as grim as during recent months [written in early 1950], readers may wonder whether this advocacy of 'irresponsible' individualism is not sheer escapism. It would be insufficient to answer that 'escape', like 'compromise' or 'appeasement', has become a bad word to the crusaders for political and group commitment. It would perhaps be a better answer to observe that if America is to be saved from destruction or self-destruction, it will be by preserving, as part of our armory of significant escapes, our humor and creativity and sense of perspective.

I recognize, of course, that many Americans feel guilty about their 'luxuries' if others are forced to fight and suffer, and so would welcome a kind of edited hardship as an alleviation of their guilt. But though this is understandable and, in many ways, desirable, it provides the privileged countries and groups with much too limited and hence too easy a morality. The present international dangers menacing America (real enough in the view I hold of Stalinism) can obviously be used by many people in America to rationalize their partiality for the shared hardships of war against the solitary hardships of developing their individuality in time of peace.

Again, it should be obvious to the reader that I speak in a social context in which anarchy and 'unbridled' individuality are much less likely prospects (except on the international scene) than the all-too-evident danger of the 'garrison state'. This danger must make us particularly sensitive to the fact that we depend for advance, in morals no less than in physical science, on individuals who have developed their individuality to a notable degree. We must give every encouragement to people to develop their private selves – to escape from groupism – while realizing that, in many cases, they will use their freedom in unattractive or 'idle' ways. Our very abundance makes it possible for us, even in the midst of war, to take the minor risks and losses involved in such encouragement as against the absolutely certain risks involved in a total mobilization of intellect and imagination.

Yet in these remarks I find myself, as a final irony, addressing the defense of individualism to some presumed director of unselective service: I am using, Adam Smith style, group-survival arguments to justify the 'selfish' living of an individual life. (Much of the same irony overtakes many devout people who 'sell' religion as a variety of group therapy – because it is good for morale rather than for morals.) Possibly I am thereby revealing my own arguments against my own guilts. But I think more is involved. I am trying to answer Dostoevsky's Grand Inquisitor in terms that he would understand, as well as in the transcendent terms that his interlocutor, Jesus, understands. I am insisting that no ideology, however noble, can justify the sacrifice of an individual to the needs of the group. Whenever this occurs, it is the starkest tragedy, hardly less so if the individual consents (because he accepts the ideology) to the instrumental use of himself. . . .

Social science has helped us become more aware of the extent to which individuals, great and little, are the creatures of their cultural conditioning; and so we neither blame the little nor exalt the great. But the same wisdom has sometimes led us to the fallacy that, since all men have their being in culture and as the result of the culture, they owe a debt to that culture which even a lifetime of altruism could not repay. (One might as well argue, and in fact many societies in effect do, that since we are born of parents, we must feel guilt whenever we transcend their limitations!) Sometimes the point is pushed to the virtual denial of individuality: since we arise in society, it is assumed with a ferocious determinism that we can never transcend it. All such concepts are useful correctives of an earlier solipsism. But if they are extended to hold that conformity with society is not only a necessity but also a duty, they destroy that margin of freedom which gives life its savor and its endless possibility for advance.

> *Individualism Reconsidered* (1954), abridged paperback ed. (Garden City, Doubleday, n.d.), pp. 22–7.

Paul Goodman
(1911–   )

SOCIETY MADE WHOLE AGAIN

Imagine that these modern radical positions had been more fully achieved: we should have a society where:

A premium is placed on technical improvement and on the engineering style of functional simplicity and clarity. Where the community is planned as a whole, with an organic integration of work, living and play. Where buildings have the variety of their real functions with the uniformity of the prevailing technology. Where a lot of money is spent on public goods. Where workers are technically educated and have a say in management. Where no one drops out of society and there is an easy mobility of classes. Where production is primarily for use. Where social groups are laboratories for solving their own problems experimentally. Where democracy begins in the town meeting, and a man seeks office only because he has a program. Where regional variety is encouraged and there is pride in the Republic. And young men are free of conscription. Where all feel themselves citizens of the universal Republic of Reason. Where it is the policy to give an adequate voice to the unusual and unpopular opinion, and to give a trial and a market to new enterprise. Where people are not afraid to make friends. Where races are factually equal. Where vocation is sought out and cultivated as God-given capacity, to be conserved and embellished, and where the church is the spirit of its congregation. Where ordinary experience is habitually scientifically assayed by the average man. Where it is felt that the suggestion of reason is practical. And speech leads to the corresponding action. Where the popular culture is a daring and passionate culture. Where children can make themselves useful and earn their own money. Where their sexuality is taken for granted. Where the community carries on its important adult business and the children fall in at their own pace. And where education is concerned with fostering human powers as they develop in the growing child.

In such an utopian society, as was aimed at by modern radicals but has not eventuated, it would be very easy to grow up. There would be plenty of objective, worth-while activities for a child to observe, fall in with, do, learn, improvise on his own. That is to say, it is not the spirit of modern times that makes our society difficult for the young; it is that that spirit has not sufficiently realized itself.

In this light, the present plight of the young is not surprising. In the rapid changes, people have not kept enough in mind that the growing young also exist and the world must fit their needs. So instead, we have the present phenomena of excessive attention to the children as such, in psychology and suburbs, and coping with 'juvenile delinquency' as if it were an entity. Adults fighting for some profoundly conceived fundamental change naturally give up, exhausted, when they have achieved some gain that makes life tolerable again and seems to be the substance of their demand. But to grow up, the young need a world of finished situations and society made whole again.

Indeed, the bother with the above little utopian sketch is that many adults would be restive in such a stable modern world if it were achieved. They would say: It is a fine place for growing boys. I agree with this criticism.

I think the case is as follows: Every profound new proposal, of culture or institution, invents and discovers a new property of 'Human Nature'. Henceforth it is going to be in *these* terms that a young fellow will grow up and find his identity and his task. So if we accumulate the revolutionary proposals of modern times, we have named the *goals of modern education*. We saw that it was the aim of Progressive Education to carry this program through.

But education is not life. The existing situation of a grown man is to confront an uninvented and undiscovered present. Unfortunately, *at* present, he must also try to perfect his unfinished past: this bad inheritance is part of the existing situation, and must be stoically worked through.

Let me repeat the proposition of this chapter: *It is the missed revolutions of modern times – the fallings-short and the compromises – that add up to the conditions that make it hard for the young to grow up in our society.*

The existing local community, region and nation is the real environment of the young. Conversely, we could define community spirit and patriotism as the conviction in which it is possible to grow up. (An independent and not too defeated adult confronts a broader historical, international and cosmic scene as his environment for action.)

Modern times have been characterized by fundamental changes occurring with unusual rapidity. These have shattered tradition but often have not succeeded in creating a new whole community. We have no recourse to going back, there is nothing to go back to. If we are to have a stable and whole community in which the young can grow to manhood, we must painfully perfect the revolutionary modern tradition we have.

This stoical resolve is, paradoxically, a *conservative* proposition, aiming at stability and social balance. For often it is not a question of making innovations, but of catching up and restoring the right proportions. But no doubt, in our runaway, one-sided way of life, the proposal to conserve human resources and develop human capacities has become a radical innovation.

Right proportion cannot be restored by adding a few new teachers formally equivalent to the growth in population. Probably we need a million new minds and more put to teaching. Even Dr Conant says that we must nearly double our present annual expenditure on education for teaching alone, not counting plant and the central schools he wants. And this does not take into account essentially new fields such as making sense of adult leisure.

It must be understood that with the increase in population and crowding, the number and variety of human services increase disproportionately, and the *laissez-faire* areas, both geographical and social, decrease. Therefore the *units* of human service, such as school classes or the clientele of a physician (and even political districts?), ought to be made *smaller*, to avoid the creation of masses: mass teaching, mass medicine, mass psychotherapy, mass penology, mass politics. Yet our normal schools and medical schools cannot cope with even the arithmetic increase.

Right proportion requires reversing the goal in vocational guidance, from fitting the man to the machine and chopping him down to fit, to finding the opportunity in the economy that brings out the man, and if you can't find such an opportunity, make it. This involves encouraging new small enterprises and unblocking and perhaps underwriting invention. Again, if at present production is inhuman and stupid, it is that too few minds are put to it: this can be remedied by giving the workman more voice in production and the kind of training to make that voice wise.

Probably, right proportion involves considerable decentralizing and increasing the rural-urban ratio. Certainly it involves transforming the scores of thousands of neglected small places, hopelessly dull and same, into interesting villages that someone could be proud of. A lot of the booming production has got to go into publicly useful goods, proportionate to the apparently forgotten fact that it is on public grounds, because of public investment, and the growth of population, that private wealth is produced and enjoyed. We have to learn again, what city man always used to know, that belonging to the city, to its squares, its market, its neighborhoods and its high culture, is a public good; it is not a field for 'investment to yield a long-term modest profit'. A proportionate allocation of public funds, again, is not likely to devote more money to escape roads convenient for automobiles than to improving the city center. (If I may make a pleasant suggestion, we could underwrite a handsome program for serious adult leisure by a 10 per cent luxury tax on new cars; it would yield over a billion.)

Since prosperity itself has made it more difficult for the underprivileged immigrant to get started, right proportion requires devoting all the more money and ingenuity to helping him find himself and get started. (In such cases, by the way, ingenuity and friendly aid are more important than money, as some of our settlement houses in New York have beautifully demonstrated.) And some way will have to be found, again, for a man to be decently poor, to work for a subsistence without necessarily choosing to involve himself in the total high-standard economy. One way of achieving this would be directly producing subsistence goods in distinction from the total economy.

In arts and letters, there is a right balance between the customary social standard and creative novelty, and between popular entertainment and esthetic experience. Then, to offset Hollywood and Madison Avenue, we must have hundreds of new little theaters, little magazines, and journals of dissenting opinion with means of circulation; because it is only in such that new things can develop and begin to win their way in the world.

It is essential that our democratic legislatures and public spokesmen be balanced by more learned and honorable voices that, as in Britain, can thoughtfully broach fundamental issues of community plan, penal code, morality, cultural tone, with some certainty of reaching a public forum and some possibility of being effective. For there is no other way of getting the best to lead, to have some conviction and even passionate intensity, to save America from going to managers, developers and politicians by default.

Certainly right proportion, in a society tightly organized and conformist, requires a vast increase in the jealous safeguard of civil liberties, to put the fear of God back into local police, district attorneys and the Federal Bureau of Investigation.

Here is a program of more than a dozen essential changes, all practicable, all difficult. A wiser and more experienced author could suggest a dozen more.

Let me expand one of these: Making sense of adult leisure.

What are the present goals of the philosophers of leisure, for instance, the National Recreation Association? and now imagine those goals achieved. There would be a hundred million adults who have cultured hobbies to occupy their spare time: some expert on the flute, some with do-it-yourself kits, some good at chess and go, some square dancing, some camping out and enjoying nature and all playing various athletic games. Leaf through the entire catalogue of the National Recreation Association, take all the items together, apply them to one hundred million adults – and there is the picture. (This costs *at present* forty billion dollars a year, according to the guess of Robert Coughlan in *Life*.) The philosophy of leadership, correspondingly, is to get people to participate – everybody must 'belong'.

Now even if all these people were indeed getting deep personal satisfaction from these activities, this is a dismaying picture. It doesn't add up to anything. It isn't important. There is no ethical necessity in it, no standard. *One cannot waste a hundred million people that way.*

The error is in the NRA's basic concept of recreation. Let me quote from a recent editorial in *Recreation*: Recreation is 'any activity participated in . . . merely for the enjoyment it affords. . . . The rewards of recreational activities depend upon the degree to which they provide outlets for personal interests.' (Outlets again, as in the Governor's prescription for the juvenile delinquents.) But enjoyment is *not* a goal, it is a feeling that accompanies important ongoing activity; pleasure, as Freud said, is always dependent on function.

From the present philosophy of leisure, no new culture can emerge. What is lacking is worth-while community necessity, as the serious leisure, the σχολή of the Athenians had communal necessity, whether in the theater, the games, the architecture and festivals, or even the talk.

That we find it hard to think in these terms is a profound sign of our social imbalance. Yet we do *not* need, as Dr Douglass claimed in the passage we quoted above, 'a new ethics, a new esthetic'. For the activities of serious leisure are right there, glaring, in our communities, to avoid shame and achieve grandeur.

But the question is: If there is little interest, honor, or manliness in the working part of our way of life, can we hope for much in the leisure part?

The best exposition of what I have been trying to say in this chapter is the classic of conservative thinking, Coleridge's *On the Constitution of the Church and State*. His point in that essay is simply this: *In order to have citizens, you must first be sure that you have produced men.* There must therefore be a large part of the common wealth specifically devoted to cultivating 'freedom and civilization', and especially to the education of the young growing up.

Growing Up Absurd (London, Gollancz, 1961), pp. 229–36.

Anthony Crosland
(1918–   )

OPEN-AIR CAFÉS

How far towards equality do we wish to go? I do not regard this as either a sensible or a pertinent question, to which one could possibly give, or should attempt to give a precise reply. We need, I believe, more equality than we now have, for the reasons set out in this chapter. We can therefore describe the direction of advance, and even discern the immediate landscape ahead; but the ultimate objective lies wrapped in complete uncertainty.

This must be the case unless one subscribes to the vulgar fallacy that some ideal society can be said to exist, of which blueprints can be drawn, and which will be ushered in as soon as certain specific reforms have been achieved. The apocalyptic view that we might one day wake up to find that something called 'socialism' had arrived was born of revolutionary theories of capitalist collapse. But in Western societies change is gradual and evolutionary, and not always either foreseeable or even under political control. It is therefore futile and dangerous to think in terms of an ideal society, the shape of which can already be descried, and which will be reached at some definite date in the future. Countries like Britain do not leap from one fully-fledged social system to another, but are, on the contrary, in a state of permanent transition.

Moreover, socialism is not an exact descriptive term, connoting a particular social structure, past, present or even immanent in some sage's mind, which can be empirically observed or analysed. It simply describes a set of values, or aspirations, which socialists wish to see embodied in the organization of society. One must confine oneself to saying, therefore, that society at any given moment either does or does not sufficiently embody these values; and if it does not, then further changes are required. But exactly what degree of equality will create a society, which does sufficiently embody them, no one can possibly say. We must re-assess the matter in the light of each new situation.

We can thus only venture very general statements of the objective. I feel clear that we need large egalitarian changes in our educational system, the distribution of property, the distribution of resources in periods of need, social manners and style of life, and the location of power within industry; and perhaps some, but certainly a smaller, change in respect of incomes from work. I think that these changes, taken together, will amount to a considerable social revolution.

On the other hand, I am sure that a definite limit exists to the degree of equality which is desirable. We do not want complete equality of incomes, since extra responsibility and exceptional talent require and deserve a differential reward. We are not hostile as our opponents some-times foolishly suggest, to 'detached residences in Bournemouth where some elderly woman has obviously more than a thousand a year'.[1] I do not myself want to see *all* private education disappear: nor the Prime Minister denied an official car, as in one Scandinavian country: nor the Queen riding a bicycle: nor the House of Lords instantly abolished: nor the manufacture of Rolls-Royces banned: nor the Brigade of Guards, nor Oxford and Cambridge, nor Boodle's, nor (more doubtfully) the Royal Yacht Squadron, nor even, on a rather lower level, the Milroy Room, lose their present distinctive character:[2] nor anything so dull and colourless as this.

But where en route, before we reach some drab extreme, we shall wish to stop, I have no idea. Our society will look quite different when we have carried through the changes mentioned earlier; and the whole argument will then need to be re-stated, and thought out afresh, by a younger generation than mine.

As our traditional objectives are gradually fulfilled, and society becomes more social-democratic with the passing of the old injustices, we shall turn our attention increasingly to other, and in the long run more im-portant, spheres – of personal freedom, happiness and cultural endeavour: the cultivation of leisure, beauty, grace, gaiety, excitement and of all the proper pursuits, whether elevated, vulgar or eccentric, which contribute to the varied fabric of a full private and family life.

[1] *The Tablet*, reviewing *New Fabian Essays*, 31 May 1952.
[2] On the condition, of course, already fulfilled in the case of Oxford and Cambridge, that entry into these eminent institutions is not a matter simply of lineage.

There are, after all, not one, but two good reasons for being a reformer, and on the Left. The first is a belief in the benefits of socialism. But there are many changes in society which an idealistic reformer might wish to make, but which are not to be subsumed under any defensible definition of socialism. And one is also on the Left, and a Labour supporter, because as a matter of experience most of those advocating such changes are to be found on the Left, and those opposing them on the Right.

It would be amazing if every important issue of public concern could be embraced in a socialist–capitalist controversy, or within some definition of socialism. Socialist aspirations were first formulated over a hundred years ago. Some remain urgently relevant, and have formed the substance of this book. Others have lost their relevance through being largely fulfilled. But of course new issues, not then foreseen, and increasingly important as the old evils are conquered, have arisen since; and they may be highly significant for welfare, freedom and social justice, even though not assimilable into the old socialist–capitalist categories.

This may be seen by considering the case of either the United States or Soviet Russia. In the former country, a Leftist, who was a socialist in Britain, would be much less concerned to promote more social equality or material welfare, of which plenty exists already, than with reforms lying outside the field of socialist–capitalist controversy, yet still the subject of acute Left–Right dispute: civil liberties, or the Negro problem, or foreign policy, or crime, or the sociological problems of a mass society. Similarly in Russia, a Leftist, who was even the most old-fashioned socialist in Britain, would scarcely assume that no urgent problems remained simply because nationalization and planning could go no further; on the contrary, he would concern himself with the promotion of values, notably the rights of personal freedom and dissent, which in Britain are not a matter of socialist–capitalist disagreement.

So in Britain, as we approach the socialist goals described above, the reformer will bend his energies more and more to issues which cannot be classified as specifically socialist or non-socialist, but which lie in other fields altogether.[1] There are two such fields in which social action is

---

[1] One example of such an issue, which many people already believe to be urgent, was quoted in Chapter 1 [of original source]: the issue of managerial and bureaucratic power. This has little to do either with socialism, which historically has been concerned only with the economic power of private business, or with capitalism. It is a political and sociological problem of large scale, which now presents itself as strongly in the State bureaucracy, the Trade Unions, the nationalized industries and the political parties, as it does in private industry.

already called for: the freedom of personal and leisure life, and social responsibility for cultural values.

Society's decisions impinge heavily on people's private lives as well as on their social or economic welfare; and they now impinge, in my view, in too restrictive and puritanical a manner. I should like to see action taken both to widen opportunities for enjoyment and relaxation, and to diminish existing restrictions on personal freedom.

The first of these requires, it is true, a change in cultural attitudes rather than government legislation. If this were to come about, much could be done to make Britain a more colourful and civilized country to live in. We need not only higher exports and old-age pensions, but more open-air cafés, brighter and gayer streets at night, later closing-hours for public houses, more local repertory theatres, better and more hospitable hoteliers and restaurateurs, brighter and cleaner eating-houses, more riverside cafés, more pleasure-gardens on the Battersea model, more murals and pictures in public places, better designs for furniture and pottery and women's clothes, statues in the centre of new housing-estates, better-designed street-lamps and telephone kiosks, and so on *ad infinitum*. The enemy in all this will often be in unexpected guise; it is not only dark Satanic things and people that now bar the road to the new Jerusalem, but also, if not mainly, hygienic, respectable, virtuous things and people, lacking only in grace and gaiety.

This becomes manifest when we turn to the more serious question of socially imposed restrictions on the individual's private life and liberty. There come to mind at once the divorce laws, licensing laws, prehistoric (and flagrantly unfair) abortion laws, obsolete penalties for sexual abnormality, the illiterate censorship of books and plays, and remaining restrictions on the equal rights of women.[1] Most of these are intolerable, and should be highly offensive to socialists, in whose blood there should always run a trace of the anarchist and the libertarian, and not too much of the prig and the prude. If we really attach importance to the 'dignity of man', we must realize that this is as much affronted by a hypocritical divorce law which, as Matthew Arnold once wrote, neither makes divorce impossible nor makes it decent, as by the refusal to establish a joint production council in a factory.[2] A time will come, as material standards

[1] Though if we remove these last, we should in fairness also remove unequal responsibilities from men. Women cannot claim equal rights, and at the same time continue to bring breach-of-promise or alienation-of-affection cases.

[2] Indeed many of these reforms can be justified by the simple moral judgement that

rise, when divorce-law reform will increase the sum of human welfare more than a rise in the food subsidies (though no doubt the party managers will be less enthusiastic for it). Socialists cannot go on indefinitely professing to be concerned with human happiness and the removal of injustice, and then, when the programmes are decided, permitting the National Executive, out of fear of certain vocal pressure-groups, to become more orthodox than the bench of bishops.

Much of this can at least claim the sanction of one powerful stream of socialist thought – that stemming from William Morris; though other, Nonconformist and Fabian, influences wear a bleaker and more forbidding air. For one brought up as a Fabian, in particular, this inevitably means a reaction against the Webb tradition. I do not wish to be misunderstood. All who knew the Webbs have testified to their personal kindliness, gentleness, tolerance and humour; and no one who reads *Our Partnership* can fail to be intensely moved by the deep unaffected happiness of their mutual love. But many of their public virtues, so indispensable at the time, may not be as appropriate today. Reacting as they were against an unpractical, Utopian, sentimental, romantic, almost anarchist tradition on the Left, they were no doubt right to stress the solid virtues of hard work, self-discipline, efficiency, research and abstinence: to sacrifice private pleasure to public duty, and expect that others should do the same: to put Blue Books before culture, and immunity from physical weakness above all other virtues.

And so they spent their honeymoon investigating Trade Societies in Dublin. And so Beatrice could write that 'owing to our concentration on research, municipal administration and Fabian propaganda, we had neither the time nor the energy, nor yet the means to listen to music and the drama, to brood over classic literature, to visit picture galleries, or to view with an informed intelligence the wonders of architecture'.[1] And so Sidney withheld approval from the Soviet experiment until workers' control had been suppressed, and Beatrice until the anti-abortion law had been enacted, and she could write with approval of the serious, youthful Comsomols with their passion for self-discipline and self improvement:

---

hypocrisy is bad. There is something nauseating about the shocked outcry which greets any proposal to amend the licensing laws or to allow plays to be performed on Sundays, and the sanctimonious assumption of superiority over the immoral and godless Continentals, when we consider that public prostitution is tolerated in Britain on a scale which amazes visitors from more 'godless' countries. Let us at least have a little consistency.   [1] *Our Partnership*, p. 14.

and of the emphasis on personal hygiene and self-control – 'there is no spooning in the Parks of Recreation and Rest'. And historically, without a doubt, this insistence on austerity was a vital service to a young and growing opposition movement.

But now we surely need a different set of values. Permeation has more than done its job. Today we are all incipient bureaucrats and practical administrators. We have all, so to speak, been trained at the L.S.E., are familiar with Blue Books and White Papers, and know our way around Whitehall. We realize that we must guard against romantic or Utopian notions: that hard work and research are virtues: that we must do nothing foolish or impulsive: and that Fabian pamphlets must be diligently studied. We know these things too well. Posthumously, the Webbs have won their battle, and converted a generation to their standards. Now the time has come for a reaction: for a greater emphasis on private life, on freedom and dissent, on culture, beauty, leisure and even frivolity. Total abstinence and a good filing-system are not now the right sign-posts to the socialist Utopia: or at least, if they are, some of us will fall by the wayside.

The Future of Socialism (1955), abridged and revised paperback ed. (London, Cape, 1964), pp. 147–9, 353–7.

S. M. Lipset
(1922–   )

THE GOOD SOCIETY ITSELF IN OPERATION

A basic premise of this book is that democracy is not only or even primarily a means through which different groups can attain their ends or seek the good society; it is the good society itself in operation. Only the give-and-take of a free society's internal struggles offers some guarantee that the products of the society will not accumulate in the hands of a few power-holders, and that men may develop and bring up their children without fear of persecution. And, as we have seen, democracy requires institutions which support conflict and disagreement as well as those which sustain legitimacy and consensus. In recent years, however, democracy in the Western world has been undergoing some important changes as serious intellectual conflicts among groups representing different values have declined sharply.

The fact that the differences between the left and the right in the Western democracies are no longer profound does not mean that there is no room for party controversy. But as the editor of one of the leading Swedish newspapers once said to me, 'Politics is now boring. The only issues are whether the metal workers should get a nickel more an hour, the price of milk should be raised or old-age pensions extended.' These are important matters, the very stuff of the internal struggle within stable democracies, but they are hardly matters to excite intellectuals or stimulate young people who seek in politics a way to express their dreams.

This change in Western political life reflects the fact that the fundamental political problems of the industrial revolution have been solved: the workers have achieved industrial and political citizenship; the conservatives have accepted the welfare state; and the democratic left has recognized that an increase in over-all state power carries with it more

415

dangers to freedom than solutions for economic problems. This very triumph of the democratic social revolution in the West ends domestic politics for those intellectuals who must have ideologies or utopias to motivate them to political action.

Political Man (1959) (London, Heinemann, 1960), pp. 403, 406.

Che Guevara
(1928–1967)

MAN'S FULL STATURE
AND HIS WORK

In this period of the building of socialism we can see the new man being born. His image is not yet completely finished – it never could be – since the process goes forward hand in hand with the development of new economic forms.

Leaving out of consideration those whose lack of education makes them take the solitary road toward satisfying their own personal ambitions, there are those, even within this new panorama of a unified march forward, who have a tendency to remain isolated from the masses accompanying them. But what is important is that everyday men are continuing to acquire more consciousness of the need for their incorporation into society and, at the same time, of their importance as the movers of society.

They no longer travel completely alone over trackless routes toward distant desires. They follow their vanguard, consisting of the party, the advanced workers, the advanced men who walk in unity with the masses and in close communion with them. The vanguard has its eyes fixed on the future and its rewards, but this is not seen as something personal. The reward is the new society in which men will have attained new features: the society of communist man.

The road is long and full of difficulties. At times we wander from the path and must turn back; at other times we go too fast and separate ourselves from the masses; on occasions we go too slow and feel the hot breath of those treading on our heels. In our zeal as revolutionists we try to move ahead as fast as possible, clearing the way, but knowing we must draw our sustenance from the mass and that it can advance more rapidly only if we inspire it by our example.

The fact that there remains a division into two main groups (excluding, of course, that minority not participating for one reason or another in the building of socialism), despite the importance given to moral stimuli, indicates the relative lack of development of social consciousness.

The vanguard group is ideologically more advanced than the mass; the latter understands the new values, but not sufficiently. While among the former there has been a qualitative change which enables them to make sacrifices to carry out their function as an advance guard, the latter go only half way and must be subjected to stimuli and pressures of a certain intensity. That is the dictatorship of the proletariat operating not only on the defeated class but also on individuals of the victorious class.

All of this means that for total success a series of mechanisms, of revolutionary institutions, is needed. Fitted into the pattern of the multitudes marching towards the future is the concept of a harmonious aggregate of channels, steps, restraints and smoothly working mechanisms which would facilitate that advance by ensuring the efficient selection of those destined to march in the vanguard which, itself, bestows rewards on those who fulfil their duties, and punishments on those who attempt to obstruct the development of the new society.

This institutionalization of the revolution has not yet been achieved. We are looking for something which will permit a perfect identification between the government and the community in its entirety, something appropriate to the special conditions of the building of socialism, while avoiding to the maximum degree a mere transplanting of the commonplaces of bourgeois democracy – like legislative chambers – into the society in formation.

Some experiments aimed at the gradual development of institutionalized forms of the revolution have been made, but without undue haste. The greatest obstacle has been our fear lest any appearance of formality might separate us from the masses and from the individual, might make us lose sight of the ultimate and most important revolutionary aspiration, which is to see man liberated from his alienation.

Despite the lack of institutions, which must be corrected gradually, the masses are now making history as a conscious aggregate of individuals fighting for the same cause. Man under socialism, despite his apparent standardization, is more complete; despite the lack of perfect machinery for it, his opportunities for expressing himself and making himself felt in the social organism are infinitely greater.

It is still necessary to strengthen his conscious participation, individual and collective, in all the mechanisms of management and production, and to link it to the idea of the need for technical and ideological education so that he sees how closely interdependent these processes are and how their advancement is parallel. In this way he will reach total consciousness of his social function, which is equivalent to his full realization as a human being, once the chains of alienation are broken.

This will be translated concretely into the regaining of his true nature through liberated labor and the expression of his proper human condition through culture and art.

In order for him to develop in the first of the above categories labor must acquire a new status. Man dominated by commodity relationships will cease to exist and a system will be created which establishes a quota for the fulfillment of his social duty. The means of production belong to society and the machine will merely be the trench where duty is fulfilled.

Man will begin to see himself mirrored in his work and to realize his full stature as a human being through the object created, through the work accomplished. Work will no longer entail surrendering a part of his being in the form of labor-power sold, which no longer belongs to him, but will represent an emanation of himself, which would reflect his contribution to the common life, the fulfillment of his social duty.

We are doing everything possible to give labor this new status of social duty and to link it, on the one side, with the development of a technology which will create the conditions for greater freedom, and, on the other side, with voluntary work, based on a Marxist appreciation of the fact that man truly reaches a full human condition when he produces without being driven by the physical need to sell his labor as a commodity.

Of course there are other factors involved even when labor is voluntary: Man has not transformed all the coercive factors around him into conditioned reflexes of a social character and he still produces under the pressures of his society. (Fidel calls this moral compulsion.)

Man still needs to undergo a complete spiritual rebirth in his attitude towards his work, freed from the direct pressure of his social environment though linked to it by his new habits. That will be communism.

The change in consciousness will not take place automatically, just as it doesn't take place automatically in the economy. The alterations are slow and are not harmonious; there are periods of acceleration, pauses and even retrogressions.

Furthermore, we must take into account, as I pointed out before, that we are not dealing with a period of pure transition as Marx envisaged it in his *Critique of the Gotha Program* but rather with a new phase unforeseen by him: an initial period of the transition to communism or the construction of socialism. It is taking place in the midst of violent class struggles and with elements of capitalism within it which obscure a complete understanding of its essence.

Socialism and Man (International Marxist Group, 8 Toynbee St., London, E.1) (no pagination).

COLOURFUL, CREATIVE CONFLICT

Of all factors influencing the intensity of political conflict, those of the pluralism-superimposition scale are by far the most effective. In order to assess their consequences, I shall resort, for a last time, to constructing contrasting ideal types. At one extreme of the scale thus emerging, we should find a society in which all patterns, issues and contexts of political conflict are superimposed and combined into two large hostile camps. There is superimposition with respect to the structure of authority and to the scales of rewards that make up social stratification. Whoever occupies a position of authority has wealth, prestige and other emoluments of social status at his disposal, too; whoever is excluded from political authority has no hope of climbing very far on the scale of social status. Furthermore, the conflicts arising from different associations are superimposed. Power is generalized in the sense that a homogeneous and interchangeable élite governs an identical subjected class in the state, in industry, in the army and in all other associations. Finally, such nonclass conflicts as exist in society are congruent with the conflicts arising out of the unequal distribution of authority. Political class conflict, industrial class conflict, regional conflicts, conflicts between town and country, possibly racial and religious conflicts – all are superimposed so as to form a single and all-embracing antagonism. Under these conditions, the intensity of political conflict reaches its maximum.

As with our earlier ideal types, there is no actual society in which this is fully realized. There are, however, many indications that superimposition of patterns, and the monism of social structure resulting from it, are a characteristic feature of modern totalitarian states. The ruling and the subjected groups of industry and the state are identical; the party exercises its power in both associations. With respect to the military, the same condition is aimed at, although – as the Russian example shows – it is not attained without a struggle. In any case, generalized authority is the constant goal of the state party. This generalized authority includes the attempt to monopolize every scale of socioeconomic status for the 'new class'. Its members enjoy, apart from, or perhaps by virtue of, their authority, high incomes and considerable prestige – although the latter is less subject to manipulation than the former.[1] With respect to the superimposition of class and other conflicts, no unequivocal pattern seems discernible in totalitarian countries, although a tendency to alienate minorities as well as subjected groups in terms of authority is not un-common under oligarchic rule. *Divide et impera* is an old and supposedly useful imperative of despotism; but with respect to the social structure of their countries, present-day totalitarian rulers have not followed its prescription. They have, instead, aimed at a uniform and monistic organi-zation of society. Moreover, in the Communist countries of the East they have adopted an ideology of intense conflict. The two go together well: on account of the monistic structure of conflict (and many other) relations in totalitarian countries, these relations have gained, and continue to gain, in intensity. Whatever conflicts do occur involve both rulers and ruled with their whole personalities; and if these conflicts become open and violent, the cost of defeat is too high for both parties to allow graceful retreat. 'Totality' distinguishes the totalitarian state in more than one respect, including the extent of the changes desired by those who, for the time being, are its powerless subjects.

The ideal type opposite to that of totalitarianism is that of a free society. Here, the intensity of political conflict is reduced to a minimum. The scales of social stratification are largely separate; possession of authority does not necessarily imply wealth, prestige, security. There are competing élites at the top of the various scales. Conflicts in different associations are dissociated. Leadership in the state does not imply leadership in industry, in the army or in other associations, nor does exclusion from authority in one context imply exclusion in all others. Class conflict and other clashes between groups are dissociated, too; being a member of a parti-cular minority, race or church does not automatically convey certain privileges or disabilities with respect to the distribution of political author-ity. Pluralism of institutions, conflict patterns, groupings and interests makes for a lively, colorful and creative scene of political conflict which

[1] They do not enjoy high 'job security' nor will they be able to achieve this under totalitarian conditions. In view of possible revolts and the role of the ruling class in them, this fact must not be underestimated.

provides an opportunity for success for every interest that is voiced.

Needless to say, there is no society which corresponds in all respects with this ideal-typical picture. With respect to minorities, in particular, there still is a great deal of superimposition of conflict fronts in all Western countries. Being a member of this or that church, race or ethnic group puts many people at a disadvantage in the struggle for political authority. Regarding the other two factors, however, we have seen that a pluralist structure of society is in fact progressing in the post-capitalist world. One of its symptoms consists in the institutional isolation of industry; this in turn involves some dissociation of the scales of wealth and authority. By these and similar factors, the involvement of people in political conflict decreases; individuals, veto groups and political parties can, so to speak, afford to lose; and if they win, the changes they introduce are piecemeal rather than radical. History is a permanent guest in a free society, not an unwanted intruder whose presence signals revolutionary upheavals.

I concur with the common belief that the struggle between free societies and totalitarian societies is the dominant issue of political conflict in our time. Contrary to many, however, I do not believe that this struggle is confined to international relations. The struggle between freedom and totalitarianism occurs within societies as well as between them. No real society can be found at one or the other extreme of our ideal types. There are very nearly free and very nearly totalitarian countries, but more often we find intermediate forms. In the modern world, there are such paradoxical states as democracy without liberty and liberty without democracy. Everywhere, however, the struggle between freedom and totalitarianism may be regarded as one between different attitudes toward social conflict. Totalitarian monism is founded on the idea that conflict can and should be eliminated, that a homogeneous and uniform social and political order is the desirable state of affairs. This idea is no less dangerous for the fact that it is mistaken in its sociological premises. The pluralism of free societies, on the other hand, is based on recognition and acceptance of social conflict. In a free society, conflict may have lost much of its intensity and violence, but it is still there, and it is there to stay. For freedom in society means, above all, that we recognize the justice and the creativity of diversity, difference and conflict.

Class and Class Conflict in an Industrial Society (1957), English ed. (London, Routledge, 1959), pp. 316–18.

Gabriel Cohn-Bendit (1936–   )
and Daniel Cohn-Bendit (1945–   )

HORIZONTAL RELATIONS

A society without exploitation is inconceivable where the management of production is controlled by one social class, in other words where the division of society into managers and workers is not totally abolished. Now, the workers are told day after day that they are incapable of managing their own factory, let alone society, and they have come to believe this fairy tale. This is precisely what leads to their alienation in a capitalist society, and this is precisely why socialists must do their utmost to restore the people's autonomy and not just doctor the economic ills of the West.

It is not by accident that liberals, Stalinist bureaucrats and reformists alike, all reduce the evils of capitalism to economic injustice, and exploitation to the unequal distribution of the national income. And when they extend their criticism of capitalism to other fields, they still imply that everything would be solved by a fairer distribution of wealth. The sexual problems of youth and the difficulties of family life are ignored – all that apparently needs to be solved is the problem of prostitution. Problems of culture come down to the material cost of dispensing it. Of course, this aspect is important, but a man is more than a mere consumer, he can not only get fed, he can get fed up as well. While most of man's problems are admittedly economic, man also demands the right to find fulfilment on every other possible level. If a social organization is repressive it will be so on the sexual and cultural no less than on the economic planes.

As our society becomes more highly industrialized, the workers' passive alienation turns into active hostility. To prevent this happening, there have been many attempts to 'adapt the workers', 'give them a stake in society', and quite a few technocrats now think this is the only hope of salvaging 'the democratic way of life'.

But however comfortable they may make the treadmill, they are determined never to give the worker control of the wheel. Hence many militants have come to ask themselves how they can teach the workers that their only hope lies in revolution. Now, this merely reintroduces the old concept of the vanguard of the proletariat, and so threatens to create a new division within society. The workers need no teachers; they will learn the correct tactics from the class struggle. And the class struggle is not an abstract conflict of ideas, it is people fighting in the street. Direct control can only be gained through the struggle itself. Any form of class struggle, over wages, hours, holidays, retirement, if it is pushed through to the end, will lead to a general strike, which in turn introduces a host of new organizational and social problems. For instance, there cannot be a total stoppage of hospitals, transport, provisions, etc., and the responsibility for organizing these falls on the strikers. The longer the strike continues, the greater the number of factories that have to be got going again. Finally, the strikers will find themselves running the entire country.

This gradual restoration of the economy is not without its dangers, for a new managerial class may emerge to take over the factories if the workers are not constantly on their guard. They must ensure that they retain control over their delegated authorities at all times. Every function of social life – planning, liaison and co-ordination – must be taken up by the producers themselves, as and when the need arises.

It is certain that the managerial class will do everything they can to prevent a real revolution. There will be intimidation and violent repression, prophets both new and old of every shape and form will be held up to bamboozle the workers. There will be election campaigns, referenda, changes in the cabinet, electoral reforms, red herrings, bomb plots and what have you. At the same time, the experts will preach about the dire threat to the national economy and international prestige of the country. And should the workers turn a deaf ear to them, and persist in restarting production under their direct control, the managerial class will end up, as always, by calling in the army and police. This is precisely what happened in France in 1968, and not for the first time either.

What of the future? We cannot produce a blueprint – the future alone can evolve that. What we must agree on, rather, are the general principles of the society we want to create. The politicians tell us we live in an age of technological miracles. But it is up to us to apply them to a new society, to use the new media so as to gain greater mastery over the environment. While people today simply watch television as a surrogate for the lives they have ceased to live, in the new society they will use it as a means of widening their experience, of mastering the environment and of keeping in touch with the real lives of other people. If television programmes were to be put on for their social value and not solely because they induce the maximum hypnosis in the greatest numbers, they would enable us to extend the real democracy to the entire population.

Just imagine the preliminary Grenelle talks transmitted as a whole; just imagine the 'dialogues' between the bosses and the professional trade union pundits transmitted straight to the workshops. The workers would just laugh themselves sick, and throw the lot out of office.

Or take the question of planning the economy. Clearly, even in the future, planning will have to be done, but not just for the sake of profit or balancing the books. Once the workers have learned to manage their own affairs, in full equality and collective effort, they will try quite naturally to place the whole system of production and distribution on an entirely new basis. As Vaneighem has put it: 'For my part, the only equality that really matters is that which gives free rein to my desires while recognizing me as a man among men.' (*Traité de savoir-vivre à l'usage des jeunes générations*, Paris, 1947.)

Contemporary history has shown that the abolition of the private ownership of the means of production, essential though it is, does not necessarily mean the end of exploitation. Under capitalism, wages and prices fluctuate more or less with the law of supply and demand. Hence we are led to believe that the amelioration of the workers' lot is a simple marketing (or planning) problem, and that all our pressing social questions can be solved by 'dialogues' between officials or parliamentary representatives.

Similarly the wage system hides the reality of exploitation by suggesting that pay is simply a matter of productive capacity – but how do you evaluate the productive capacity of, say, a schoolteacher?

In the capitalist system, the only standard of value is money, hence the worker himself has a price tag that fits him neatly into a social pigeon-hole and is set apart from the rest. He has become just another commodity, not a man but an economic abstraction, whose relationship with other men is governed by arbitrary laws over which he has no control. The time each worker spends on a particular job is expressed in working hours; it is only when the workers themselves take control, and appropriate the fruits, of their own production, that work will be determined by real needs and not by blind and arbitrary market forces. Social relationships will no longer be vertical – from top to bottom, from director to worker – but horizontal, between equal producers working in harmony. And the product of their toil will no longer be appropriated by parasitic organisms, but shared out fairly between one and all.

Obsolete Communism: the Left-Wing Alternative (1968) (London, Penguin, 1969), pp. 103–6. (First pub. André Deutsch, 1968.)

INDEX

absolute, absolute values, 13; considered by, Bakunin, 170 n.; Coleridge, 111 n.; Oakeshott, 378; Pareto, 233; Schiller, 75

absolutism, Bernstein on, 237–8, 241; Mussolini on, 315

actions, Popper on, 380–1

activity, Comte on, 142–3; Mill on, 153, 158; Oakeshott on, 375–6, 378, 379

Acton, John Emerich, Baron, quoted on democracy, 373 and n., on French Revolution, 374

administration, Bukharin on, 329–30; Lenin on, 281–2; Saint-Simon on, 85–6

aestheticism, 12; Comte on, 143; Marcuse on, 19, 367, 368; Schiller on, 71–6

affluent society, Marcuse on, 365, 366, 367

aggression, Freud on, 247–50, 251

agrarian reform, Babeuf on, 78

agriculture: considered by, Comte, 143; Fourier, 114–16; Mao, 357; Proudhon, 163

alienation, 14; considered by, Cohn-Bendit, 424; Dahrendorf, 422; Guevara, 418, 419; Kant, 36, 38

Anarchist-Communism, Kropotkin on, 231–2

anarchists and anarchism, 6–7; and minimum control, 8; vision of society, 8; see themselves as realists, 10; opposition to planning, 17; and industrialism, 17; continuing appeal, 17; absorb radicals, 18; opinions and reflections by, Engels, 19; Kropotkin, 10, 229, 232; Lenin, 19, 278; Orwell, 387, 388, 389; Russell, 291; Simmel, 262

anarchy: considered by, de Maistre, 59; Durkheim, 255; Engels, 189; Proudhon, 163, 164

antagonisms: considered by, Dahrendorf, 421; Engels, 188; Mao, 356; Marx, 175, 178, 179–80, 186; Morris, 221; Proudhon, 161

aristocracy: considered by, Arnold, 203; Carlyle, 138–41; Cole, 337 n.; de Maistre, 63; de Tocqueville, 149; Michels, 293, 297; Mosca, 261

aristocratic government, Arnold on, 260; Mosca on, 260; Saint-Simon on, 82

armed workers, Lenin on, 278, 280, 281–2

Arnold, Matthew, 5, 21; cross references, 21, 412; 'Democracy', 203–6

arts and artists: considered by, Coleridge, 111; Forster, 304–5; Goodman, 406; Marx, 177, 178; Saint-Simon, 81, 83, 86; Schiller, 71

association, Fourier on, 114–19

Auden, W. H., 9, 12; 'Eden', 393–4; 'Reading', 392–3; 'Vespers', 390–2

authority and authoritarianism, 8, 9; opinions and reflections on by, Dahrendorf, 421–3; Keynes, 312; Lippmann, 340–4 *passim*; Mosca, 259; Mussolini, 314–19; Proudhon, 162, 163; Weber, 272; Wilde, 242, 244–5

autocratic government, Mosca on, 259, 260, 261

Babeuf, Gracchus, 17; cross references, 21, 239; 'Manifeste des Égaux', 77–80

Bakunin, Mikhail, 8, 9, 13, 18; concept of equality, 5; 'Fédéralisme, Socialisme et Antithéologisme', 170–2

Bentham, Jeremy, 12, 15; on direct democracy, 3; salutes the new age, 14; basis of selection, 20; cross references, 21, 157, 317; 'The Constitutional Code', 54–8; 'A Fragment on Government', 53–4